Rock,Paper,Slippers

TONY SHELLEY

Edited by Julia Rolf

www.newgeneration-publishing.com

 New Generation Publishing

For Frances and Darryl with love

Acknowledgements

Special thanks to:

Kim for love, support, encouragement, belief and endless read out loud sessions

Darryl Beatson for support from start to finish and nagging me to get it written

Julia Rolf for editing skills and general advice – I couldn't have done this without you

Olivia Burren for the the proof read

Jacqui Pearce for coming up with the title

David Knowler for the jacket design

The many people who believed I could do this and continuously asked 'when?' Too many to namecheck – you know who you are

Apologies to the many people who have been a big part of my story for many years and whom I haven't managed to shoehorn in a story about – I hope you all know who you are

To be someone must be a wonderful thing

A Famous footballer or a rock singer

Or a big film star

Yes, I think I would like that

'To Be Someone (Didn't We Have A Nice Time)', Paul Weller

Introduction

I think it's important that we get off on the right foot straight away, so I'll be honest with you – I don't really consider myself to be much of a writer. I wrote essays at school, but only when I had to. Usually I just write lists. Not useful, 'to do' type lists or anything handy like that, I write totally pointless lists – mainly Top 10 lists: 'Top 10 Songs with Leg in the Title', 'Top 10 Potato-Based Snacks of all Time', 'Top 3 Interesting Scenes from *Eldorado*' (well you try coming up with more than three) – that sort of caper. Basically, anything that keeps me away from tackling the things that would actually be on a 'to do' list, if I could be bothered enough to write one. I once deliberated for two hours over whether Shane McGowan or Dave Hill out of Slade should be number one in my list of 'Top 10 Ugliest Pop Stars'. The upside of all this list making is that if I should ever be asked what my seventh favourite vegetable is, I am there, ready with the answer (parsnip).

I've never really had any great ambitions to become a writer either, although I've always quite fancied being the bloke that writes the puns for the headlines in *The Sun*. Mostly, I only ever wanted to be a pop star or a footballer. As far as I was concerned they were the only jobs worth doing. I'm reconciled now to the fact that if I were destined to become a pop star or a footballer, it probably would have happened by now. There are many reasons why I never managed to become either, the main one being that you either have it, or you don't. I don't.

Whilst this is not strictly an autobiography, I do have some stories to tell – doesn't everyone that has lived long enough to own a bald patch? My tale is of growing up in Essex, England during the sixties and seventies (and in my case the eighties as well), culminating in actually becoming a fully-fledged grown-up by the time the naughty nineties and the slightly better-behaved noughties came along. As a backdrop to my own adventure, there's the chronicle of an ever-changing world; a world that has gone through perhaps its most volatile period of transformation in modern history, and I have been lucky enough to have been there, done that and tie-dyed the t-shirt.

Proper writers have to know who their target audience is, and I suppose that's the one thing that I have in common with them. What I'm striving to do here, is to test the water to see if we fit, if we gel, if we can get along, maybe even be friends.

It may be that, unlike me, you have never had the yearning to play professional football or be in a pop group but are just simply part of my generation. I'm not saying that you have to be as old as me to enjoy this book ... but it would probably help.

Do you remember huddling around a transistor radio on the school fields, your stomach taut with tension as Johnny Walker announced the new Top 20, hoping for all you're worth that your favourite song is this week's number one, or going into a sweet shop and digging deep into your pockets and finding just enough money for a bag of sherbet pips and a Jubbly? I used to think that constituted a decent meal.

Did you adore the adverts featuring the guffawing Cadbury's Smash aliens, loathe the Shake n' Vac lady, and irritate grown-ups who annoyingly asked you what you wanted to be when you grew up by saying 'a proper little madam'?

How about this? Whenever anyone within earshot utters the words 'watch out', is your immediate reaction still to shout back: 'There's a Humphrey about!'?

Have you ever lost a week of your life trying to solve a Rubik's Cube? No? Me neither. Rubik's Cubes were for Maths swots, right?

Ever dreamt of scoring the winning goal in a Wembley Cup Final, and rehearsed the routine for your goal celebration? Of course you have.

Remember coming home from school having been awarded parental rights over a stick insect in a jam jar, or using the sun and a magnifying glass to burn a hole in a piece of paper? Remember the pain you felt when a mistimed 'Klacker' shuddered across your already swollen knuckles?

Here's a tester: while watching re-runs of *Are You Being Served?*, do you still snigger at one-liners involving Mrs Slocombe's pussy?

Perhaps you were once the proud owner of a Harrington jacket, a 'Frankie Says' t-shirt or a pair of sideburns that made Noddy Holder's look like an understatement. Did you shed a little tear the day you reluctantly binned off your bottle-green high-waisters and squeezed yourself into a pair of bondage trousers?

This might be awkward, so take a deep breath. You've probably never come clean about the time you spent in front of your bedroom mirror playing cricket bat guitar or singing into a hairbrush, but you know you did it, I know you did it, so let's just get it out there in the open right now.

And what of those poignant memories that stirred something deep inside? Geldof standing motionless with his fist raised high at Live Aid, the floral tributes blanketing the pitch at Anfield following Hillsborough, Gazza's tears in Turin or possibly even Thatcher's tears as she shuffled miserably out of Number Ten. If any of these snapshots of days gone by have punctuated your life too, then we probably share similar memories, even though we have never met, and you are perfectly positioned to allow yourself a wry smile at the way we were, as we take a light-hearted stroll through our back pages together.

Talking of pages, now we are on the same one – calendar-wise at least – and seeing how we have already bonded, I'll let you into a little secret. A few years back, I had a bit of a crisis. Middle age hit me hard. I wasn't expecting it and it certainly wasn't invited. It just showed up, like a door-stepping Jehovah's Witness, or that Vesuvius-like spot that miraculously appears on the end of your nose on the morning of a first date.

So there I was, belly button-deep into what I could only assume was my very own mid-life crisis. I didn't buy a sports car or suddenly decide that it was high time I learned to play the saxophone; my crisis manifested itself in other ways. Directionless, dissatisfied, overly emotional and reflective: that's how I was. The very opposite, on all four counts, of how I'd been in the forty-odd years that had preceded it. I called my crisis Colin. I needed to give him a name, an identity, just so I could call him a bastard behind his back. We hated each other's guts, but he still hung around for two years, waiting for me to crack: mithering and pecking away in a battle of wits like no other I had ever faced.

However, it was the reflective part of my so-called crisis that turned out to be the catalyst for this collection of memories that you are now about to read. In twenty or so years' time, middle age will have packed its bags and crept out of the back door, despite me begging it to stay for a few more days. As my memory banks suffer their inevitable withdrawals, I don't want to be sitting around trying to remember why I did this, that or the other, or the name of that kid at school who could turn his eyelids inside out! So I decided to get it all down in black and white, while I still had the use of my general faculties and could remember everything. It felt like the right time.

And then there's the music. I've grown up with pop music and for a while it grew up with me, but now it seems that pop is going through its own mid-life crisis. Pop calls its crisis Simon – Simon Cowell. A man who is even older than I am but still believes that pop music is solely for the young and beautiful and must be formulated in the image of Beyoncé. But he's wrong; pop is no longer created or devoured exclusively by young people, and while people of my age continue to buy or download it by the truckload, it appears to me that maybe youth was just pop's little way of turning up its collar and slipping on a pair of shades to try and act cool.

I'm well aware that pop was supposed to be a teenage phase – one of those you grow out of, like heralding the arrival of each newly sprouted pubic hair – but it has been an unrepentant obsession that began to consume me from the age of twelve. It's the longest relationship I've ever had, and although we're both totally different now from how we were when we first met, it seems unlikely that we are ever going to split up due to musical differences. I'm not saying it's been easy – we've had our fair share of ups and downs, but since when did love travel an unblemished road? Pop is a passion, which, in its own preposterous way, has swept aside all other pretenders to the infatuation throne with transcendent ease.

Back in our early days, its three-minute frenzy of adrenalin forced me to shake my fist, my head and my body down to the ground. It encouraged me to play imaginary guitar to imaginary audiences, in imaginary stadiums, but most of all – just to imagine. I also know that I am supposed to like opera by now, but a group of overweight actors singing about things that I cannot relate to, in a language that I can't understand, cannot make me laugh, cry or cover me in goose-bumps like pop music can.

I hesitate to use the phrase 'soundtrack of my life' – it's an expression that is used far too often for my liking – but it does make the music sound important and, to me, it is. Everyone uses that phrase, abuses it even, but my 'soundtrack' is played just that little bit louder than the backing track of those that take it for granted. It's the lover and friend that has always been there when I've needed it and even when I've been foolish enough to think that I didn't. It has even forgiven me for those regrettable first dozen years when I ignored it, the years in which Batman, Daleks and the exact distance between a set of goalposts somehow seemed more important. In return I have forgiven it for reminding me that I was a womble.

So you won't find any apologies for the amount of musical commentary between these covers – or for the record collection agonising, or for my attempts to somehow fix the moustache and silly glasses to pop's Mr Potato Head.

Bearing that in mind, if your record player wasn't the most important object in your bedroom or pop music generally isn't your thing, you may well find yourself waving the white flag of surrender in the middle of no man's land, which in pop terms lies somewhere to the south of Gilbert O'Sullivan and to the east of Sting. But as I see it, you have two choices. You can slip this book back onto the shelf – I don't think anyone noticed you pick it up anyway; walk away now and we'll say no more about it – or you can read on and discover what all the fuss is about.

I am about to enter completely unchartered territory. The last time I wrote anything of any substance – something that could vaguely be described as being essay-esque – was on 21 June 1977. That was during my geography O-level exam, in which I discussed glaciers and the Canadian prairies. Neither of those subjects are covered here.

I have never kept a diary, although I now wish I had. I'm far too shambolic for such organised administration, so everything here is how I remember it.

George Harrison once sang 'if you don't know where you're going, any road can take you there' – a profound statement and one that seems absolutely spot-on to me. I'm just about to find out if he was right, so never mind the bollocks, here's my book.

Birthday

Today is my birthday and I am fifty years old. Fifty! Saying it out loud helps. I suppose it's a bit like an alcoholic at an AA meeting – facing up to the problem is the first step to recovery. Except surprisingly, it's not a problem for me, which is just as well, as there is no recovery from this. I'm fifty and I'm ok with it.

What have I got to be miserable about anyway? My wife Kim has just handed over her present – tickets to see El Clásico: Real Madrid v Barcelona at the Bernabéu Stadium in Madrid – and tonight I'm having a party. Not only that, but at that party, my old band, The Fabulous Heseltines, are back together again for one night only and we will be playing live for the first time in nine years.

I thought hard, but admittedly, not for very long, about the band playing at my party. Such an act does have a faint whiff of self-indulgence about it. You see, being in a band is showing off at the best of times, but playing to a captive audience, who have no choice but to cheer and whoop the birthday boy is showing off of the highest order.

As musicians, we forget, that being in a band is not very important to people who are not in a band, whereas to us it means everything. Most of my friends who will be at the party would probably rather have a bit of chinwag with others there who they haven't seen for ages. Most of the girls would rather form a circle and dance to 'I Will Survive', whilst pointedly shouting the lyrics at their oblivious menfolk, than watch us lot put 'Hanging on the Telephone' through its paces. But there'll be no 'I will surviving' at any party of mine – not on your nelly, mate. It's a bit of a shame really, because when it comes to showing off, we forget that one of the primary reasons why we joined a band in the first place was to show off to girls, and now we are going to spoil their evening with several great big dollops of lumpen rock music. But sod 'em, it's my party and I'll play if I want to.

The band arrived at the venue, Buckhurst Hill Village Hall, around midday, which gave us time for a decent sound check and a chance to run through a few songs that were bound to prove troublesome later. The members of this band are scattered all over the country these days – that's the reason we split up in the first place – but we still managed to squeeze in three rehearsals during January and February. The rehearsal jogged a few memories but we were still rusty as hell, so any kind of run-through during the afternoon was going to be useful.

We set up and started testing the sound levels. Rob struck out the opening guitar riff to David Bowie's 'Heroes', but as soon as the rest of the band came in to join him, the power cut out and we were plunged into a worrying silence. The hall had a decibel meter with an automatic cut-out facility if the volume limit was breached, and we had immediately triggered it.

This sent me into major panic mode. The Heseltines sound could be described as boisterous at the very least, and we didn't really do quiet – in fact, back in the day we had a 'no quiet songs' policy. There was no way we could play this gig at low volume; we had to find a way of overriding the decibel meter and worry about the consequences later. We traced the source of the meter to a microphone placed high in the rafters of the hall and decided that somehow we had to either disconnect that mic – or at least try and muffle it, to give us a bit of leeway to be noisy. We even thought about cutting the cables, but that really had to be our last resort.

Kim and a few of our friends were also down at the hall helping to get things ready for the evening's festivities – putting up old photos on the walls of me with varying degrees of embarrassing hairstyles, blowing up balloons and clustering them together to form multi-coloured latex genitalia – they assumed this sort of thing was being helpful anyway.

One of their number, Pete, our resident 'go-to' man for fixing stuff, had a bit of a reputation for innovative constructions and always had his van full of the most ridiculous materials that he kept on board, just because they may at some point in his life come in a bit handy.

Pete went out to his van, and came back with several lumps of foam – the type you find in middle-class people's garden furniture. 'All we've got to do lads, is get this, up there' he said, pointing to the mic nestled about fifteen feet above our heads.

We then spent some time building a precarious tower of trestle tables and chairs, whilst Pete constructed the longest pokey thing he could make out of broom handles and gaffer tape. He tried desperately to poke the foam into position so it would muffle the offending microphone. But whichever angle he came at it from, he just couldn't get the foam off the pokey thing and into position, without hands up there to help guide it.

After about two hours of trying, and our afternoon of rehearsal ebbing away, I suggested 'Should I just go to a tool hire shop and hire a filthy great ladder?' At which point Pete piped up: 'No need, I've got a filthy great ladder at home'. We just all looked at each other and fell about laughing. So, after just the right amount of ridicule, Pete was dispatched to get the very ladder that he could have gone and got two hours ago; the mic was duly muffled and the band were able to crack on with some much-needed practice.

On the night, once all my friends and family started to arrive, I became more anxious. That nervous feeling that I used to get whenever we played live had returned. I hadn't been this nervous about a gig for years. I really wanted us to be good – both for those that had been regulars at our gigs back in our pomp, and for those that hadn't and were seeing us tonight for the very first time.

The food that we had laid on was a buffet provided by a local Indian restaurant, but I couldn't eat a thing. I greeted my guests and moved around the room, chatting, just trying to relax. Each group asked the same question, just like they did when they came to our gigs several years previously – 'what time are you going on?'. There was an air of expectation in the room.

When 9 o'clock came, the lights dimmed further. Kim took to the stage and announced into the mic: 'Ladies & Gentlemen, please welcome ... The Fabulous Heseltines!'. The welcome we received was a mixture of 'welcome back' and 'ok, if we really must'. But regardless, it sounded great to these ears. I'd missed it.

'Good evening Buckhurst Hill, it's great to be back!'. Not that we'd ever played in Buckhurst Hill before, but I've just always wanted to say that – as if we'd been on a world tour and this was the final gig in my home town. In reality, it had been many years since we had all stood on a stage together, and so it did feel great to be back – that was what I really meant.

With a '1, 2' and a cruuuuhh, urrhhh, cruuuuhh on the snare and kick drum and we launched ourselves into 'Teenage Kicks' by The Undertones. It's the perfect song to open any set because it's dead easy, everybody in the audience knows it – and of course every fiftieth birthday party should kick off with a song about teenagers wanking.

It's always a bit tricky picking the opening song of a live set – it has to be chosen carefully. Song one should be a bit of a teaser, a little taste of what's to follow, because you don't want to reveal your hand too early and play your best songs early on, yet at the same time you need to get off to a flyer. When playing in a pub full of strangers, a band can fly or fall on the strength of their opening number. Kick off with the wrong song and you might find yourselves playing to the bar staff and the bloke in the corner on the fruit machine for the rest of the night – get it right and the crowd could be with you till the bitter end. It's a dilemma that has tortured the set-list compilers in bands for decades. Another thing to consider is that in a way, the first few songs are almost wasted because no one is drunk enough to get up and dance just yet. At the height of Britpop we always opened with 'The Riverboat Song' by Ocean Colour Scene – a hugely popular song at the time, but the combination of the stop/start nature of the song and the tricky 6/8 time signature made it impossible to dance to, even if anyone wanted to. Audiences usually have to be coaxed onto the dance floor with a cocktail of alcohol and the comfortably familiar.

But this time 'Teenage Kicks' was welcomed with a packed dance floor and heads bopping up and down like the crowd at Live Aid during 'Rockin' All Over the World', but with less hair and fewer shoulder pads.

The loudness of the 'Wah-hey' at the end of the song, settled us down and I allowed myself a modest smile of relief, but inside my head there was a little Stuart Pearce screaming with delight like he did after scoring that penalty in Euro '96: 'Yeeeeeeeeessssssss!'.

As we raced through our songs it occurred to me that although primarily this was The Fabulous Heseltines re-kindling their rock history, we were also dipping into my friends' pasts too and maybe that's another reason why they were responding so enthusiastically to the songs we were playing.

Sitting at the back, behind the band, is a great place to observe what is going on in front of you. Not just within the band, but in the audience too. Drummers can look up all the time; we don't have to look down at guitars to make sure our fingers are in the right places on fretboards and stuff like that. My mind has been known to wander when I do this and I kind of go into autopilot. I started thinking about a few people that should have been there; my friend Mark, who was possibly the funniest bloke I have ever met – a natural wit, who had died suddenly in 2007 at the tender age of 41; and my good friend Darryl, who had intended to fly in from New Zealand just for my party, but had been diagnosed with cancer earlier that very week. Life can be a total shit sometimes.

I also thought about my mum, who had died five months earlier. It occurred to me that not once had I ever invited her to come and see me play in any of the bands that I had been in. I'd been playing in bands for years and years, and she had never seen me doing the thing that I love most – now it was too late. This was a stark contradiction to my earlier dalliances on the stage, when I insisted that she attend the ear-shattering shrill of my recorder recitals, or come to watch me aimlessly wander around the stage forgetting my lines in my school plays. I wanted her there for that, because the whole point of being in those sort of things was so your parents could see how great you were. But as far as playing pop music goes, I didn't want her anywhere near. Well, you wouldn't, would you? Pop music is for us, not for our parents – that's one of the things that makes it so great. That's what my kids tell me anyway. I'm not sure what she would have made of this. She would probably have hated it and thought that we were too noisy, but she did love a good party.

My dad was there though – watching me play for the first time. At 81 years old he was too hard-of-hearing to tell whether we were too noisy or not, but still managed to deliver a moment of absolute joy when I spotted him up and dancing to 'The Boys Are Back In Town' – the very song that I was playing in my bedroom all those years ago, when he burst in and swiped the needle across the record in a fit of rage because he 'couldn't hear himself think'. I'm not really sure what thinking sounds like, but the older you get, the more you need to hear it.

It occurred to me that all around this room is my history. This is my fiftieth birthday and so here it is – my fifty years all laid out in front of me, in people form. Little pockets of friends and family, from all the various stages of my life. Some have been with me for almost forty years, others have arrived more recently, but every one of them have played their part somewhere down the line in my joyous story.

As we headed towards the business end of our set, we rattled our way through The Clash's 'I Fought the Law' – the only surviving song from the very first set I ever played with this band, and one that our rhythm guitarist John swore he would never play again back in 1996 (because musicians are a bit like that), but here he is in 2011, jumping up and down to it as he thrashes out the chords like he's 15 again. At the back of the room, I spotted the other four members of my current band, Black Market Clash, watching our every move with great intensity. No doubt, analysing and critiquing behind cupped hands, because musicians are a bit like that too.

At the end of the song our singer, Phil, led the guests in a rousing chorus of 'Happy Birthday' and they encouraged me to leave the drum stool and make a speech. I'd never stood at the front of the stage before and it felt strange to be there with the band behind me. This was me metaphorically taking off my cap and raising my bat as a ripple of applause fills the room, acknowledging my maiden half-century. I did all the usual thank yous and introduced the band – another first for me. We never used to do the whole 'introducing the band' thing when we were a going concern. I made sure I didn't precede each name with the extremely irritating 'Mr' that seems to have become pop law.

I have no idea why whenever a singer introduces his band members, their names have to be preceded by 'Mr', but apparently they do. 'Mr Eric Clapton', 'Mr Keith Richards', etc. I blame this trend entirely on the eighties – a time when some pop stars were so androgynous that you could never be 100% sure which type of winkle they owned – thus making the 'Mr' prefix quite helpful. But I wasn't doing it. I especially wasn't doing it to introduce our other singer Jo – what with her being a girl and everything – that would just be rude, although I do quite fancy introducing the lead singer of The Police as Mr Sting.

We finished our set with a couple of Beatles songs: 'I Saw Her Standing There', and a little mash-up that we had come up with years ago that segues 'Sgt. Pepper's Lonely Hearts Club Band' and its reprise, held together with a ridiculously long guitar solo. The lyrics of the reprise make it the perfect set-closer: 'We're sorry but it's time to go', and all that.

It had all gone rather well, considering, and we all loved it, but now it was time to enjoy the rest of the party and have a drink and a plate of cold curry.

Sometime during the following week I received a letter in the post from the Buckhurst Hill Parish Council;

Dear Mr Shelley,

I understand that the hire of the hall overran by almost 2 hours on Saturday 19th March and into the morning of 20th March. As the caretaker advised you, an additional charge will be made and therefore I will deduct the amount of £77.76 from your deposit.

The caretaker has also made me aware that there is a large amount of foam material lodged in the rafters of the hall and evidence that our sound level detecting equipment has been tampered with. However, this seems undamaged so there will be no further cost.

In view of the breach of the Council's regulations of conditions of hire, I have to advice (sic) you that should your next hire overrun, you will be banned from hiring any of Buckhurst Hill Parish Council's premises in future.

Yours sincerely

Pauline Davis (Mrs)
Clerk to the Council

Now while I'm perfectly aware that this is hardly Keith Moon driving his Roller into his swimming pool, The Sex Pistols and The Stranglers got banned by councils didn't they, so in some small token way, maybe this was the pub rock equivalent? A laughable threat I know, but I don't think it does my rock CV any harm at all. And so inspired by a book I was reading at the time called *The Timewaster Letters* I responded:

Dear Mrs Davis,

Yes, I'm afraid that the foam and the sound level equipment tampering was us. I'm wondering whether you should consider making it easier to disconnect it and then we wouldn't have to have spent quite so much time trying to defeat it. It took us over two hours, the exact amount of time we overran by. Let's just call it the domino effect.

I was also wondering whether this could be enough to incur a ban now without me having to go through the business of another hire? Because despite your letter sounding as if it's aimed at a toddler, I am in fact 50 years old and therefore don't know if I have enough time left to earn the ban through your proposed method. Please have a think about it; I have a reputation to uphold you know.

Yours hopefully,

Tony Shelley (Mr)
Drum Specialist – The Fabulous Heseltines.

On reflection, this was a pathetic final attempt at rebellion from a rebel without a clue and needless to say I didn't get a reply. A final attempt to kick ass, as the youngsters might say. The trouble is, these days, I'm doing all my ass-kicking with slippers firmly on my feet.

If you wouldn't mind bearing with me at this point, and try to imagine that this is the film of the book: the screen is fading out and going all wiggley and wavy, and harps are playing arpeggios, because we're about to go back in time and head to another world they called 'The Sixties'. So everybody say 'Wooooooooooo!', and I'll see you there.

Our House

You know what drives me nuts? That expression – 'If you remember the sixties, you weren't really there.'

Firstly, I hate the way it's used in such a knowing, smug, way that insinuates that the entire world spent the whole decade off its head. I also find it irritating that those that feel the need to shout the loudest about 'being there' – perhaps to try somehow to gain some sort of kudos from their children, probably spent the sixties either doing their homework, selling insurance or doing some other mundane activity, and weren't actually 'there' at all.

The expression dismisses the contribution of anyone that didn't embrace the drug culture of the time or wasn't totally groovy, as if they had no part to play in the way in which the world changed during this period. There were plenty who were there and can remember it. They believed they could change the world and, in so many ways, succeeded because they were out there doing something positive rather than simply sitting in a field getting stoned. In many ways it's these people that define the sixties, not the stoners.

So who was it that came up with this foolish little idiom? It was a guy called Paul Kantner, and scholars of sixties psychedelia will identify him as being 'that bloke out of Jefferson Airplane'. But you'll be with the majority if you're thinking 'who?', as he's not exactly someone that wove too many stitches in rock's great tapestry. It's altogether rather pleasing that his nine-word throwaway sentence is more famous than he was.

I will concede that Paul and his mates were amongst those who did fry their brains to such an extent that they probably don't remember much about their halcyon days, and therefore he isn't derogating the expression in the same way that Mr Insurance Salesman is.

I don't want to come over all stuffy about the sixties drug scene; in fact, it's one of the things that I find most fascinating about the whole mid-to late-sixties period. It was certainly responsible for helping to produce some of the most amazing and memorable music ever written (hardly any of which was created by Jefferson Airplane, I hasten to add) and it changed how artists, musicians, poets, actors and writers went about their creativity; and to be honest, with my addictive nature, there is every possibility I would have adopted it head-on. But the whole point for me is, if I had been old enough to enjoy the sixties culture as it happened, I would have wanted to be able to savour it, remember it, and say 'I was there' and hopefully have something a little more meaningful to boast about than just having spotted a purple aardvark playing the flute.

If I'm being completely honest though, the most frustrating thing for me about this whole 'being there' thing is that I wasn't there. We're a funny lot, us kids who were born in the sixties. We were there, but at the same time, we were too young to be there. It's all rather irksome. We were so close we could almost smell the joss sticks, but if you were to give me a time machine, I'd take being a 12-year-old boy in 1962 rather than a 12-month-old baby, in a heartbeat. Baby oil for patchouli oil – sounds like a good swap to me.

I have a rose-tinted view of the sixties that I think partially stems from missing out on all the madness, but I don't think I'm alone. My initial interest in sixties culture started in the mid-seventies when I discovered The Beatles. That was a life-changing encounter, which I will discuss in much more detail later – probably when we get to the mid-seventies.

I'm not sure what it is that draws so many people so strongly to the sixties, but I don't think that any other decade has the ability to encourage folk that weren't even born when it ended, to go back and discover it. As someone who has been enslaved for over thirty years by the songs of The Beatles, The Rolling Stones, The Who, Bob Dylan, Small Faces and The Kinks, I tend to believe that it's the music that entices everybody else too. I think the music was important, but for people that aren't drawn in by the music, there are other fascinating aspects to the decade outside the world of pop music: the Space Race, the Cold War, the Kennedys, mods and rockers, the hippy counterculture, the emergence of the satirists, the growth of television and modern theatre, the causes and protest rallies, the fashions – or maybe they just have a thing for dear old Julie Andrews in a habit, but there was something there for everyone.

Just because I wasn't 'really there', there is no harm in pretending that I was. In my mind, I have travelled back to the sixties many times. I have it all mapped out, my sixties – how it would have been, had I been old enough to enjoy it. I would have been a mod. Of that I am certain. The mod movement had that classic combination for a teenage fad: great music and fabulous clothes. The powerfully thrashy yet danceable music of The Who and Small Faces, and the kitchen-sink dramas within the songs of The Kinks – combined with the opportunity to wear two-tone Tonic suits, button-down Ben Sherman shirts with an inch-wide tie – it would have proved way too much for me to resist. Even the thought of having to wear a pork-pie hat or Hush Puppies doesn't put me off. I have my reservations about my modness though – it's the scooters. I don't really fancy the scooters. I've always seen myself as more Lamborghini than Lambretta. I'm not sure I would have been up for the beach battles with the rockers that wreaked havoc at seaside towns up and down the country every Bank Holiday Weekend either – I would have been a bit too namby-pamby for that, but I would have been there, down at Brighton beach, maybe doing something a little less fervid. Maybe just a bit of chanting or some aggressive pointing. Later, I would have been a hippy, with a huge ginger Afro. No beard though; a ginger beard might be ok if you're the drummer in Cream, but it's not for everyone.

I don't really have too many clear memories of my own about the early sixties, what with me not being there and all that, but my parents have relayed various stories of those years, and there are a few bits and pieces that have stuck with me.

I grew up in a three-bedroom terraced house on the Eastern Avenue in an area called Gants Hill, which is in the district of Ilford, Essex. The Eastern Avenue is a busy dual carriageway, better known outside local circles as the A12. All in all, it stretches from Great Yarmouth in Norfolk right though Essex to the Blackwall Tunnel. Our stretch was incredibly noisy and without the luxury of noise-cancelling double glazing, we lived amid the constant hum of traffic hurtling down the road at great speed all day long. It's the sort of noise that you get used to after a while, but visitors to our house would often comment about it. In 2007, Cornhill Insurance named the A12 as the worst road in Britain – which was nice of them.

My parents bought our house in 1960 for £2,700. I have vivid memories of how our house looked; the picture has been preserved in my mind. We had a galley-style kitchen that contained a blue Formica table with a couple of uncomfortable matching chairs tucked alongside it. The sink overlooked the back garden and seemed to have the omnipresent shape of my mum standing in front of it. There were two living rooms downstairs, front and back. As far as I can remember, the front room was redundant and empty; everything happened in the back room. There was an armchair and a table and chairs in there, and I would sit at the table doing jigsaw puzzles or sorting out my Captain Scarlet bubble-gum cards.

There was a fireplace, which wasn't used for real fires, but in it stood an electric bar fire. I used to play this game where I'd stand with the back of my legs as close to the fire as possible, up until that point where the back of my knees were so hot they were stinging. Then very slowly shuffle away, desperately trying not to let the cloth of my trousers touch my skin, because you know if it does, it's going to hurt like hell. I think this was a game only boys could play. There were a couple of French doors (Jean-Pierre & Claude), which led out onto the back garden, and in front of them stood a black-and-white television. It was a really old set. None of that modern push-button convenience for us; this was one of those TVs where you had to turn a dial, radio style, to tune in the channels and then stand in front of it for ten minutes, moving the aerial until you got a half-decent picture. My dad was a TV engineer and it always puzzled me why we had such a rubbish telly when he was in the trade, but I suppose if you work as a Jaguar salesman it doesn't mean you can afford to drive one, and we had the best telly we could afford. The unloved front room had a ceiling that had been damaged somehow during the war and had bare floorboards and ripped wallpaper. My bedroom was large and sat directly over the back room. Between the floors were fourteen stairs covered in a deep-red flecked carpet.

I know what you're thinking – fourteen stairs? Well yes, as a kid, I had a close relationship with the stairs. I know there were fourteen, because I had an obsession with counting them. It was like some sort of ritual that I put myself through. I would count them going up and count them back down again – just to check there were still fourteen of them, obviously. I amused myself by inventing as many different ways of descending them as I could think of. On my stomach, on my back, on my knees, rolling sideways – but whichever method I selected, each step had to be counted on the way down. You'd be amazed how quickly you have to count to get from one to fourteen when you're rolling down a flight of stairs. The stairs held no fear for me, we were great mates. Years later, I would collude with them and hurl myself down them in an attempt to convince Mum that I had slipped and injured myself in numerous attempts to skive off school. This tactic rarely worked; she wasn't easily fooled, mainly due to my unconvincing limping skills.

Directly after they got married, and because they were having major building work carried out on their new home in Ilford, Dad's youngest brother Ivan and his new wife Estelle came and stayed with us for a while. Ivan had a great sense of humour and was quite a skilful mimic. Estelle also had a great sense of fun and possessed an incredibly loud and dirty laugh. My mum remembered this as a fun time in their lives and enjoyed having them around, not least because Estelle liked spending time with me and that must have taken the pressure off a little.

As I began to string a few words together, Estelle tried to teach me a few nursery rhymes. She would give me the first few words of a line and expect me to complete the rest of the sentence. This was a constant source of amusement to her and she would emit huge shrieks of laughter, as my underdeveloped speech would invent new and much funnier verse such as 'hickory clickory cock'. When she would return to the house of an evening, she would insist that I should be awoken from my slumber and brought downstairs in order to rattle off a few ditties in my half-awake state. After the performance, I would be taken back to my cot and put back to sleep.

My early days were spent being pushed around the shops at Gants Hill or around Valentines Park, where I would feed the ducks. The park was just around the corner from our house and is one of the biggest and most beautiful parks in the London area. It was famously immortalised as 'Itchycoo Park' in the Small Faces song from 1967 and it was somewhere that I would spend a huge amount of time during my older childhood. Because of this personal connection, and because I'm a sentimental old sod, the song makes me feel happy and is my favourite Small Faces tune. Despite the sentimentality though, it does, according to my Top Ten Rock

Grunts list, contain a moment from Steve Marriott at 2:19, where he lets out the 7th greatest grunt in rock. Thinking about the song now, it seems rather cool to think that while I was feeding the ducks (stale bread, rather than a bun), Steve Marriott and Ronnie Lane, the writers of the song, might have been getting off their (small) faces elsewhere in the park at the very same time.

Mum told me that during these trips total strangers would peer into my pram and sometimes give her a few coins with which to buy me something. She said it was because I would give them a huge smile as they gawped at me. I suspect it was nothing to do with the smile and more likely because they had never caught a glimpse of a real live ginger kid before, and considered the donation to be like the entrance fee for the freak show they used to have at fairgrounds in the nineteenth century!

I would tend to fall asleep during these journeys out in the pram, and when we returned to the house I would be left outside in the front garden to continue my nap to the throbbing noise of the traffic hurtling down the road a few yards away. It wasn't considered risky to leave a child unattended in those days: something that seems inconceivable now.

There were no dedicated children's channels on TV back then and for pre-school kids like me, just a couple of programmes a day. Twenty minutes or so would be spent in the company of a bizarre collection of toys that were the stars of *Play School*: Big and Little Ted; Hamble, a particularly ugly doll; Jemima, a rag doll with stripy legs; and Humpty, an egg-shaped gonk (very 60s) with checked trousers. Hamble really was quite ugly with her vile puffed-up face and her piggy-eyes; I couldn't take to her at all. I once read that the presenters hated her too, and she would often be out of the show for weeks on end being repaired, following injuries caused by the off-camera kicking she would sometimes receive from the presenters! I don't know if that story is true, but I hope it is – she was asking for it. The presenters would sing songs, tell us the date and talk to the toys and then hold them up to their ears to receive their response. The programme would always start with the same opening sequence that went:

'A house with a door, windows – 1-2-3-4. Ready to knock? Turn the lock – its *Play School*'.

Each day of the week would be dedicated to a different activity. I can't remember all of them but Tuesday was dressing up day, which would involve both the presenters and the toys dressing up (like they weren't wearing strange-enough clothes in the first place) and performing a story. Every day there would also be a short educational film covering a different topic, such as milking a cow or an aeroplane taking off. To get to the film, we were told that we had to look through one of three windows: the square window, the round window or the arched window. The presenters always built the tension up for this bit by saying 'so which window will we look through today?' I used to shout at the screen 'the arched window'. I always hoped it would be the arched window – it was the nicest.

The other children's programme that aired around lunchtime each day was *Watch with Mother* – a banner that was used for lots of different programmes that had been running on the BBC since the fifties. *The Woodentops*, a family of wooden puppets whose strings were quite clearly visible, were regulars. They had a mental Dalmatian called Spotty Dog, who walked like the soldiers in the Russian army (but on all fours and without any kind of furry headgear), twins that declared that today's dinner would be 'sawdust and hay' during a rather repetitive chanting session and a baby whose only character trait was throwing his blanket out of his pram (is this where the expression 'throwing your toys out of the pram' originated from?).

Then there was Andy Pandy, another puppet with visible strings, who lived in a picnic basket with Teddy – who was… well, a teddy. There was also a rag doll (there's a pattern emerging here, I think), called Looby Loo. She would only appear when Andy and Teddy weren't around. We weren't told where Andy and Teddy went and it seemed rude to ask. When she appeared, we would be treated to the narrator singing her very special song:

Here we go Looby Loo
Here we go Looby Light
Here we go Looby Loo
All on a Saturday Night

Seemed all very reasonable back then, but I'm tempted to consider these lyrics more carefully now. 'Here we go Looby Light?' What does that mean, precisely? And what was the point of going all Looby Loo on a Saturday night? Andy Pandy was only on during the week, so she could have gone as Looby Loo as she bloody well liked, but we would never have known anything about it, so what's the point of that? If anyone's going Looby Loo, I want to witness the Looby-Looing, not just be tantalisingly told that's it's going on at a time when I can't see it.

The Flowerpot Men starring Bill and Ben was the most awful children's programme of all. We were told that Bill and Ben lived in the two enormous flowerpots at the bottom of the garden. So enormous in fact, that the plinky-plonky percussive sounds played to indicate the differences in size between the enormous pots and the small and medium-sized pots was almost frightening. We were informed that behind the pots lived a 'little weed', who was imaginatively called 'Little Weed'. Little? Little Weed was taller than the really enormous flowerpots, so not so that little at all. I'm not sure how this programme ever got made – nothing ever happened. Little Weed would say 'weeeeeed' a lot, for no apparent reason, and Bill and Ben would talk to each other in a language that, with the greatest will in the world, no one could understand a word of, and that was it. How did they get away with that? Try to explain Bill and Ben to the kids of today, and they'd never believe you. Not only would they not believe you, but more to the point, they wouldn't tolerate it. These days kid's channels show a never-ending supply of cartoons, which was exactly what we wanted.

Because of this rather rudimentary and quite frankly rubbish selection of TV programmes available, my main source of entertainment in these early years was my record player. I can remember this magnificent box of loveliness incredibly well. It was brown with a wooden lid and had a single speaker at the front and a plastic handle on the side for carrying it from one room to another, although it usually lived in my bedroom. The turntable was a little bigger than a 45-rpm record and was made of metal with a felt mat that sat on top. The arm was also metal and beige in colour. The needle (it pains me to say needle, I know it's a stylus, but in this case, it was so crude, it should definitely be referred to as a needle) had a sticky-out tab at the side, which could be flicked to play either 45s or 78s. I can't remember which one you were supposed to choose if you were lucky enough to own any LPs.

The centre of the turntable was furnished with a six-inch spindle, upon which records could be loaded. As one record finished, the next was supposed to automatically drop down, leaving the other loaded records in place, but this rarely happened and they would usually all come cascading down at once.

I had records, mainly singles, and few old 78s. Dad provided most of these, I think, but my passion was well publicised and some may have arrived via relatives and possibly some from a young teenager called Betty who lived next door. I would spend hours at a time playing with my favourite toy, fascinated by both the mechanics of the machinery and the sounds emanating from that single speaker. 'Do Wah Diddy Diddy' by Manfred Mann, 'Needles & Pins' by the Searchers, 'Sun Arise' and 'Jake the Peg' by Rolf Harris, 'Bachelor Boy' and 'Summer Holiday' by Cliff Richard and 'Right Said Fred' by Bernard Cribbins were some of the records that I clearly remember having. There were also a couple of Disney stories: *Peter Pan* and *Sleeping Beauty*. These were 7-inch singles but had to be played at 33 1/3, which was a little confusing, and were accompanied by a picture book that contained illustrations of the scenes being described by the narrative on the disc. 'Tinker Bell' the magic fairy would indicate when a page should be turned, by playing a little signature on the xylophone. Later, 'Puppet on a String' by Sandie Shaw, 'Lily the

Pink' by Scaffold and 'They're Coming To Take Me Away, Ha-Haaa!' by Napoleon XIV were in the collection. I distinctly remember the Napoleon XIV one because the B-side was the A-side recorded backwards! It was 1968 after all. They did things like that in 1968.

My mum considered me to be a child genius. I had a skill, an unfathomable skill that she delighted in imparting to anyone who would listen. It didn't matter if you had heard the story countless times before – she would tell you anyway, like it was the first time you'd heard it. When she started, it was best to go with it, she wasn't really a 'stop me, if you've heard this one before' kind of girl.

She insisted that in my pre-school days I was able to decipher one record from another before I had the ability to read the label. She would give me a song title and then I would be instructed to sort through the pile of records and deliver the said record back to her. I rarely got one wrong, apparently. She marvelled at this wonderful talent, and how she had no idea how I managed to pull it off. I'm not sure either, but I suspect it might have had something to do with the colour of the record labels. My mother had high hopes that I might one day turn out to be a doctor, but felt comfortable that if that didn't work out, a career as the next Tony Blackburn was more or less in the bag.

As a little aside: when I first got into sixties music, in the mid-seventies, I was keen to find all these old records that I once owned. Dad suggested that they might be stored somewhere in the loft, so I went up there to investigate. Buried deep within the collection of old mattresses, bags of discarded photographs and birthday cards that would never be read again, and that old blue Formica table, I found just one record: 'I Feel Fine' by The Beatles. I had only just discovered The Beatles, but they had already begun to consume every part of me. With trembling fingers, I slipped this little slice of my childhood out of its green Parlophone sleeve. There it was, in my hands – a real, live, original Beatles record from the sixties, scratched to within an inch of its life, no doubt caused by the countless times that it had crashed down that spindle on top of the works of Harris and Cribbins more than a decade before, together with the years of dust collecting it had been through in the loft.

I excitedly descended the stepladder and the 14 stairs, and placed my newly found relic on the stubby, short spindle of Mum and Dad's Panasonic Music Centre, which resided in the now-inhabited front room. I lowered the stylus on to the damaged plastic and nervously retreated to the sofa. Nervously, because I had my doubts as to whether this sophisticated new equipment would have the ability to play the blemished vinyl with which it was being presented. I had visions of the stylus skating across the record in an act of modernistic rejection and a deep voice coming out of the speakers saying 'What the fuck was that? Do you not know who I am?' But my fears were ill placed. As my ears were filled with the now-familiar sounds of the feedback intro, segued into George Harrison's distinctive guitar riff, the hairs on the back of my neck came alive and that initial cold shiver was quickly replaced with a warm grin of satisfaction that spread from ear to ear. I'm not sure why I reacted like that – I knew the song like the back of my hand; it wasn't the song that excited me so much, but perhaps the thought that I was reacquainting myself with something from my past of which I had no recollection – something that was totally relevant to me, now I was a fully-fledged Beatleshead. The real revelation was when I flipped the single over to have a listen to the B-side, 'She's A Woman' – a big, fat belter of a song. I had already begun my mission to own every single thing the band ever recorded, and thus, already knew, that this track didn't appear on any Beatles album – the only place you could get the track was on the back of the 'I Feel Fine' single, so it was a huge bonus to have come across it so easily. I still have the single now; I never play it – there's no need – but I take a look at it from time to time.

Waterloo Sunset

I'm wondering whether there has ever been a cooler place to be than London in 1966. If you're the sort of person that likes to live in a place where everything is buzzing and exciting, and you were around in the early years of the first century, then Rome would have been that place. Similarly, in the late seventies it would have been New York City, but in 1966, London swung like a great big swingy thing.

For once it wasn't New York or Paris that dictated what we should be wearing or how we should be furnishing our homes. There had been a distinct shift of power in pop music too; American artists no longer dominated our charts and the American Billboard Hot 100, in contrast, was full of British acts.

If anyone was in any doubt that it was one of the apexes in our modern cultural history, the events of a couple of weeks during July of that year well and truly rammed it home. England hosted the football World Cup – and we only went and won the blighter.

The World Cup is one of the few gifts we have been given in life that can unite an entire nation in an overwhelming bond of excitement and patriotism, with people from all walks of life coming together for a common cause. I can't even begin to imagine what it was like to breathe and taste the atmosphere that was generated around the country during that fortnight; I've experienced a similar passion during Euro '96 and the World Cup semi-final of 1990, but they both ultimately ended in disappointment rather than the euphoric climatic triumph of 1966.

England started the tournament slowly and looked anything but world champions in the group stages, but victories over Argentina and Portugal in the knockout phases saw us come face-to-face with the old enemy West Germany in the final at Wembley Stadium.

I have no idea what I was doing that Saturday afternoon. I'm sure Mum and Dad would have watched the game, despite not having any interest in football whatsoever – it was just one of those things that you had to watch wherever you were, and I suspect the whole country came to a virtual standstill during those couple of hours; unfortunately, I have no personal recollection of it whatsoever and, to be perfectly honest, I'm quite cross about that.

While the rest of the nation endured their 19th nervous breakdown watching the drama unfold on the telly, I was probably upstairs in my bedroom, stomping around in time to Nancy Sinatra's 'These Boots Are Made For Walkin'' or attempting to 'Bend It' like Dave Dee, Dozy, Beaky, Mick and Tich. (who, if you don't know, were a 1960s pop group, despite sounding like the subs bench for the Seven Dwarfs football team).

Over the years, I have managed to convince myself that I am the only

English person alive on 30 July 1966 that didn't watch the World Cup final. I put this unfortunate fact totally down to really bad parenting. My dad was never a football fan, in fact I could demonstrate numerous occasions during the early seventies, after I had become seriously afflicted with the football disease, that proved he positively loathed the sport. As a teenager I became somewhat suspicious of any man that didn't like football. I assumed that as owners of testicles, it was every male's birthright to consume the beautiful game in vast quantities; anyone that didn't clearly had something wrong with them and should not be trusted. As time went on and more and more women – who clearly weren't endowed with the aforementioned collection of dangly trouser objects, became interested in football, I was forced to re-think this theory.

However, on this particular day – this very special day – any parental disdain for football should have been set aside, and I should have been plonked down in front of the TV and forced to watch those historic moments develop. As a five-year-old with no football leanings whatsoever, I would have hated every minute of it of course, but that's not the point.

I may not have been able to watch this match live but obviously I have seen the footage from this game many times. The TV companies have wheeled it out prior to every World Cup tournament since, in an attempt to get England fans in the mood for the forthcoming footy feast. The knock-on effect of this is that it instills false optimism in a nation that believes once again that this is to be 'our year'. I guess they will continue to do so until we win the thing again. It's funny, because whenever I watch the game, I can still feel the tension in the match even though I know exactly what is going to happen. I can feel the head-in-hands disappointment and almost hear the deafening anguish of an entire nation all shouting 'fuck' in unison, as the Germans equalise in the dying seconds of the match, sending the game into extra-time. Similarly, I can't help myself from beaming like a rafter at that moment the players and crowd go crazy when they realise that the Russian linesman has decided that Geoff Hurst's thunderous shot against the crossbar for the third goal bounced over the goal-line rather than on it.

The fourth goal, in the final moments, also scored by Geoff Hurst, will forever be immortalised by the words of Kenneth Wolstenholme, the BBC commentator that day. 'Here comes Hurst, there's people on the pitch – they think it's all over' and then as Hurst crashes the ball into the back of the German net for the third time that afternoon – 'it is now'! Perfect! Just like Paul Kantner, Wolstenholme's words ended up being more famous than he did. I've always felt a bit of sympathy for poor old Hugh Johns, the ITV commentator for the final. This was the greatest moment in England's sporting history and what did he come up with? 'Here's Hurst, he might make it three. He has! he has ... so that's it ... that is it'. It doesn't quite capture the moment or do it any kind of justice whatsoever. Not only was this the winning goal in the World Cup final, but also it was ENGLAND'S winning goal. In addition, it was the first time that anyone had scored a hat-trick in a World Cup final – a record that still stands today. How Johns must have kicked himself afterwards; I dread to think how many times he replayed that goal in his head, every single time coming up with a better way to describe it.

Earlier that year, I had begun my education at Gearies Infants School in Gants Hill. I had attended a pre-school nursery but apart from some trouser-wetting there isn't really very much to report. The school was a rather grey, old-fashioned looking building. Well it would be, it was built in the late 1920s, but what I mean is, it looked old-fashioned to me even in 1966. The classrooms felt cold and unfriendly, with high ceilings and those sash windows that the teachers had to open using a long pole with a hook on the end. I remember finding it highly amusing watching my teacher, Mrs Adler – a frail old lady who must have been 80, if she was a day – struggling to thread the hook on the end of that huge pole through the loop on the window – like an oversized version of that fairground attraction where you have to hook a floating duck to win a goldfish.

All of the classrooms were accessed via the stone-floored corridors that echoed every footstep, with each class having its own colour-coded door – presumably so us kids could identify them easily. At the end of one of the corridors was the school hall. I had never seen a room as big as that before and the gym apparatus that skirted two of the walls looked very exciting. However, my one remaining anecdotal memory of the school hall is not a pleasant one. I might say at this point that those of you with a weak stomach should look away now, but a more practical piece of advice would be to skip the next paragraph.

We were having an appalling winter (1967/68) and this particular morning there had been a heavy blizzard. I had the obligatory stinking cold that generally goes with these things. Morning assembly took place in the school hall and we would sit in rows cross-legged on the parquet floor and be preached to in the usual school assembly way. It crept up on me suddenly without any warning of either its arrival or its immensity. Before I had a chance to extract my hanky from my pocket, I let out the most enormously loud, head-turning sneeze, which was unfortunately accompanied by a globule of snot that was so mountainous, it wouldn't have surprised me if I'd spotted several members of the royal family taking a winter ski break on its lower slopes. This is a most appropriate metaphor because it was the white knitted skiers on Alison Greenwold's red cardigan that halted the flight of the aforementioned snot-rocket. I was beside myself with embarrassment and far too scared to inform her that I had blemished her cardy. I wanted to get my hanky out and dab away gently at the mess, but I thought that this would just draw attention to what I had done, so didn't bother. I'm not sure why none of her friends told her, but I suspect that they were too repulsed to speak. By the way, I knew you wouldn't skip this bit.

There were no playing fields at Gearies, just a grey concrete playground surrounded by more greyness in the form of railings around its perimeter. The infant school was flanked by the junior school that I would attend from 1969–72 on one side, and by Gearies Secondary Modern for Girls (which I didn't attend at all) on the other. The infant and junior schools had adjoining playgrounds. We weren't allowed any ball games in the infant school, which rendered the cricket wicket that was painted on to one of the playground walls completely pointless – it was there just to tease.

It all happened in that playground though. Being an old school, the toilets were located outside. Games of 'It' were started by pushing someone into the girls' toilets, which, come to think of it, is maybe a little strange. It was deemed to be the shame of shames for a boy to be thrown into the girls' loos by their classmates, and one would struggle against the mob for dear life to avoid this terrible fate. The person that ended up in there had 'the lurgi' and was proclaimed to be 'It' – this was clearly because girls were dirty and smelt of poo. The person 'infected' with 'the lurgi' would then chase someone around the playground and try and touch them, thereby passing on 'the lurgi' and making that person 'It'. There were ways to avoid being 'It'; having something crossed like fingers or legs was known as 'fainites' and this made you immune from catching this dreadful disease, despite being caught by the carrier. Thinking back on it now, I love the get-out clauses that were desperately brought in to avoid being lurgified. Some of these included:

1. If you were caught without 'fainites' that is without anything visible being crossed, you might simply claim 'I can't be 'it' because I had my hair crossed!'.

2. Injected for life without touch – A completely meaningless phrase that, despite its meaninglessness, actually meant that you didn't have to cross anything whatsoever, rendering 'fainites' completely pointless.

3. And my personal favourite – and this should be said without pausing for breath – 'I can't be 'it' because I did fainites in 1964 and it lasts for ten years and I know you didn't see it but I did it and if you don't believe me, you can ask my mum'.

The boys' toilets were the setting for the first bout of ridicule I can remember suffering. This would almost certainly have taken place on my very first day at school. The purpose of the trouser-fly had not yet been explained to me, and I wasn't aware at this point that it was possible to have a wee without lowering one's shorts and pants. So I took my first school pee much in the same manner as I would at home. Much to my dismay and eternal embarrassment, the older boys that were populating the loos at that precise moment thought it was hilarious to see my bare bum exposed to the crowd. As they ran out of the loos, no doubt to round up more of their friends to come and laugh at my arse, a lad my own age, Paul Margolis, came to my rescue. He demonstrated there and then (using his own winkle, you'll understand) the correct procedure for peeing in public. It was the start of a beautiful friendship.

In terms of ice-breaking and opening gambits, Paul 'Mongo' Margolis' was probably unique, but nevertheless we moved on from this episode and he became my first friend. I'll be honest and say that I'm struggling to remember any other school stories about him that are worthy of repetition, but he did show up again in the late seventies after being mercilessly sacked as the drummer from another friend's band. I recently bumped into his parents, who proudly informed me that he is now a professional drummer in a death-metal band called Septic Tank II, after suffering many years as a drug addict. That's nice, I thought – living the dream. However, a million miles away from the world of death metal, it was he that told me my first-ever joke; it was so childishly contrived, that it's almost still funny:

A man loses his dog who is called 'Willy'. So he reports his loss to the police. The policeman asks the man for his address and rather conveniently, he informs the copper that his house is called 'Hairy Bum'. So the copper says 'have you checked around the house to make sure he's not locked in a cupboard?'. To which the man replies 'yes, I've looked all over my hairy bum, but I can't find my willy!'

It's quite bizarre really; I am normally terrible at remembering jokes, even ones that I only heard a week ago, yet I remember that one so clearly.

Apart from the unfortunate toilet incident, I don't remember starting school being too much of an ordeal and I think I settled in ok. I was good with numbers and learnt to read fairly easily. My mum took me to join Gants Hill Children's Library, which was a cavern of wonder to someone whose world had just been opened up to the power of the written word. The *Cat in the Hat* series, several titles by Enid Blyton and all sorts of Ladybird books were the sort of stuff I cut my teeth on – just like most kids I suspect, but I do recall reading lots of books and nagging Mum on a regular basis that we needed to go to the library to change them. Mum was a keen reader too and I can certainly remember hanging around the adjacent Adult Library while she chose her new books and thinking how dull they all looked, with their tiny writing and lack of pictures.

Unfortunately, the reading bug didn't stay with me for long and within a few years other things took over. As far as fiction is concerned that is still the case, I have never returned to it. I consider myself to be extremely poorly read. In terms of 'the classics', I have read very few. This is something that bothers me, but clearly not enough for me to do anything about it. I rarely read a novel – all the books I read these days tend to be about music, or biographies of people I admire.

I was pathetically hopeless at anything arty at school: drawing, painting, modelling anything remotely creative, I struggled with. It was very frustrating to look at the marvellous creations of my peers and then observe the mess sitting on the desk in front of me. I'd love to be able to make things or draw well but it's just not something that has ever come naturally to me. Generally, though, at this stage I enjoyed school.

I think my teacher at infant school may well have thought of me as a sensible type. I don't think there was any hard evidence to support this notion – maybe I just had sensible shoes. A new boy joined my class halfway through one of the terms. His name was Mark Karpel and he arrived from his previous school with a reputation for being a bit of a tearaway. I was given the responsibility of 'looking after' him, as maybe they thought that I would be a calming influence. I can't remember what being his minder entailed, but I guess it's always hard for kids to join an already established group and this arrangement gave him an instant friend. He didn't really need me – he was much more outgoing than I was – but I was impressed with his naughtiness and sense of fun. We became really good friends and would go around to each other's houses to play after school. He had a younger brother called Spencer – yes, they really were called Mark and Spencer! Spencer was even naughtier than Mark. I'm not sure whether it was because of the Mark and Spencer thing but Spencer was known as Spud. Even his mum called him Spud. When I would go to their house, they only ever wanted to play rough-and-tumble type games. It wasn't what I was used to, but it was fun and I loved going there although I was always slightly relieved when Dad would arrive with the car to collect me. Mum and Dad didn't really like Mark and didn't like me playing with him; they considered him to be a ruffian.

Around this time, I caught German measles. It was vile; I had to have a nurse come to the house every day for about a week and administer an injection of some sort into my bottom, which was both very embarrassing and rather painful. I was covered from head to toe in spots, and as someone that was already very freckly; I must have looked like the fall-out from an explosion at a dot-to-dot book factory. Needless to say, I was absent from school during the illness and bored silly. I asked Mum whether Mark could come round and play and reluctantly she agreed. While he was over, we'd been doing one of those colour-by-numbers pictures together. After he left, I couldn't find the felt-tip pens that we had been using and asked Dad if he had seen them anywhere. He guessed straight away that Mark had nicked them and was absolutely furious. I insisted that Mark wouldn't do such a thing but dad was adamant and put me, still wearing my pyjamas, slippers and dressing-gown, in the car and drove me round to Mark's house. Dad went steaming in, all guns blazing, and sure enough there on the floor were Mark and Spud colouring in with my pens. Dad collected the pens up and told us that we not to play with each other anymore. It was all very disappointing and when I went back to school things were a little bit awkward between us. But after a while, our friendship got back on course; he apologised for the theft and I apologised for going round to his house in my pyjamas. We ignored the parental warning, and everything was ok from then onwards. By the time we moved up to the junior school we were in different classes and drifted apart a bit as we gathered new friends, but there was still a bond. He became one of the tough kids at school, but not a bully; there was something honourable about his toughness and he stepped in to rescue me from sticky situations once or twice – never more so than the last time I saw him.

It was around 1979, a time when football hooliganism was at its most rife and I was on my way home from a match decked out in my West Ham scarf. As my tube train pulled into Leytonstone station and the carriage doors opened, I heard the yobbish overtones of what sounded like around seven or eight Tottenham supporters chanting on the platform. They entered my carriage and I kept my head down but they immediately spotted me before I had a chance to bury my colours within the confines of my jacket. My heart sank and they surrounded me. I knew what was coming next and mentally prepared myself for hospital food.

'A fuckin' 'ammer', skilfully observed one of the crew. 'Gis that piece of shit yer cunt' spat another pulling at my scarf and jacket collar. (Scarf nicking was a common form of trophy collecting amongst rival football supporters back then).

I unknotted the scarf and as I looked up to shamefully hand it over, I instantly recognised one of the shaven-headed Neanderthals hovering over me.

'Alright Mark?' I said, desperately hoping that he would recognise me. 'You been to the match?' Why the hell did I say that? Where else would he have been – the Ideal Home Exhibition? It was just one of those things that you sometimes say for the sake of saying something and you know it's wrong the moment you hear the words leaving your lips.

He gazed at me for a second or two and a smallish smile crept across his face. 'Anthony Shelley?'

'Alright?' I replied, this time a little more confidently.

I had heard about Mark's reputation through the grapevine. He and Spud were well known in football fan circles as two of the hardest thugs in the Tottenham crew.

'Leave him alone, he's alright,' he said in an authoritative manner, and the pack instantly stood down. I got up from my seat, more than a little relieved that my erstwhile chum had recognised me despite me having considerably more hair than when our paths had last crossed. We chatted for the remainder of the journey back to Gants Hill, mainly about football, and I spoke in that slightly more exaggerated cockney accent that I use when trying to appear harder than I actually am. This involves being looser of jaw, dropping more letters than is actually necessary and throwing in the odd wink or two. Fortunately there was no mention of felt-tip pens or pyjamas. When we arrived at Gants Hill we both said how great it had been to bump into each other, but at that particular moment, I felt my need was greater than his. We shook hands and parted company. I never saw him again.

As I walked home from the station along the Eastern Avenue, it hit me that I had just had a very lucky escape and I reflected on the irony that our friendship had started all those years ago with me as Mark's minder and had ended with him being mine.

Other friends that I should mention from around this time included the 'Caped Crusaders'; my record player took a bit of a back seat once I had discovered the delights of Batman and Robin. I was Batman mental. How come no one ever coined the phrase Batmania? I read all the books and comics, collected the bubble-gum cards and had a most fantastic toy Batmobile that fired orange bullets when you pressed a button located on the boot (or trunk as Bruce Wayne would have called it).

Saturday nights offered a double televisual bonanza – *Batman* followed by *Doctor Who*. I'd be so eager for this feast that I'd always switch on the TV too early and catch the tail-end of *Grandstand*, meaning I had to suffer the agonising wait as that familiar voice droned its way through the afternoon's football results. I sat there urging him to finally get to Scottish League Division Two. I thought that by reading out the results at twice the speed that he did, I could somehow help him to get to the all-important Stenhousemuir-Arbroath result quicker, and then it would all be over.

I accepted *Batman* for what it was at the time, and it wasn't until I watched the series again in my teens that I appreciated how brilliantly tongue-in-cheek it was. The actors, Adam West and Burt Ward, must have had so much fun making the series. The scripts were so funny and fabulously corny. Whenever Batman and Robin were in trouble, or whenever they got the better of the Joker or the Penguin, there was always a quip, high on punnery, to go with it.

'It's no use Joker! I knew you'd employ your sneezing powder, so I took an anti-allergy pill! Instead of sneezing, I've caught you cold!'

And Robin always had a 'holy' expression appropriate to the sticky situation in which they had got themselves into: 'holy fancy-dress party, Batman'; 'holy quails eggs, Batman'; 'holy rusty metal, Batman'.

I was loyal to Batman. I liked Superman but he didn't quite cut it for me and I don't remember *Spiderman* being on TV in Britain during the sixties. In any case, *Spiderman* was a silly idea whichever way you looked at it. Batman was a far more believable comic-book hero than silly old Superman or Spiderman – and with his mask, cape and 'tasseltacular' elbow-length leather gloves that could magically emit a 'pow' and a 'bam' balloon from them when they made contact with the face of The Riddler's henchmen, was far better dressed too. He was the holy grail of comic-book heroes – and the holy quail.

With the reemergence of new episodes of *Doctor Who*, there has been a lot of nostalgia for the original series. The common memory that gets trotted out time and time again is that of watching the programme from behind the sofa (nobody calls it a couch anymore – why is that?), due to its scary content. I don't have that memory of it at all. I can quite clearly picture myself sitting enthralled right in front of the telly and being told by my mum to move further back because sitting so close would give me square eyes, which, to be honest, was a far scarier prospect than anything *Doctor Who* had to offer. Dad never complained about me being too close to the telly. In the days before remote controls he probably considered it handy having me close by to switch the channels for him. Actually, we didn't call them channels; it was always 'sides'. 'Let's see what's on the other side, Anthony'. The other side always referred to either BBC1 or ITV, despite there being a third channel – there was never anything much on BBC2.

I've never liked science fiction – never really understood what the fuss was about – but I loved *Doctor Who*. I think this was mainly because his enemies were so brilliant. The Cybermen, who were very scary chaps; the Yetis, who seem to have been completely overlooked and lost in the mists of time; and the Daleks, who were by far my favourites of the nasties. I wanted to be a Dalek. I made a Dalek outfit out of a cardboard box, using kitchen utensils for the arm things. I perfected the voice and everything, but no one ever asked me to be one. The Doctor and I didn't stick with each for too long. Patrick Troughton was the Doctor when I was a big fan; by the time Jon Pertwee took over the role, I'd had enough and moved on.

Despite not being allowed to take up a career as a Dalek and the World Cup final business, I have very little to complain about regarding this period of my life. My early childhood was more or less perfect and I grew up in a loving and secure environment, which is all you can ask for really.

I don't remember my parents playing with me much when I was a kid, but the interaction with them that I do recall vividly is the days out in London. Dad was very much into history and I think this is where my love for it came from. These trips usually took place on a Sunday, as Dad worked on Saturdays, and we visited all the sights: the Tower of London, Trafalgar Square, St. Paul's Cathedral, Big Ben, Westminster Abbey, the

Monument in Pudding Lane and Buckingham Palace (in those days you could only look at it from outside). Dad would impart all his knowledge about these buildings and I would get a sense of the historic values of these beautiful places from what he was teaching me. There is a fabulous photograph somewhere of us standing outside the Post Office Tower (now called the BT Tower), in which my sister Mads and I are posing holding a very small primate, which of course would be illegal now. There always used to be photographers outside these tourist attractions wanting to sell you photos of your visit. I love this photo, not because of the monkey but because of the black winklepicker shoes with elasticated sides that I am wearing in it. They were very cool and no doubt housed a compass in the heel. The monkey wasn't at all cool – he was wearing a knitted tank top.

We would take a stroll along the Embankment, eating ice-cream, or browse the paintings hung up over the railings of Hyde Park. We'd sometimes go and listen to the assorted lunatics spouting nonsense at Speaker's Corner. If we were lucky, a Sunday outing would end with pancakes at 'My Old Dutch' in Holborn.

I think these trips into London were responsible for the start of my love affair with the city – to me, it's still a very special place. All the history helps and I think you would be hard pushed to find another city in the world steeped in so much of it, with so many beautiful monuments within such a small area. My favourite building is Tower Bridge. I think if you're looking for an icon that screams 'London' then that's the one I'd go for. Some would go for Big Ben, I know, but Tower Bridge is far prettier. I love London at night. To get the best view, I like to be situated on the south side of London Bridge with the illuminated Tower of London and Tower Bridge to the right and the huge dome of St Pauls slightly to the left. The reflected lights in the Thames make the city look so tranquil, and disguise the filthy brown water of the river and the throbbing busyness of the metropolis by daylight. The contrast is stunning and I'm not quite sure how the city manages it.

The finest song ever written about my city is 'Waterloo Sunset' by The Kinks. This beautifully understated song, skilfully crafted by Ray Davies, somehow within its three brief minutes manages to capture all the atmosphere of mid-sixties London so evocatively through brilliant imagery, without ever being blatantly obvious about anything. It's a song that looks at both positive and negative images of London, from the perspective of a lonely man doing a spot of people-watching and reflecting on his own situation. It's a very touching and emotional lyric from Davies and one that can make me quite misty-eyed from time to time. Of all the millions of songs that I have heard during my life, this one is one of the very best.

I can't imagine ever being able to live too far from London – I would miss it terribly. I tried living in Oxford for two years in the late eighties and was completely out of sorts. New York is the only other place that I've been to where I could envisage myself living. It has a similar sort of vibe to London, so maybe that's why I might find the transformation easier.

The final memory I have about my home life in the early years was the birthday parties, and my sixth birthday party in particular. It was not extraordinary in itself, but in later years my mum used to recall her memories of this party more than any other. It was marred for her by the behaviour of one of my guests, David Freed. I think he was invited because his mum was friendly with mine; I don't think we were friends for any other reason, because he was a year older than me and therefore not a classmate like the rest of the partygoers. She used to tell me how this boy, perfectly behaved and well-mannered within the boundaries of his own home, released all his pent-up energy and went completely crazy at ours. This included climbing on to the table (that blue Formica one), throwing food, bursting the balloons and refusing to drink the orange squash that was on offer, demanding that he would only drink Ribena. He sounds like a vile little shit, doesn't he, but remember the name – he'll be cropping up again a bit later. Although he won't have any idea that he did, that boy changed my life.

It's All Too Beautiful

California in 1967's Summer of Love sounded like a great place to be if you were in your late teens, so it's a bit of a shame that I was only six and living in Essex. I don't think I even had a pair of sandals as a token gesture. I think my cousin was a hippy though, if that counts? She was the right age and I've definitely seen photos of her wearing a floral mini-dress. I'm not sure if she took the actual magic bus to the 'mystic East', but today, her daughter is a yoga instructor, so she probably did.

I think being a hippy is one of those things that sounds really great in theory, but in practice leaves you smelling unpleasant for long periods of time, which is less great. They had good intentions, but I suppose in the end, their ideals were a little too … well, idealistic. But along the way they had some lovely festivals, didn't they? Nice clothes, too.

As with any other youth culture, the hippies had their own uniform of psychedelic paraphernalia that we are all familiar with, but it's interesting to note that this was the period when the cross-over between men and women's clothes became most cross-overy. In terms of hippy chic, it was the boys that embraced the girls' wardrobes more than the other way around, which may have caused a surly eyebrow or two to be raised by the cosmically challenged. Take the kaftan for example – it's just a big dress and, quite frankly, just an excuse for boys to not wear trousers without having to be Scottish. Men grew their hair halfway down their backs, and beards halfway down their fronts, which was at least nice and symmetrical, if a little high maintenance. Sounds great so far, doesn't it.

The hippy buzz-words of 'peace and love' were passed around the globe like one humongous spliff and before you could say 'make love, not war', there was a whole new set of hippy-inspired words invading our language. But the real key to speaking fluent hippy was to punctuate every sentence with the word 'man' as regularly as possible. 'Bread' was no longer just something that you ate, and although 'tripping' now meant something completely different, it still usually resulted in one being left flat-out on the floor. A woman could be referred to as 'man' even though she was woman, and a man would likewise be called 'man' despite the fact that he had hair like a girl. Both men and women could be referred to as 'cats', although this wasn't a reciprocal arrangement with the feline world, whilst dogs on the other hand, regardless of gender, were not called 'cat' or 'man' and were generally still called Rover.

I'm not aware that the Summer of Love ever made it to Gants Hill. It probably had a peek, spotted the number of burly cab drivers that lived there, decided there was nothing it could do and fled back up the old A11 to Leytonstone, scared out of its wits. Pop history certainly doesn't record any rock festivals in Valentines Park during the late sixties, which is where

I spent a lot of my time at weekends and during the school holidays. But had the Jimi Hendrix Experience or Cream been noodling away in Melbourne Fields, I doubt I would have noticed anyway. I don't hold any grudges against those bands for not playing in Valentines Park; The Kinks, The Who and The Beach Boys were all no-shows too. Even the Small Faces didn't turn up to play their beloved Itchycoo Park.

Valentines Park may not have played host to the glitterati of pop, but it did see Blakey from *On the Buses* make a celebrated appearance – and Black Beauty, he came too. Both of them came for one purpose – to open the 12th Ilford Scout and Guide Groups' annual garden fete.

You may be thinking that Blakey (real name Stephen Lewis) from *On the Buses* and Black Beauty (real name Jet Black – not the one that later played drums in The Stranglers – no horses were ever in The Stranglers) from *The New Adventures of Black Beauty* are a strange duo of celebrities to open a garden fete – and you'd be right. You're probably speculating how on earth these two major stars, with their enormous egos, could co-exist on the same stage? Would they be bustling with each other for prime position on the rostrum with all the autograph-hunters? Would they be trying to outdo each other with crowd-pleasing specialities: Black Beauty neighing, tossing his mane and counting to ten by stamping his hooves, whilst Blakey rattled out a couple of fist-clenched catchphrases like 'I'll do you for this, Beauty' and throwing in a few 'aww my gawds' for good measure? Well, fret about it no longer, as Blakey and Black Beauty didn't actually open the fete together. They performed their fete-opening duties in different years – consecutively, if I remember correctly, and as far as I'm aware, these two showbiz colossi have never met each other. Of course, those of you with more enquiring minds will simply be wondering, how the hell does a horse open a garden fete?

I had joined the 12th Ilford Cub Pack around the late sixties and Mum and Dad had become heavily involved too – Dad as the Group Treasurer and Mum as a Brown Owl of the Brownie Pack that my sister belonged to.

I was very excited as the day of 'Blakeyfete' approached; I'd never met anyone off the telly before and I was a huge *On the Buses* fan. As Dad was involved in the organisation of the day's proceedings we had to be at the park early, and I was commissioned to do a few odd jobs. When Blakey arrived he was holed up in a frame tent, which was where he would be carrying out the autograph signing later in the day. Someone official asked me to take him a cup of tea and a couple of biscuits to sustain him before the hoards arrived – a job that resulted in my first one-to-one with a real live celebrity. I don't recall it as being remarkable in any way, I just remember being surprised that he didn't speak with Blakey's voice, which was disappointing. I ached to ask him to do the laugh that he did on the show, but I just didn't have the nerve. Still, that never stopped me from dining out on our meeting and showing off my autograph when I got back to school the following Monday.

Meeting Black Beauty the following year was even less distinguished. I didn't get to serve him his hot beverage of choice and he had a 'no autographs' policy. To be honest, the equestrian hero held very little interest for me. Anna Sewell's book was really for girls, and the TV show was a kind of costume drama – a genre that I detest even now I'm old and supposed to like that sort of thing; as far as I'm concerned, almost any drama in which the actors are wearing clothes that pre-date the 1960s is a costume drama and I don't touch it. So all in all I was less than star-struck about meeting Black Beauty; it was one of the oddest choices that could have been made in terms of celebrity fete-openers, and despite having been there, I still can't answer the question of exactly how a horse opened a garden fete. On the upside, it was the only time I've witnessed a celebrity having a shit.

I'm not sure whose idea it was to order 200 copies of the *New Adventures of Black Beauty* soundtrack LP – 189 of which remained unsold – but the fact that they came home with us and spent the rest of the seventies in several unopened boxes in our garden shed, makes me point the finger of suspicion squarely in my dad's direction. How was this ever a good idea? It's not as if the beast was able to sign the LPs, thus making them some sort of collector's item that might suddenly be stumbled upon by an unsuspecting record fair goer whilst he thumbs his way through the Barclay James Harvest bootleg crate. I also wonder what happened to those eleven sold copies? Did the purchasers ever play them or did they end up cast asunder, jammed at the back of someone's wardrobe with the Ker Plunk and Buckaroo? Maybe they are still loved and serve as a reminder to their buyers of the day they met Black Beauty? The thought that just one person who bought the record that day is now an obsessive record collector and currently displays the LP neatly sandwiched between his Beautiful South and Black Sabbath albums is too delicious to totally dismiss.

Back at school I had a new best friend – Ray 'Scuzz' Scurry. We first met in the first year of Gearies Junior's and our initial common bond was that we both thought the word 'humbug' was utterly hilarious and guffawed our way through Mrs Wyatt's readings of *The Phantom Tollbooth*, in which the Humbug character appeared. We were also united in our hatred of Mrs Wyatt. Teachers in the junior school were that little bit stricter than they had been in the infants and that came as quite a shock to me. Being sent out of the class for talking too much, laughing too much or just generally being too much was a regular occurrence. Mrs Wyatt was a very art-orientated teacher and, as I've said, I was rubbish at that sort of thing; she enjoyed ridiculing my efforts. I didn't know it at the time but, thinking about her now, she was most certainly a hippy. I can picture her now in a pink crocheted mini-dress with a fake gold chain belt around her waist. She wore far too much make-up and she stank of what I now think was probably patchouli oil. Yes, she was a hippy, but she didn't send much love and peace in my direction.

Scuzz was one of those very athletic kids; he could run faster than shit off a shovel, and was great at the usual boys' things like climbing trees and skimming stones, and knew about fishing and motorbikes. He could do almost everything better than I could and I suppose I was a little bit in awe of him. One thing that I particularly remember about him was that, even at the age of eight, he was very aware of how friends should behave towards one another, as if he had had a very strict moral code drummed into him. This kind of makes him sound like a goody-goody type, but he was far from that. We were thick as thieves throughout junior school.

We used to egg each other on to do more and more daring things in class. This might begin with poking the person sitting in front us with a ruler or hitting someone at the other side of the classroom with a tiny ball of paper that had been sucked tightly together with saliva and shot, pea-shooter style, through a Bic biro shaft that had had the ink refill removed. Sometimes things might progress to asking Mrs Wyatt if we could go to the toilet and when permission was granted, walk out of the classroom with a slightly more ludicrous limp than the last time we'd asked. The discovery that a swear word could be shouted out disguised within an exaggerated cough came as a revelation, and was often employed. The dares didn't stay within the boundaries of school, and jumping off the roof of Gants Hill Odeon is quite possibly the most ridiculous thing that I ever did.

When I have told this story in the past, I always say 'jumping off the Odeon roof' for dramatic effect, but in reality it wasn't quite as dangerous as that. Gants Hill Odeon sat proudly on the crown of the Eastern Avenue, about half a mile from my house. The fire exits from the cinema opened up onto an alley that ran around the back of the building. On a good day, you might find one of these exits left ajar and you could sneak into the cinema without paying, and spend the afternoon watching a film over and over again. We always used to check just in case, but usually ended up disappointed. On one such occasion, Scuzz thought that it would be a great idea if we climbed the iron staircase that ran around the back of the building and jumped, stunt-man style, from the flat roof that was about twelve feet off the ground onto the stony surface below. Sounded simple – looked terrifying. But a dare is a dare, and if he was doing it, I was bloody well doing it too. In one of his less honourable moments, it was deemed that I should go first. So I had a look, shuffled my way to the end of the roof and, in a split-second of ill-advised bluffness, threw myself off.

I landed awkwardly, spraining my ankle quite badly in the process. As I writhed around on the gravel in absolute agony, I was acutely aware of Scuzz following me down and executing a perfect landing, which would have probably been rewarded with an ensemble of 5.9s and 6.0s from the judges, had there been any. Why he chose to take the short route down after seeing my fate I'm not quite sure, but there was never any doubt that he would be able to do it better than me, and perhaps that was the reason. He helped me hobble back home in his usual honourable way. I can't remember how I explained my injury to my parents, but whatever the story was, it was a lie.

Come to think of it, I was quite an injury-prone kid and the sprained ankle, despite the dramatic style in which it was achieved, pales into insignificance when compared with the permanent damage caused by the Great Swing-Boat Incident of 1969.

Corrine Miles was my first girlfriend. Well that's not strictly true. I mean obviously we played the 'you show me yours and I'll show you mine' game, but we never kissed or anything serious like that. But in terms of friends that owned a different shaped winkle – she was the first. She didn't care much for dolls houses, ponies or reading *Bunty*, and she certainly wouldn't have entertained the idea of going to see silly old Black Beauty open a garden fete – she preferred more boyish pursuits, so for a girl I thought she was fairly cool. We would often go to Valentines Park on our bikes and do boyish things like building dams in the streams there and collecting sticklebacks in a jam-jar. She provided a nice contrast to doing these types of things with Scuzz, as it gave me the opportunity to be top dog, for a change, and generally to show off a bit.

There was a great adventure playground at the park with the usual sets of brightly coloured swings, slides and roundabouts. The centrepiece of the playground was the swing-boat; a huge, cast-iron structure like a big see-saw. Whilst most of the kids would sit astride the contraption, there would be one kid on the ground at either end, pushing it for all their might, trying to get the boat as high as possible. Once the boat got a bit of height, the kid at each end would grab the pushing handles with both hands as it came towards them and thus be lifted clean off the ground. This was great fun and far more interesting than sitting on it like a normal person. On one such occasion, I was pushing the boat while Corrine was standing beside me waiting for her turn to get on. I was so busy trying to show her how hard I could push it and how high I could be lifted, that when I turned to face her – just to check that she was suitably impressed – I completely forgot about the oncoming mass of metal and as I turned back the swing-boat caught me with full force, square in the mouth.

There was blood everywhere as it claimed a diagonal lump from one of my two front teeth. Not only did this hurt like hell but it was also particularly galling as I had only recently cultivated the tooth and it had now been transformed into a fang that Count Dracula would have been proud to call his own. The upshot of this careless act of self-cosmetic surgery was that about six months or so later, the tooth turned black with decay and had to be removed; because the tooth was one of my 'grown-up' teeth, the choice was either to have a huge gap or become an eight-year-old kid with a false tooth.

I plumped for the latter of these options. I had a great dentist. His name, most comically, was Mr Sucker. A better name for someone that takes teeth out for a living I couldn't imagine, but he was a brilliant dentist, very gentle, and I thought he was a genius – so much so that for quite a few years following this episode, I wanted to be a dentist too. He made me my tooth and I was extremely proud of it. It amused me at first that I could scare unsuspecting people by dangling it out on the end of my tongue, but later I went through stages of unease with it; in my teenage years I was highly embarrassed when it used to accidentally fly out of my mouth and land on something inappropriate across a classroom during uncontrollable fits of laughter or coughing. As I got older I grew to like it again, when I was able to make my kids laugh with tricks of disappearing teeth.

I was less impressed with our family doctor, Dr Wallach. He was a horrid man, very matter-of-fact and unsympathetic to whatever ailment you might have; he was short and Jewish, with a thick Germanic accent that lent itself more to sounding scientific than in any way compassionate. His name was pronounced 'Wallock' which led to Mads and I later giving him the rather obvious nickname of 'Wallach-the-Bollock'. To be fair, we also called Mr Sucker, 'Sucker-the-Fucker' – not because he was one, just because it was funny.

It was via Wallach-the-Bollock that I discovered that something rather spectacular had happened in space in July 1969. Mum had some trouble with her knees and Wallach-the-Bollock had prescribed some sort of pill as its cure. That's all he ever did – send you off with a prescription for some vile medicine or a bottle of tablets. When Mum complained that she had difficulty swallowing pills, his less-than-sympathetic response was:

'Vot, you can't svollow a leetal peeel – a man has yust valked on za moon, ant you can't svollow a peeel?'

It could have happened the day before, the week before or even the month before, but I had been completely unaware of the exploits of Neil Armstrong and the rest of the Apollo 11 crew until Wallach-the-Bollock's inadvertent newsflash. Like the 1966 World Cup Final before it, I feel now that it's something I should have been made to watch, but I wonder how impressed I would have actually have been. At eight years old I believed there was already a man that lived in the moon and it was perfectly normal behaviour for a cow to jump over it, so I somehow think I might have been slightly underwhelmed to see a man simply walk on it.

Television Man is Crazy

As 1969 slipped into 1970, the dawning of the new decade had a slightly back-down-to-earth eeriness about it. There was much wailing and gnashing of teeth as The Beatles announced they were calling it a day. I didn't care – I'd barely heard of them – but history records that everyone else was a little bit cross. It seems to me that the seventies announced their arrival like your parents coming home early from holiday and interrupting the party you'd organised without their knowledge – I don't think anyone was ready for the festivities to be over just yet.

From a personal point of view, I don't remember the early seventies as being a particularly depressing time for the country but looking back now at the news stories of the time, it seems that, politically, everything was going wrong.

As the economy recovered slightly during the early months of 1970 and as Labour were well ahead of the Conservatives in the opinion polls, Wilson decided to call a General Election. It was the first election since the voting age had been reduced to eighteen. Armed with the vote of rebellious youth, the Conservatives won a surprise victory and the posh Edward Heath became the new resident at Number 10. So much for the spirit of Woodstock.

I wasn't really interested in reading all that boring old election stuff, or watching the news bulletins on TV. Watching the news was very much an adult pursuit and one that, in the case of my dad, was carried out with as much enthusiasm as my avoidance of it. I would often be forced to scuttle away from my position in front of the telly as Dad insisted on the channel being switched mid-programme, so that he could catch the latest broadcast. 'Stay and watch it – you might just learn something' he would say in a not-nearly-persuasive-enough tone. Sometimes I hung around and watched and even managed to pick up on a little bit of what was going on, but it mostly went over my head – it just seemed too grown up to really grab my attention, with its dull set of presenters telling tales of misery. Dull they may have been but I do remember some of those presenters (or newscasters as they were known): Richard Baker, Peter Woods, Reginald Bosanquet, Kenneth Kendall, Gordon Honeycombe and Sandy Gall.

Kenneth Kendall was a bit of a dark horse as it turned out. These days the media discuss the sexuality of TV celebrities with the same matter-of-factness as they do their diet regimes, but who would have guessed back then that boring old Kenneth Kendall was as gay as a maypole? In fact, it wasn't until a whole gaggle of newsreaders and TV presenters did their 'Nothing Like A Dame' routine on *The Morecambe & Wise Show* that it was officially confirmed that newsreaders had anything at all below their concealed waistline, let alone did anything rude with it.

The *News at Ten* on ITV was a slightly sexed-up version of its BBC counterpart. It had those dramatic 'bongs' of Big Ben heralding each of the main points of the news at the start of the programme so that you knew what was coming later, in the hope that you would keep watching. *News at Ten* also introduced the concept of two newscasters to present the bulletin rather than the traditional one. At the end of the programme, as they shuffled their papers and the studio lights faded, the two silhouetted presenters would pretend to have a conversation, which we were expected to believe was about the news stories they had just read. They were probably just speculating on what they might be having for their tea, but most disappointedly, not once did they use this darkened opportunity to make shadow puppets.

The 'on-the-spot' reporters on *News at Ten* would 'glam up' their reports by personalising their sign offs. 'Andrew Gardener, News at Ten, Saigon' – it gave the viewer a slight taste of the exotic, except when Andrew was in Dagenham covering the latest strike at Ford.

When I did feel obliged to obey my Dad's request and watch the news, all the stories that filled the screens seemed to be so depressing: Vietnam, people being blown to bits in Northern Ireland, starvation in Biafra, fat dictators taking over in Uganda, strikes, strikes and more strikes. Everyone was going on strike: postal workers, ship builders, firemen – and when the bin men and gravediggers followed suit, Britain hit an 8.5 on the mingometer and the army were called in with their Green Goddesses to clear up the mess.

The dreariness of the news stories of the day didn't seem to affect my life to any great extent – apart from when the power-cuts meant no telly for several nights a week. So despite all these troubles in the adult world, and all the ridiculous fashions, the seventies were my decade. They were the decade of my youth and as much as I hanker after the sixties, it's the seventies that played host to my salad days and I'm not too disappointed about that. They were great times and it wasn't all kipper ties and platforms shoes you know.

I was never really that taken with kids' TV, but I was partial to the sitcoms and sketch shows that were shown in the early part of the evening. *On the Buses, Please Sir! Love Thy Neighbour, Are You Being Served? Man About the House, The Dick Emery Show* and *The Benny Hill Show* were all firm favourites with me. These shows were not really aimed at children; they were sexist, racist, stereotypical, obvious and packed with sexual innuendo and double entendres, and therefore perfect for the adolescent schoolboy. I adored them all.

It was here that I learned that women really enjoyed being referred to as 'crumpet' and in early seventies comedy there were only two jokes – breasts and homosexuality. To writers and audiences alike, huge breasts were hilarious. They were never referred to as huge breasts of course –

knockers, bristols, bazookas or charlies was the correct seventies comedy terminology – but a sitcom just couldn't be funny unless at least one member of the cast possessed a chest the size of Geoff Capes' breakfast that jiggled around like a couple of Space Hoppers.

Are You Being Served?, set in the Grace Brothers department store, was the epitome of an early seventies sitcom that included most of the prerequisites I have just mentioned. There was innuendo flouted across every episode and its biggest contributor was Mollie Sugden, who played the blue-rinsed battleaxe Mrs Slocombe (although on our black and white telly, I was unaware of her hair's wondrous hue). It seemed that it was compulsory for her to make references to her pussy in every episode; in fact, I wouldn't be surprised if it had been written into her contract: 'My pussy got soaking wet last night and I had to dry it out in front of the fire,' or 'I'm sorry I'm late, but there was a fireman crawling along my ledge trying to grab hold of my pussy'. We all knew she was talking about her cat but the startled expressions on her colleagues' faces indicated that they didn't, and every mention of Mrs Slocombe's pussy was greeted with guffaws of laughter up and down the land.

The breasts gags were made at the expense of Miss Brahms, played by a young Wendy Richard, who spent most episodes being lusted after by the quiff-headed womaniser Mr Lucas (Trevor Bannister). 'You don't get many of those to the pound,' he would observe, gesturing with his thumb at her ample bosom whilst winking at Captain Peacock. Meanwhile, Richard's role in the show mainly consisted of her sticking her chest out and speaking in an over-exaggerated cockney accent. I doubt it was her skill with the accent or her voluptuous chest that later landed her the role of the dowdy Pauline Fowler in *Eastenders* a decade later. In fact, it's almost impossible to reconcile the sexy strumpet of Grace Brothers with the cardigan-clad, downtrodden Fowler of Albert Square.

Although homosexuality was gradually becoming more accepted and openly discussed in Britain, the reality of homosexual sex was still considered too controversial to be openly referenced on early seventies TV. Britain wasn't quite ready for cocks and bums and certainly not before *World in Action*, if you don't mind. So the introduction of gay characters in a television series was something that had to be presented in a certain way so that even the most dedicated of homophobes could enjoy the show and warm to the character. Enter Mr Humphries, played by John Inman – possibly the first stereotypically gay character on British TV.

There were rules for the manufactured TV gay. He needed to be camper than a Volkswagen van on its way to Glastonbury, in both voice and flamboyant appearance. Then there was the walk – the more effeminate the better: a very pronounced bottom, swaying from side to side, accompanied by the omnipresent hand on hip. Gay characters were required to call straight men 'ducky' and say things like 'ooh I've come over a little queer,' and gesture with the hand that wasn't glued to their hip, in a flapping, limp-wristed manner. Mr Humphries had a catchphrase all of his own too, and like Mrs Slocombe's pussy, it had to be used with, ahem, gay abandon. 'Are you free, Mr Humphries?' one of the other characters would enquire. Mr Humphries, quite obviously bereft of customers, would look to both sides to check his availability and announce 'I'm free!' in his campest of tones. Inman did little else of any substance during the remainder of his career and we could say that his work appointment diary was 'freer' than he would have liked. Poor old John was defined by those two words and I'm sure he carried the phrase through to his life after *Are You Being Served?*. I have this scenario in my mind that his agent would be forced, when enquiring about Inman's availability to take on some upcoming work, to go through a premeditated and predictable routine that would go something like this:

Agent: John, can you do a voiceover for Findus Crispy Pancakes on the 18th?
Inman: No darling, ask me properly.
Agent: Findus Crispy Pancakes voiceover on the 18th. Are you free?
Inman: I'm free!

He dined out on it for many years to come, managing to get himself cast as the archetypal pantomime dame and making the odd appearance on seventies game shows such as *Celebrity Squares* and the utterly pointless *Blankety Blank*. In 1977 he even released an album, most unastonishingly entitled *I'm Free*.

Are You Being Served? was early seventies British humour at its absolute worst. The programme quite incredibly lasted for 13 years, spanning ten series, but it doesn't really make us thirsty for seventies nostalgia in the same way as other shows from that era. This is not just because it is now considered to have been so crass, but also because of the constant re-runs that the BBC have thrust upon us over the years. We are all too familiar with the escapades of Mrs Slocombe's pussy and Mr Humphries' bottom. *Dad's Army* suffers a similar fate.

A series that as far as I am aware has never been re-run is *Man About the House*. I'm not sure why this is, as it was immensely popular at the time and everybody at school watched it. The situation here was that Robin, played by Richard O' Sullivan, lived in a flat with two girls – Jo (Sally Thomsett) and Chrissy (Paula Wilcox) – and spent most of his time trying (unsuccessfully) to park his flares and cheesecloth shirt over the back of Chrissy's bedroom chair.

Their landlords George and Mildred Roper – brilliantly performed by Brian Murphy and Yootha Joyce – lived downstairs. The bumbling and henpecked George disapproved of the mixed-sex accommodation going on upstairs, whilst the sex-starved Mildred liked the idea of finally, in some small way, being part of the promiscuous society that she'd heard so much about. Although it's not necessarily the place of situation comedy to engage in social commentary, the situations depicted often reflected the changes going on in society and *Man About the House* rammed home the fact that in the real world of 1973, men and women co-habiting out of wedlock had become a common occurrence. Of course in this programme Robin, Jo and Chrissy weren't actually living as a ménage-a-trois (except in the fevered imagination of George Roper, who assumed it was orgies galore in the flat upstairs), but the inference was always there, never more so than at the end of the show. As the credits rolled, little pictures symbolising a man living with two women would flank the names of those involved: two pairs of knickers and a pair of Y-Fronts, two stilettos and a hobnail boot. However, the implication made by what I assumed were two cats and a chicken went straight over my head.

Jo was blonde and Chrissy a brunette, and like with the two girls in Abba, it was essential that you nailed your flag firmly to the mast of either one or the other ... so to speak. I liked Jo, just as I liked Agnetha from Abba. An early preference for blondes, I now note.

The TV blonde thing was a new awakening for me. Previously, I had rejected outright Sharon, the sex-mad blonde in *Please Sir!* played by Penny Spencer in favour of the sweetly pretty, god-bothering yet somewhat nymphomaniacal brunette Maureen Bullock, played by Liz Gebhardt. Everybody else fancied Sharon but I only had eyes for Maureen – my first celebrity crush. Maureen was sexy; I knew that even at the age of twelve. She flirted shamelessly with her reluctant teacher Mr Hedges – it was a bit like the kid in the Police song 'Don't Stand So Close To Me' – but with gags. She would brazenly unbutton her blouse to entice him, but then hastily button it up again, replacing her cleavage with her crucifix in a flustered pang of guilt when she decided that a quote from *The Bible* was required to ease a tricky situation. Maureen was lovely, and it's quite probable that the unbuttoning of her blouse caused my very first trouser-stirrings. Even though I hadn't thought about her once in over twenty years, when I read in 1996 that she had died from cancer, something in my heart went ping.

Please Sir! was my absolute favourite show and in my opinion remains an underrated classic. It followed the adventures of the teachers and pupils of Fenn Street School through their formative years and then later through early adulthood in the spin-off series *The Fenn Street Gang*. We were expected to believe that class 5C was inhabited by fifth-formers played by actors that were quite clearly in their early twenties at the very least. The characters (apart from Maureen of course) were all one-dimensional: Sharon Eversleigh, the sexy dolly bird (as they were called back then – but mostly by middle-aged men); Eric Duffy, the hard (but fair) man; Frankie

Abbott, who was a hard man in his own imagination but in reality a mollycoddled mummy's boy, whose mother referred to him as 'my little soldier'; Peter Craven, was the smoothie who fancied his chances with the ladies; and Dennis Dunstable, the slightly retarded but lovable one whose party piece was to impersonate farmyard animals in a slightly retarded but lovable way.

Their teacher, the hapless Bernard Hedges, (cleverly nicknamed Privet rather than Benson) was played by a young John Alderton prior to his role in *Upstairs, Downstairs*. Hedges was a fresh-faced teacher straight out of training college who had big ideas about how to teach unruly inner-city kids; however, when these ideas were applied to the likes of 5C at Fenn Street, things never went entirely to plan. But then again, things going to plan is rarely funny.

Another role of note was that of the formidable Doris Ewell, splendidly portrayed by Joan Sanderson, who made battleaxery her business and who famously went on to play the deaf woman that requested a different view from her Torquay hotel bedroom window in *Fawlty Towers*. But I hardly noticed the lack of depth in the characters and found the show very funny. I still have genuine affection for *Please Sir!,* so much so that when I spotted a few years back that ITV were running repeats of the show for the first time since the seventies, I couldn't bear to watch. I knew it would appear dated and less amusing and I didn't want my fond memories being tarnished, so I gave it a miss. However, looking back it's interesting to note that a recurring theme in the piece – love-sick schoolgirl Maureen's relentless pursuit of her teacher Mr Hedges – is something that comedy writers wouldn't dare write into a sitcom today.

Another topic that wouldn't get anywhere near our TV screens these days was the one employed by the hit series *Love Thy Neighbour*. The blatant use of racist insults that defined this show ensured that it would never get a repeat run on mainstream TV, and for that we should be eternally grateful. But it was yet another sitcom that referenced what was going on in the real world in the early part of the decade. There had been a huge influx of immigrants arriving in Britain from the West Indies and Asia since the late sixties, and there were 'real-life' Eddie Booths on almost every working-class street, actually believing that their little castles were now worth next to nothing since the black family had moved in next door.

During my research for this chapter I revisited clips from some of these shows that introduced me to my favourite comedy genre, and whilst I don't mind admitting that the very mention of Mrs Slocombe's pussy induced an unexpected smile across my face, I have to conclude that *Love Thy Neighbour* had little to recommend it. It seems painfully unfunny now and I feel somewhat embarrassed about liking it quite as much as I did. It relied almost exclusively on the use of racist name-calling between Eddie Booth

(Jack Smethurst) and his new neighbour Bill Reynolds (Rudolph Walker) for its laughs; Sambo, Nig-Nog, King Kong, White-Honky and Snowflake were amongst the insults that would be batted across the garden fence with alarming regularity. It seems unbelievable that this sort of terminology was considered perfectly acceptable for family viewing in 1972, but it was, and we sat there as a family and unashamedly laughed out loud. The knock-on effect on society of believing that this was admissible stretched from the playground to the football terrace to the workplace and back again.

Since its demise, there have been those that have made a case for the programme and its writers (Vince Powell and Harry Driver), stating that Eddie Booth was always made to look stupid and ignorant and rarely came out on top, or that he was a walking contradiction of a man, who claimed to be a working-class socialist yet spouted the dubious philosophies of Enoch Powell. All this is true. It's even true that it was only the two men that had this dispute – their wives put aside their husbands' differences and got on quite well in an attempt to show their old men that black and white people could live together in perfect harmony without any interference from either Paul McCartney or Stevie Wonder. But even in today's world, where political correctness has gone a bit mental (if that's not too politically incorrect), these excuses seem very lame and only disguise the fact that the bigotry of the show's main characters probably didn't do race relations any favours during a time in which a disdain for a multicultural Britain was gathering momentum. I don't believe this was the intention of the writers, but by the same token I don't think they used the series to make a point of exposing the ignorance of bigotry in the way Johnny Speight had achieved most deftly in the excellent *Till Death Us Do Part*. Powell and Driver used racial insults as their main currency and converted them into cheap laughs for primetime TV. They had form – they'd written racial stereotyping into their previous creation, *Never Mind the Quality, Feel the Width*, using a stereotypical Jewish tailor as a central character and, in the case of Vince Powell, his next work after *Love Thy Neighbour* was the pitiful *Mind Your Language* – a series that took ethnic stereotyping to a new low.

Sad as it now seems, these were my early introductions into the genre of the sitcom, as TV became an important part of my life. Watching TV was a much more precious activity than it is these days. If I had to miss an episode of my favourite programme for whatever reason, it was if my whole world was about to cave in. There were no video or DVD recorders or magical Sky+ boxes back then. If you missed your programme that was it – it was gone and it would have been little consolation to me in 1972 to be told to hang on for thirty years and I'd be able to catch up on that missed episode of *On the Buses* on ITV4.

I do wonder how the invention of TV recorders has affected the advertising industry. I can't remember the last time I sat through an advert.

I tend to record programmes that appear on the commercial channels so I can avoid them. Watching adverts takes up too much valuable telly-watching time. As that little black and white symbol appears in the top right-hand corner of the screen, I have the remote ready and aimed in anticipation of watching millions of pounds worth of brilliantly conceived advertising ideas flash by me at thirty times their original speed. In the seventies, the ad breaks mostly signified a convenient time to go to the loo, but unless you had a bladder similar in size to that of a small gerbil, at some point in the evening you were going to have some adverts thrust upon you.

The ads back then were no less inventive than they are today – they just cost a lot less to make. But because we were forced to watch them over and over again they stuck, and are now instantly recognisable when we are reminded of them. They will probably remain imprinted on our brains forever. On a slow telly night, which for me might include the likes of *Panorama*, *Armchair Theatre* or anything with spaceships in it , the ads were more enticing than the actual programmes.

One method of product association in adverts was to make us laugh. I was a big fan of the Cinzano Bianco adverts, featuring the much-missed Leonard Rossiter and Joan Collins, in which Collins would usually end up with a cleavage full of vermouth. Then there was the Cadbury's Smash alien family (which, if I remember correctly, also included a cat and dog), rolling about on their backs with their limbs waggling furiously in the air as they laughed uncontrollably at the fact that we still ate real potatoes, peeled them with our metal knives, boiled them for 20 of our earth minutes and then smashed them into tiny pieces. It was pretty funny stuff, and when put like that our methods did seem a little bit antiquated. However, what our alien friends failed to tell us was the fact that the perennially lumpy instant muck that they were trying to flog us was actually the worst idea since George Harrison decided to take Eric Clapton home to meet the wife.

Another method was through the slogans and jingles that created an immediate association with the products, which is of course the whole point. We were informed that Mars helped you work, rest and play, Roses grew on you, we should go to work on an egg and that Heineken refreshed the parts that other beers couldn't reach, which seems a strange selling point, as I think they were referring to brewer's droop.

Sex sells, (even floppy winkle sex, apparently) and as a sign of the times, adverts in the early seventies began to exploit this. The Cadbury's Flake ads featured a gorgeous young woman and used imagery that implied that she was seductively performing oral sex on the crumbly chocolate stick rather than simply eating it. The Denim aftershave ad employed the image of a female hand inside a man's denim shirt as she unfastened his buttons, revealing an overly hairy chest. But probably the ad responsible for more teenage erections than even Maureen Bullock could lay claim to was one for Manikin cigars in which a scantily clad woman thrashed her way through jungle growth with a big knife, threw asunder her top, revealing her dimpled back and just a hint of bum cleavage, and then proceeded to roll the cigar on her thigh, which just for good measure was covered in beads of sweat. The slogan – 'Manikin brings sheer enjoyment'. I had no idea what a cigar tasted like back then, but as far as I was concerned the ad alone lived up to its slogan.

The other side of the advertising coin was to make the products cosy and wholesome. TV advert wives and mums were the centrepiece of such campaigns. The Oxo mum, Linda Bellingham, became famous for the magic she could perform by crumbling a stock cube between her thumb and forefinger; the Shredded Wheat mum ever-so-sweetly sang 'There are two men in my life, to one I am a mother, to the other I'm a wife', and of course there was the Bird's Eye Trifle mum, who before presenting the pudding to her family danced the can-can on the table, singing 'it's one of those afters, you get now and then…'.

But there were two middle-aged women who achieved cult status for their crimes against the advertising industry: the Odor Eaters woman, who declared 'my Bert's a sweet man … except for his feet', in an ad that always seemed to have something wrong with its lip-synching, as if it had been dubbed from Chinese into English like one of those kung-fu movies that were so popular at the time; and then there was arguably the worst ad of all time – the legendary Shake 'n' Vac debacle. The song was bad enough, but the dance, which, with its hip-thrusting and leg-kicking, looked like something 'The Young Generation' dance troupe might perform on *Bruce Forsyth's Big Night Out*, was the sort of thing you could only watch through a small gap in your fingers, as your hands covered your face in embarrassment for her. How could she do that to her real family? It was her kids that I felt sorry for. They probably watched those ads through the gaps in their fingers too. Oh, the shame of it. I dread to think what those poor kids had to put up with at school. I imagine they were mercilessly nicknamed 'The Shakenvackies' by their classmates, and had to skulk their way into school each day, heads bowed in discomfort at their mother's antics, secretly wishing that she was something altogether more respectable – like the Beanz Meanz Heinz mum … or a prostitute.

I once bought a house that had been previously inhabited by a huge Alsatian called Seth. The carpet stank of this dog and after trying several different methods to get rid of the smell, I finally arrived at the last resort – the Shake 'n' Vac. It's funny; because of the way in which the three holes are positioned on the lid of the carton, it is actually impossible to get the stuff out without performing a similar dance to the lady in the ad (although it can be achieved without the hip-thrusting and the leg-kicking), and so as I administered the treatment, I felt some of her humiliation. More to the point, the odour left by this repugnant product was far worse than the dog smell I was trying to get rid of.

From *Monty Python* in the seventies, *The Young Ones* in the eighties, through *The Office* and all the way up to *The Inbetweeners* of recent years, the reciting and regurgitating of last night's telly was and always will be a staple part of playground culture, no matter which decade you hail from. But in the early seventies, the jingles and slogans of the adverts also came to school with us the next morning. In some extreme cases we even referenced these slogans to invent ways to insult people. For example, a girl that was up for a snog and a bit of a fumble behind the bike sheds might be nicknamed 'Martini', because she liked it 'anytime, anyplace, anywhere'. I make it sound like I knew a lot of 'Martinis' – I didn't, and by the time I did, I didn't have a bike to park. Adopting a jingle and changing the words to something much ruder was always fun. The one that springs instantly to mind is the ad for Trebor Mints. The original went 'Trebor mints are a minty bit stronger', to which we added the line 'stick 'em up yer bum and they'll last a bit longer'.

It's not beyond the realms of feasibility to claim that some advert jingles that used new words set over old songs became more recognisable than the original song. I suspect that there were folk who discovered Elvis Presley's back catalogue, following his death in 1977, who were both baffled and heartily disgruntled to find that his reworking of 'It's Now or Never' employed an identical tune to that of the 'Just One Cornetto' ad.

I doubt the advertising men would have dared to dream about the longevity of their sloganeering and jingle tunesmithery. I'm prepared to believe that, forty years later, there are people of my age all over the country that still find it difficult to take the pickle jar out of the fridge without chanting 'Bring out the Branston', and countless grown men that still can't apply aftershave without muttering 'splash it all over' like Henry Cooper did in the Brut advert. These are the same people that probably find it impossible to snap open a bar of Cadbury's Whole Nut without shouting 'nuts, whole hazelnuts' and swiftly follow this up with 'Cadbury's take 'em and dey cover dem in chocolate' sung in a cod West Indian accent. Try offering round the biscuit tin containing a variety of Club biscuits to friends of a certain age and I guarantee that, without any hesitation, one of them will burst into a quick rendition of 'If you like a lot of chocolate on your biscuit, join our club' – probably with arms outstretched and, in extreme cases, using jazz hands. To be honest, it wasn't until 1984 that I managed to wean myself out of the habit of trying to work out whether or not an attractive girl I'd just passed in the street was using Harmony hairspray.

Probably the most bizarre advertising campaign of the seventies was that of Unigate milk's 'Humphreys'. What were Humphreys? They were red and white striped straws that secretly sneaked up on you and stole your milk through the method of sucking. The slogan – 'Watch out, watch out, there's a Humphrey about' – was on every child's lips as the country exploded into Humphreymania. There were Humphrey mugs, glasses, badges and of course straws, and every kid under the age of 12 wanted Humphrey stickers on their exercise books. The demise of the Humphrey was rather fittingly for the times caused by a mild case of sexual innuendo, when Unigate's new advertisement campaign was fronted by the slogan 'Are you getting enough?'.

Soft drinks were always promoted with good adverts. My favourite from this period was the 'R. Whites secret lemonade drinker' ad, in which the dad, looking a little like Hank Marvin, sneaks down the stairs in the middle of the night in his pyjamas, carefully avoiding the sleeping dog and singing the jingle[1] as he goes. When he arrives at the fridge, he pours himself a glass of lemonade and then proceeds to use the bottle as a microphone as he sings the rest of the jingle, not noticing that his wife is standing there watching his every move. Anyone that had been caught by their mum singing into a hairbrush in front of their bedroom mirror shared his deep shame.

Coke and Pepsi always brought out new ads every summer. There was no Diet Pepsi or Pepsi Max back then, it was just Pepsi. Well not just Pepsi, it was actually, lip-smacking, thirst-quenching, ace tasting, motivating, good buzzing, cool-talking, high-walking, fast-living, ever-giving, and indeed cool fizzing Pepsi. You don't learn detail like that with a TV remote control glued to the palm of your hand whizzing through the adverts. You just need the splendour of youth, agility of palate and several hours of playground time to try and perfect it.

* * *

Sometimes in life we are handed manna from heaven on a gilt-edged plate. Whilst researching the episode data for *Are You Being Served*? I couldn't believe my luck when I discovered that a show that relied so heartily on its sexual innuendo ran for exactly 69 episodes. Gifts like that don't come along too often and I wonder now whether it was intentional for Grace Brothers to finally shut up shop after episode 69. If so, it was the subtlest example of cap-doffing to the unsubtle world of comedic sexual innuendo ever associated with any such show. I wrote that passage on the programme during the afternoon of 1 July 2009. Later that evening I learned that dear old Mollie Sugden had opened her final tin of Whiskas that very same day, proving that the lord of comedy giveth a gag with one hand, whilst snatching (very much a bit of sexual innuendo intended) it

---

[1] Written and sung by Elvis Costello's dad, with a young Elvis himself on drums and backing vocals.

away with the other. A huge coincidence, of course, but it felt very strange – as if I had somehow contributed to her passing by writing some sort of demeaning obituary before she had actually died. Silly really, but one thing's for certain – I won't have been the only person checking out the compilation video of her pussy gags on YouTube on that particular day. But I may have been the first.

Back Home

TV at home was still in black and white, so for the full Technicolor experience I went to the cinema. There were a few in the area, including ABCs at both Barkingside and Ilford, but they were both a bus ride away. Gants Hill Odeon, on the other hand, was a five-minute walk from my house, so when I wasn't jumping off its roof, I'd take the trouble to go inside and stare at its huge screen.

Dad had taken me to see my first ever full-length feature film there back in the early sixties – Disney's *Snow White and the Seven Dwarves*. He has reminded me many times how scared I was of the wicked stepmother, and cried through most of it. But I didn't let that put me off; we went back a few months later so I could cry through *The Wizard of Oz* too. It's a witch thing – they're so pointy ... and witchy. By the time we went to see the comparatively witch-free, *Sound of Music*, I had stiffened my resolve and made it to the end completely dry-eyed.

By the time the seventies came around I was allowed to go to the Odeon unaccompanied. On Saturday mornings they put on a special show for kids, where we would sit quietly sucking on our Toffee Strips during the first half, watching cartoons and old black-and-white short American comedies such as *The Three Stooges* and *The Laurel and Hardy Show*. At halftime, mayhem would break out as hundreds of kids spent the entire interval running around the cinema, engaging in human bundles and sliding on their knees down the aisles, making it hard for the usherettes to restore order after the break. The unruliness of the interval always used to spill over into the second half, which featured one long film – usually some sort of dull Western or animal movie – when really what was required was some more Foghorn Leghorn. The entertainment during this section of the show mainly consisted of shouting out inappropriate remarks and lobbing the remainder of our pick'n'mix at both the screen and the kids who liked cowboy movies.

The Odeon was an imposing building. It opened in 1934 and had seating for just over two thousand people in its two tiers. I loved the place, we have history – I had my first back-row snog there and eventually, after being turned away too many times to recall, saw my first 'x-rated' film there (*The Exorcist*). I've seen crowds queuing around the block on such auspicious occasions as the opening night of a new James Bond film or *Saturday Night Fever*. I must have seen hundreds of films there over the years. I saw my favourite film of all time there, *Midnight Express*, and loved it so much I went back the very next night and watched it again. It was a proper cinema with uniform-clad usherettes and cashiers that sold you entrance tickets that spewed out of their metal cash desks and were so miniscule that you'd lost them the second they were housed in the pocket of your jeans. The usherettes had torches and escorted you to your seats as if you weren't quite capable of managing an alpha/numeric combination all on your own, and in the interval they sold you tubs of raspberry ripple ice cream from a tray suspended from their shoulders. I always enjoyed looking at the film posters displayed outside the cinema after I'd seen the film; it was rewarding that the random images I'd stared at while queuing to get in suddenly made sense. But, despite all the cinematic delights I experienced, my favourite Odeon memory comes – unsurprisingly – courtesy of rock'n'roll.

In the late seventies the Odeon was sporadically used as a rock venue, playing host to Ian Dury & The Blockheads, Graham Parker & The Rumour, Dr. Feelgood, the Tom Robinson Band and even Cliff Richard. There was a rather large empty space that separated the stage on which the screen was mounted from row A of the stalls, which worked brilliantly as a purpose-built dance area when it was commissioned for pop concerts.

So there we were, bouncing away near the stage that night in December 1978, during Ian Dury's legendary gig at the venue, when midway through 'Billericay Dickie' a small section of the floor gave way under the strain of teenage enthusiasm. It was very exciting, and about as rock'n'roll as things ever got in Gants Hill. Dear old Ian was concerned for us all, bless him; he issued warnings and found it hard to concentrate during the rest of the gig, forgetting huge paragraphs of his masterful lyrics. The moment was recorded for posterity and you can hear the whole drama unfold on the album *Straight from the Desk*. I add the drama of nearly falling through the floor to my other adventure of nearly jumping off the roof on my list of Top Ten Things that Nearly Happened at Gants Hill Odeon.

By the time the Odeon was finally put out of its misery in 2002 it was a sad shadow of its former self, having been converted into an extremely poor multiplex cinema in 1981 in an attempt to keep up with other cinemas that had gone through the same conversion process all over the provinces. It's now a block of modern apartments. We were lucky to have had it as long as we did; it was one of the last surviving bastions of the 1970s Gants Hill of my youth. The town has gone through an incredible period of deterioration over the last couple of decades, as one by one the big high-street names that once inhabited its thoroughfares shut up shop and moved to bigger and better premises elsewhere, leaving the place as little more than a haven for takeaways and corner shops.

The centrepiece of Gants Hill is its huge roundabout, which is like the hub of a bicycle wheel, its eight exits appearing as the spokes. The tube station, with its barrel-vaulted halls of pedestrian subways sits underneath it.

The shops were a mixture of smaller versions of familiar names – such as Boots, Woolworths, Tesco and W.H. Smiths – and a collection of independently owned shops. There was an old-fashioned Sainsbury's that boasted 'groceries and provisions' over its doorway. The shop was divided into two sections: one that sold all the regular grocery-type products and the other a dedicated delicatessen (easier to write than it is to say), which had sawdust on the floor and men and women behind the counter who wore silly hats and cut off lumps of cheese from huge slabs of the stuff with cheese wire. That half of the shop absolutely stank of exotic cheeses, whose names I had never heard of.

Mum would often send me 'up the top' (as we called it), to get a few bits of shopping (as she called it), and I would be left feeling quite nauseous whenever I had to go into the smelly part. I still can't look a blue cheese square in the nose without feeling queasy. I've never really understood why anyone would want to eat cheese that had huge lumps of mould embedded in it. This is just food that's gone off, isn't it?

There was also Halfords, the bike shop, which in those days sold only bicycles. I bought my first proper bike there. I was always browsing its windows and one day spotted a metallic red Raleigh with 20-inch white tyres. I saved for it for months, using the money that I earned running errands and that had been given to me by relatives. I remember that it cost exactly £20 and it was a proud moment when I went in there, handed over the cash and rode my new bike home.

Although there were nowhere near the number of eateries in Gants Hill then as there are today, we did have a Wimpy Bar. It was a slightly intimidating place that always had older teenagers hanging around outside. I was introduced to the world of the hamburger by my friend Antony Weinberg, who was nicknamed 'Bergy' (as an abbreviation of his surname, rather than a reference to his fondness of hamburgers). It would be around another three years before the first McDonalds would arrive in London, so the Wimpy was the only place where you could indulge in such Americana. If you ate in the restaurant you would eat your burger from a plate, with a knife and fork, at tables that were adorned with a ketchup dispenser in the shape of a giant tomato. The discovery that their frankfurter in a bun was hilariously named 'The Bender', was a sniggersome gift that just kept on giving.

There was also a restaurant on the Woodford Avenue called 'Shelly's Grill' – a slightly ponsed-up Greasy Joe's café that served chips and a lettuce leaf with everything and which, by some strange coincidence, had almost the same telephone number as us. I used to get so fed up with fielding off their customers that, on a busy night of misdialled calls, my exasperation would force me to take the booking anyway, sometimes embellishing my unwanted role as their receptionist by asking if the caller would like a window table.

Perhaps one reason why all these smaller shops eventually disappeared was that nearby Ilford had bigger and better versions and a lot more besides. You could get a bus from outside W.H. Smiths in Gants Hill and be in Ilford in fifteen minutes. It was a trip that Mads and I took with my mum almost every Saturday afternoon. Unspectacular as this usually was, the return journey on Saturday 11 April 1970 was punctuated by a particular comment made by the squinty-eyed bus conductor who was taking our fares – an off-the-cuff remark that turned my world on its head.

'Shopping in Ilford? How did she talk you into that?' he questioned, gesturing with his head at my mum as he curled out our tickets from his machine. I looked away shyly, not knowing what he was on about and slightly wary that he was winking at me.

'Wouldn't you rather be at home watching the telly?' Now that was something I could understand and nodded, still avoiding any one-eyed contact. When I got home, I immediately switched on the TV to find out exactly what it was that I was missing.

BBC1 – football, BBC2 – a film with old people dancing, ITV – some men dressed in white shirts and shorts cuddling each other. I continued watching to discover that ITV were showing the same thing as BBC1, something that I'd not seen before. This must be important if both the main channels were showing the same programme, I thought to myself, and gathered that this must be what the squinty-eyed conductor was referring to. I switched from channel to channel just to check that something different wasn't happening on one of them. I'd been vaguely aware of football, but never thought I liked it much. I didn't really understand the rules for a start, and hadn't participated in the games that went on at school in the playground at break times. What I had just witnessed on ITV were the celebrations following Jackie Charlton's opening goal for Leeds United against Chelsea in the 1970 FA Cup Final. I watched on, intrigued. The pitch was an absolute quagmire and tackles were flying in from all angles. These tackles looked as if they hurt, but the recipients seemed to just shrug them off and get on with it. The game was intensely exciting, with Chelsea equalising just before half time and another goal from each side in the final five minutes of the match taking the game into extra time. I was actually quite excited at the prospect of another thirty minutes of this, despite the fact that it meant that *Doctor Who* would have to be put on hold. The game produced no further goals, ending in a 2-2 draw, and the commentator told me that this meant that the game would have to be replayed. What a stroke of luck!

I couldn't wait to get to school on the following Monday and discuss my new discovery with Scuzz. He too had witnessed his first game over the weekend. He had been encouraged to watch the game by his Chelsea-supporting father, so he had his colours firmly nailed to the Blues mast. It hadn't really occurred to me that when you watched football you were supposed to support one team or the other, but if Scuzz was now a Chelsea supporter then so was I. With hindsight, if I had known what I know now about the Chelsea and Leeds teams of 1970, I would have probably come to the same conclusion, but in a less sycophantic way. I would have picked the flamboyant, free-flowing, stylish football of Chelsea over the hard and uncompromising, gritty methods of Leeds. If ever there were two teams that lived up to the stereotypical image of the areas that they hailed from, it was those two.

It was an excruciatingly long wait of almost three weeks until the replay came around. I watched it at home and yet again it was a rough match, full of incident, and again went to extra time with Chelsea winning 2-1. The winner was scored by an unlikely hero, right-back David Webb, who bundled in a header following a ridiculously long throw-in from Ian Hutchinson, whose arms windmilled like a Pete Townshend power chord as he hurled the ball into the box. I read a few years ago that David Ellery, a modern-day referee, sat through the video of the entire game and concluded that by applying today's refereeing standards, only five of the players on the pitch that day would have avoided being sent off – and two of those were the goalkeepers!

But that was it for me; I became totally consumed by football. I wanted to play it, talk about it, read about it and watch it at every possible opportunity – and that's exactly what I did. The most important thing in my new world seemed to be to learn the colours, nickname, stadium name, ground capacity and playing squad of every team in the English leagues.

I could hardly believe my luck – I had just discovered football, and the Mexico '70 World Cup was only weeks away. England were world champions and expectations were high, with pundits claiming that the 1970 squad was even better than the team of 1966. Esso, the petrol company, launched their England World Cup Squad coins and I just had to collect them. Drivers could get one free coin with every four gallons of 4-star petrol that they bought. I had everyone that had a car on the case for me: Dad, Uncle Ivan and Mark from next door all contributed. The first coin I got was Gordon Banks, which turned out to be the hardest one to get round our way. Kids whose dads were cab drivers, and had therefore been showered with coins at the end of each working day, would turn up at school with bags full of these things ready to swap for the elusive Mr Banks. You could more or less name your price for a Gordon. Tempting though it was, I wisely refused to part with my Gordon Banks coin, even when offered a Paul Reaney, Brian Labone, a Bobby Charlton and a Francis Lee in exchange. The gamble paid off and I managed to collect the set and proudly placed them all in the presentation card in time for the start for the tournament. The England squad was even at Number One in the charts with their spirited song 'Back Home'. Everything was set for a feast of football.

The problem with being nine and the World Cup taking place in Mexico was that half the matches were on while I was asleep. I was not allowed to stay up to watch England's group matches against either

Czechoslovakia or Romania, both of which were won 1-0 by England, but I did catch the game with Brazil that was shown on a Sunday evening.

I didn't realise it at the time, but that Brazil side were probably the greatest football team I have ever seen. They went on to win the tournament, annihilating Italy 4-1 in the final. They had some amazing players: Pelé, Jairzinho, Carlos Alberto, Tostao and Rivelino, but England were a match for them that day despite narrowly losing the game 1-0. The game is remembered for the unbelievable save made by Gordon Banks from a powerful downward header from Pelé, where he somehow managed to get from one post to the other in the nick of time to turn the bouncing ball over the bar. Banks was hailed as the greatest keeper of all time because of that save and instantly became my first footballing hero. From that moment on, I wanted to be a goalkeeper and a collectable World Cup coin.

Despite losing to Brazil, England made it to the quarter-final, where they played West Germany. Rather inconsiderately, my cousin Doreen had decided to get married on the same day as the match. Although it didn't cross my mind at the time, it must have been really irritating for her to find fifty or so of their guests decamped in the cloakroom of the reception hall, huddled around a single transistor radio listening to the match. I doubt, however, that she was more upset than we all were after England carelessly let a two-goal lead slip and lost the game 3-2. It was my first taste of bitter disappointment caused by the beautiful game. In some ways it was good that I got this disappointment in early – it would stand me in good stead to cope with all the other miserable let-downs the game would inflict on me over the next forty years. Football is like that: it's a bit of a bugger. It gives you precious Cup Final wins with one hand, and with the godlike other, punches the ball over Peter Shilton and into the back of the net. It's a harsh lesson, but one I learnt in a cramped cloakroom in Edmonton.

I spent the 1970–71 season feverishly following Chelsea. They had a superb team that included the likes of the free-scoring Peter Osgood, the outrageously talented Alan Hudson, wizard of the wing Charlie Cooke and one of football's real hard men, Ron 'Chopper' Harris, who looked angelic with his short back and sides haircut at a time when footballers' hairstyles started mimicking those of rock stars. But Chopper could break a man's leg if he looked at him in a funny way.

The early seventies was a great time to become interested in football. The game seemed to be infested with entertainers, characters and players that were blessed with monstrous amounts of talent. It seemed that almost every club in the first division had at least one player that home fans would be happy to pay money to see when their teams came to town: George Best of Manchester United, Rodney Marsh of Manchester City, Stan Bowles at QPR, Frank Worthington at Huddersfield Town and the aforementioned Alan Hudson. Yet all of these players, with the exception of George Best, never really fulfilled their potential. The money that could be earned by footballers back then was a tiny fraction of what average players in the lower leagues earn these days, yet compared with the man in the street, these were rich young men and with their wealth came the distractions of drink and gambling – that much hasn't changed. The only difference is that these days, the minute a footballer gets the faintest whiff of a sweet sherry, he is whipped into rehab for two or three weeks until he sees the error of his ways. In the seventies, footballers' addictions went unchecked by their clubs and they were allowed to slip into oblivion unnoticed. When I look at these wayward geniuses it seems hard to fathom that not one of them managed to make it into double figures in terms of England caps. What makes this even more ludicrous is the fact that an utter donkey like Phil 'bloody' Neville (everyone calls him that in order to distinguish him from his brother, Gary 'bloody' Neville) has 59 of the things all to himself.

It's not as if England didn't need those players. Failing to qualify for the 1974 and 1978 World Cup tournaments meant that the aforementioned quarter-final against the Germans in Mexico would be the last match England would play in a World Cup for twelve years! But the excesses of all these players became a liability for their clubs and country and by the mid-seventies, broke and broken, they had all left England in search of the dollar in American 'soccer'. But while they were here I loved watching them play. Flawed they might have been but they weren't machines like today's top players – they had personalities, which they expressed on the pitch and in their cheeky after-match interviews. You never heard them utter such banal clichés as 'we'll take each game as it comes' or 'it was a game of two halves'. These players rarely lasted for two halves.

It's funny: as the football pundit, Rodney Marsh is a bit of a bell-end, but as a young man he was witty and clever. My favourite Marsh story is one of an exchange that he had with England manager of the time, Sir Alf Ramsey. Ramsey was a bit of a stuffed shirt, a bit old- school; he'd won the World Cup and it wasn't really the done thing to give him any cheek, but that didn't seem to bother the young Rodney Marsh.

In a pre-match team talk Ramsey told him 'I'll be watching you in the first half and if you don't work harder than you did in the last game, I'll pull you off at half time,' to which Marsh replied: 'Crikey Alf, at Manchester City all we get is an orange and a cup of tea'. He never played for England again.

Scuzz introduced me to his Chelsea-supporting neighbours, Gary and Danny, who soon became good friends. We would play the game endlessly on the grassy area opposite Scuzz's house in Martley Drive, known locally as 'the rec'. It was a handy place to play as it was on the way home from school and lots of kids would go there as soon as school was over, so there would always be a match going on. Convenient though it was, the rec wasn't an ideal place to play football – the grass was littered with broken glass from where older kids had smashed bottles against the concrete tunnels that bordered the climbing frames and swings. You needed to be careful exactly where you put down your jumpers that marked out the goalposts or you would be going home with rips in your trousers and a bloody knee – especially if you were a goalie.

Goalkeeping seemed to be the thing that I was best at so I concentrated on that. I wasn't afraid to throw myself about in attempts to make saves, exaggerating them wherever possible to make them look good. The over-egging of the simple save, though essential to gain the applause of my team-mates, was my undoing when I tried out for the school team. My PE teacher told me I was over-complicating things and should keep it simple, and the job went to Barry Barnett. I was miffed and reassured myself that he was only picked ahead of me because he was taller. It made it an easier pill to swallow.

Football on TV was limited to highlights of two games on *Match of the Day* on a Saturday night and three on Sunday afternoon's *The Big Match*. There would sometimes also be a midweek game shown on *Sportsnight with Coleman* but unless it was during the school holidays I wasn't allowed to stay up for that. Instead I would listen to games in bed on my transistor radio. I wasn't allowed to do this either, but the invention of the single ear-plug was a wonderful thing, and I sneakily listened to the frustrating commentaries under the covers, wishing I could see the images that went with those vivid descriptions.

This was all very well but what I really wanted was to see a live game. I persuaded Dad to take me to Stamford Bridge as a birthday treat. As I've previously said, he wasn't a football fan and it took a few months to talk him into it. We went to see Chelsea play FC Bruges in the European Cup-Winners Cup Quarter-Final second-leg. We bought tickets for the North Stand, which in those days was an uncovered open terrace. Whilst I was quite enjoying the pre-match atmosphere of the singing and bustling of the crowd, Dad wasn't happy about standing up for the whole match and told a steward that I couldn't see anything from where we were standing. Amazingly, for the price of a pound sneaked into his back pocket, the steward agreed to let us through the gate and into the unnumbered benches in the lower part of the East Stand. Chelsea were 2-0 down from the first leg so they needed to win by three goals to go through to the semi-final. It was a great game with an electric atmosphere, as Chelsea pulled back the two-goal deficit to take the game into extra time, and a further two goals from Peter Osgood secured their place in the semi-finals. Even Dad enjoyed it – not enough to turn him into a football fan, but I think he understood why I liked it so much.

Chelsea went on to win the European Cup-Winners Cup that season. The final, against Real Madrid, was held in Athens and on the evening of the match my Uncle Ivan said we could come over and watch the game at his house on his new colour telly. This sounded perfect to me, but the plan was thwarted by the fact that on arrival it became apparent that the invention of colour TV had not yet stretched as far as Greece and the game was broadcast in black and white.

A few weeks earlier, on Good Friday, Ivan had taken me to see West Ham play West Bromwich Albion. The Hammers were fighting off relegation but managed to win the game 2-1. We sat up in the West Stand and the view of the pitch was amazing. Unlike Stamford Bridge, Upton Park was a tight little ground, with the crowd very close to the pitch. The advertising hoardings around the pitch were rendered useless because you couldn't read what any of them were supposed to be advertising due to the combination of the claret and blue scarves and the arms of the kids that were draped over them. Before the match, and at half time, we were entertained by a brass band. Ivan tried to convince me that this was a good thing, but I wasn't so sure. I liked the strip that West Ham played in: claret shirts with light blue sleeves and brilliant-white shorts and socks. In the team that day were England World Cup-winning heroes Bobby Moore and Geoff Hurst. I found it hard to fathom that a team with these champions in its line-up were fighting relegation, but I was very excited to see these two players in the flesh. What was even more puzzling was the quality of football that this team played. They passed the ball about with such finesse and attacked in waves that made you believe that they could score every time they went forward, so how could they be struggling so badly? The main reason being that despite their attacking flair, their defence had more holes in it than one of Norman Stanley Fletcher's string vests.

The other thing that I remember very clearly from my Upton Park debut was the amount of swearing that emanated from the fans around us: 'Referee, you're a cunt'; 'Lampard, you bearded cunt!'; 'Fuck off Albion, you Black Country cunts!'. I'd never heard so many cunts in my life. It was as if a new law was going to be passed in an hour that was going to deny them their right to use the word, and they had to get as many in as possible while they still had the chance. I was slightly embarrassed to be honest; I'd heard all the swear words in the playground – I just wasn't sure my uncle had. My naivety was reassured however when he, without prior warning and rather loudly, reminded Harry Redknapp what a useless fucker he was!

Jimmy Greaves scored one of the goals that day. Greaves, ironically, was the player that was dropped from the England team after the group stages of the 1966 World Cup, allowing Hurst to take his place and grab all the glory. Now they were teammates after a deal that took the Hammers' other World Cup hero, Martin Peters, to Tottenham in part-exchange. It was unknown at that time that Greaves was a raging alcoholic, whose career would be more or less over a few weeks later. It seemed a little unfair that Tottenham got a player that had once been described as being ten years ahead of his time, whilst West Ham got the footballing equivalent of Oliver Reed.

The winning goal for West Ham was scored by Bryan 'Pop' Robson. Robson was lethal in front of goal and had a habit of being in the right place at the right time, ready to slam any loose balls straight into the back of the net, hence the nickname – always there to 'pop' in a goal or two. It should be noted that this Bryan 'Pop' Robson is not the perennially injured and rather rubbish Bryan 'Pop' Robson that captained England more times than he deserved to during the eighties. West Ham's Bryan 'Pop' Robson was a small, balding man who had a wispy length of hair combed across his shiny bald head – a style that I was convinced had been pioneered by my dad, in collusion with Bobby Charlton. Windy days were tricky for all three, as a sudden gust would take control of the flimsy growth, leaving the owner with an extremely lopsided effect of long straggly hair on one side, and nothing but an ear on the other. A style famously adopted by Phil Oakey of The Human League throughout the eighties and unfairly claimed as his own – it's about time he came clean and confessed the origins of his famous hairstyle. Fans of early seventies football and my dad have always known the truth.

I came away from Upton Park that day feeling a little bit confused. There were a number of things that I had really enjoyed about being in this ground and watching this club that I hadn't felt when I watched Chelsea a few weeks previously. I had laughed at the comments being shouted from the crowd around me – witty stuff, sometimes clever, sometimes obvious, sometimes downright insulting, but mostly humorous. There were no grand expectations from these people. They expected West Ham to lose, they expected it to all go wrong, as if their experienced eyes had seen it all before – and they probably had. There was something charming about their attitude to their team that appealed to me. It was if they were perfectly aware that the team were never going to win very many matches but they played the game how it was supposed to be played – with style and panache, and that was enough. I liked this idea of supporting the underdog. I was also impressed with this very small ground where the crowd were almost on top of the pitch and could pat their heroes on the back when they came to the touchline to take a corner or a throw-in. As we walked back down Green Street to the car, Ivan tried to persuade me that this should be my club. I wasn't completely convinced but after what I'd experienced that day, I was wavering. But why would I start supporting this struggling team when Chelsea were near the top of the league, had great players throughout, were the FA Cup holders and on the verge of winning a European trophy as well?

On the night that Chelsea won the Cup-Winners Cup, Ivan badgered me throughout the game about how I should not be supporting Chelsea as they were from West London and how I should always support my local club –

that was how it worked. That in itself didn't convince me, but when he mentioned that I could get to Upton Park by taking the 147 bus from Ilford or the 101 from Wanstead, it dawned on me that I was allowed to take buses on my own, whereas the comparative long-haul journey to Fulham Broadway tube station involved the drawn-out process of relentlessly begging someone to take me. I thought about it long and hard over that summer and came to the conclusion that my desire to attend as many matches as possible, coupled with what I had witnessed at Upton Park that Good Friday, were enough to justify my decision. From the start of the 1971–72 season, I became a West Ham supporter.

Scuzz, Danny and Gary were unimpressed at first but they soon got used to the idea. It was especially enjoyable for them as the Hammers slipped to three straight defeats at the start of that season, while Chelsea got off to a flyer. The rivalry between friends supporting different football teams and the never-ending banter that it brings is another one of life's joyous gifts.

I felt justified in my decision. Choosing your football team is an important process and not one that should be taken lightly. There is one hard-and-fast rule, which states that you must support the same team as your dad – that is the law and it must be obeyed. There cannot be a more heartbreaking feeling for a lifelong Manchester City fan than the moment in which his beloved son breaks the news to him that he is a red. For me that wasn't an issue. No interest from Dad meant I had carte blanche, I could support whichever team I liked. Given an open page, there can be many reasons why we choose our colours, but rash decisions can be made if you're not careful. It's easy to fall into the trap of choosing a team simply because they are the current holders of a trophy. There will be men now in their late twenties who may regret becoming Blackburn Rovers fans on the back of their title win in 1995. Some people will choose their club because it's the team that their mates support, as I did with Chelsea – or perhaps because it's a team who are the greatest rivals of the team their mates support. Other reasons can be more extreme – my friend Martin became a Tottenham supporter simply because Martin Chivers and Martin Peters played for them.

Maybe it's admissible to have a little window to find your footy feet, but it's not really the done thing to change your allegiance in the way that I did. I was young and I didn't have that parental hand to guide me in the right direction – just an uncle who had a mate with a season ticket who just happened to be sunning himself on the Costa Brava on a day when the Hammers were in a seducing mood. If I need an excuse, then that's it, and it's going to have to do. But if you're going to change clubs, the decision has to be made early to be credible. When my brother-in-law Glen announced at the ripe old age of forty that he was no longer an Aston Villa fan, and now wished the world to acknowledge him as a fully-fledged

Gooner, we, his friends and family, felt it was our duty to make him feel as uncomfortable as possible about it. It felt wrong to indulge him. The reason he gave for swapping allegiances was that he wanted my yet-to-be born nephew to support a decent team that will win trophies. Fourteen years later and Charlie has yet to grace the Emirates Stadium with his presence. He doesn't even like football!

It has crossed my mind over the last few years that had I stuck with Chelsea I would have had many more trophy-winning days by now. However, I would have missed out on the emotional roller coaster that is the very essence of what being West Ham supporter is about. I embrace it, it's character-building and it's fun – well as much as fun that is born out of the womb of misery can be. Continuous success must surely become tedious after a while, whereas an occasional moment of glory is a precious and wonderful thing. I have never really openly discussed my dark and murky Chelsea-supporting past since that initial colour-swapping period. There will be people that have known me for many years that will have no idea of this dirty secret. Admitting to be the adulterer in a football divorce, is as shameful as confessing to owning a Chris de Burgh box set, but I will never regret marrying my little bit on the side.

School's Out

If you were a football fan in the seventies, it's almost certain that you would have owned the game Subbuteo, and if you didn't own it you will have at least played it with someone who did. Thirty years BC (before computers) and the invention of games like *FIFA* and *Football Manager*, for the football fan, there was only Subbuteo. Well, that's not strictly true, there were things like *Blow Football* – a very silly game that involved hurling huge globules of phlegm through a straw at your opponent. There was also Waddingtons *Table Soccer*, which was slightly more thought-through than its huff and puff counterpart, and at least included a pitch, some proper players, a counter and a rule book. But for the authentic footy game – and I say that in the loosest possible sense – there was only Subbuteo. Just how realistic the game was may have been largely reliant on your concept of reality, but if you could ignore things such as the fact that the ball was as big as the players, you were halfway there.

The basics of the game would be that you would flick the players against the ball to move it around the pitch. 'Just flick to kick' – that was Subbuteo's strapline. The game was played on a green cloth pitch, which was usually laid out on the carpet. The serious player would have his pitch glued to a piece of hardboard to avoid all those flick-incurring creases in the cloth that would occur during the course of the game. Me? I was strictly an on all-fours-on-the-carpet man.

Serious Subbuteo players were easy to identify as they were inflicted with a compulsion to carry out the thumb and forefinger flicking action during their everyday life – a bit like how golf enthusiasts will play out an imaginary chip onto the 17th green with an imaginary sand wedge while you're talking to them about something completely unrelated at the office coffee machine. You could spot a serial flicker a mile off.

I got my Subbuteo set as a Christmas present from my parents. We had an annual ritual of going to Hamleys toy store in Regent Street every December, where Mum and Dad would allow me and my sister to choose our own present. One thing only, and there was a budget of course. This might seem a bit clinical but at least it avoided disappointment on Christmas morning. The previous year I had chosen a chemistry set and I have no idea why – probably because Scuzz had one.

You could buy Subbuteo sets in varying levels of included accessories. These packages were called things like 'Club Edition', 'Continental Edition' or 'World Cup Edition'. I had the 'International Edition', which came with everything you could need, but importantly the most sought-after accessory of them all – the battery-operated floodlight pylons. The only trouble was that it only came with two of them instead of the minimum of four that could be found at every real football stadium. This meant that if you were playing an evening kick-off game – i.e. you had the bedroom lights switched off – you had to move the pylons to where the ball was or you couldn't see a thing.

One of the things that made this game so popular was the range of accessories that could be bought for it. You could send off to the manufacturer (Hasbro) for their catalogue, which had pictures of all the bits and pieces that you could buy. Just like the photographs of the burgers displayed above the counter at McDonalds, these items never looked quite as good when they were set up on your own bedroom floor as they had done in the catalogue. I had the scoreboard, which came complete with a set of cut-out team names that you could slip into the slots on the board, and a dial to turn that displayed the score as the goals rattled in. I also had the green plastic perimeter fence that you had to build yourself using the little brown connecting pieces. The fence was a brilliant idea – in fact it was almost an essential. Those that didn't have one would spend most of their playing time scrambling under their bed looking for lost balls, after an overly zealous flick had sent it hurtling past the static ball-boy figures. It even included a few fence panels that had advertisements on them for that extra bit of authenticity. The problem with the perimeter fence was that although it looked fantastic when the game was being played, it was a complete pain to pack up and re-assemble, so the novelty of it soon wore off.

There were also specialised corner kickers and throw-in takers that were designed to raise the ball into the air at set pieces. It was a nice idea but there were two major flaws in the design: firstly, these specialists were four times the size of all the other players, which looked somewhat odd; and secondly, they would hurtle the ball with height into the penalty area at around 500 mph. This rendered their skills completely pointless as all the other players were only one inch tall and had their legs glued to a semi-circular base, which made jumping to nod the ball in at the far post quite tricky. In fact, the ball came in so fast that it was more likely to take awaiting players' heads clean off their bodies than result in a goal. Imagine Peter Crouch on stilts sending over crosses for Wee Jimmy Krankie and you'll get the picture.

All Subbuteo sets came with two teams – reds and blues. With a bit of imagination you could just about believe that the match you were playing was Manchester Utd. v Everton but that was about it. However, you could buy teams with the authentic kits of more or less any club in the world. There was a chart of all the available teams placed underneath the glass on the counter at Toys & Prams in Ilford. I called the shop 'Toys & Prams' – everyone knew it as 'Toys & Prams'. This was because it had a huge sign hanging outside that read 'Toys & Prams', but the store was actually called Worrickers. They sold toys and prams.

Each team cost 60p and whenever I had some spare cash, I would take myself off to Ilford and pick a new team for my collection. This made playing the game more realistic for me, but at the same time opened up the world of fantasy by allowing me to stage matches like Brazil v Leeds or, even more unrealistically, West Ham v Barcelona.

The key to buying teams in their proper strips was to go for clubs that shared the same colours. For example, the all-white strip of Leeds United could double up as Real Madrid and similarly the red and blue stripes of Crystal Palace could also be Barcelona. This of course was the early seventies, a time when football clubs kept the same kit season after season, and didn't change them to simply add an extra stripe or change the design of the collar, thus convincing their ever-gullible fans to part company with fifty quid every August. I assume that Subbuteo is far too primitive to interest the kids of today, but if it does, the collection of Subbuteo teams must be a financial nightmare for them.

I always used to draw the numbers one to eleven on the back of the players' shirts in a black felt-tip pen. This was for player identification purposes during my commentary of Subbuteo matches – there always had to be a commentary. I'm not sure why, it just seemed appropriate. Goals would be greeted with a loud exhaling of breath, which did sound a little bit like a cheering crowd. If you have just tried this to see if I'm right, I hope you're not reading this on public transport.

The accompanying schoolboy commentary was also commonplace whilst playing real football – not just by me, reassuringly, everyone did it. This was particularly handy for me as a goalkeeper, as it meant I knew what an opponent was about to do. If the player on the ball yelped 'here comes Rivelino' in an excited fashion as he sprinted towards me, I could expect him to approach, dribbling the ball in an attempt to take it round me. The call of 'Lorimer ... LORIMAR', mimicking the identical commentary of *Match of the Day*'s Barry Davies, told me that I was about to face a thirty-yard thunderbolt. Peter Lorimer, the former Scotland and Leeds United player, was a long-shot expert who thundered in many a goal from distance during his career. He could kick a ball even harder than a Subbuteo specialised corner kicker.

Back in those days there were no such things as squad numbers and players wore shirts numbered one to eleven with the substitute wearing number 12. Not 27, 43 or 96 – always, always number 12. Unfortunately, there were no substitutes in Subbuteo. A huge oversight on behalf of the manufacturers, due to the fact that Subbuteo players were more injury-prone than Darren Anderton on a skiing trip. The very nature of a game that was played on the floor meant that too many players had their careers cut short by a stray knee or a tartan carpet slipper. Sometimes a blob of glue on the treatment table could extend a player's career if the injury was a simple severing of his head or arm, but for those unfortunates whose legs snapped clean from their bases, it was curtains, and they were either consigned to the dustbin or placed in the Spurs Subbuteo team. Had superglue been invented it might have been a different story, but Bostick was no magic sponge. Attempting to glue the severed legs of players back on to their bases resulted in them returning from injury with their bodies fixed at an angle of 45 degrees, giving the impression that they were either about to launch into a diving header or perform a ski jump. On their return to action, a forceful flick would see their bodies take off, leaving their base behind as they hurtled head first into the perimeter fencing.

In perhaps an early forerunner for fantasy football, I would supplement a team that had suffered player fatalities with a player from a team that had a similar strip, and thus, Pelé became a regular up front for Norwich City. An interesting career move for the Brazilian, that in real life would have packed Carrow Road to the rafters, although I'm not too sure how the flamboyant Pelé would have coped playing for their perennially colourless manager, Ron Saunders.

Subbuteo has even made the crossover into the world of pop music. The Undertones most famously mention the game in their hit 'My Perfect Cousin'. Less well known is a song called 'All I Want for Christmas is a Dukla Prague Away Kit' by Liverpool's half indie, half parody band, Half Man Half Biscuit – the point being that the away kit of the former Czechoslovakian champions was one of the few not to be made available in Subbuteo.

At the start of the new century Hasbro announced that it was ceasing production of Subbuteo. There was such an outcry from tearful middle-aged men, waxing lyrical about cloth pitches and specialised corner kickers in newspaper columns and Internet forums, that they actually reversed the decision and began manufacturing the game again. There is still a healthy market for original Subbuteo memorabilia on eBay. One of the most popular items is the eighties Argentinian team. I'm not sure whether its popularity is due to the nice light-blue and white striped shirts or a glut of still-angry Englishmen desiring to own it just so they can break off that offending arm of Diego Maradona.

Back in the world where people didn't have to rely on being flicked to get about, Britain had gone decimal. Out went the old pounds, shillings and pence and we were presented with a whole collection of shiny new coins to get used to. There were now only 100 (new) pence in the pound instead of 240, and five pence in a shilling instead of twelve. It was supposed to make things easier and once we all got used to it, made perfect sense, but conversion charts were confusing. Leading up to decimalisation, and for quite a while afterwards, every shop displayed a conversion chart explaining how the new money compared against the old. The thing that was hard to fathom was how 1p could convert to both 2d and 3d. But we did get used to it, and within a few months it was as if the old system had never existed. I can remember the very first thing that I bought with the new money. It was a Galaxy Ripple which I chose because it cost two-and-a-half pence, which meant that I could use the newly introduced halfpenny coin. I bought it on the way to school from the sweet shop on the corner of Gants Hill Crescent, on the morning that we went decimal – Monday, 15 February 1971. The shop was one of those that we would probably refer to these days as being an old-fashioned sweet shop – one which sold sweets from big jars that were kept on shelves above the counter. You could buy them by their weight, but if we didn't have enough money for a quarter they would sell us three pence worth. They sold delicacies such as Sherbet Pips, Lemon Bon-Bons, Cola Cubes and Flying Saucers, the latter of which were made out of god knows what, filled with sherbet and stuck to the roof of your mouth for the rest of the day. Back then you could also buy sweet cigarettes; not the feeble imitation that these days goes under the insipid name of Candy Sticks, but proper sweet cigarettes – with filters and the orange-coloured lighted bit. You could buy eight Black Jacks and Fruit Salad chews for a penny and Gobstoppers that were the same price and would last for about a month if you took them out and wrapped them in a tissue whilst you ate proper food.

I had a new teacher for my last two years at Gearies, Miss Bocking. Of all the teachers that I had throughout my schooling, I would single her out as the most influential on my education. She was absolutely lovely and although I can't remember too much about her teaching methods, all I know is that under her tenure I went from being a very average student to somewhere near the top of her class. I do remember that she taught me how to do long division sums – the absolute git of the arithmetic suite. When she explained something she made it seem so simple, as if anyone could do it. Everyone in the class loved her; nearly all the pupils would bring in presents for her on her birthday and at Christmas, and she would reciprocate. A real 'apple-for-the-teacher' teacher, at a time when it really wasn't cool to like your teacher. But there was something unique about her, something that she managed to tap into that made me want to learn when I had never really been that fussed before.

I also had two new friends, both of whom were in my class for these last two years: the aforementioned Wimpy-munching Bergy, and his neighbour Howard. Bizarrely, these two chaps also lived in Martley Drive, a few doors away from Scuzz, Danny and Gary. It was as if the whole world lived in Martley Drive and I was starting to wish that I did too.

Bergy was a small lad who wore National Health glasses and had hair that generally looked like it hadn't entertained a bottle of shampoo for some time. He was a brilliant chess player and a mathematical genius who could magically add up huge numbers in his head in seconds – a sort of stumpy Carol Vorderman. To be honest, he was a bit of a show off. Not in the performing sense, but he was a bragger and not without reason as he was one of those kids who was always first to get things. It wouldn't surprise me in the slightest if in later life Bergy had had the Internet before Bill Gates! Whatever was new and exciting – he was in there. The pocket calculator for example, which was a fairly new invention – he had one before everyone else. Not just a simple one either; his was one of those Casio mathematical jobbies that had things on it that we didn't yet understand, like tangents and cosines. I wouldn't have minded, but he could do most of those sums in his head anyway. As far as I was concerned the primary function of a calculator was to tap in the number 58008, turn it upside down and laugh uproariously as the screen revealed the word 'BOOBS' in LED.

Bergy was also the first person I knew who owned a Raleigh Chopper. Come to think of it, he was the only person I ever knew that owned a Raleigh Chopper. The Chopper was *the* bike to own in the early seventies. It was the most beautiful thing on two wheels and went on to serve time as an icon of the seventies. It looked so different from other bikes – a little bit like a motorbike but without an engine. It had U-shaped drop handlebars and a big long padded saddle with a high back, which made it perfect for giving 'saddlers'. The most unusual thing about the bike was that it had a big fat wheel at the back and a smaller wheel at the front, but somehow still managed to look cool. Bergy was very protective over his Chopper, (and who wouldn't be), and would never allow anyone to have a go on it … except me, which obviously used to really rile Howard, but how could I refuse?

Howard was very different from Bergy. He was quiet and shy and in 1972, as everyone else's hair was getting longer and wilder, he remained loyal to the most famous of schoolboy hairstyles – the 'Pudding Basin'. There's no two ways about it, Howard was a geek before it was chic to be a geek. He knew about buses and their routes and could name every British monarch from William the Conqueror to Queen Betty in order, together with the years in which they reigned.

On an after-school visit to his house, Howard once attempted to indulge me in a football-related game that he had invented. He presented me with a jumbo W.H. Smiths pad (one of those that had the *World in Action* logo on it – I never understood why) that was chock-full of handwritten football results and self-calculated league tables. On closer inspection, I noticed that all the teams were characters from those five-minute TV programmes that used to be shown in the seventies just before the evening news, such as *The Magic Roundabout*, *Captain Pugwash* and *Hector's House*. So a round of results may have read something like:

Zebedee 2	Captain Horatio Pugwash 1
Zsa-Zsa 1	Bayleaf the Gardener 4
Sir Prancealot 5	Florence 2
Cut-Throat Jake 1	Crystal Tipps 3

Commentating whilst playing Subbuteo matches against myself might be considered by some to be a little leftfield I'll admit, but it pales into insignificance compared with this form of self-amusement. For any younger readers, who might have picked this book up by mistake, I should point out that this isn't generally the way that that young lads entertained themselves in the seventies whilst we waited for the iPad to be invented.

He explained, in all seriousness, how the scores were determined by a throw of a dice and how problematic this was because of the lack of a zero, and how he was considering using the six as a zero next season in an attempt to make it more realistic, because in real football more teams scored nil than they did six. The irony of him trying to drag realism into matches played between a moustachioed red face on a spring and an overly hairy dog that moved around only in excited little circles seemed to have passed him by completely. In my mind I was lost for words, but in a moment of pure insanity I found words helplessly dripping from my lips. 'Why don't you make your own dice out of a sugar cube and draw the numbers on it with a felt-tip?'. He was delighted with my impromptu solution to his 'nil' problem – I felt utterly deflated to have sunk to the level of indulging him in this madness, but managed to keep my mouth firmly shut tight about the fact that there was absolutely no way on earth that Crystal Tipps would ever, ever beat Cut-Throat Jake at football – especially not away from home.

Bergy and Howard had grown up together, lived opposite each other and more than anything were incredibly competitive with each other. I often found myself in the middle of their personal battles, and while I had great times with them both, I grew tired of refereeing their conflicts. As a trio, our friendship didn't survive much past the summer of 1972. However, there is one gift that Bergy bestowed upon me that I will be eternally grateful for.

The 11 Plus exam had been abolished a couple of years before we were due to take it and replaced by something much more comprehensive called the Verbal Reasoning Test. We'd done a mock exam earlier in the year and I had topped the class with 98% – yes, I was surprised too. The real test would determine whether we finished our education at a grammar school, or what was known back then as a secondary modern school. Due to the previous Labour government's initiative, which was to offer a flat level of education to all children, grammar schools had been disappearing faster than the Roadrunner being chased by an ACME van, so places were hard to come by. There were only two non-fee-paying grammar schools left in the borough of Redbridge: Ilford County High and Beal Grammar School.

On the day, the exam went well and shortly afterwards a letter plopped on to the doormat informing my parents that I had passed the exam and had qualified to apply for one of the grammar schools. The letter was accompanied by a prospectus of all such institutions in and around the London area. Bergy had also passed the exam and, to his delight, Howard had not. Howard was desperately disappointed as it meant that he was destined to go to Gearies Secondary Modern School for Boys, which had a reputation for being a rough school where the bullying of the weak was its most successful product. I felt sorry for him and doubted whether he was steely enough to withstand such a school, but Scuzz, who had also failed and was going there too, insisted that he would take care of him, in his usual gallant manner.

For those of us that passed, we were instructed to choose our top three schools and send off the form. Bergy did all the research, decided that Beal should be top choice and persuaded me it was the best school for us. Mum wanted me to go to Ilford County High, as it had the reputation as being the top school in the area, but they wore pink blazers and I stood firm and insisted on Beal as first choice simply because Bergy had made it sound so appealing. One of its top selling points for me was that it had three full-sized football pitches with proper goal posts and nets. Playing football on pitches with goal nets was an absolute luxury in 1972.

There were only 120 places available, so it was going to be a tall order to get my first-choice school. We were never told of our score in the final exam, just whether we had passed or failed, but when the letter arrived to say that I had been accepted at Beal, we assumed that my score must have been a big one. And so my fate was sealed: I would attend Beal Grammar School for Boys after the summer, and I owed that decision to Bergy. Ironically enough, our friendship would more or less taper off once we got to Beal, but the debt that I owe him is for directing me there. I formed many friendships at that school, some of which have lasted to this day – friends whom I love dearly, and without whom my life would have been a much poorer existence.

The last few months at Gearies were a bit of a doddle. All the hard work had been done and it was winding-down time. We were given strange projects like looking after stick insects. We had to take them home in an empty jam-jar and write up what they did – the shortest essay I ever had to write. I think stick insects must become invisible to humans over the age of eleven. I have yet to see another stick insect since the day mine popped all six of its clogs. Maybe it's because they go around disguised as sticks – I don't know, I'm no entomologist.

As far as pets go, stick insects are hopeless; cats were much more my thing and around this time we got ourselves a Siamese cat that we called Taurus, which was an odd choice – he was a Capricorn. My mum was skeptical about us getting a cat; she was not really an animal person at all, but as it turned out she became the most kitten-smitten of all of us. To her, Taurus was the most intelligent beast on earth. To be fair, he was a dab-paw at getting into the notoriously difficult-to-open Dairylea triangle, but according to my mum he was far cleverer than that. She would insist that he spent half the week working as a solicitor and the other half as a driving instructor. I kid you not. I can picture her now sitting with her legs up on the sofa and stroking him as he sat on her lap, asking him if he'd had a hard day at the office.

Those final few idle months at Gearies would be the last that I would spend in the regular company of girls for five years. Girls were still a mystery and remained as uninteresting to me as I did to them. All except Ruth Feldman, that is. Whereas most girls in my class seemed to be very insular and unwilling to let you borrow their felt-tips or let you have a go on their klackers, Ruth was always encouragingly nice to me, engaged me in conversation and joined in with our footy games in the playground and over the rec. As an added bonus, I thought she was very pretty. She had shoulder-length mousey hair, big blue eyes and freckles – not too many and not the big blobby sort that all merged into one, like I had – small ones, and just the right amount to qualify her as cute. She was the first girl apart from Maureen Bullock out of *Please Sir!* who I had any sort of real crush on. The problem was that she fancied Jeffrey Levy, but that was ok, because most girls fancied Jeffrey Levy and he had his heart set on Kay Crowther anyway. This, I thought, meant that there was still a chance for me. Almost all the lads in my class fancied Kay Crowther – mainly because she already had properly formed breasts.

During the summer holidays following that final term, Scuzz and I plotted the best method for me to ask Ruth out. This involved a lot of hanging around outside her house, too scared to knock on her door, with an already-prepared speech planted firmly in my brain should things go to plan. Thankfully, she never emerged – she was always out – probably hanging around outside Jeffrey Levy's house, with a mental crib sheet of her own.

Crunch time came when she finally showed up at the rec after we'd all finished playing football and were lying on the grass staring up at the sun-filled sky, sucking on quickly diminishing Jubblies. Scuzz advised that it was now or never and his plan needed to be fulfilled. The only thing that I wanted to fully fill were my pants.

The fool-proof scheme that he had concocted was that he would ask her out first and would obviously be sent away with a flea in his ear, leaving the way clear for me. As a cunning plan, this one lacked a certain amount of cunningness and how we ever imagined that this was any sort of plan, I have no idea – but it was the best two wet-behind-the-ear nitwits could come up with. So there we were, and there was she. How could she possibly turn down the orderly queue of sweaty eleven-year-old boys presented before her?

The first part went to plan and Scuzz was duly turned down, so nervously up to the mark I stepped. It was probably a mistake to offer her a suck on my Jubbly before I popped the dreaded question, and unmuddied knees were doubtlessly the minimum requirement for such a demonstration of commitment, but I don't think either of these basic errors affected her decision. At least my refusal was full of humility and accompanied by an explanation that probably involved something to do with Jeffrey bloody Levy, but it was all rather embarrassing nonetheless, and it didn't seem like a good time to mention Kay Crowther's breasts.

And so we turned away shame-faced and carried on playing football as if nothing had happened – the perfect antidote. And as if to make up for the disappointment, and to offer some sort of consolation prize, Ruth asked if she could play too. God, she was bloody brilliant.

On reflection, the only saving grace of the whole sorry fiasco was that I wouldn't have to face her at school again. In 2015, Howard organised a reunion for Miss Bocking's former pupils. There were eleven of us there from the class of '72, including Ruth. As we posed for a photograph with our old teacher, I stood in the back row with one arm draped around Ruth's shoulder and the other, most ironically, around Jeffrey Levy's. The photographer called for more volunteers to sit in the front row alongside Miss Bocking to balance the photo up. No longer embarrassed in the presence of my erstwhile crush, I quipped: 'I've waited 43 years to put my arm around Ruth Feldman – I'm not giving it up now!'.

Ruth, like many girls in my class, was an exponent of the white-plimsoll-pop-star-love-declaration-graffiti brigade. This involved pinning their hearts to their footwear in support of their favourite; 'I love David' (Cassidy) or 'I love Donny' (Osmond) were the most popular slogans that adorned the female foot in the summer of 1972. There were a few stragglers – you might occasionally see an 'I love Michael' (Jackson), but these were much rarer.

This was about the time that I started to become aware of pop music again. David Cassidy and Donny Osmond were very much in the news – not because of their music but because of the teenage hysteria that they caused every time they appeared in public. The media made comparisons with Beatlemania but failed to come up with a decent 'mania' catchphrase for them and they just became known as 'teeny-bopper' artists. Although Cassidy was in his early twenties, Donny Osmond and Michael Jackson weren't much older than we were. Donny and David were a kind of throwback to the teen-idol pop stars of the late fifties, both in the way that they looked and performed, and the style of songs that they recorded. Meanwhile, Jackson, easily the most preferable of the three, was also styled retrospectively – this time with a nod to the Tamla Motown groups of the sixties.

I had no interest in any of these young pop-tarts – they were strictly for girls. It was quite clear to me that the girls in my class were interested in this new breed of pop star because of their looks. It couldn't possibly have anything to do with their music, surely? They seemed obsessed with these creatures and talked incessantly about them; their schoolbooks were covered with little drawings of foppish boys wearing tank-tops with shirt collars that overlapped their shoulders. There were also hearts with arrows through them bearing the legend 'David 4 Me', or something similar.

I thought I should take an interest and wondered whether there were any gorgeous female pop stars that I could similarly align myself to. There wasn't. The best I could come up with was Mary Hopkin, but it's probably fair to say that on reflection I wasn't looking hard enough, and, besides, my plimsolls were black.

It's funny how girls seem to discover pop much quicker than boys. I don't think this has ever changed. Laura, our babysitter, was 15. She was too old for the likes of Cassidy and Osmond, and when she got her homework books out while sitting for us, I noticed that her textbook graffiti of choice was TREX – I asked why. Trex as far as I was concerned was a cooking fat – I'd seen it advertised on the telly. She informed me that somewhere in the seventies-style bubble writing was a dot and it actually read T. Rex. I was still none the wiser – a T. Rex was a dinosaur, wasn't it? It wasn't until she went into an unstoppable barrage of superlatives that mainly concerned the gorgeousness of some fellow called Marc Bolan that I gathered we were back to this bloody pop business again. She confirmed her undying love by showing me the inside cover of her rough book, which had 'I love Marc Bolan' written very neatly about fifty times, as if she'd been made to write it as a punishment for talking in class.

Glam rock was in its infancy and provided a boyish alternative to the 'teeny-boppers'; I accidentally decided to give pop a chance. I started watching *Top of the Pops* – not religiously, just when I thought about it. On this programme I could see the likes of Bolan and Gary Glitter, both of whom appeared to be dressed from head to foot in Bacofoil, with glitter and make-up on their faces and high-heeled silver boots – and this, remember, was the boyish alternative. The music was rather stompy and maybe it was the stompiness that gave it its laddish appeal.

A week or so after I left Gearies a song called 'School's Out' by Alice Cooper replaced 'Puppy Love' by Donny Osmond as the number one record in the charts. How appropriate, I thought. Time passes so slowly during the school summer holidays and it felt as if it was number one all that summer, but in actual fact it was only top for three weeks. Alice looked a bit scary in his leather cat suit and thick black eye make-up. It was as if he'd fallen out of a horror movie and landed in the *Top of the Pops* studio by mistake. Whereas Marc Bolan had worn a pink feather boa around his neck, Alice's choice of neck apparel for the show was a live python. He looked as tough as any man whose name was Alice possibly could. 'School's Out' may only be three-and-a-half minutes long, but in those three-and-a-half minutes Alice Cooper did what every writer hopes to achieve – to capture a moment in the listener's life. That moment was when the school bell rings on the last day of term, and the feeling of euphoria that signifies the start of seven weeks of sunshine and freedom fills your heart with unadulterated happiness. That books thrown in the air, slamming down of desk lids, dashing for the school gates moment. The moment that can't be bought. Yet for me, and the thousands of other kids that left school in the summer of 1972, Alice Cooper sold us that moment – sold us a memory.

I would find out much later that there is nothing quite like pop music for illuminating a memory and aligning you to that point when you heard a song for the very first time, locking you into that moment forever. I had no idea in 1972 that pop was capable of that – that it could be so powerful – even more powerful than a Peter Lorimer 30-yarder. I still didn't completely trust it, and as far as I was concerned, compared with my obsession with football, it was still well and truly on the subs bench. But it would only be a matter of months before it would be asked to take off its tracksuit, start limbering up and told in no uncertain terms: 'You're going on, son'.

We Don't Need No Education

I didn't have a clue where it came from, and to be honest, I didn't really care. All that mattered was that one evening, towards the end of the summer holiday, Dad huffed and puffed his way in through the front door carrying a colour telly. His heavy breath punctuated with a gasped warning that it was only borrowed and was going back to whence it came the minute the closing ceremony was over. But a colour telly. At long last, a colour telly.

The ceremony to which he referred was that of the 1972 Munich Olympic Games – the first Olympics to be broadcast in colour. Dad is a big fan of the Games and Munich '72 was the first that I can remember watching with him. As with most people, there were some sports that interested me – such as the track and field, volleyball and the swimming – while others bored me rigid.

Due to the novelty of our temporary acquisition, I watched more of these Games than I would normally have bothered myself with, so I do remember them quite vividly. These were the Games in which swimmer Mark Spitz won seven gold medals, Olga Korbut, the tiny Soviet gymnast, won the hearts of millions and took home three golds of her own, and Northern Ireland's Mary Peters won the gold medal for Great Britain in the pentathlon. I hadn't quite got used to the whole Great Britain Team thing. It was all right for *Jeux Sans Frontiers*, which as far as I was concerned was far more important than the Olympics anyway, but as a football fan, watching the Home Internationals at the end of every season, the four home nations felt like very separate beasts.

Sadly, the Games are also remembered for the massacre of eleven members of the Israeli team, who were taken hostage in the Olympic village and subsequently murdered by the Palestinian terrorist organisation Black September. It was the first time a terrorist attack had been broadcast live on TV and we all sat around it and watched the events of September 5 1972 unfold in grainy colour. The image of a man in a red tracksuit carrying a machine gun along the roof of a building is as vivid to me now as it was then.

The news over the next few days was full of the whys and wherefores of what had happened and, understandably, there was considerable outrage felt amongst the large Jewish community of Gants Hill. There was a lot of talk about how the Germans had bungled the two rescue attempts and how the Games should be abandoned in light of the tragedy. It was a public relations disaster for the Germans, who – almost 30 years later – were still trying to repair the damage to their reputation caused by the Second World War, and had hoped that these Games might help to pave the way. Instead, they were blamed for the disaster as seventeen people (including five terrorists and a German police officer) lost their lives.

In terms of headline-grabbing news items, the day after the massacre may have been somewhat less dramatic, but it held its own significance for me as it was the day that I started my new school. We had been sent a long list of clothing requirements in advance, and these had been duly purchased from Lucille and David – 'The School Uniform Specialists' – in Gants Hill. It felt strange to suddenly have to wear a uniform after the casual attire of Gearies.

Beal's uniform consisted of a tan blazer complete with school crest, black flannel trousers and a yellow and brown striped tie. My school shirts were in varying pastel shades and made of nylon, itched like crazy and didn't lend themselves well to the sweatiness of an adolescent boy. There was a whole host of sports gear that was needed too, and hence I got my first pair of football boots. Horrible things they were: R.P. Ellen's own budget brand. Ellen's was the shoe shop near the corner of the Cranbrook Road that had a few years earlier supplied me with several pairs of 'Clarks Commandos' – complete with handy-to-use compass hidden in the heel. I'd always got my shoes there and they sold football boots, so it was a done deal. They had a big fat rounded toe that made it virtually impossible to kick the ball in any way other than the trusted toe-punt. These boots weren't made for walking – let alone running – as they would take huge slabs of skin from your ankles as quick as look at you. They had to go and were quickly usurped by a beautiful pair of Adidas Beckenbauers, which had the three Adidas stripes in bright yellow rather than the traditional white. I loved those boots and had them for years.

I took a briefcase to school on that first day. Mum assured me that, with this being a grammar school, everyone would have one. Inside was the prerequisite requirement for every kid's first day of term – a W.H. Smiths 'Back to School Kit' that included a pencil, a ruler and a pencil/ink rubber. The ink half of the rubber was an imposter and had no business being in there at all. There was no such thing as an ink rubber, and its idea of eradication amounted to shredding the paper it was being used on until the mistakes, and indeed the page itself, no longer existed. Also included were a collection of strange objects, the likes of which I hadn't seen before: a setsquare, a set of compasses, a protractor and a plastic stencil that had random shapes of things such as a test-tube, a hexagon and something that vaguely resembled the planet Saturn. I don't think I ever used the stencil, or the setsquare for that matter, and as for the compass – it spent far more of its short lifespan being held upright on the classroom chair in front of me, waiting for an unsuspecting bottom to land on top of it, than it ever did creating perfect circles.

I met up with Bergy at Gants Hill station on that first morning and we took the 144 bus to school together. I was surprised that he had gone for the optional school cap and suggested that this may have been a mistake.

The school bus was an intimidating experience – full of older boys, looking much scruffier than we did in their worn-in uniforms, and sporting ties with knots as big as tennis balls, loosened so far from their collars that it was clear they were no longer on speaking terms. Some of them were even smoking – they were that grown-up. One lad almost immediately grabbed Bergy's cap and he and his mates began mercilessly throwing it around the upper deck as Bergy haplessly chased after it. He never wore that cap again.

When being fitted for my school uniform, I too had toyed with the cap option – my mum thought it would be nice. But by this time my hair was long and wide and of no fixed style – just a big bright orange curly mass, and so when I donned the ill-fitting headgear, it looked ridiculous. Mum described it as looking like a 'pimple on St. Pauls'. She had a few regular expressions like 'who's she – the cat's mother?' or 'there's no such thing as "can't"', but this was a new one on me and a fairly accurate analogy at that. I was quite thankful that I had cast all ideas of cap-wearing to one side. School caps, worn backwards or otherwise, were far from being 'street'.

The school was a forbidding-looking building that housed around 750 pupils up to the age of eighteen throughout its three floors and separate metalwork, woodwork and art shops, although the football and rugby pitches, cricket nets and tennis courts that occupied its acres of green land somehow managed to soften the stern expression on its face. The most daunting thing about the place was that were so many huge boys clip-clopping around its unfamiliar corridors in their 'Blakey' heeled shoes, and it felt intimidating to be an anonymous face amongst them all. I expected this school to be full of posh, swotty kids, and I remember being surprised that it had a fair smattering of scary hooligan types amongst its older ranks too.

Following a gathering of the new intake in the school hall, I was despatched with my new classmates to Annexe One, which I was told would be my form room. Form room? The form thing was a little baffling at first. I thought I was in the first year but apparently I was a first former in the first form, and what I had always referred to as a class was now also called a form, and there were three other forms in the first form, each with a form room all of their own.

All very confusing, but everything was done differently here and it took a little bit of getting used to. There were no girls around the place for a start, and that made everything seem that little bit harsher – a little bit more serious. If you wanted school dinners, you had to buy a dinner ticket, which cost the princely sum of twelve new pence per day. This was different to the simple handing over of a week's worth of dinner money to your teacher on a Monday morning, as we had done at Gearies. Dinner tickets were actually a great idea, and meant that you could dip in and out of school dinners as and when the menu took your fancy. There would be no more uncomfortable stand-offs between me and a crusty old square of cheese pie (which is what we used to call quiche in the olden days, kids), no more pointless manoeuvring of it around my plate with my fork, not knowing whether the next substance that I was about to dispense would be tears or vomit, and no more threats of having to sit there until the entire abomination was devoured – a scenario that I was once forced to go through by a particularly despicable dinner lady at Gearies. No sir, it was to be spam fritters all the way for me.

Hilarious as it was for a bunch of giggly adolescent boys to discover that lessons were now called 'periods', the person that strung together my first timetable was certainly no Eric Morecambe. It told the sorry tale of double art followed by double woodwork on a Monday morning. If there was anything that was going to bring me down with a bad case of the Sunday-night blues, it was going to be those two nasties. There was even worse news – homework was now on the agenda too. The subjects that I took were the standard fare of maths, English, geography, history, French and science. They all seem pretty staid compared with all the magnificent vocational subjects that kids are able to study at schools, colleges and universities these days; things that might actually be a little bit more fun and ultimately more useful to learn about than the formula that enables us to work out the area of a trapezium (half the sum of the parallel sides, multiplied by the distance between them). So far, in the forty-odd years that have passed since I learnt that formula, I have never yet needed to find the area of a trapezium. They're not the sorts of things you find generally hanging around just waiting for their areas to be calculated, are they? I'm not even sure if I would know a trapezium if it came up to me in the street and introduced itself, holding an outstretched hand and saying, 'Hello, I'm a trapezium'. However, if one did happen to cross my path and I needed to know its exact area, I'd be ok.

I suppose that is the reason that we had to learn such nonsense – the just-in-case factor. What worries me more is the fact that, all these years later, I still know this formula. For this, the responsibility lies squarely on the shoulders, or perhaps the nimble toes, of my maths teacher Mr Brandon – or 'Pukebomb', as he became christened, due to the fact that his touchy-feely mannerisms were enough to make even the strongest of stomachs want to throw up in explosive fashion. He would prance around the classroom, performing silly dances in a poor attempt at public relations, reciting mathematical formulae over and over and over again in a rhythmic pattern, like some early rapping prototype of Jay-Z. Pukey-B, perhaps.

The kids of today will still be having these formulae drummed into them one way or another, but, for them, it's not such a huge leap from logarithms to rock rhythms. When Pythagoras turns his back, there will be a group of students huddled somewhere excitedly editing a music video that they will have filmed and directed for a song that they will more than likely have also written and played. Somewhere else, another student will be tinkering with the final sentences of her essay 'David Bowie – The Ziggy Years'. And all this during school time! How did these things manage to find their way into the school curriculum? Do their timetables try and disguise these wonders from their parents, or do they just come right out with it: maths – history – double jazz-funk? You can almost picture the horror on young Kyle's face as he arrives for his lesson only to discover that his mum has mistakenly packed his woodwork apron instead of his flange pedal.

When I was at school pop music was not welcome in the classroom; music lessons at Beal were exclusively of a classical nature – the works of composers such as Brahms, Mozart and Schubert. We were forced to listen to something like Brahms' 'Symphony No. 4 in E Minor' and then have to listen as Mr Timms, our music teacher, droned on endlessly about its wonder. And then, as if to add insult to injury, we would have to write an essay about it for homework and come up with a whole bunch of new reasons why we thought it was great too.

Mr Timms wouldn't entertain the idea of pop music. There would be no rolling over of Beethoven – not on his watch anyway. I remember on one occasion, as he got out the record player prior to yet another classical recital, Ian King held up a copy of Jethro Tull's *Aqualung* and asked, 'Can we listen to this sir? – It's a classic'. Clearly there was never a realistic chance of Timms allowing this and it just gave him his cue to wax lyrical about the marvels of classical music over the puerility of pop. I hated the way in which he pooh-poohed pop as if it wasn't relevant as a musical medium. He was more than just a little bit smug about classical music's 400-year history, and would have been surprised if 'The Tull' had lasted till the end of the week.

But things have changed, and whilst I'm not quite prepared to accept that we have arrived at the stage where the lyrics of 'One Less Bitch' by NWA are dissected as part of a poetry lesson, the mellowing towards pop in schools is undeniable. In my day pop was left to rot, kicking its heels on the wrong side of the school railings, but now, the education system is welcoming it in from the cold, putting a leather-elbow-patched-arm around its shoulders and giving it its own locker with a big capital 'P' on the door. I'm not entirely sure how I feel about this. There's a part of me that is insanely jealous of today's kids being able to incorporate pop music into their studies and learn the drums or bass guitar during school time. Another part of me is secretly proud of pop's progress in so much as it has finally been acknowledged as being important enough for serious study. Yet there's another part telling me that this is completely wrong – that pop was always fundamentally anti-school, a war between young and old, a dinosaur-sized bone of contention that has somehow evolved into the powder of collusion with its traditional enemy, and it should never, ever be an experience that you share with your teachers.

If I could have a conversation with Mr Timms now, I might have the nerve to ask him: what is so clever about classical music anyway? It is after all just a bunch of tunes strung together – does that make it any cleverer than, say, side two of *Abbey Road*? Then there's the lyrics issue. I find it hard to get emotionally attached to any piece of music, pop or otherwise, without words. I love lyrics; words are one of the most powerful tools we have to express ourselves, and therefore form an important part of any piece of music that is going to draw me in. It made me laugh how Mr Timms would tell us that some sort of story was being depicted by certain passages of an instrumental classical piece. This may well have been true in some instances, but any such interpretations are always going to be subjective to the listener. One man's meat is another man's cheese pie – as they say. With pop, the lyrics are there to tell the story for themselves and, of course, these can be subjective too, so why would I accept Timms' ramblings on the classical genre as being perceptions cast in stone? I'm not saying that classical music isn't without merit – there are some beautiful pieces – but what I am saying is that I'm not having it that classical music is in any way cleverer than pop or has the right to look down its nose at it. Music doesn't have to be complicated to be good. Simple can be beautiful and forceful too.

I am aware now that this school was equipped with every facility to enable me to excel – in fact, I knew that then too, but I didn't use it to my advantage. Maybe I wasn't as clever as I thought I was, but things went terribly wrong with my education at Beal.

I particularly felt this in maths, a subject in which I had previously been pretty successful. I had a couple of days off early on, missing the introduction to algebra, and found on my return that I had no idea what was going on. I didn't ask for extra help from my maths teacher, Mr Anderson, who was also our form teacher and to be honest, a thoroughly decent bloke who would probably have given it. He was young and straight out of teacher training college – a real-life Bernard Hedges. I suppose I didn't want to feel stupid in front of my new classmates, so I kept quiet and let it all wash over my head as I fell further and further behind. I don't know why I wasn't able to catch up; I just couldn't. I started to feel like I was out of my depth and I don't think I ever fully recovered.

During those couple of days I had off I also missed the trials for the school football team. I was desperate to play in goal for the school and was gutted to have missed the trials. Mr Ramsden, a brash northerner, was the games teacher who ran the football team and was also my geography teacher. We had already established a hate/hate relationship during our first geography lesson, after he told me that my handwriting was appalling and informed me that unless I got my hair cut by the next lesson I would face a detention. He was the type of games teacher that spent his entire career in a tracksuit, even when he was teaching geography, and his odour told the story of football-pitch-to-classroom continuity. When I asked him whether it would still be possible to still try out for the football team, he made it quite clear that this would be a huge inconvenience to him but reluctantly agreed to a special one-to-one try out.

It took place the next day during the lunch break and I met him on the football pitch. There he was, tracksuited as ever and going through his routine of ball juggling, which was either him just showing off or an attempt to intimidate me. If the latter was his intention, it worked; I was incredibly nervous – this was important to me. He proceeded to blast a few venomous shots at me, most of which I got nowhere near. I think he was trying his hardest. Then he started to take penalties, which again sailed past me and into the net. Then when I did eventually stop one, he told me that I had moved before he had struck the ball and therefore it didn't count. It was a bit like that football pitch scene from the film *Kes*. Needless to say, I didn't make the team and my chance was gone. I was really furious with myself for letting my nerves get the better of me and knew I could have done better, but that was that.

Bergy, who had now been handed a new moniker – 'Ronnie', as in Ronnie Corbett, due to the fact that he was very short and wore black-rimmed glasses – had been dispatched to a different class from me and thus our friendship, whilst not petering out completely, did tail off as we both made new friends. When thrust into a new environment, we tend to hang onto the familiar or at least the slightly familiar. I gravitated towards Marc Preston, who I had known at Gearies, but we weren't what you might class as good friends then; however we sat together in Annexe One throughout that first year and became just that. He would egg me on and encourage me to carry out all the unruly classroom antics of the naughty schoolboy that he didn't dare to be. He was a smart kid and far more sensible than I was, and tried to help me with my schoolwork in exchange for the odd Kraft cheese slice and piccalilli sandwich. But as my academic confidence steadily dropped, I quickly got myself out of the habit of learning anything and into messing-about mode during lessons, in attempts to make others laugh.

My greatest accomplices in this mission were the two lads that sat directly behind Marc and me in Annexe One – Martin Gaffney and Colin Baldwin. Both were West Ham supporters, and Colin was a scout too so there was plenty of common interests to help us bond. Martin also fancied himself as a bit of a joker, but unlike me he was clever enough to know where to draw the line between being silly and getting his work done. He won popularity with his classmates by performing the worst impersonations of Frank Spencer, Harold Wilson and Frankie Howerd I have ever heard. Colin's party trick was his bizarre ability to turn his eyelids inside out. He did this by holding out his eyelashes between his thumb and forefinger and blinking hard. It was a disgusting trick that saw half his eyes covered in limp bloodied tissue, and made me feel quite nauseous. He would try and catch me unawares by tapping me on the shoulder, resulting in me turning round to face him, only to be greeted by this preposterous sight. The three of us did however work studiously together on creating new and rather rude lyrics to well-known tunes. One of our early successes was a re-working of the song 'The Farmer and the Cowman', which oozed classiness and, if I remember correctly, went something like this:

The penis and vagina should be friends,
Oh the penis and vagina should be friends,
One man likes to push it in,
The lady likes to pull it out,
That's no reason why they can't be friends.

I think that as a class, once we got to know each other, we were a pretty sound bunch that generally got along quite well. There were no bullies as such but there was one kid, Ian White, who seemed to irritate the hell out of everybody. There was a whole manner of ways in which he achieved this – one of which was coming over to your desk and leaving it furnished with one of his big slimy bogies. I don't know why he was on this mission to annoy everyone – attention-seeking perhaps – but there were always consequences to pay for his actions and things usually ended up with him cowering in the corner in tears. Once, a couple of years later, he wound up Mark Anderson to such an extent that Mark picked up his desk and hurled it across the classroom at him. But none of this ever seemed to deter Ian; he went about his business in a relentless fashion regardless. He was an odd chap who didn't seem to be a part of any of the cliques that were forming but used to linger like an unwanted smell on the periphery of everybody else's groups. He once tried to court favour from his classmates by bringing one of his dad's dirty books into school. It was called *Sexy Party Games* and was the first piece of pornographic literature I ever saw – it was rubbish. It had photos of the sort of games one might play at an orgy, and gave them titles that played on the names of games that were usually associated with children's parties such as 'Blind Man's Cock' or 'Postman's Fuck'. It became hot currency in Annexe One and Ian briefly became everyone's best friend as he allowed anyone that wanted to take it home, for a little go on it in private, to do so.

One particular session of 'White retribution' almost resulted in disaster for me. During a rainy break-time, someone extracted his still-damp swimming trunks from his duffle bag and the entire class proceeded to lob them around the classroom while he flapped about from desk to desk trying to retrieve them. It was like a 30-man game of piggy-in-the-middle. When the trunks arrived in my hands, I attempted to send them over to the far side of the classroom, but as I hurled them skywards they got caught on one of the iron girders that supported the corrugated roof of the annexe, and to everyone else's great amusement, there they remained.

The period immediately following that break was to be RE, taught by the almost senile Mr Gaskin. He was around 175 years old, and rumour had it that he only had one lung. He had no control over any class that he taught and his lessons generally dissolved into chaos, with everyone doing whatever they fancied. Even the swotty kids took advantage and used his lessons to make an early start on their homework. He did try and exert his authority, and would often tell offending boys to go the secretary's office and bring him back the cane and punishment book. This would result in those boys leaving the classroom, taking the rest of the lesson off and not returning until after Gaskin had left to go to his next lesson. He never questioned their prolonged absence, probably because he had forgotten that he had sent them out in the first place. We were all surprised that in his two hundred years of teaching he hadn't worked out that he probably wanted to send someone that wasn't actually about to be the recipient of his anger to fetch the cane. Or maybe he was cleverer than we thought, and that was just his way of getting disruptive boys out of his class.

Had the trunks not been trapped above our heads, it would have been perfectly conceivable that the trunk-chucking game would have continued throughout Gaskin's lesson, regardless of him attempting to teach us something Jesus-y. However, ten minutes after the lesson was due to start, there was still no Gaskin. We did start to wonder whether he had got lost along the way, but our curiosity was quelled in horrific fashion as the towering presence of the headmaster Mr Manuel entered the annexe, bringing the tomfoolery to an abrupt standstill as the class fell into an immediate respectful silence.

Mr Manuel was a huge mountain of a man that demanded immediate attention. He was one of those teachers who would either speak to you in a very soft genteel voice or, when angered, with veins almost bursting out of his neck and his face red with rage, would shout directly in your face with such venom that its airy force could pin back the recipient's facial skin as tight as a ten-session course of Botox. It was rumoured that a dose of the cane from him could reduce even the hardest of boys to tears and I really didn't fancy confirming those stories. His nickname, unsurprisingly, was simply 'Manny'. It was impossible not to know this, as the outside wall of the gym was emblazoned with the legend 'Manny is a Cunt' in big white spray-painted letters. It was there on my first day and there it remained until my last. In fact, when I went back to the school to pick up a reference for a job in 1986 and took a nostalgic stroll through the grounds, it was still there. Why he never had it removed, I don't know – he must have walked past it a squillion times. Perhaps he approved of his image or, at worst, agreed with it, or maybe he was the only person in the entire school who didn't know it was his nickname.

As he took up his position at the front of the class, he explained that Mr Gaskin was ill and that he would be taking us for our RE lesson. I found it almost impossible to concentrate as my eyes were firmly anchored to the pair of damp trunks hovering above him and praying like mad that he didn't spot them or, worse still, find himself wearing them on his head. At one point during the lesson (for reasons that escape me now) he asked the class if anyone had watched the previous night's TV adaptation of the book *The Last of the Mohicans*. However, as he struggled to find the word 'Mohicans' and proceeded to ask if anyone had seen 'The Last of the …The Last of the … The Last of …', one quick-witted soul intercepted with 'The Summer Wine, Sir?', prompting much mirth from the rest of us. As 'Manny' rolled his eyes towards the ceiling in disbelief, my heart was in my mouth, as I felt certain that he would catch sight of the suspended swimming gear. How could he miss them? But somehow he did. It was a closer shave than even Victor Kiam could have provided, and I escaped that particular incident without having to experience the Manny 'hairdryer', and with my bottom untanned. Manny would eventually have his day with me four years later, but by then I was much better equipped to deal with it. More of that later.

This is Pop!

Away from school, my life was about to take a dramatic turn. The venue for such a game changer: the scout hut in Gants Hill; the time: a Saturday night in February 1973. I was persuaded by Laura the babysitter to attend a disco that was being DJ-ed by her boyfriend Steve. I've since noticed babysitters always have boyfriends called Steve. Attending such an event seemed to be against my better judgement; after all there were going to be girls there, who would be expecting to be asked to dance, and after several months of my new all-male environment that was quite a scary prospect. But I buckled and went along decked out in my first pair of platform shoes, which I can distinctly remember were mainly black but with a red suedette upper inset, and had a modest two-inch heel. To complement them, I wore a pair of bottle-green flares and a yellow t-shirt, which had a smiley face printed on the front and 'be happy' written on the back, both of which had been bought from Mr Byrite in Ilford during a shopping trip with my mum that very afternoon. I loved those shoes to death. How could I not have looked good in a pair of shoes like that?

I can clearly point to this night as being the moment when pop came back into my life and decided to stay. I had never before been exposed to several continuous hours of thumpingly loud music. I stood and observed for a while, sipping from a plastic cup of orange squash as I leaned nonchalantly against the perimeter wall in a gap that was uninhabited by the stacks of metal chairs. The air was thick with teenage hormones and the pungent merged aromas of Brut and Smitty. I nodded my head in time with the music at what seemed like appropriate intervals, trying my best to convince both myself and anyone that happened to be watching that I knew what I was doing. The music was overpowering and it was impossible not to feel intoxicated by the depth of sound that emanated from the huge speakers. 'Cum on Feel the Noize' by Slade, 'Do You Wanna Touch' by Gary Glitter and 'Blockbuster' by Sweet were all songs that were played over and over again that night and each time were greeted by air-punching cheers, thunderous foot-stomping and shouty singing from the mass of those brave enough to move along to them on the scout hut's dusty lino that formed the dance floor. I wanted to be a part of this. I sidled up to where a couple of boys I knew from scouts were dancing and joined them. I didn't have a clue how to dance and just awkwardly tried to copy what they were doing. Unfortunately, they were clueless too – it was like the blind leading the blind, and the dancing, if that's how it could be described, mainly involved staring at the floor, shuffling nervously from side to side, and moving one foot to join the other.

I found myself dancing next to a girl who told me through a cupped hand that her name was Debbie and that she was twelve. Not wanting her to think that I was some wet-nosed kid, I told her I was too. Twelve that is – not called Debbie.

It's never really a good thing to start a relationship with a lie, but in the grand scale of lying to a girl, exaggerating my age by four weeks was probably forgivable. Debbie talked about anything and everything, which was handy, as I had no rehearsed chat-up lines. She talked about the music – which songs, singers and bands she loved and which ones she hated, while I tried to appear knowledgeable and pretend that I too was a regular reader of *Jackie*. We seemed to be getting on like the proverbial blazing home. I think she must have been attracted by those shoes – probably too shy to say so, but it felt great whatever the reason. I didn't even feel awkward when she grabbed my waist and drew me closer to dance slowly to Harold Melvin's 'If You Don't Know Me By Now', a song that would from that moment forward be forever associated with my first kiss. She placed my hand on the small of her back, which felt excitingly damp. We kissed – a proper, full on, lip-to-lip snog. I'd seen it done on the telly so knew what was required. It felt naughty and terribly grown-up, and even at that age I was aware that wiping the wetness away from my lips afterwards probably wasn't the polite thing to do – so I resisted the temptation. And so Debbie became my first proper girlfriend; we lasted around six weeks.

Prior to our respective dads coming to collect us after the disco, we agreed to meet the following afternoon at Gants Hill Odeon. We saw *Fiddler On The Roof*, but I was more interested in practicing my snogging technique than listening to Topol yodelling. Fortunately, she did too. After the film she said that she was going home to tape the top twenty from Radio One. I liked the sound of this and thought I might do the same – it would be like re-living the previous evening's excitement and I could keep it forever. What an old romantic.

When I got home I asked dad if I could borrow his tape recorder. It was one of those old reel-to-reel jobs that had a complicated mechanism whereby you had to thread the tape through all the recording heads. It had a detachable microphone and I had previously used it to record my own football match commentaries over muted editions of *The Big Match*. Come on, everyone has done that, haven't they?

I pilfered the radio that usually lived in the kitchen, took it up to my bedroom and found Radio One. I put a sign on the door that said 'shhh recording in progress' (although it's possible that I used a lot more 'h's' than that) and hoped that no one would come into my private recording studio. That was the thing about detachable microphones, you had to be completely silent whilst taping or the recording would be permanently blighted with chatter or creaking floorboards. The severest case of this I ever heard of is one that my wife Kim recalls, which occurred during a recording she made of 'Bohemian Rhapsody' in 1975. Her mother chose the quiet 'nothing really matters' refrain close to the end of the song to bellow Kim's name up the stairs, to indicate that her tea was ready. Consequently, she now finds it impossible to listen to the song without inserting an ear-shattering 'Kiiiiiim!' at that exact point. It's how she heard the song time and time again as a kid, and how she will hear it forevermore.

Tom Browne's show *Solid Gold Sixty* ran on Radio One from 4pm to 7pm every Sunday. The important bit was the hour between six and seven, in which he played this week's top twenty in its entirety; it was a must for every pop fan up and down the country, most of whom were probably sitting there like me in deathly silence, crouched over their radios with their detachable microphones poised against its speaker, praying that their mum wouldn't call them for their tea.

I can remember almost every song that was in my first top twenty – 'Roll Over Beethoven' by the Electric Light Orchestra, 'Whiskey In The Jar' by Thin Lizzy, 'Cindy Incidentally' by The Faces, 'Daniel' by Elton John and 'Feel the Need in Me' by the Detroit Emeralds – and I delighted in almost all of them. I must have played that tape two or three times a night during that week, learning all the words and singing along. Slade's 'Cum on Feel the Noize' was the number one record and I adored it, from its opening screams of 'Baby, baby, baaaaybeeeh' to its fading choruses. Much in the same way as I had chosen Chelsea in their pomp as my football team, I decided that Slade, on top of their game, should be my band. Sweet were the other contenders, but there seemed to be something dishonest about them – too much make up, too manufactured, too much funny-spoken-bit-in-the-middle-y.

Slade were from the Black Country and had started life as a skinhead band. They were still a bit of a motley crew of ruffians (as my mum might have described them), but not in a threatening way. The sort, I imagine, that if you walked into their local, they would fall over themselves to buy you a pint and welcome you into their gang, and not let you leave until you'd had a jolly nice time. They'd had plenty of hits during 1971 and 1972 but were just about to embark on their most successful period. In a little over 18 months they would be gone, but for now they were the kings of glam rock.

They were quite an ugly band; Noddy Holder, the lead singer, with his top hat and huge whiskery sideburns, looked a bit like a younger version of Mr Bumble out of the film *Oliver!*. But that voice – what a voice. I'm not even sure if I mean that in a good way or not. All I know is that I had never heard anything like it before – or since, for that matter. A great big, raspy thing it was, that seemed to arrive at the microphone having travelled up for the day from his stack-heeled boots via his power-boosted lungs; a controlled screaming that somehow managed to stay in tune. I tried to not allow myself to be put off the band by guitarist Dave Hill, who I thought was a bit of a nob. Dressed from head to toe in silver, with enormous buckteeth and a silly pudding-basin fringe, which had probably been cut by his mum, he looked like an oven-ready beaver. His pre-planned back-to-back guitar posturing with bassist Jimmy Lea on *Top of the Pops* seemed excruciatingly ill-fitting for a band singing words such as 'you know how to squeeze me, whoa-oh, you know how to please me whoa-oh'. But despite loving all their singles up to what I consider to be their final hoorah, 'How Does it Feel?' (which, incidentally, I still think is a little belter), it wasn't until I bought a compilation CD of their hits in the nineties that I owned any of their records.

I'm not sure why that was, but it brings me nicely around to the subject of the first record that I ever bought. As aging fans of pop music, its reasonable to expect the topic of 'what was the first record you ever bought?' to crop up in conversations at fairly regular intervals over the course of a lifetime. This subject might be particularly prevalent when in a group of work colleagues, or during a reunion of old friends following a decade or two apart. In the case of your work mates, it is more than likely that the answer you gave to this question was the first lie that you ever told them (discounting the rubbish that you spouted at the interview of course), and in the reunion scenario the record that you tell them was your first now is unlikely to be the same as the one you told them about in 1975.

If you know me and you've maybe tinkered with history by lying to me about your first record – it's ok, I understand, we're cool. I get why you did it and I'm well aware that the potential that pop offers for truth-bending is almost without boundaries. By the same token, I hereby apologise now for my own pop porkies that I may have laid at your doorstep. My lies weren't even consistent; one week it would be 'Drive-In Saturday' by David Bowie, the next Alice Cooper's 'No More Mr Nice Guy'. My first record wasn't either of these and, most lamentably of all, I'm afraid it wasn't the truly wonderful 'Superstition' by Stevie Wonder either. I'm sorry. I wish it had been, but go and have a flick through my singles and you won't find any of these records in the form of a 7-inch piece of vinyl. There may have actually been a point where I had totally convinced myself that Stevie's opening drum beats that lead so perfectly into his funktastic clavinet riff on 'Superstition' were the first sounds that I heard when the dust was eventually blown off that old record player from the sixties. But alas no, I lied too. I can hear its title dripping from my lips even now. I did it almost without thinking – and for many years at that. Isn't that shocking? It's quite obvious why we re-invent this momentous event, or at least it seems obvious to me. Your first record is an indication of just how quick you were out of the starting blocks, how switched on and – dare I say it – how hip you were. It marks the exact point in time where you first welcomed pop into your life; where you invited it in to share a bag of Quavers and a bottle of Cresta, showed it your stack of football programmes that you were intending to sell in order to buy even more pop music, and discussed all the things you were going to do together in the future.

At this point, it might also be worth considering those poor sods that don't actually have to lie about their first record. What if your first record really was 'Bohemian Rhapsody', 'Strawberry Fields Forever/Penny Lane', 'Like a Rolling Stone' or some other staggeringly breathtaking slice of groundbreaking pop music? Would you believe them? Such an announcement to their chums would surely result in some exaggerated chin rubbing, coupled with a few audible 'chinny-reck-ons', forcing the purveyor into a bizarre reversed universe where he or she has to think of a truly dreadful record in order not to be declared a liar? Is the world full of people whose first record really was Marvin Gaye's 'What's Going On' but are falsely claiming it was 'Chirpy Chirpy Cheep Cheep'?

And so on to my real first record. Well the actual first record I ever bought doesn't count – no really, it doesn't, I'll explain. I spotted it in the window of Woolworth's at Gants Hill: my eyes drawn towards it by the blonde lady who adorned its sleeve kneeling in the sea in just some red bikini bottoms and a white cheesecloth shirt which was so soaked through that she might as well have not been wearing it at all. *16 Chart Hits – Volume 5* was the name of the album I found myself staring at, and to the right of this beautiful creature was a list of songs that excited me almost as much as she did: '20th Century Boy', 'Cum on Feel the Noize', 'Hello Hooray', 'Killing Me Softly with His Song', 'Cindy Incidentally', 'Twelfth of Never', 'and many more', it proudly boasted. It was almost an exact replica of that first top twenty that I had taped off the radio. And the price emblazoned on a star-shaped ticket for such a pop feast – 79 of your newest pence. A bargain, without a doubt.

I had no hesitation in handing over the cash and excitedly took it home. But when I played the opening track of side 1 – '20th Century Boy' – it didn't sound right. The thunderous opening chord and Marc Bolan's yelping 'owwww' sounded so much weedier here than I had remembered from the T. Rex record I'd heard on the radio. I played it again before progressing further and my fears were consolidated. This wasn't the corkscrew-topped Adonis at all, but some sort of makeshift Marc. Playing through the rest of the album revealed further horrors. A counterfeit Cooper, a simulated Slade, a fake Flack and a fraudulent Faces (featuring of course a replica Rod Stewart). I still couldn't really believe that these songs were not by the original artists and combed the sleeve (trying not to linger for too long on the beach blonde) for clues, details of who the hell was filling my bedroom with this horrible noise. I tried to convince myself that I'd got it wrong and I was in fact listening to the real deal. But it was no use; I had to face the fact that I'd bought a lemon.

This particular musical violation was part of a series that was put out by the budget label Contour in the seventies and there were many other labels releasing similar abominations, most notably the *Top of the Pops* series on the Hallmark label, which had absolutely nothing to do with the TV show. I came across a *Top of the Pops* album that emanated from 1980 at a record fair I attended in the early nineties. It was priced at 20p and I thought, what the hell, and bought it for old times' sake. I thought it might make me laugh – I wept. So getting back to my original point, an album of anonymous cover versions can't possibly count as a proper record as it amounts to the same thing as a tape by a pub band being flogged by their bassist after one of their gigs at the Red Lion. The great news is that if your first album was also one of these budget-label jobbies and you've been harbouring the guilt for 30 years – congratulations, you're off the hook, you've just had your pop history re-written – it never even existed.

Debbie, bless her forever, gave me a 50p EMI record token for my twelfth birthday (she got over the fact that it was my second twelfth birthday quite well). So off I went to Guy Norris Records at Gants Hill to buy my first real record. Guy Norris was the most brilliant of record shops. It was a real throwback to the sixties, with its listening booths and racks upon racks of empty LP sleeves housed in protective PVC covers. I loved going into the listening booths. You could just go up to the counter and ask to hear a record before buying it. What a great way to while away some time, and a safeguard against coming home with an album of extremely poor cover versions done by a bunch of sound-alikes that clearly didn't. The try-before-you-buy facility has only recently come back into fashion and I can't help feeling that, had it been available during the eighties, it could perhaps have prevented the pain inflicted on people that bought the albums of T'Pau and Level 42 on the strength of their lead-off singles.

'Booth four mate – two minutes'. By the time you'd settled yourself down, music would come flooding through the speakers hidden behind the perforated hardboard walls of the booth – fabulous. Sellotaped to the counter under laminated plastic was this week's Top 100 singles, as compiled by the British Market Research Bureau. But on this day there was no need for the thumbing down of lists or a try-out listen in the booth, I knew exactly what I was getting with my token.

I strode up to the counter and, unthreatened by the long-haired youth behind it, came straight out with it – '"Get Down" by Gilbert O' Sullivan, please.' And there you have it – my first record. Ok, it's not 'Superstition', and to be fair, it's not really very good at all, but I loved it at the time with its thumping piano, ridiculously catchy melody and actually, now that I think about it, quite clever middle eight.

I always suspected that Guy Norris Records was one of the selected stores whose single sales were used to compile the official charts. I based this theory on the fact that every Wednesday (the day after the new chart was announced), in an attempt to boost sales, singles cost only 45p rather than the usual 50p. And so on the Tuesday following my purchase, as the new chart was announced, I took great delight in celebrating the fact that I had helped 'Get Down' reach the number one spot. The song is mainly remembered for the hilarious but appalling dance routine performed by Pan's People on *Top of the Pops*, in which the choreography was a literal translation of the lyrics and featured a group of dogs sitting on a bench, whilst the dance troupe pointed to the floor every time Gilbert sang the words 'get down', and wagged their fingers at the poor pooches during the 'bad dog baby' bits.

Gilbert was considered to be a bit of joke in the seventies – unfairly I think. It could have been the frizzy mop of hair, which in truth, was not that unlike my own. It could have been that red-and-white sweater with the big 'G' emblazoned across the chest that he always wore on *Top of the Pops* and in photo shoots for the magazine *Jackie*. It could have even have been the fact that he started his career trying to look like the little boy from the Hovis adverts, with a short back and sides, wearing a cloth cap, shirt, tie, tank-top and hob-nail boots. Quite why he wanted to look like a Yorkshire schoolboy from a bygone age when he was a 27-year-old man from Swindon is anybody's guess. But whatever the reason, he never received the acclaim that some of his songs deserved. At least there was nothing manufactured about Gilbert. He was a proper piano-playing singer/songwriter with an ear always for a fantastic melody and very occasionally for some decent words. 'Nothing Rhymed' was an absolute beauty, as was 'Alone Again (Naturally)'. I would officially like to throw my hat (or perhaps more fittingly, cloth cap) into the ring, and nominate 'Alone Again (Naturally)' as the saddest record of all time. During its perfect three minutes and forty-one seconds, Gilbert finds himself left in the lurch on his wedding day, contemplates suicide, abandons his faith and, as if that wasn't enough, both his parents die too. On a brighter note, the song can almost certainly lay claim to being the last in which the term 'gay' is used to mean happy.

I revisited the works of Gilbert O'Sullivan in 2001. I bought a compilation CD of his hits and was surprised at how many great tunes were on it. Songs that you just know you shouldn't really like, but Gilbert has this unique ability of delivering them in such a way that you end up defying common sense and liking them anyway. He can take you on a journey from the sublime to the ridiculous in five minutes flat. That bit in 'Alone Again' where his mother dies of a broken heart gets me every single time; his little-boy-lost voice commands the hairs on the back of my neck to stand to attention, as he forces me to drown in his sorrow with him. Yet a couple of minutes later I feel obliged to laugh in his face as he bangs on about noses being caught in gates on 'Ooh-Wakka-Doo-Wakka-Day'. And this is where he gets really annoying, because it's when he is at his most trite lyrically that he is at his most potent melodically. This is how he gets away with the nose/gate interface thing: by wrapping it up in a tune so catchy that it only takes one listen, and you'll be ooh-wakka-doo-ing, all wakka-day long.

That same year, I went along to see him play a gig in London with my friend and former band mate Ian. Before the gig I wondered how Gilbert had been all these years, what he'd been up to, and if he was still alone. Without wishing him any malice, that's what I'd secretly hoped for. A happy and contented in middle age Gilbert would somehow seem meaningless and no use at all. I needed him to be just how I remembered him if this reunion was going to work out. I didn't want him bald and fat, married with kids or – worse – grandchildren. And if he still had that sweater with the big 'G' on it – that would help. He strode out on to the stage with a couple of cheery waves to the smallish audience and sat down at the piano. Gilbert at 56 looked fantastic – exactly the same as he did in 1973. This was a good start. All he needed to do now was play the oldies, but instead he insisted on playing us his latest recordings, mostly from an album that he had inexplicably named *Piano Foreplay*. We waited, and waited … and waited, getting more and more irritated as 'Alone Again', 'Get Down' and 'Nothing Rhymed' failed to show. After an hour and a half of excruciatingly dull music, Gilbert announced a break and out we trotted. Whilst being somewhat impressed that he was prepared to deliver a close-on three-hour show, we deliberated whether or not we could stomach another ninety minutes of this drivel. What if the hits never came? Or worse still, what if they were being saved for the encore and were to be delivered in the form of a snippet-styled medley?

Whilst chewing the fat over a pint and cigarette on the doorstep of the theatre, I spotted a man maybe half my age wearing a cap-sleeved tee-shirt and sporting a tattoo of Gilbert's face on his tricep; a moment to savour in an otherwise uneventful evening, and an amusing distraction from our dilemma. I hadn't for a second considered that Gilbert would have hardcore fans, let alone ones that weren't even born when he was in his first flourish of fame. A tattoo of cuddly old Gilbert seemed utterly preposterous to me. You have tattoos of Keith Richards or Jimi Hendrix, or some other axe-wielding rock icon, not Gilbert O'Bloody Sullivan. Gilbert's not a tattoo type of person, surely? You take your Gilbert curled up on the sofa with a cup of tea and a couple of Hob-Nobs, not with a line of coke and bottle of Jack Daniels.

We were still undecided about the second half and settled on allowing the toss of a coin to determine our fate. The coin chose that we must return but we inserted a caveat that Gilbert had six songs in which to deliver the goods. After twenty minutes and still no hits we walked out. He'd left us no choice. There is nothing worse than an artist who lets their so-called artistic integrity, not to mention the promotion of a new album, get in the way of playing the songs that gave them all their wealth, fame and fans in the first place. It's just plain disrespectful. So I apologise, Gilbert, for walking out of your gig, but let that be a lesson to you, you great big cloth-cap-wearing buffoon.

However, for exposing me to a night of *Piano Foreplay*, you are forgiven and for 'Get Down', I no longer deny you, and it would be churlish in the extreme not to thank you now for puffing the wind into my sails at the very beginning of my wonderful pop odyssey.

Losing My Religion

I'm on stage. What's more, I'm on stage and about to sing. There are two or three hundred pairs of eyes watching my every move and a similar number of ears hanging on to every word. The majority of the audience has fingers tightly crossed, willing me to be word and note perfect. The remainder are sniggering at my dilemma. It's my first gig – the biggest in terms of spectators in which I ever performed. But this isn't the Hammersmith Odeon or the Rainbow, lamentably; it's the Beehive Lane synagogue in Gants Hill. The date is March 30 1974 and this, folks, is my Bar Mitzvah, and I long to be far, far away from here, or alternatively sat at home in my pyjamas watching the lovely Sally James on *Saturday Scene*.

I'm wearing a navy blue suit and my hair has been cut for the first time in over a year. My mum insisted on it. I stamped my feet in protest for a few days and then trudged off to the barbers, like she knew I always would. They fashioned it into a brushed-back quiff. I'm Elvis – The Ginger Years.

My shirt is white, with motifs of a little chap riding a penny-farthing bicycle dotted all over it, and its big collars are tucked well underneath the wide lapels of my jacket. There is of course a kipper tie, tied with a knot the size of a small planet – navy blue again, with swirling paisley shapes of gold. Those great shoes with the red suedette inserts have been usurped, for the occasion, by a pair of new black ones with white stitching around the toes and a three-inch heel. It wouldn't really have mattered if I'd been wearing grapefruits on my feet, as the length and width of my flared turned-up trousers leave my shoes completely invisible to the naked eye.

My nerves are forcing me to shake like a thirsty alcoholic standing naked on the ice somewhere on the Antarctic Peninsula. My voice, with the comedic timing of Ronnie Barker, decided to begin its breaking process just three days ago, and as the first notes escape from my mouth, the sounds that emerge resemble those of a lederhosen-clad alpine yodeller, or that bloke out of the Dutch group Focus on the song 'Hocus Pocus'. There is muffled laughter from my friends in the stalls. I attempt to ignore it.

The build-up to the whole event had been a huge strain on everyone concerned. The family had been gearing up for it for a couple of years and it seemed to be the focus of everything that was talked about for ages and ages. There was the huge party to be organised and paid for, outfits to be bought, caterers to be booked, guest lists drawn up, invitations to be sent out and table plans to be carefully charted, ensuring that any feuding relatives were kept well apart.

The pressure was building on me, too. I had to attend Hebrew classes three times a week, with an additional evening taken up by Bar Mitzvah classes. It would be gone seven o'clock on most nights before I could even begin my homework, and then there was still so much telly to watch. Something had to give and it wasn't going to be *The Benny Hill Show,* so I fell even further behind with my school work.

There was also a Bar Mitzvah exam to be passed before I would even be allowed up on to the stage on the day, and then there was the onslaught of all the new teenage hormones that were raging their way through my body to contend with as well. I was struggling to balance it all and, more pressingly, I was not getting to grips with the verses that I was to perform in the synagogue. My parents' solution to this problem was to send me to Mr Aidlekopff for extra tuition and to try and cure me of my ambivalence towards the whole sorry business.Thus another couple of nights a week struck off my social calendar.

Mr Aidlekopff was the scariest of teachers. He was a huge bear of a man, always suited – a black three-piece, with the waistcoat buttons trembling under the strain of his enormous stomach. He had an extensive bushy black beard too, which made him look a little like a Jewish King Henry VIII. Although he probably didn't order any actual executions, I was still terrified of him and having lessons on a one-to-one basis with him in his home extenuated that fear. He taught at the Hebrew classes that I attended and, depending on which rumour you believed, he had either been to prison for assaulting one of his pupils or had spent some months in a mental institution following a rather unfortunate incident in Sainsbury's, in which he had allegedly broken down in tears, dropped his trousers and furnished one of their aisles with a small poo. I'm not sure if either of these tales was true but he was in his fifties and still lived with his mum – a fact that suggested to us a certain social ineptitude and left the rumours hanging there, wrapped up in suspicion. But despite his possible social misgivings, my utter fear of the man got me through and I finally learned my part with only a few days to spare.

On the day, and apart from the yodelling, it seemed to all go rather smoothly and I breathed a huge sigh of relief when it was all over. This was supposed to be my big day, during which I would get up in front of all my family and friends and recite my portion of Jewish law. It was meant to symbolise my religious coming of age and a consolidation of my Jewishness. All organised religions have their own various methods of suckering you into believing that you need them, and I was told by my Hebrew teachers how this occasion would instil the feeling of belonging to something important, to a tradition and to a lifestyle. But as I stepped off that stage, my immediate thoughts were: 'Right, I've done my bit – fulfilled all my obligations, so now can I get on with my life and be like everybody else, please?'.

There would be no more Hebrew classes, no more Bar Mitzvah lessons, no more one-to-ones with fat King Henry, and I couldn't have been happier about that. To me it felt like an ending rather than a beginning. I acknowledged that it was a proud day for my parents and grandparents and I wished, for their sakes, that I could have felt warmer about the whole business and about my religion in general, but I couldn't. I'm not going to pretend that at the age of thirteen I had got anywhere near understanding why I felt differently to everyone else in my family or to most of my Jewish friends that were going through the same thing, I just knew that I did. I had a very strong suspicion that everything that this religion was based on – i.e. The Bible – was a great big fib. Stories of talking snakes, boats carrying thousands of animals and a bloke decending a mountain carrying two filthy great rocks in a pair of sandals, made absolutely no sense to me at all. I just didn't believe there was a man who knew and saw everything, living in the sky. If Santa and the fairies were made up, surely there was a huge question mark hanging over the head of this fella too?

If I look back at the photographs of my Bar Mitzvah day, I see myself against the backdrop of our brilliantly white net curtains, a frown ingrained on my forehead as I'm dressed in full religious regalia: a skull cap, prayer shawl, holding a prayer book and looking extremely uncomfortable about the whole ordeal. I didn't want to be photographed like that – it just wasn't me. There is one photo in which I am supporting the book with just my index and middle finger. I am subtley 'flicking the Vs' at the official photographer, his camera and quite probably at myself too. I did this on purpose and it now looks like a very small act of rebellion from a rather spoilt brat; half of me now feels slightly ashamed, but the other half is pleased that the photograph exists.

Much later, when I heard the R.E.M song 'Losing My Religion', it felt very personal and totally resonated with me because it captures perfectly how I felt on that day:

That's me in the corner
That's me in the spotlight
Losing my religion.

My Bar Mitzvah party took place the following day. The traditional dress code for such an occasion is black tie, but this was the mid-seventies and against the better judgement of my parents, I plumped for a purple crushed-velvet dinner jacket with matching bow tie and some black trousers with silk stripes running down the legs – an outfit that made me look like a varicose vein in a pair of platform shoes. Despite this lack of dress sense, with the pressure now off I did thoroughly enjoy my Bar Mitzvah party. Mum had ensured that no stone was left unturned and no expense spared during her organisation of the event and I recall it as being a very happy day for us all. Bar Mitzvah parties are generally quite lavish occasions, with mountains of food, a free bar and an invite to distant elderly relatives who would announce their unfamiliarity by squeezing a large section of your cheek skin between their thumb and forefinger, and yelling 'my, haven't you grown since I last saw you'. (This is mainly because the last time that they saw you, you were wearing a bib and dribbling like an excited Alsatian). Without wanting to generalise, I think it's fair to say that Jews on the whole are not really big drinkers, so a free bar at a Jewish function is a little bit like having free celery at a Weight-Watchers meeting. Still, I had plenty of friends there who were only too happy to chance their arms and try to get served with alcohol, and if the food fight that ensued later in the evening was anything to go by, I would say that most of them succeeded.

There was also a band. I wanted a disco with a DJ, but Mum insisted there had to be a band. I had seen the sorts of bands that entertained at such dos and had been appalled by most of them. They had names such as 'Pina Colada', or 'The New Jersey Jazz Men' (even though they no doubt hailed from Cockfosters), or 'Mickey Music (I'm guessing that this probably wasn't his real name) and the Paradise Players'. They played laid-back jazz or the easy-listening sounds of Frank Sinatra and Dean Martin. There may have been the occasional side-step into the world of pop, maybe a 'Yellow River' here or a 'Congratulations' there, but that would be their only concession to what they assumed to be catering for the youngsters. The lead singer would usually end the evening by saying something like: 'Thank you and goodnight – if you've been drinking, please don't drive and hey, if you're driving – don't forget your car'.

As is traditional at Bar Mitzvah parties, I opened up the evening's dancing (or 'ball', as it was rather grandly referred to on the invitations) by awkwardly waltzing around the dance floor with my mother, whilst my dad danced with my sister. The remainder of the guests watched from the sidelines and applauded in feigned admiration. This wasn't a problem for me at all – it was the next bit that filled me with trepidation; that bit halfway through the tune, where my dad would take my place and glide across the floor properly with Mum, leaving me to dance to the rest of the tune with my sister – an act that would have consumed us both with repugnance in equal measures.

You see, Mads and I had a difficult beginning to our relationship. To describe it as merely a sibling rivalry is a bit like saying that the miners thought that Margaret Thatcher was a bit of a spoilsport. It hovered around the perimeter fence of hatred. I'm not sure where all the venom came from, but we couldn't get on at all. There were some glories though – the game Skid Patch for instance: a pre-bedtime game that we devised between us in a moment of reconciliation, that consisted of running at top speed from the front door, through our hall and skidding on our socks across the adjoining kitchen lino whilst screaming 'skiddy, skiddy, skiddy, skiddy, skiddy,

skiddy, skiddy, skiddy – skid patch!' to the tune of the Batman theme. Our parents banned this game because it was bloody dangerous and these games generally ended with one of us injuring ourselves by crashing into the back door or a Hygena kitchen unit. I'm sure our parents must have noticed the outline of children in their pyjamas running at high speed past the glass lounge door as they watched TV, but probably just thought 'sod it, at least they're not knocking seven bells out of each other for once'. These were our together moments and they were few and far between. The rest of the time we preferred wind-ups, insults and violence as our primary form of communication.

I'd try to include Mads in my interests. Well that's not strictly true; I would attempt to force her to recite the names of the entire West Ham team – in order mind – numbers one to eleven. Her act of defiance during this fruitless exercise would be to deliberately announce number three as being Frank Lampost rather than Frank Lampard (this being the rather hairy seventies full back who looked a little like Animal out of the Muppets, rather than his good-looking son that girls will have heard of). As punishment for this I would sit astride her, my knees pinning down her arms, which gave me free access to her face as I slapped out the rhythm of Gary Glitter's 'I'm the Leader of the Gang (I am)'on her cheeks. That was how things worked.

Thinking back now, she was rather ballsy, preferring to take the slapping rather than pander to my stupid demands. We learned perfectly how to press each other's buttons and winding each other up became an art form that I have seldom seen matched by other siblings. I would get her in such a rage that she would grab a lump of my hair and pull me clean out of my chair, proceeding to drag me across the living room carpet, still hanging onto the ginger mass.

Being forced to hand over my beloved bedroom didn't help either. My mother justified my eviction by saying that because Mads was a girl she needed more wardrobe space. I never understood this – had she not seen the size of my flares and platform shoes? Regardless, me and my 'Lionels' were dispatched to the tiny box room and I wasn't happy about it. It meant that I now had to gain her permission to set up my Subbuteo pitch on my old bedroom carpet, and also gave her the right to kick me out whenever she pleased, forcing a premature final whistle and a hasty gathering up of perimeter fencing.

Although it's nothing unusual for young siblings to have strained relationships whilst growing up, ours was pitiful. There were some other moments of tolerance, though. I liked her best friend Jacqueline. She was feisty, funny and not intimidated by me in the slightest, despite being fully aware of the manner in which I treated her best friend, and she actively encouraged my involvement with the pair of them whenever she was at our house. Hostilities were put on hold when she was around and I enjoyed the opportunity to show off a bit and teach them both things such as the full complement of my profanity vocabulary. A few years ago I got back in touch with Jacqueline after around thirty years of non-contact and was delighted to find that she was still feisty and funny, and still held me responsible for her excellent command of bad language.

But then, around the time when Mads was in her mid-teens, unexpectedly it all changed. I cannot put my finger on exactly when, why or how, it just did. One day we were sworn enemies and the next, the best of mates. The rules changed overnight and neither of us can remember the reason why. But change they did. It was amazingly refreshing and a bit like suddenly getting a new best friend that you could spend as much time as you liked with because they didn't have to go home for their tea. We had a lot of ground to make up, far too many lost years and we instantly became close. We started to have friends in common and therefore were able to go out in a crowd together. It may have been the point when I started to fancy her friends, or perhaps when she started to fancy mine, but with my pop head on I like to think there was some sort of spiritual coming together the day she came home with a copy of Bob Dylan's single 'Baby, Stop Crying', a few days prior to me going to see him at Blackbushe.

Normally kid sisters are hopeless when it comes to pop. Kid sisters in the mid-seventies tended to be fans of the Bay City Rollers and mine was no exception. Consequently, I hated Woody and the gang far more than was actually necessary, purely on the basis that she liked them. Older brothers, on the other hand, add unlimited value to their younger siblings and I wanted one. Older brothers bring home grown-up rock music and whilst they probably still won't let you actually borrow their records, they do inadvertently give you the benefit of hearing the likes of David Bowie and The Stones blasting out through their bedroom walls when you have no business being familiar with such great music. They leave copies of *Melody Maker* in the loo so you read about bands and records that *Disco 45* wouldn't dream of touching. They get you into 'X' films and take you to gigs and football matches. They also punch people that call you 'Duracell Head'. Little sisters don't.

However, I now note that later, some of Mads' pop purchases had a direct correlation to the stuff I was listening to. Sometime in 1978, we both arrived home carrying a copy of 'Rat Trap' by The Boomtown Rats that we had separately bought that same day. My copies of The Beatles' *White Album* and *Sgt. Pepper* were regularly to be found taking up residence in her bedroom, and it wouldn't be long before we would become a two-*Abbey-Road*ed family. So maybe it really is possible that my unintentional passing on of pop was perhaps responsible for Mads and I finally finding some common ground.

Pop was a passing phase for her – like it is for most normal people, and I doubt very much that she gives her old record collection a cursory glance these days. If she did, she might notice that it no longer includes her copy of 'Roxanne' by The Police on blue vinyl, just my boring old black vinyl copy.

I don't believe that it's purely by coincidence that in 1988, whilst watching my sister's wedding video, I discovered that I had the beginnings of a bald patch. I had no idea until I saw myself on the tape. Right at the back it was – a horrific moment and possibly a legacy of the hair-pulling years. 'What goes around, comes around' and 'life goes round in circles' might only be clichés, but nothing says circles like a freshly discovered bald patch can.

Old Friends

Although I didn't consider 1974 to be my religious coming of age, it was a year in which I made many important new friendships, true friendships; some that have lasted from that day to this – and that's a lot of days. It's not until you undertake a project like this that you stop to really consider how or why we make certain connections with people and why the bonding process is ongoing – a lifetime's work in progress. Nevertheless, friends come and go as the years pass, and some of those that disappear for a while turn up again later, and stick around. It's not even worthy of consideration to question why you lost touch in the first place – it doesn't matter, the important thing is that you are able to pick up where you left off all those years before. And when you do, you know you're in it for the long haul, still laughing hysterically at your shared past, and in our 'wiser' middle years, discovering that we all secretly harbour the same fears for the future, just like we did when we were clueless, pimply teenagers.

I didn't hate going to school, far from it – that's where all my friends were; it was just the learning things bit that I couldn't stand. We were streamed during the second year at Beal and I was dumped into form 2D, a class for below-average pupils. I was lucky to have been thrown together by first-year academic sluggishness with some people that made putting in all those tough long hours as a teenager a much easier job to do.

We were allocated the science lab as our form room and a science teacher, Mr Hilton, as our form master. He was a strange chap. His nickname was 'Tick' (as in tock) or 'Robot' due to the fact that he spoke in a very deliberate, broken-syllable manner. He wasn't particularly strict, but he was no pushover either. He did have a sense of humour though. He would regularly dish out his favourite punishment to boys that misbehaved or mimicked him in class, which was to send them on cross-country runs around the school fields. He would yell out in class 'Shel-ley, which day do you have games?' If I said 'Thursday' he would follow it up with 'Su-per, bring your cross coun-try kit in on Mon-day'. But when you turned up on the fields ready for your run, he would often be nowhere to be seen. Sometimes he would show, sometimes he wouldn't, depending on his mood. He kept you on your toes like that. You couldn't take the risk of assuming that he wasn't going to be there, just in case he was. I think he just got pleasure from making kids bring in a load of gear that they didn't really need.

The science lab did not make a good form room as it just had workbenches and stools rather than proper desks and chairs. This meant that most of our lessons took place away from our spiritual home. The lab did lend itself well to schoolboy pranks, though. It had strange furnishings, like gas taps on the benches and black blinds on the windows. One of the lads, Mark

Anderson, who was a talented artist, had a particular skill for the female form and took to drawing naked ladies in white chalk on the blinds, so when Mr Hilton asked for them to be lowered prior to showing a scientific film, the room was suddenly transformed into the cover art from the Jimi Hendrix album *Electric Ladyland.*

Those blinds were also responsible for my favourite Robot moment. One lunch break one of the geekier kids, Mark Woodard, was set upon by several of his classmates. He was gagged, his hands bound with several smelly football socks, and then tied by his ankles to the cords from the blinds at the very back of the science lab. When Hilton arrived after lunch to take afternoon registration, as he called out each name all he could hear was muffled yelps coming from the back of the lab. He made purposeful strides towards the back of the room to investigate, as the rest of us stifled our giggles of anticipation; on gaining sight of the vexed nerd writhing about on the floor and unable to free himself, Hilton simply uttered 'get up Wood-ard, you im-bec-il-ic fool'.

Games lessons were the only time that we all came together as an entire year, with over a hundred boys making up the numbers for several rugby and football matches. It was a strict rotation system: rugby in the winter term, football in the spring, cricket and athletics in the summer. I couldn't get to grips with rugby at all. Far too rough. A game in which you could flatten your opponent by jumping on top of him and then run with the ball tucked neatly under your armpit seemed strange – where was the skill in that? If football was the beautiful game, then rugby was Nana Mouskouri's uglier sister.

During the first year, I had often found myself on the rugby pitch standing alongside a tallish gangly youth called Ray Pearce. We would bemoan the dreaded game together as we stood around shivering and hoping that the ball wouldn't come our way, so that we could avoid being squashed by the over-zealous chubbies who were now claiming the sport as their own. However, when it came to playing football, Ray and I were magically transformed from shirkers into strikers and found that we seemed to have an instant understanding when we played together, scoring and creating goals for each other at will. Our conversations in those early days on the rugby pitch had been guarded at first, which was very typical of us both when around new people, but on discovery that we were both West Ham supporters and both had more than a keen interest in the finer points of piss-taking, we soon hit it off on a social level as well as a footballing one. Ray was a natural mimic – he still is. He didn't do voices, but would pick up on people's mannerisms very quickly. You needed to be on your guard around him, because if he spotted anything unusual: the way you walked, talked, blinked or scratched yourself, he'd be on it. His sense of humour appealed to me. It was subtler than mine, a drier humour, less obvious but always funny. In the second year, thrown together in 2D, we got to know each other very quickly and within a few weeks we were sitting alongside each other in every lesson with the single objective of making each other laugh. He did nothing for my education but made the dullest of lessons so much more bearable.

Ray lived in a ground-floor maisonette in nearby Goodmayes, which was a couple of bus rides away. His parents had divorced a couple of years prior to us meeting and he shared that flat with his dad and younger brother, Alan. Strange as it may seem bearing in mind today's statistics, I didn't know anyone at that time whose parents lived apart. At thirteen, you don't ask questions and so we never really spoke about it. However, it was very apparent that, because he'd been thrown into this domestic situation he was more worldly wise, more mature than I was, and far more self-sufficient. He could cook and bought his own clothes, whereas my culinary skills stretched to Dairylea on toast and I still went shopping with my mum.

At first my mum considered Ray to be a bad influence on my diction. She claimed that since I'd become friends with him, I'd started speaking 'more cockney' – dropping my 't's' and 'h's', and she threatened that if I started walking around with my thumbs clasped behind the lapels of my blazer and demanding jellied eels for my tea, she was going to stop me from hanging round with him altogether. But when Ray came to our house he was so well mannered and charming that he won her over in no time at all.

John 'Billy' Budd was the new boy in our class. Having recently moved into the area, he'd missed almost all of the first year. It's difficult coming to a new school later than everybody else when friendships have already been formed. You're desperate to make new friends but don't want to look like you are. But John used his presence and wit sparingly – he played it right. Lanky of legs and crew-cut of hair, John wasn't into football but give him a notebook, a furry-hooded 'Parka' and a busy platform at Paddington Station and he'd be in his element – on the face of it, not a natural contender for our gang, but the more I got to know him, the more I liked him. His full acceptance into our little crew was consolidated on the day he gave Beal's resident pop star a thoroughly deserved spanking that had us and the rest of his classmates reaching out to shake his hand and slap him on the back.

Bradley Palmer, along with his younger brother Stewart, were The James Boys. Never heard of them? Well if you haven't, you clearly didn't see the centre spread in the *Daily Mirror* from sometime in 1973, in which the red-top declared them to be 'Britain's Answer to The Osmonds'. As it turned out, unsurprisingly, The James Boys never really troubled Donny and his brothers, but they did become very popular in Germany, which probably reveals about as much about them as you need to know. Could they sing? Not really. Could they dance? If marching and performing ninety degree turns counts, then yes, they were experts. Could they carry off a hooped t-shirt and a pair of dungarees? Absolutely.

Bradley was in our class. Well, he was when he wasn't being jetted off to Germany or some other European pop wilderness, or appearing on *Lift Off with Ayesha* or *Junior Showtime*. He was a reasonably pleasant lad before pop got hold of him and encouraged him to wear brown-tinted glasses for school. He revelled in his new-found fame, and would start conversations that begged our interest with lines such as: 'So Alvin – you know, Alvin Stardust, said to me …'. He also boasted about all the new sexual activity he was now enjoying since he'd been on the telly. He once asked me without a hint of shame, 'So Shelley, do you think someone like you will ever get a blow job?'. It was comments such as this that riled his classmates, and when our poppy peer picked a fight with the unknown quantity of Billy Budd, almost the entire class were delighted to see the new boy triumph in style – a sort of flying fists, windmill style.

Laurence 'Milly Molly' (don't ask) Nesbitt was primarily a friend of John's. He was the shortest boy in our class but one of the funniest and a merry prankster to boot. He wasn't a shout-things-out-in-class type like Ray and me; his humour was more measured. He would do things like subtly draw or write something on your book whilst you were reading from it aloud in class, forcing your speech to erupt into uncontrollable giggles. His signature drawing was not the schoolboy standard, the ejaculating cock – that would have been too obvious for Laurence – but a bowler-hatted man who had one normal leg, whilst his other leg emerged from his jacket sleeve rather than his waist, and was furnished with an enormous shoe on the end of it. A shoe that was almost as big as the man himself. He would leave this little man everywhere, and you might get home and suddenly find one inhabiting the blank page of an exercise book that you were just about to fill with homework. Finding these little drawings in the most unexpected places never failed to make me laugh, no matter how many times I'd seen them before. It was a bit like discovering romantic messages from a lover hidden in unsuspected locations around the house – but with orthopaedic shoes.

Fraser Cooper had lived merely a few yards away from me all his life – just around the corner in Lynton Crescent – yet we'd never met until the day he joined my scout troop. We didn't really talk much at first there either, but one July evening in 1974, as I smashed a tennis ball against a garage wall opposite his house, he came out wielding his own racquet and another lifelong friendship was born. Tennis wasn't really my thing – my racquet had mostly been employed to simulate guitar playing in front of my bedroom mirror – but I had been inspired to give the sport a go by the brilliance of Jimmy Connors, who had won the Men's Singles Championship at Wimbledon that very day.

The close proximity of our houses meant that we could spend a lot of time together. It took seventeen seconds to get from my house to his. I know this because seventeen seconds was the record, and one that I tried to break (no running allowed) every time I made that journey. (I stopped attempting this by the time I'd reached my early twenties.)

On the evidence of our first few weeks of being friends, I would never have predicted that our friendship would still be going strong today. Two years my junior, Fraser was far more passive in his approach to life than I was. I preferred to be outside, in the streets, where we could generally make nuisances of ourselves playing Knock Down Ginger or scrumping fruit from neighbours' trees, away from parental eyes, whereas Fraser liked to stay in of an evening and watch telly with his family. I wouldn't like to estimate the number of episodes of *Hawaii-5-0* and *Kojak* (programmes that I would never have otherwise watched) that I have sat through with him and his family. I spent a lot of time in that house – it was a very welcoming place and I got to know his family very well. His younger sister Donna was always allowed to hang around with us and join in with whatever we were doing. She was a straight talker. If she didn't like your trousers or you smelt a bit funny, she'd tell you. I took to her immediately, which was rather odd bearing in mind the awful relationship I had with my own sister at that time. She's still that straight talker today; she rarely tells me that I smell these days but what she does say is usually worth listening to.

Playing football was a bit of a non-starter with Fraser. He loved the game, but couldn't kick a ball to save his life. On the upside, his talent for lighting his own farts is unsurpassed. In the absence of football in the park, we made our own entertainment. The 'having a fit' game was one of Fraser's inventions. This involved one of us running up to total strangers, and rolling about on the grass in front of them, frantically waggling limbs about and grunting and groaning in an indecipherable manner. Said strangers would generally just ignore the imbeciles at their feet, step over us and carry on with their pleasant walk through the park.

The 'No Education Flid' was another of Fraser's creations. For this character, he would bend his arms so that only his elbows were poking out of his t-shirt sleeves, whilst shouting in a somewhat angry Jamaican accent (no idea why), 'you've got no education, you'. I loved the 'No Education Flid' – thought he was utterly hilarious and encouraged Fraser to do him over and over again. This, which seems like shockingly inappropriate behaviour now, was comedy to us back then. It's all rather tragic to admit that we found the plight of the disabled a source of amusement, but the seventies were such unforgiving times. Times change, but in 1974, we thought nothing of it.

Pop music was now well and truly a going concern in my life. A transistor radio was an essential piece of kit at school every Tuesday, when we would tune in during the lunch break to the Johnny Walker Show on Radio One and gather around the radio to hear the new Top 20 as it was announced, desperately hoping that something decent was that week's number one.

I was totally absorbed by the charts – the songs that were going up, which ones were going down, which were the new entries – and I seemed to have a mind that revelled in all these statistics and one that was able to store all these unnecessary facts and figures. My maths teacher once remarked, on overhearing a conversation in which I was relaying to one of the gang that week's movers and shakers, that it was a pity that my brain couldn't remember mathematical formulae with the same accuracy that it could a record's position in the charts.

By now I finally had a decent cassette recorder. I wanted a music centre. They were the very latest in music entertainment systems: a stereo record player, cassette recorder and radio all contained in one slim-line deck that came with a couple of loudspeakers. The absolute killer stroke with these marvellous new pieces of kit was that you could record directly from the record deck or radio straight onto cassette without the use of a microphone or the need to hang silly 'Shhh recording in progress' signs on the door. I could bounce around my bedroom like Leo Sayer dancing barefoot on hot coals, and not a single whimper would blight the recording. Genius! Dad said he would get me one (I think it was a softener for being ousted to the box room), but what he actually came home with was a Sony stereo cassette deck.

Although not what I really wanted, it was in itself a thing of beauty. I'd never seen anything that looked quite so sophisticated. It had volume sliders for each channel, just like a proper recording desk, and two microphones that linked to two recording volume meters, whose needles would keep me amused as they jiggled back and forth with the swell and retraction of the music whilst recording. All this black and chrome marvellousness was contained within a smart teak-coloured wooden outer case. There was a plastic carrying handle on the side of the casing, should you ever want to take the recorder out of the house, and in such an event, the two teak speakers could be placed on top of the machine, face down, and clipped securely to it. I was delighted with it, and no doubt this recorder was of a far higher quality than one that would come as part of a music centre, but it meant that I still had nothing decent to play records on, and I also still needed my 'Shhh' sign.

With this new piece of equipment, I threw myself fully into the recording of the Sunday night Top 20 countdowns on Radio One, perfecting the skill of knowing exactly when to stop and start the recording to avoid capturing the DJ's inane chit-chat. I rarely missed a Sunday recording session and compiled dozens of cassettes in the process.

My involvement with the Top 20 didn't begin and end with the recordings either. There was meticulous cataloguing of it too, in a collection of exercise books. Top of the page – the week, Tuesday 8 May 1974 to Monday, 13 May 1974. Then the list of the Top 20 singles. Green felt tip pen for the songs going up, red for those going down and black for the stuck-in-the-same-positioners. A logical choice of colour scheme, I now note. I never felt the need to go beyond the Top 20 – those songs outside of it would get their chance in the list if they were good enough, and I thought it best to stick with the big guns just in case I ever had to make an entry for The James Boys (luckily, their biggest hit, 'Over and Over', peaked at number 39).

I would sit poised on my bedroom carpet, an empty page at the ready, and as Tom Browne played each song (in reverse order), with page-flicking reference to its position in the previous week's chart to determine the colour of felt tip required, and into the book it would go. Song title, artist and last week's position in brackets, written slowly and carefully, so that the recording would not pick up the scratching of felt tip on paper. See, this is what pop does to you once it's wormed its way into your life. It's obtrusive and bossy and you have to keep an eye on it. It gets under your skin, gets a grip on you, sinks its teeth in and draws you into its world, and before you know it, it's made you want to be Dave Lee Travis and turned you into a fucking librarian.

Taping records from the radio was my main source of pop. I didn't have a Saturday job, and so with pocket money as my only income, and West Ham matches to attend, there wasn't much cash left over to spend on pop. I bought singles occasionally: 'Crazy' by Mud, 'Hello, Hello I'm Back Again' by Gary Glitter, and 'Roll Away the Stone' by Mott the Hoople (an early triumph) were a few that had boosted the collection early on. Along with the cash issue, still having to play records on that old record player from the sixties put me off throwing myself fully into record buying. But help was soon at hand.

A few months after the arrival of the Sony cassette recorder, I finally acquired that music centre that I'd wanted so badly. It was secondhand and came via my dad's shop, when a customer randomly came in and asked if he wanted to buy it. It was made by a company called Bush, which was an appropriate name because the sound quality was absolute gash. But that didn't really matter because it also had those all-important slider controls – bass, treble and balance and that's what counts. I worked out that if you angled the speakers correctly and fiddled with the balance of the channels, when I took up my listening position (horizontal on my bed), I could get the perfect stereo mix, where the sound appeared to come directly at me from the centre of the two speakers. It even had one of those Perspex lids, which made it look a lot better than it sounded. And as I placed the speakers on my bedroom windowsill, that old sixties record player was finally put out for the bin men.

For those of us that were around in the seventies, the names K-Tel and Ronco will be forever synonymous with that huge collection of totally useless gadgets that they endlessly advertised on TV: the 'Brush-o-Matic', the 'Buttoneer', something else that gave you a quick haircut that I can't quite remember the name of but was probably called something like the 'Snipotronic', and another gadget that wiped all the dust from your records. But both these companies also produced a string of LPs that compiled the hits of the day and packaged them up in neat little album-sized bundles. They had titles such as *22 Dynamic Hits* or *Super Hot Hits*, and came packaged in sleeves that usually had little bubble-sized photos of the artists involved and boasted 'original hits by original artists' – presumably so they weren't mistaken for those cheap 'soundalike' LP's which had so badly burnt my fingers earlier. These albums were the prototypes for the *Now, That's What I Call Music* series of albums that are available every few months these days, and I bought myself a few of them. It seemed to be a cheap way of getting lots of singles in one go.

But I'd not been thinking in terms of buying proper albums. Hadn't even given them a second thought – it was all about singles and the singles charts for me, and it hadn't really occurred to me that beyond the charts that there was a planet-sized bucket of music just waiting to be discovered – but where do you start?

When I flick through my densely populated album collection these days it's almost as if every album has a story to tell – mostly stories about the reason I bought them in the first place. There's a whole magnitude of reasons why I own these records, some deliberate and some whimsical. Maybe I could try a radical new filing system for them categorised by those very reasons. What might these categories be?

Well, there'd be the albums I bought from the record store at the station after a drunken night out, while I killed time waiting for my train home; the albums that I bought because I liked the single but when I got them home, they stank and I never played them again; the unwanted birthday and Christmas present albums, which, with a bit more thought from the donor, could have been lovely record tokens; the albums by artists that I'd only heard of by reading about them in the music papers and thought I'd give them a go and champion them for a bit as a testimony to just how trendy I really was; the albums that remind me of being in a certain place at a certain time; or the album brought back to the office one lunchtime by the gorgeous girl with the legs, that I went straight out and bought too so I might be able to engage her in conversation about it over a quiet drink after work – a category that should be avoided at all costs. It's the exact reason how married men in the eighties ended up owning Simply Red albums.

Of course one of the biggest sections would be the 'I can't possibly have bought this' category. These are albums that I can't for the life of me remember what possessed me to go anywhere near them, vis-à-vis *More Miles Per Hour* by John Miles. But then the three other John Miles albums sitting right alongside it fill in the gaps and remind me that I did at some point in the past actually have a bit of a John Miles phase. A bit more than a phase to be honest – I was once so familiar with him that I used to refer to him in conversation as 'Milesy' without so much as a flinch.

But to get back to the 'where do I start?' question, the answer is simple: we go for the records that our friends like or recommend that we should buy. Pop is very much about popularity amongst one's peers, and a record is pretty much judged by someone we know either getting behind it, or hating it with a passion. Sometimes it's difficult to tell where the line crosses over. Do your friends choose your records for you, or do records choose your friends?

My friendship with Ian 'Monty' Montague certainly had its origins in the former. Monty was the Pop Meister General of our class – a self-styled Doctor of Rock. He was more grown up than most lads in our class, which was reflected in his love for grown-up music, whilst we were still flapping about with glam. He sang and played guitar in a band and instinctively knew which bands it was ok to like and which ones should be given a wide berth. He was the cool one, the foppish, good-looking one, and the guv'nor as far as musical knowledge was concerned. He didn't give much away, which made him difficult to get to know at first. He was the first to show any trace of facial hair, often sporting the beginnings of a bum-fluff moustache, which at thirteen was pretty impressive, and he also had a mole on the side of his stomach that he insisted was a third nipple. When he wrote, he drew his 'a's' with a curly tail at the top, like they appear in print, and his sevens in a European style with a line through the middle. For Essex in the mid-seventies, this sort of behaviour was almost considered to be avant-garde. He went hitch-hiking long before any of the rest of us dared to – an activity that almost got him seduced by a German driver, who answered his lift request with 'ja, and you show me your villy on ze vay?'.

Before I knew him well, I'd imagined that at home he sent his dad out to buy him those coloured cocktail cigarettes, whilst his mum served him margaritas as he sat watching *Crossroads* from the comfiest chair in the house, wearing a smoking jacket and slippers. None of this was probably true – Monty was not your classic slipper wearer.

He mainly hung out with a small gang of like-minded musos, which included Drew Adamson and Mark Anderson – guitarists both and who played in Monty's band, The Thin Yoghurts. We called them 'The Heavies' because they were into bands like Led Zeppelin, Genesis, Jethro Tull, Deep Purple, Yes and Pink Floyd. In our ignorance we assumed these to all be heavy rock bands. Ray was the link between Monty and me; they were already friendly from travelling on the bus to and from school together and Ray had already made that musical connection, having owned *The Dark Side of the Moon* since it came out and was already cultivating a healthy collection of David Bowie albums, which sat well with Monty.

I think that at some point in their lives, all pop fans have their own personal Doctor of Rock – someone to guide them in the right pop direction. Doctors of Rock are very snobby about their musical tastes and this is a good thing. I needed a helping hand with my record buying; it had been fairly unfocused up to this point and Monty was only too happy to run his rock stethoscope over my collection. All Doctors of Rock have a rock stethoscope, and those outside of the doctorate recognise it simply as a tool of ridicule.

The latest additions to my collection – 'A Walking Miracle' by Limmie & The Family Cooking (ridiculous name for a group), Hot Chocolate's 'Emma' and 'Seasons in the Sun' by Terry Jacks – were not considered healthy for my musical education and so Monty took it upon himself to bring into school a handful of selected listening for me to run my ears over: the Genesis album *Selling England By The Pound*, *Tales From Topographic Oceans* by Yes and of course the key album from this period, Pink Floyd's masterpiece *The Dark Side of the Moon*. I was being thrown head-first into the swimming pool of prog with only my water-wings of pop to keep me buoyant. It was a test in which I would either drown without a trace, or survive the whole ordeal and earn the right to swim freestyle.

I hate pigeonholing pop music into genres. I like to call it all pop, whether its rock, country, glam, punk, heavy metal, soul or whatever – it's all pop to me. It somehow sounds more wholesome that way. I base this theory on the little footnote that you will find on most of the Deep Purple LPs from the seventies – a clear instruction to record shops from one of the heaviest of heavy rock bands: 'file under pop'. However, I will make the distinction for the purposes of discussing the albums that Monty encouraged me to listen to in order to get me into 'proper music'.

Progressive rock, aka prog rock or simply prog, was one of the most ludicrous genres that pop ever took the time to embrace. I can understand why the pimply and unwashed, lank-haired youths of the seventies loved it so much. They could drone on about how talented the musicians were, and of that, there is no question or room for debate. They could argue that these tracks (never songs) were 'pieces' or 'movements' and therefore far more sophisticated than silly old pop. Prog was a bit like classical music but with rock instruments. Pompous rock would have been a much more descriptive name for the genre.

Prog rock albums usually had a theme or a concept – classically about mythical beasts or historical battles – all very relevant for 1974. Tracks were typically full of long, droning, trippy, drawn-out instrumental noodling and tricky drum patterns, and if they didn't clock in at something over fifteen minutes, they were clearly selling themselves short. Take a solo, by all means take a solo. Those eight bars in the middle of the song will be perfect, sixteen tops, but don't take half an hour over it because I'm going to need a wee.

Tales From Topographic Oceans was a double album, with a concept based on Shastric scriptures of some ancient Yogi (God help us). It had just four tracks – one on each side of its two LPs, with each one tipping the clock at around twenty minutes. That is simply preposterous. If you can't say it all in less than five minutes, it's probably not worth mentioning. Ok, I'll admit there are quite a few notable exceptions to this rule, but I'm drawing the line at eight minutes, and only then in extreme cases of genius such as 'Hey Jude', 'Desolation Row' or 'Stairway to Heaven'.

Song titles with brackets was another one of prog's irritating little traits. All the tracks on *Topographic Oceans* have bracketed titles, and the text within these parentheses do nothing to enlighten us further as to what the hell the song might be about – their job is to confuse and to make the tracks seem even more cosmic and less accessible. Prog was full of all these types of excesses that just give pop a bad name. Put simply, this was pop lopping its cock out, showing off and being a little too clever for its own good. And let's face it: one of the best strategies that pop employs is to be a bit of a thickie. The fans of prog delighted in the fact that their bands rarely released anything that troubled the singles charts and referred to their heroes as being 'album bands', which was just another way of saying that they were unable to develop a catchy hook or a half-decent chorus. It's one of pop's most beautiful ironies that progressive rock, a genre that relied on so many excesses and demanded so much complexity from its musicianship, was finally put to death not by one of its mythical beasts, but by a very real one that was so basic it could barely string three chords together – punk rock. Prog rock, rest in piece (or movement).

I didn't like *Selling England By The Pound* much and I couldn't find anything in *Tales From Topographic Oceans* to hang on to, but I didn't let on. I agreed with Monty when he spoke about unusual time signatures and multiple key changes as if I knew what the hell he was talking about. I refused to even give either of those two albums cassette space, but *The Dark Side of the Moon* was different. It didn't grab me straight away, but after a few plays I began to get into it. This wasn't really prog rock at all, was it? The songs had melody, sounded crisp and in some cases even punchy, and I was pretty sure that almost every track was in a straight 4/4 time. All the weird little sounds and abstract voices sounded fantastic even on my primitive equipment, as they hopped from speaker to speaker. There still weren't any choruses but the concept – how the various stages of human existence are accompanied by the ever-present threat of madness, was at least a little easier to grasp. How getting old makes you go mad

('Time'), how greed makes you go mad ('Money') and how going mad makes you go mad ('Brain Damage'), with all this cheeriness neatly bookended at the start and the end of the album by the sound of a human heartbeat. However, I didn't rush out and buy a copy of my own (I would do that a couple of years later) and I didn't feel the need to investigate the work of Pink Floyd any further (I would do that later too). The album made a mild impression on me but it wasn't really what I was looking for. I grew to love *The Dark Side of the Moon,* but for now Pink Floyd and the rest of the prog rock lot were just names that I wrote in bubble writing on my Adidas school bag and exercise books to fit in with everybody else. Another pop porkie – they weren't really for me; I wanted something different, I just wasn't sure what it was yet.

I found it on *Top of the Pops* some time during the spring of 1974. By now, the programme had become essential viewing for me and therefore every Thursday evening the rest of my family had to endure it too. Dad hated it and my enjoyment would often be punctuated with comments of disdain such as 'look at the state of him, what is he wearing?' and 'you can't understand a bloody word he's singing ... if you can call THAT singing'. Mum, on the other hand, would periodically come in from the kitchen with a tea towel draped over her arm and mock-waltz with it around the room in time to the music. I liked the fact that Dad didn't like it – that made me feel all youthy and edgy.

This particular edition of the show featured an American band called Sparks performing the song 'This Town Ain't Big Enough for The Both of Us', and I was mesmerised. Russell Mael, the curly haired one, posed and postured like a caged tiger, singing in an absurd falsetto voice, and on this rare occasion, my dad was actually right – you really couldn't understand a word he was singing. But the real intrigue lay with his brother Ron, the keyboard player and principal songwriter. Ron Mael sat behind his electronic keyboard, with his head slightly tilted to one side, wearing a shirt and tie, his hair slicked back and sporting a toothbrush moustache. He looked like a 1930s throwback but he was just twenty-nine years old. When the cameras focused on him, his face would stay deadpan but defiantly moved his eyes to the left and then to the right. 'He looks like bleedin' Hitler', my dad complained, and he did a bit, but the song was delicious. Starting quietly with just keyboards that simply followed the vocal line, and then out of nowhere, just after the 'and it ain't me who's gonna leave' bit, the whole band came thumping in raucously as if their lives depended on it. I loved it: the song, the performance, the fact that my dad loathed it, everything. This was it. The next day, everyone at school was talking about those three minutes of pop telly, and to a man, everyone agreed they were fab – even Monty.

For once I didn't mess about with the single, I went straight for the album from which the single came, the beautifully punnily titled *Kimono*

My House – my first proper album. I loved its brashness, its thudding qualities and the lyrics that were full of wit and not too much wisdom. It was an album that, with its hard-hitting guitars, thumping bass and pounding drums, demanded volume and I obeyed faithfully. Some pop music should come with instructions that simply say 'play fucking loud', so it can wash over you and allow you to lose yourself within its depths. It can make your heart thump and your pulse race and, when you're lying on your bed just trying to meet the criteria of being a teenager, up to your eyeballs in uncertainties, loud pop music is perfectly qualified to persuade you that's it's all going to be ok and take you to somewhere lovely. Much later, when Colin (the bastard) arrived, I realised that pop was also capable of doing the complete opposite.

My dad would bang from downstairs with a broom handle on the underside of my bedroom floor and yell for me to turn it down, until out of pure frustration he would reluctantly have to take the trip up the stairs, fling the door open and be confronted with the full complement of decibels emanating from my speakers. 'Does it really have to be this loud? It's just a bloody racket,' he'd complain. Ahhh yes, but it was *my* bloody racket.

One of things that I really like about pop is its 'no loyalty' rule. Pop groups are not like your football team or your friends; you don't have to stick with them through thick and thin. There's no 'wedding vows' type agreement. No monogamy, no sickness and health, richer or poorer or good times/bad times promises. It's perfectly acceptable to like bands when they are doing the business, but as soon as that stops we are totally at liberty to go off and buy the records and attend the concerts of somebody else. No questions asked.

Sparks would go on to deliver albums of diminishing returns. I bought their next album *Propaganda* and, although not quite as good as *Kimono My House*, there were many exciting moments on it and some very good songs. However, the difficult third album (mine not theirs) *Indiscreet* was wretched. Hardly a decent song on it. I should have known, really – the album's lead-off single, 'Get in the Swing', had seen Russell appear on *Top of the Pops* barefooted and in a pair of hot pants – but I bought it anyway. I tried and tried with *Indiscreet*, playing it over and over again hoping that suddenly it would click, but I found it hard to get past the song called 'Tits'.

That was the deal breaker for me and Sparks, and we went our separate ways from there. Sparks went very quiet for a few years, resurfacing in 1979 with an album of disco music called *Beat the Clock*, but there's no coming back from a song about bosoms.

Ray and Monty went to see Sparks play live in the summer of 1974 at the Rainbow Theatre in London: 7 July 1974 to be precise. I didn't go; I can't remember why – either money or possibly parental forbidding. But while they went to see my favourite band, I stayed at home and watched the 1974 World Cup final between West Germany and Holland. I was that annoyed at missing out, that it still rankles enough for me to remember what I did as an alternative. I also remember that they were hugely disappointed that Sparks only played for 45 minutes that night. At least I got 90 minutes' entertainment, but it seems somewhat odd to me that I know exactly what my friends were doing on 7 July 1974, whilst I doubt very much that they do. Sometimes I astound myself by the sheer quantity of useless information that is stored in my head as far as pop music is concerned.

Fortune's Always Hiding

It didn't really take me that long to work out that I was never going to be the next Gordon Banks. I'd kind of fallen out with Gordon anyway; he'd broken my heart that cold January night in 1972 when he spectacularly saved a Geoff Hurst penalty in the dying minutes of a League Cup semi-final at Upton Park and denied me my first trip to Wembley. I went right off him. Later that year, poor old Gordon was involved in a car accident that claimed the vision in his right eye and his career was over. Despite the bitterness caused by the penalty affair, I was desperately upset to hear the news. He didn't deserve that. The timing was awful – I was only eleven and no fit size to take over. Peter Shilton got the gig.

I turned my back on goalkeeping – not permanently, I would come back to it later – but I had a new footballing hero, West Ham's inspirational captain Billy Bonds. 'Bonzo' was a highly committed, engine room type of footballer, who chipped in with a fair number of goals too. He was the sort of player that had a never-say-die attitude, playing with his shirt untucked, his socks rolled down and his chin unshaved. He wore short-sleeved shirts for freezing cold night matches in Newcastle and tackled his opponents as though someone had threatened to kneecap his sister if he didn't. Everyone wanted to be like Billy Bonds – me included.

I was never going to be the next Billy Bonds either, but that was hardly the point. I quite fancied myself in the role of midfield general – directing things masterfully from the back, getting myself forward to pop in a couple of goals, and throwing myself wholeheartedly into muddy sliding tackles. And so I started playing in midfield, rushing around the pitch with my shirt untucked and my socks rolled down to my ankles, arms outstretched and hands randomly pointing at things that I thought needed to be pointed at.

The Hammers had made a sluggish start to the 1974/75 season, just like they did every season, but this time it was sluggish enough for Ron Greenwood to be replaced as manager by his relatively unknown assistant John Lyall. It was a transitional period for the club. The old guard of Hurst, Peters and Moore had all moved on and our best striker, Bryan 'Pop' Robson had also left the club. Fresh blood was needed and Lyall acted quickly, bringing in three virtually unknown players – Billy Jennings from Watford, Alan Taylor from Rochdale and Keith Robson from Newcastle United's reserve team. Finding unknown players and turning them into decent footballers would prove to be Lyall's forte over the years. Jennings and Robson made an immediate impact and West Ham started to climb up the table. It was an exciting time to be a West Ham fan, we were playing some great stuff and, as ever, we imagined that we might be on the brink of something approaching success.

I'd been going to football matches almost every week during the couple of seasons prior to this one – mostly with Gary and his grandfather, who would drive us to matches in his old Austin Cambridge. We would stand on the terrace at Upton Park one week, and then when the Hammers were playing away from home, go to watch Second Division football at Orient.

It was during the 1974/75 season that Ray suggested that we should all go to football together. He, Colin (not the bastard, the other one, with the eyelids) and me were the real football fans and formed the nucleus of this tight football-attending crew but Billy and Milly were starting to get into it too and would come along sometimes – mainly just as an excuse to wear their newly acquired Dr. Marten boots.

Attending football matches in the seventies couldn't have been any more different to how it is today. Stadiums have changed beyond all recognition – they still have the same white lines on the pitch, but that's about it. Back in the day those arenas catered for a predominately male working-class crowd, feeding us on manky old 'Westlers' hot-dogs and watering us with cups of tea or Bovril in polystyrene cups. There were no posh sandwiches or punters with Lady Grey in their Thermos flasks. You could smoke in the ground; in fact, it was almost essential if you wanted to look hard. There were no all-seater stadiums and there was none of this buying of tickets weeks and weeks in advance for the price of a small hatchback either. We paid at the gate on match days, and it cost just twenty-five pence to stand on the North Bank at Upton Park, where we would jiggle and jostle for a decent vantage point on the narrow steps of terracing, sometimes only being able to see a fraction of the action through a gap left in between the sea of heads in front of us.

We were packed in so tightly that there was absolutely no chance of leaving your standing position to go to the toilet, for fear of never getting back again. So for those that were of a drinking age and found themselves full of fizzy lager mid-way through the first half, taking a piss exactly where they were standing – right there on terraces – was a common occurrence. The close proximity of fellow football fans caused other problems too. Whenever there was any goalmouth action, everyone used to tumble down the steps together as we all strained to see what was going on. You couldn't help it, you just felt yourself being flung forward onto the person in front, like some sort of grand scale game of human dominoes. You could end up yards away from your original standing position during one of these man-cascades, and when the moment of excitement had passed, hundreds of blokes would begrudgingly make their way back up the terracing – hoping to be reunited with their friends without soaking the bottom of their flares in the puddles of wee. But seeing the action wasn't wholly the point – it was all about the atmosphere and being there with your mates, the hilarious banter, the singing, the licence to shout obscene remarks very loudly, and going so crazy with excitement when a goal was scored that the rush of blood to the head made you see stars. It felt bloody brilliant.

And so we couldn't see the game, ate terrible food and stood in a lake of piss – and those were the good bits. These were the halcyon days for football hooliganism and every Saturday afternoon, violence was rife at every football ground around the country. Before it got totally out-of-hand and organised with military precision, football hooliganism was mainly about 'taking your opponents' end' – which whilst sounding as if it might be an alternative way of describing bottom sex, it actually meant getting into the home terrace of your opponents with a large number of your most violent yobs and, once in situ, singing very rude songs about doing so. Going to games, particularly away games, could be a very scary experience.

West Ham fans had a reputation for being one of the hardest 'firms' of hooligans in the country and its fair to say that their fans could claim many more victories on the terraces than the team ever could on the pitch. Because of this reputation, not many gangs of other teams' fans chanced their arms at Upton Park, and consequently there was rarely any real trouble inside the ground. Most of the football-related violence that I have witnessed took place on the road – at away matches or between the ground and the station. Mobs of angry neanderthals, gathering like a pack of hungry wolves at their local station, just waiting for our train to pull in, and as the doors of those old Inter-City trains flung open, there would be a huge roar of intent as the echoes of chanting thugs filled the subway corridors and platforms of alien stations. I have seen battles up close that make me shudder if I think about them for too long and been chased by gangs of louts through the streets of some of this country's most miserable locations.

None of us were what you might describe as being 'hard'; leafy Gants Hill was hardly the front line, and therefore fell short in trying to turn its residents into toughies, but we all embraced the hooligan ethos to a certain degree without ever wanting to get involved in anything that might actually hurt. We were pretenders. That is, we were prepared to chant the chants and point fingers angrily in unison at the opposing supporters; we were even prepared to wear the clothes. We each bought ourselves a pair of Dr. Marten boots to look the part – not that those boots had any intention of kicking anything that had a face; we wore smart Harrington jackets and obeyed the strict dress code of wearing a woollen scarf hanging from the belt-loops of our jeans and a silk one tied around our wrist – it was all about fitting in. Now there's a funny thing – football scarves made of silk. Thugs beautifying themselves in silken scarves is a bit like kitting out ballet dancers in donkey jackets.

We had our favourite spot on the terraces – somewhere right near the back of the North Bank, directly behind the goalposts – and would squeeze and weave our way through the masses to find it. Being a bit of a shorty, I found it even harder to see the game than the others, and if I happened to have some huge great hulk standing in front of me, I had no chance. Other small kids used to take milk crates to stand on to gain a better vantage point, but a milk crate was not an image-enhancing accessory and would have defeated the object of trying to look the part. It would have been a bit like a skinhead trying to hide a 'cut-here' throat tattoo with a lovely cravat.

We would often find ourselves standing shoulder-to-shoulder with one skinhead in particular, who would be decked out in full thuggish regalia: Ben Sherman shirt and jeans purposefully hitched up so high by his braces that his twelve-lace-holed 'bovver boots' were revealed in all their glory. After a few anonymous conversations at various matches, he finally introduced himself as 'Meat-Head'. We sniggered (privately of course).

Meat-Head was non-discriminatory. He hated everybody. 'Blacks, Pakis, Yids, Northerners, Paddys, Jocks – I fuckin' hate 'em all,' he would boast. He was a few years older than us and heavily peppered every sentence he spoke with derivatives of the word 'wankers' at inappropriate intervals. It was as if he wanted to say the word as many times as possible, regardless of whether or not it fitted into context. He would try and entertain us pre-match with tales of taking the Shed at Chelsea or the Paxton Road end at Tottenham like he'd carried out these battles single-handedly. 'Yeah – wankers' we would interject trying to make it not sound as if we were taking the mickey. 'You wankers should come with me next wankering time' he suggested on one occasion. I think we started hiding from him at matches after that, just in case he wankeringly insisted.

When it comes to singing at football matches, I have to confess that today's fans are a lot more inventive, cruel and therefore funnier than they used to be in the seventies. Back then, the songs tended to mostly be about fighting with other supporters, whereas now, with fan violence almost gone from the game, the focus of the fans is more on ridiculing the players and the opposing supporters without the threat of kicking anyone's head in. There is genuine humour in the songs these days and football fans are good at laughing at themselves – plus, to everyone's delight, today's footballers are not.

I remember on one occasion David Beckham got so agitated with the 'Posh Spice takes it up the arse' song that during a game at Upton Park he started responding by taking pot-shots at goal from ridiculous distances. He figured that the best way to answer the abuse was to score a spectacular goal. But as his attempts from thirty-five and forty yards got more and more wayward, his manager, Alex Ferguson, decided to spare his blushes and take him off the pitch rather than watch him continue in his fruitless quest.

In the early nineties, the football world was surprised when champions Leeds United sold their best player, French international Eric Cantona to their archrivals Manchester United. All became clear later, when the news leaked out that Cantona had been shunted out of the club because of his affair with top scorer Lee Chapman's wife – *Men Behaving Badly* actress Lesley Ash. Chapman was then provoked up and down the country with chants of:

He's French, He's Flash
And he's shagged Lesley Ash
Cantona, Cantona

The consequence – Chapman lost form, was dropped from the Leeds team and became so utterly hopeless that he ended up playing for West Ham.

Inventive as the songs may be in more recent times, the move from terraces to all-seater stadia has curtailed the atmosphere felt at games in years gone by. Back in the seventies, the singing at matches was a good enough reason to be there; united in voice in support of the team made us feel we were part of something – even if it wasn't necessarily part of something good.

Very few clubs have a terrace song that is internationally known, but uniquely associated with them. Liverpool have 'You'll Never Walk Alone', Portsmouth 'The Pompey Chimes' and West Ham 'I'm Forever Blowing Bubbles'. In the seventies, 'Bubbles' was always sung with scarves held between outstretched arms above our heads, and the gently swaying sea of claret and blue was a sight to behold. There were times when being part of several thousand people singing it in unison could give me an inwardly warm glow of pride and could deliver goosebumps without too much trouble at all.

Although the terraces were usually a place where we could let off steam and shout and sing obscenities at extremely loud volumes, they were awash with policemen on the prowl, eager to eject anyone behaving in a threatening manner, and so you had to watch your 'f's' and 'c's' – a process that Ray once fell foul of during an easy League Cup win against Barnsley.

Whilst in full voice during a chorus of a rather sweary variation on *The Liver Birds* theme tune, he got his collar felt by the long arm. We never really understood why it was Ray that was singled out, as we were all singing it – us and about a thousand others. But singled out he was, and we watched, somewhat thrilled and bursting with pride, as our mate was paraded around the perimeter of the pitch and down the players' tunnel, with his arm pinned tight against his back by a burly constable.

The next day at school we interrogated him about the ins and outs of the whole affair. As it turned out, he wasn't charged with anything – he just had his name taken and was then ejected from the stadium. He explained, however, that he had picked the wrong game to be thrown out of. His dad rarely went to football matches, but on this occasion, and unbeknown to Ray, he had been given a last-minute ticket for the game by a workmate and had been sitting up in the stand with his chum, watching in horror as his son was frogmarched out in front of him.

We all thought this to be hilarious and it inspired Billy and Milly to get to work on one of their piss-taking drawings. Whenever anything funny happened you could always rely on those two to crystallise it in artwork. The scene depicted in the picture was Ray's dad looking on horrified amongst a sea of heads, with a speech bubble coming out of one side of his mouth that read ''ere, Raymond!' and another coming out of the other side saying 'that's my boy'. The drawing inspired us to immediately begin work on a league-table-style code for future ground ejections in which we could all compete.

It was deemed that every time that one of us was thrown out of a football match, we would receive an ''ere' to precede our name (as in 'ere, Raymond'), and we should always be addressed as such in future. Two ejections and the recipient would become an ''ere, 'ere', and on a third ejection the ''eres' would be converted to an 'oi' – the highest accolade available for such behaviour. I seem to remember Milly receiving an ''ere' at Highbury, but sadly I have to record that I didn't become an ''ere Tony' until I got thrown out (again for swearing during a song) in 1988, by which time I was 27 years old and a father.

Although West Ham supporters had that reputation of being hard, the same couldn't be said about the team. A string of embarrassing cup exits at the hands of lower league opposition had led them to be known as a bit of a soft touch. Four years had passed since I started supporting the club, and in that short period they somehow managed to get themselves knocked out of the various cup competitions by Huddersfield Town, Hull City, Stockport County, Hereford United and Fulham, all of whom back then hailed from the old Third and Fourth Divisions.

Every season the cup competitions are renowned for throwing up the odd cheeky result or two, and as a supporter you expect that at some point your club is going to succumb to the act of 'giant-killing'. It's happened to the best of them. Even the mighty Leeds United in their prime suffered at the hands of Fourth Division Colchester United in 1971, and non-league Hereford's 1972 defeat of First Division Newcastle is one of the F.A. Cup's most celebrated moments. So once in a while you can just about stomach it, but humiliating cup defeats seem to go hand in hand with West Ham, and for us to suffer in this way every season since I started supporting them was hard for me to swallow. Having said that, it set me up nicely for the many more embarrassing cup exits I would have to suffer throughout the next thirty-odd years. I'm used to it now, and so when the Hammers come out of the hat, drawn away to Darlington or Tranmere Rovers, I expect the worst – and usually get it. The hardest kick in football is the one it gives you straight in the goolies.

However, the 1975 F.A Cup competition was different. It started with what looked on the face of it like a tricky away tie at Second Division Southampton. Although recently relegated, Southampton included the former England player Mick Channon and ex-Chelsea striker Peter Osgood amongst their ranks, and would go on to win the trophy the very next season. So they were no easy touch, and this was just the sort of game that West Ham would typically lose, but on this occasion we came away with a 2-1 victory.

We went to the fourth round tie at home to Third Division Swindon Town full of expectation. Surely even West Ham couldn't struggle at home to such a lowly team? We drew 1-1.

I remember listening to the commentary of the replay on the radio, sitting at the breakfast bar in our kitchen, constantly hopping on and off the bar stool as the action got more and more intense. I'm not sure why I felt that I had to get off the stool as West Ham closed in on goal. It's not as if I was able to help them out by taking up position in the penalty box and waiting for Trevor Brooking to float over one of his inch-perfect crosses for me to ghost in on the blind side and nod it into the net at the far post, but it just felt like a natural instinct to not be seated during those close-call moments. It was certainly handy being on my feet when Pat Holland knocked in the winner, as it made the dance of excited little circles that I performed around my mum, who happened to be in the kitchen at that precise moment making a cup of tea, seem a little less pre-meditated.

The not-so-great outdoors kept me away from Upton Park for round five. There's no skirting around the fact that I am not, and never have been, the outdoor type. I don't mind the countryside in small doses, but I feel a general uneasiness about huge expanses of greenery that you can only get to on a horse – an uneasiness that I've never quite got to the bottom of. Nice to look at on a warm summer's day, but it seems to me that the countryside is on a personal mission to make life as uncomfortable as possible for its visitors during winter. Someone should have a word with it and persuade it that rather than stiles and dollops of steaming horse shit, it may like to consider punctuating its footpaths with a comfy sofa or two instead – maybe somewhere to shelter from the elements and the odd telly here and there wouldn't go amiss, either.

Bearing this in mind, I can't remember what it was that possessed me to agree to go camping with the scouts in the middle of February 1975. I have a sneaky suspicion that Fraser may have talked me into that one. The draw of teenage boys farting under canvas was obviously too tempting an attraction to turn down.

It rained relentlessly. Thunder, lightning – the lot. I'd never seen such a torrential downpour, let alone been exposed to it. It rained so persistently hard that I think Noah may have floated past our tent on his ark at one point, and even he looked a little distressed. The rain was so powerful that it forced its way into our tent and everything we owned was drenched, and so with no possible means of drying anything, we slept in wringing wet clothes inside soaking wet sleeping bags. It was miserable – the wettest I'd been since the whole Ruth Feldman debacle.

The whole camping thing seems like utter madness to me now. These days, I'd have to take delivery of a huge pile of cash by way of a bribe before I even thought about going camping in the height of summer, let alone freezing February. I've been putting off going to the Glastonbury Festival for years now, just because I can't face the thought of the camping. Book me into a spa hotel nearby, feed me a nice buffet breakfast and drive me onto the site every morning and I'd be there in a jiffy. But wallowing in a mud swamp and holed up in a tent for four days? Perish the thought – not even in the name of rock.

And so as West Ham prepared to take on Queens Park Rangers in the fifth round, I was spending the weekend at Gilwell Park, wallowing in mud, miserable as sin's more miserable brother and looking very much like a ginger Afghan hound that had just retrieved a stick from a very dirty lake.

By lunchtime on the Saturday, and with the rain still coming down in sheets, the camp was abandoned and several teenage boys thankfully dismantled soggy canvas and awaited their parents' warm saloons to pull up on the gravelled car park. When Dad arrived I asked him if he fancied making a short detour and dropping me off somewhere near Upton Park so I could make the match. He informed me that I was in no fit state to stand on freezing terraces in the driving rain for two hours. I took that as a 'no'.

I got home and crashed out on the sofa. Mum supplied me with a cup of tea and some Dairylea on toast and informed me that as soon as I had finished them, I was having a bath. The next thing I was aware of was waking up a couple of hours later with a blanket draped over me. As I came round, the first thought to cross my mind was the match. I hurriedly turned on the TV just in time to see 'West Ham 2 QPR 1' typed up teasingly, letter-by-letter, on *Grandstand*'s teleprinter. I punched the air with delight and the horrors of the past 48 hours were instantly forgotten. We were in the quarter-finals of the F.A. Cup.

It seemed like an agonisingly long wait from then until the match highlights were shown on *The Big Match* the following afternoon. It was an edition that would live long in my memory, not because of the quality of the football – to be honest, I can't really remember much about the match at all – but because of the moment when Gerry Francis, the Queens Park Rangers captain, leaned back against the advertising hoardings ready to take a corner at the North Bank end. There, in the shot, was Ray standing on the terracing behind him, giving him the two-fingered salute. A keen lip-reader would have been able to tell that Ray wasn't complimenting Gerry on his gorgeous sideburns. I roared with laughter, jumped out of my seat and ran towards the telly as if to confirm that it really was my mate on the screen. There was no doubt. If ever there was an instance where I needed the video recorder to be invented, it was then.

A footie trivia question: When and why did West Ham start wearing their all-white away strip?

Answer: 8 March 1975, and the reason? Because they forgot to load their proper kit on to the team bus!

This is absolutely true. As the team disembarked from the coach at Highbury, their kit was still sitting in a hamper on a pavement somewhere on the Barking Road. Only West Ham could turn up for such an auspicious occasion as an F.A. Cup quarter-final against Arsenal without a thing to wear. And so the Hammers took to the field wearing an all-white training kit, borrowed from their hosts.

We'd all been to Highbury for the league game earlier in the season, in which we were thrashed 3-0. That match had been my first ever away game, and we'd stood in the Schoolboys (how sexist) enclosure because it was the only place in the ground where kids could get in for half-price. We had spent most of that match trying to avoid getting embroiled in the fighting that was going on all around us, and so in anticipation of the team getting another thumping on the pitch and us getting one on the terraces, we thought it was best not to put ourselves through that again.

No one gave West Ham a hope in hell of winning this match. Our decent early season league form had deserted us since Christmas and we were sliding back down the table faster than a whippet wearing a pair of roller skates on a very steep hill. How appropriate, then, that Alan Taylor, a footballer who was as wiry looking and as lightning quick as one (but in football boots, rather than skates) was about to turn our season on its head.

Taylor, who up until now had hardly played, found himself a surprise inclusion in the starting line-up for the Arsenal game. He scored both goals in a shock 2-0 victory. The game was played, yet again, in torrential rain on a quagmire of a pitch. When the jubilant Hammers left the pitch at the end of the game, every one of them was caked in so much mud that there was barely an inch of that borrowed kit that was still white. The fans that occupied the open terrace of the Clock End at Highbury went home soaked through to the bone, but happy in the knowledge that a new Hammers hero had been born that day.

We were drawn to play Ipswich Town at the neutral Villa Park in the semi-final. The club announced that tickets for the match would be limited, and that they would be handing each fan a voucher as they went through the turnstiles at the next home game. These vouchers would then go into a draw and the holders of the winning vouchers would be entitled to buy a ticket for Villa Park.

The decision therefore, to attend the Burnley game (a 2-1 victory, Taylor scoring again) was made for us, and we duly collected our vouchers and hoped for the best. Ray, Colin and I got lucky, and so the following Sunday morning we took our winning vouchers to Upton Park and joined the longest queue I'd ever been in. It stretched from the ticket office, out of the forecourt, along Green Street and around the corner – probably about a mile long in total and in typical disorganised West Ham fashion, it moved at the pace of an aged tortoise with a heart condition, carrying a very heavy backpack on its shell.

Several hours later we finally arrived at the front of the queue and bought our tickets. As we walked away, we teased the hordes still waiting in line by proudly holding our tickets aloft as if they were the F.A Cup itself. We hotfooted it straight down to the office of Lacey's Coaches in the Barking Road and booked our seats for the journey on the big day.

The build- up to the semi-final was intense and very exciting and it took an eternity for the day to arrive. I'd never been out of London for a football match and so going on a special football coach to Birmingham felt like a step into the exotic.

The *Ilford Recorder* and the *Evening Standard* were full of articles and photos in the days leading up to the game, and this just added to the excitement. With the sense that I was about to witness history in the making, I decided to cut these out and stick them into a scrapbook. This I now recognise as being the beginnings of the archivist in me, a trait that would announce itself fully when adapted to pop music. The scrapbook eventually spilled over into a second volume as I continued with the cutting and sticking routine well into the following season.

Of course this is me we're talking about, and simply cutting out and sticking articles relating to West Ham from newspapers was never going to be enough. The weekly 'Hammers Page' in the *Ilford Recorder* was a good source of material but insufficient for my need to fill the scrapbook as quickly as possible. I expanded the scope of my scrapbook to include match info and statistics on my most local of football clubs, Ilford FC.

At the end of the previous season, Ilford FC made it to Wembley for the final of the very last Amateur Cup. Although the stadium was only half-filled, it seemed like the whole of the town was at Wembley that day to see Ilford lose 4-1 to Bishop's Stortford. However, going to that game ignited my interest in the club and the following season I started attending their matches on a fairly regular basis. They had a pretty decent team and were doing well in the Rothmans Isthmian League, which was a couple of leagues below the old Football League Division Four. Ilford's home ground was at Lynn Road in Newbury Park, which was about a fifteen-minute walk from my house. Fraser, who is a Tottenham supporter, would come and watch them with me, and the fact that we could go to football together and support the same team was reason enough for us to keep going.

My scrapbooks still survive today, although most of the cut-outs are now hanging loose as the yellowing Selloptape has given up the struggle against the forces of time. I'm thumbing through it now for the first time in over thirty years and getting a little glimpse of the fourteen-year-old me, my initial thoughts being that I was a bit of a nob – a likeable nob, but a nob all the same.

I'm cringing at the comments that I have written as captions for some the pictures, the coloured-in drawings of the West Ham and Ilford football kits and an entry on the inside back cover that simply reads (for reasons that I'm now finding hard to fathom) 'your [sic] gonna get your f--kin heads kicked in'.

On page 17 is a photo in which my caption reads: 'Billy Bonds spread-eagled after another crunching tackle', and I'm now concluding that the scribbling in blue biro between his legs was a result of Fraser bestowing upon Bonzo an extravagant addition to his groin area, and me consequently obliterating it upon discovery. On reflection, I was wrong to use the word 'tackle'.

But it gets worse: The *Ilford Recorder* didn't have match reports on Ilford's games every week, and so when the newspaper didn't provide one, I would write my own. I quote from a match report, which is headed up Ilford 1 Dover 0:

'A record attendance of 484 for a friendly, crowded into Lynn Road for the match against Dover. How this happened after Ilford's disgusting performance at Romford last week, I will never know'.

484! How could I have possibly known this? It's not as if Ilford's attendances for meaningless friendly matches were recorded the next morning in the *Sunday People*. Did I count them during a dull moment in that game? Of course not, I made it up – just as I made up that it was a record crowd for a friendly. And what, I wonder, might the team have done at Romford the previous week that I deemed to be so disgusting – flashed their winkles at shoppers at the market?

Most embarrassing of all, though, is the set of statistics scruffily written out on page five of Volume II, entitled 'My Games in Games'. A snappy little title, I now observe – short, sweet and deliberately obtuse. Yes, these were the results of the matches that I'd played in during games lessons at school. I even recorded the goalscorers. A typical entry:

'7/10/76 Blues v Reds - Won 9-1 Guise (2), Pearce (3), Shelley (pen), Baldwin, Levy (2)'
The huge stench of shame fills my room once more.

Back in the world of proper football, semi-final day finally arrived. The coach journey to Villa Park was full of anticipation. There was lots of singing, ours fuelled by the two cans of Watneys Red Barrel that we drank on the way, but I remember feeling incredibly nervous about the football to come.

The team wore the white kit again – this time, their own. It was now dubbed the 'lucky' kit and adopted permanently as their new away kit, usurping the traditional light blue with claret hoops. We sang ourselves hoarse in the stadium, willing the team on to score the goal that would take us to Wembley, but despite the lucky kit, the match ended in a dull 0-0 draw and the feeling of deflation filled the coach on the journey home.

None of us could afford to go to the replay that took place at Stamford Bridge the following Wednesday, and so if the Hammers were to go on and make it to Wembley, they were going to have to do it without our help. I wasn't confident. Ipswich were a good side riding high in the league and would eventually finish in third place come the end of the season. I couldn't bear to put myself through another agonising radio commentary and so I avoided the score and waited to watch the highlights of the game on *Sportsnight With Coleman* later that evening. That's not to say that it wasn't a nail-biting match to watch on the telly – it was, and when Billy Jennings deflected an Ipswich corner into his own net to equalise Alan Taylor's opener, things got a whole lot tenser. But Taylor raised his hero status that little bit higher, when he popped in the winner with just ten minutes of the match left, and I celebrated with a victory dance around the dining room table and a glass of Tizer. I couldn't really believe that we'd made it to Wembley and suddenly all those defeats against lower league opposition paled into insignificance.

We were all desperate to get a ticket for the final. Who knew when we would next reach a cup final? It could be a once in a lifetime opportunity. There were only 25,000 tickets available, and at that time the club was averaging 38,000 fans every home game, so another voucher ballot was organised. This time only Colin was successful.

Ray and I were gutted but we tried to console ourselves in the fact that we would be able to watch the build-up to the final on the TV. This was one of things that I enjoyed most about cup final day. It would start early in the morning with a football-flavoured edition of *Multi-Coloured Swap Shop* (still *Black and White Swap Shop* in our house). *Grandstand* and *World of Sport* would start an hour earlier on cup final day so as to incorporate all the footy-related treats such as *It's A Cup Final Knockout* and the interviews with all the players on the team bus as it made its way to Wembley.

In the week before the match, cup final fever seemed to explode in Gants Hill. People were decorating their houses in anticipation of the big day. Pictures of the team were displayed in front room windows and claret and blue scarves and banners hung from every available fixing point. I wanted to join in with this display of colour loyalty, and so I tied my scarf to the latch of my bedroom window, poked it out through the louvre panes and watched it flap about in the gusts of wind caused by the traffic flow rattling up and down the A12.

Ray and I had planned to watch the match and the entire build-up together, but a phone call from my Uncle Ivan on the evening before the match threw those plans into disarray. Unbeknown to me, my Dad had asked Ivan (who worked in the markets of East London, and therefore knew a few geezers, who knew a few geezers) to keep an eye out for a ticket for me. His search during the preceding two or three weeks had been fruitless, but at the eleventh hour and as the stallholders were packing up their wares for the evening, he was offered a terrace ticket for behind the goal for £3. Despite this being twice the face value of the ticket, he snapped it up, and I was on my way to Wembley.

The news was so unexpected and I felt a rush of euphoria as he told me. I can't remember whether I danced the now traditional dance of triumph around the dining room table before or after I hung up the phone, but I felt so light-headed and shocked about the whole thing that it wouldn't have surprised me if I'd left Ivan hanging on the other end of the phone while I celebrated. It somehow felt fitting that the man who had started it all for me – the man responsible for most of my football-related misery – was now delivering the ultimate reward.

I rang Ray immediately. He gave it his best shot at trying to sound pleased for me, and I had a stab at trying to disguise my excitement. I did feel a little guilty about it; he'd been to more games than I had that season, and deserved to be there more than I did.

I met Colin on the Central Line platform at Stratford station the following morning, and we made our way towards Wembley. As the journey progressed, the tube became packed with expectant West Ham supporters, drinking and singing and larruping all over the usual Saturday morning collection of shoppers and day-trippers. As we came out of the station at Wembley Park, all we could see in front of us was a sea of claret and blue making its collective waves along Wembley Way towards the stadium.

We still had a slight conundrum to overcome. The ticket that I had was for a different section to the one Colin had, and the man on the turnstiles refused to let us both in through the same turnstile. Fortunately, there were plenty of other groups of friends encountering similar situations gathered outside the gates; a simple swap of tickets with one of these lads solved our problem, and in we went.

As we took up our position on the terraces, we started to soak up the atmosphere of the occasion and our thoughts turned towards the game. Our opposition for the match was second division Fulham, and West Ham were firm favourites to win. I wasn't so sure. Not just because we had already been knocked out of the League Cup by Fulham earlier in the season, but mainly because today's Fulham team had Bobby Moore at the heart of its defence – playing his last-ever game in English football. The F.A. Cup is notorious for creating stories that even Hans Christian Andersen would struggle to dream up, and what could be more fairy-tale like than West Ham's former captain and greatest ever player, winning the cup against his old club in his last-ever match?

Although my fears were understandable, they were unfounded. The first half was a dull affair without many chances and no goals, but after an hour Alan Taylor scored yet another cup goal and we all went crazy. Not quite as crazy as we went four minutes later when he scored the second. Even West Ham couldn't throw away a lead like that. Twenty or so minutes later, the final whistle was blown – grown men wept, skinheads embraced as if all their toughness had instantly melted away and we all celebrated being the new F.A Cup holders.

I was full of pride as I watched Billy Bonds lift the cup high above his head and direct the famous trophy towards the claret and blue end of the stadium. 'Bubbles' rang out around Wembley louder than I'd ever heard it before; I savoured the moment and wondered if I could ever be any happier than I was at that precise moment, or whether I would witness scenes like this ever again.

I'm Not In Love

'Forgive me O Great God of Rock – for I have sinned. It has been two chapters since my last pop confession.'

'For what is it that you seek forgiveness, man?'
'It's 10cc, your Rockygodness. I am a 10cc fan.'
'10-bloody-cc? Oh do fuck off!'

I'm not really sure what the absolution for being a 10cc fan might be. A dozen 'Our Fathers' with a couple of 'Hail Mary of the 4th Forms', thrown in for good measure, perhaps? Maybe I should be made to sit in an isolated room for a week, wearing a set of headphones – the volume cranked up to excruciatingly painful levels, and forced to listen to the entire works of Supertramp until my eardrums refuse point blank to digest any more abhorrent seventies music and start oozing rivers of blood in protest. Yes, that would teach me to be sensible – logical, oh, responsible, practical.

As it happens, my conscience is clear as far as Supertramp are concerned. Their back catalogue is generally remembered with the same degree of uncoolness as 10cc's, but I stayed well clear. I did own their 1977 album *Even In The Quietest Moments ...* I'll grant you, but it wasn't my fault. A birthday present – an unwanted birthday present, from friends of my parents, and that's the worst kind of unwanted birthday present you can receive. It was delivered whilst I slept, and placed proudly propped up on my bedside table ready for early morning discovery, like a secretive deposit of some sort of pop Santa Claus. It wasn't even wrapped.

Something that I always did with new records was to inspect the vinyl the moment I got it home. Trying to make excited fingers stretch across the vinyl so they touched only the label top and bottom and thus not dishonouring the album with a sweaty fingerprint was always a bit of a challenge. It was a necessary ritual in the seventies. You had to check for scratches and flaws, but I just loved the look of new vinyl – crisp, clean and virginal-black. I did it from day one, right up until the time when I stopped buying records. With much less satisfaction, and without sufficient reason, I still examine new CDs. It's a hard habit to break. However, on inspection of the Supertramp album, it was obvious that this record was not blemish-free. It had been played before. Clearly this was a second-hand present.

Having not shown the faintest flicker of interest in Supertramp thus far, I wondered why anyone would choose to give me one of their albums, and so I invented my own scenario as to why it had been bestowed upon me. I figured that my parents' friends were passing on their own son's unwanted birthday present. A present that they had bought for him after having a nasty trick played on them by some smart-arse shop assistant in Our Price Records. Picture the scene:

Parents' Friends: 'Hello, we'd like to buy a pop record for our son. Can you recommend something – ha-ha – cool, that the youngsters like?'

Smart-Arse Our Price Dude: 'Yeah man, you'll be wanting something by either Supertramp or Paper Lace'.

A mind-sketch that was never corroborated, but one that I wouldn't mind guessing wasn't too far from the truth.

I played the record twice. The first time just to make sure that I couldn't be persuaded to like Supertramp, and once this test had been satisfied with a negative result, a second to try and create a new world record for balancing a Subbuteo player on a Supertramp album playing at 78rpm. But during a time when I was building up my record collection it was all about quantity, not quality, and a record was a record – even if it was a really crap record that I was never very likely to play– and so I allowed *Even In The Quietest Moments ...* to remain in my collection for a number of years.

The great flaw in the whole confessing of musical misdemeanours from days gone by is that, in the case of 10cc, I have proved time and time again that I am unwilling to repent and don't really deserve any kind of absolution. A guilty pleasure they may have been – terrible one minute, but bloody brilliant the next – but I just couldn't help myself. Common sense might strive to make me deny the very existence of their music in my record collection, but left alone with an iPod and a pair of noise-isolating headphones, I find myself in a secret world in which no one else knows about the indefensible music I still consider acceptable to listen to. A world in which life is compromised, life is shameful and where life is quite frankly, a minestrone.

When I first heard 'Rubber Bullets', I was unmoved. I liked it, but there was no mind-blowing moment of realisation. Their follow-up single, 'The Dean and I', had much more of an impact. I adored that record. I found it a fascinating journey to follow its twists and turns as it meandered its way through three minutes of pop excellence. I'd not really heard a song like that before – a song where each section was different to its predecessor. I thought it was totally original, and I bought it. 'The Dean and I' oozed fun and filled my head, and my bedroom, with unfamiliar Americana.

10cc were four hairy men from scruffy Stockport, Lancashire, but you could be forgiven for thinking that they came from somewhere overtly American such as California or Texas. Their early singles were sung, in the main, by guitarist Lol Creme. He sang – and let's be honest here – like a girl, and his voice hosted a broad American accent. In 'The Dean and I' he rhymed the word 'mom' with 'senior prom', and spoke of 'graduation', 'soda pop' and 'rolling in dollars'. I had no idea what a senior prom was. The only prom I'd ever heard about was the one at Southend-on-Sea, and Lol, in his native Greater Mancunian accent, was more likely to refer to his own mother as 'Mam' anyway, but none of this stopped me from tagging along for the ride.

But no matter how standoffish we want to be about 10cc now, there is no denying the fact that they were immensely talented and completely innovative. Here was a band where all four members could write songs, they all had strong enough voices to be lead singers and they were all multi-instrumentalists – even the drummer Kevin Godley. Admittedly, they did have image issues in so much as they didn't really have one. They all looked like someone else we knew. Lol Creme sported a John Lennon-circa-*White-Album* centre-parting hairstyle, whereas Eric Stewart looked a bit like Jim Morrison (pre bathtub death). Kevin Godley's look appeared to be modelled on Cut-Throat Jake from *Captain Pugwash* and poor old Graham Gouldman was all bug-eyed and bushy-headed, and had a sort of flat face that looked as though it had been belted full-on with a frying pan.

But 'The Dean and I' wasn't really the record that persuaded me to whole-heartedly buy into 10cc. That came a couple of years later. In the summer of 1975, they released their epic moment – the single 'I'm Not in Love' – and I was hooked. It would take me a full five years to finally let go of the bait.

'I'm Not in Love' is much maligned these days – somewhat unfairly I think, but the issues are two-fold. Firstly, I blame the devaluing of its stock, and its subsequent association with cheesy pop, on the fact that it's always the first name on the team sheet when record companies are putting together those hideous compilation CDs that get re-vamped and re-packaged every year just in time to cash in on Valentine's Day. You know the ones – big hearts or silhouetted couples kissing on the beach on the front cover, and usually sporting titles such as *The Greatest Love of All* or *Eternal Love*.

The second reason, and maybe this comes about because of the first, is that we're just sick to death of it. We've heard it so many times that the novelty has worn off and complacency has replaced enchantment. We've been I'm Not in Loved to death.

But when the record first arrived at our ears in 1975, its sound was fresh and summery. That's how I'd rather remember it. Those layers upon layers of rich Beach Boys-inspired harmonies that were stacked so high you could almost see them floating away to join the clouds – they were key, and gave the song the most spine-tingling atmosphere I'd ever heard on a pop record. Those exquisite harmonies were fronted by Eric Stewart's understated lone lead vocal, in which he manages to sound as if he's just about to burst into tears, and could blow at any moment, yet is somehow managing to hold it together. And all this was underpinned with that dreamy Mellotron part that sounds all wobbly and shaky, as if its player knew that the song was so special that he was almost too nervous to play it.

10cc's earlier singles, lyrically, had all been a bit tongue-in-cheek, full of wordplay and punnery and, to be honest, bordering on being a little bit too smart-arsed for their own good. The lyrics to 'I'm Not in Love' dropped all the tomfoolery. There were no jokes. It was a love song disguised as an anti-love song. It was clever without the need to ever be smug. The single shot to number one in the charts and 10cc were catapulted into the stratosphere, and I claimed them as my very own.

They were the first band that I had a lasting relationship with. I put a picture of them on my bedroom wall – it hid a nasty stain that was lying there. They were the first band to be afforded such homage. Nothing extravagant mind, just a centre-page spread pulled from one of Mads' *Jackie* magazines.

Posters were one thing, but records were more important, and as usual when something sparked an interest I threw myself into it wholeheartedly, or at least what I imagined to be throwing myself into it wholeheartedly. The ensuing years would prove that my '10cc phase' was merely stroking pop's kitten rather than taming its lion. But for now, the most important thing was identifying my favourite member of the band (Eric Stewart), and collecting the records – I needed to have them all.

I started in the obvious place: *The Original Soundtrack* – the mother album of 'I'm Not in Love'. This album was funded by my dad. Well my purchase of it was – he didn't actually put up the cash for the boys to spend six months in the studio recording the thing. That would've been ridiculous, he hardly knew them. A free album for the collection – a good thing you might think; this is true, and after all, you'll remember that he did buy me some of those singles back in the sixties. But my dad didn't buy me records just for the hell of it anymore. There was no value in challenging me to see if I could still tell one record from the next – not now that I could read, anyway.

To say that my dad wasn't really a fan of pop music is a bit like saying that Ben Elton wasn't really a fan of Mrs Thatch. Dad was fairly fond of easy-listening stuff like Shirley Bassey and Frank Sinatra. He generally didn't really approve of pop music – particularly, the pop music that spurted out of my bedroom at great volume and invaded his evening's TV viewing.

And so on that day in 1975 when he planted a fiver in the palm of my hand and said 'Anthony, next time you go to Guy Norris, can you get me that "I'm in Love" [*sic*] song,' I was somewhat taken aback. This scenario placed a whole host of dilemmas at my doorstep and as a 14-year-old boy, with a record-collecting passion gathering pace at the rate of an over-excited whippet on amphetamines, there was no way I was equipped to deal with them satisfactorily:

1. Do I tell him that this household already owns a copy of the 'I'm in Love' song? Give him that and bag the cash for something more LP-shaped?

2. A fiver to buy a single? No, if he just wanted the single he would have given me a pound, surely? And as far as I was aware he had never bought a pop album in his life, so clearly the handing over of the fiver was a statement of intent – a willingness to finally climb aboard the magic bus to pop utopia and turn his back on Burt Bacharach forever.

3. The fact that he didn't buy albums meant that he probably wouldn't be aware of the price of an LP, and almost certainly wouldn't notice if I came home from Guy Norris Records with some other goodies sharing carrier bag space with *The Original Soundtrack*.

Apart from all these dreadful moralistic issues over whether or not I should spend his money on boosting my own record collection, lurking deep beneath pop's lake of rebellion was the horrific realisation that my dad liked the same record as me – and at the same time, too. He'd crossed the line as far as I was concerned, broken the unwritten rule without a second thought of how I might deal with this sorry situation or how it might look to my mates. This was not usually how fathers and sons bonded in the seventies. They stood shoulder to shoulder on the terraces, they shadowboxed, and they battled with each other in a game of wits to see who could be heard loudest over the drum intro to 'Can the Can'. They did not, under any circumstances, share the same taste in soft rock.

This was the moment where our two worlds collided head-on, and we were probably both scratching our heads wondering how the hell we got there. The moment where *Deep Purple in Rock* fucks *Shirley Bassey is Really Something* and produces 'I'm Not in love' as its bastard lovechild … a frightening prospect indeed. Was this the start of some sort of coming together in the name of pop for us? I thought maybe I could try him on something less substantial and see whether this was just a one-off, or I was really dealing with Pop-dad on a stick. A lid needed putting on it that was for sure. I was concerned. Where would it end? 10cc today, Gary Glitter tomorrow? Was I about to come home from school one day to find my father dressed from head to foot in tin foil, stomping around the house in stack-heeled boots insisting that he was the leader of the gang?

I needn't have worried. Our pop reconciliation was to be short lived. My dad's flirtation with pop in the main began and ended with 'I'm Not in Love'. The next record he would buy would be 'Xanadu' by Olivia Newton John and the Electric Light Orchestra in 1980. It would be his last.

It was all ok again. Business as usual.

I took that fiver and exchanged it at Guy Norris for not only *The Original Soundtrack,* but also 10cc's previous album *Sheet Music*. A small gesture of rebellion that, under the circumstances, I felt needed to be displayed. Dad was furious. He had only wanted some change and the 'I'm in Love' song, after all.

Sheet Music was a better album than *The Original Soundtrack*. It turned out to be their best. It's the one with 'The Wall Street Shuffle' and 'Silly Love' on it. It also boasts the delightful 'Old Wild Men', 'Somewhere in Hollywood' and a typically clever yet silly song called 'Clockwork Creep', which played out as a conversation between a time bomb and the aeroplane it was about to blow up. Needless to say, the plane had an American accent.

I went back for their eponymous debut album. It was the beginning of a trend for me – I have discovered so much great music retrospectively. However, I didn't like the *10cc* album much, despite it including 'Rubber Bullets' and 'The Dean and I', and I hardly played it.

By the time *How Dare You!* arrived in the shops sometime in 1976, 10cc were no longer my favourite band; my ears had started to wander in several other directions and I was enjoying my new role as a disloyal pop flirt. That didn't stop me buying it and trying my best to love it, but it was a mostly disappointing record. They were still making fabulous singles, but their albums had always been a bit hit and miss and *How Dare You!* was no different. It did count 'I'm Mandy, Fly Me' and 'Art for Art's Sake' amongst its ranks though, and it's pretty reasonable to conclude that plenty of bands would kill for a couple of tracks like that on the same album. But what band with any sort of self-respect would make a song like 'I Wanna Rule the World' available for public consumption? 10cc had included some silly songs on their albums in the past but this one was beyond reproach. Set to a jerky tango beat, littered with all the silly voices the band could muster and a repeated refrain that droned on about being the biggest boss in the whole wide world.

There was nothing remotely defendable about this song. I started to question whether or not 10cc and I had a future together.

How Dare you! was to be the last album to feature 10cc's original line up. Shortly after its release Lol Creme and Kevin Godley left the band. They had been developing a new musical instrument called the Gizmo, which was a kind of synthesiser for the guitar, and off they popped to go and make a typically overblown triple album called *Consequences* to showcase it. No one has heard of the Gizmo since.

In hindsight, to abandon 10cc at this point would have been perfect. The band were in tatters, their records had become increasingly inconsistent and some might say that with the departure of Godley and Creme the band had lost its driving force in terms of originality. It would have been a convenient point for me to draw the line.

But 10cc were far from finished. They came back reinforced with four new members (including not one, but two drummers, for Christ's sake!) and a brand new album called *Deceptive Bends*. I bought it, of course. It included a song called 'You've Got A Cold', which, as it turned out, was actually about somebody having a cold. They tried to dress up the fact that they had written a song about somebody having a cold by underpinning it with a rather nice funky rock riff and a cracking guitar solo, but the fact still remains that once you have sung the words 'foreign bodies in yer Kleenex' you are indeed singing a song about bogeys, and no amount of pop camouflaging can save it. It's hard to imagine the point at which this song ever seemed like a good idea. But yet *Deceptive Bends* swaggered around with what just might be their greatest ever song – 'Feel The Benefit (Parts 1, 2 & 3)'. They were doing just enough to keep the flame alive.

They went on the road, and I saw them play at the Hammersmith Odeon – which meant that I also had to buy the resulting live album from that tour, *Live and Let Live*. A couple of the tracks on that album were recorded at the gig I went to. They delivered like milkmen that night, and I thought they were brilliant. I cheered loudly at every song, hoping that somehow I might make a premature recording debut. I've appeared as a cheering and clapping extra on quite a few live albums down the years, but you always remember your first time.

When punk came along I feared for 10cc. How on earth would they survive it? They surely weren't equipped to fight off the likes of Rotten and Strummer. Punk had already claimed the scalps of the prog rock lot and the mighty David Soul – even Showaddywaddy were starting to struggle.

My worries were not unjustified. While punk rock made a nuisance of itself by grabbing the UK pop scene by the scruff of the neck, forcing it to bend over in order to give it a good old rogering, 10cc disappeared. Not up their own backsides (although this had been an accusation that had been levelled at them for most of their career) – this was just a temporary hiatus. They went quiet for a year, no doubt retreating to their country piles to lick their collective wounds. And when 10cc came back, they were in a defiant mood and armed with a cowbell.

'Dreadlock Holiday' was a flimsy slice of white reggae that told the story of a white man being hassled by a black gang whilst on holiday in Jamaica. It played on every preconception of the white man's fear of the Caribbean and employed just about every cliché in the book. (I like the way that 'every cliché in the book' is in fact a cliché.) Here were white middle-class men singing as if they were from the ghetto, accompanied by congas, marimbas, tales of muggings, drug deals and the drinking of coconut-based cocktails. The song's huge hook was the 'I don't like cricket/reggae/Jamaica – I love it' bit where the victim tries to schmooze his way out of trouble.

Thankfully, they managed to stop themselves just short of 'I don't like bananas', but probably only because it didn't scan.

It didn't matter that I wasn't completely satisfied with 'Dreadlock Holiday', I bought it anyway. It didn't sound like a number one record to me at first hearing, but it was a grower and it made it to the top of the charts in the week that 10cc rolled into town to play a couple of gigs at the Wembley Arena.

Fraser and Ray had been willing enough victims, and easily allowed me to persuade them to spend some time with 10cc too. They joined me for the Wembley gig, but the band put in a lacklustre performance that night. They played all the hits and a huge selection from their largely flabby new album *Bloody Tourists,* but it felt as if they couldn't really be arsed, and were doing us all a huge favour by being there at all. Here was a band that was living the dream – playing in front of 8,000 adoring fans, having the number one record in the charts – but they didn't seem to be enjoying it all that much. When they played 'Dreadlock Holiday', in true 10cc tradition they smothered the song in a huge dollop of cheese by ending it with 'We don't like Wembley – we love it!'; however, their lack of enthusiasm on stage indicated that they clearly weren't loving it at all, and it felt dishonest.

Marry this up with all the other things about this band that had begun to irritate the hell out of me: the faux Americana on the early stuff (never, ever call the motorway a 'freeway' when you come from Stockport), the pointless throwaway tracks that littered their albums, their insistence on swapping musical genres, several times, mid-song, and of course their career-long love affair with smart-arsery. I knew, deep down, that the game was up.

I couldn't see a way forward for 10cc and me. We were over. That poster of them on my bedroom wall had long been replaced, but had it still been there, I would have looked them square in the eye and said 'look lads, I'd like to say I'm sorry, it's not you, it's me ... but actually – it is you'.

They never rang; they never wrote, nothing – for over 18 months – not a word. I was free. I was ready for other things by then and 10cc let me get on without interference. But then, in the spring of 1980, the music papers brought news of their forthcoming album, *Look Hear?* and I knew a test of my resolve lay ahead. This is where, I suppose, I bought my first 'loyalty' album. The signs of the loyalty purchase are very easy to spot, but despite the overt nature of these clues, we rarely take heed of them and buy the record anyway.

Buying records was a serious business, and when money is tight, it's not something that can be indulged in with free abandon. The cash had to be saved, the next album purchase had to be carefully planned and thought through, and days leading up to release dates had to be crossed off calendars. This whole build-up process helped to make buying records the joyous occasion it was. When you hand over an empty record sleeve to the guy behind the record shop counter, and he disappears behind the racks and racks of LPs en-route to filling it with the vinyl of your choice – if that moment doesn't fill you with that little twang of excited expectation, you are either buying a record for someone else or making a loyalty purchase. It wasn't so much that I felt trapped by 10cc; no one was holding a gun to my head. I had been free to leave at any time. It just seemed that as a fan, albeit a waning one, I owed it to them to try their latest offering, because as long-term fans of pop groups, we are constantly waiting for that next album, the return to form, the one that is going to make everything all right again.

Unfortunately, *Look Hear?* possessed no such reconciliatory attributes. It was an absolute stinker. There are albums – probably terrible, terrible albums – by artists that I love to bits that I am prepared to state a case for, argue the toss for, and defend till I'm as blue in the face as a very cold Smurf eating a sky sandwich. We make allowances, accept compromises, compose excuses for our favourites, and say things like 'Yeah, it may be a shit album but 'House of the Undead' is the best thing they've done since 'Tarquin's Waistcoat' off the first album'. But with *Look Hear?* I gave up pretending that this record was defendable on any level. I was a willing and submissive partner when I first got into bed with 10cc in 1975. By 1980, I was no longer prepared to sleep on the wet patch.

I don't recall there being a single decent track on side one and I'm not entirely convinced that I ever made it to the end of side two. The sleeve was a shocker too: a tried and tested pop trick, designed to distract the listener away from its dreadful contents. It had the words 'ARE YOU NORMAL?' emblazoned across it in huge block capitals, and as I lay on my bed listening and trying my best to draw something positive from this monstrosity, I contemplated the fact that this record was my eighth 10cc album (which added up to a grand total of ... well, all of them), and conceded that the horrible artwork that I held in my hand may just have had a point.

I tried to figure out why the hell the sleeve also featured a small photograph of a sheep sunbathing on a chaise longue by the sea. On failing to come up with a truly satisfying conclusion, I realised that the important question was not why it was there, but why, oh why, with – let's face it – a frankly over-populated minstralsy of six, did not one member of this band stand up and say 'no sheep, no soft furnishings and definitely no songs about Vietnamese boat people called 'Don't Send We Back'?

And so this time there would be no going back. *Look Hear?* finally marked the end of the road for 10cc and me. They continued to release albums throughout the eighties; I ignored them all and to this day, I have still not heard a single song of theirs released post-*Look Hear?*. This time I was truly liberated.

Looking back retrospectively, I can see the reasons why I loved 10cc so much, yet chose to keep this little part of my pop past under wraps once I grew tired of them. They could write, they could play, their songs were meticulously arranged with multiple layers of instrumentation, and they had immaculate studio craft. They were master knob twiddlers, and their music was very accessible.

The passing years do funny things to your pop sensibilities. On the one hand they make you reflect on the stuff that you used to love and wonder how the hell you ever found that music acceptable in the first place, but then on the other, they mellow you, and the pop that you once rejected for being 'far too commercial' when you were young and trendy and a bit of pop-snob, now seems to be ok and you start to think, 'hmm, a banjo solo – not bad!'.

There are limits to all this mellowing business of course. No one is suddenly going to start finding a space in their lives to rekindle the flames for Peter Shelley's 'Love Me, Love My Dog' or rummage through the back catalogue of Brotherhood of Man. But maybe it was time for me to re-appraise the works of 10cc.

When I did so, I found that I no longer cared that they started their career under the delusion that they were American, and sang those early songs in a vocal style that can only be described in strict musical terms as being a couple of decent-sized gonads short of a scrotum.

I didn't mind that most of their albums were patchy at best – perennial three-star-ers, they were neither terrible nor fantastic, but somewhere in between. I was reconciled to the fact that for every 'The Second Sitting for the Last Supper' there was a 'Film of My Love', for every 'Waterfall', a 'You've Got a Cold' and for every 'Old Wild Men' a 'Hotel'. That was how it was with 10cc – I had learned to live with it once, I could do it again, couldn't I? 10cc were pop's equivalent to that poem 'There Was a Little Girl' by Henry Wadsworth Longfellow – when they were good, they were very, very good, but when they were bad – they sucked a biggun.

In some ways it doesn't really matter that on their albums they committed unfathomable crimes, because their singles still stand up against those of their contemporaries as a body of wonderfully crafted abstracts of pop magnificence that is hard to beat. In particular, 'Life is A Minestrone' is a song that I have never grown tired of and I find it totally acceptable to marvel at the cleverness of its punnery –

I'm leaning on the tower of Pisa,
I had an eyeful of the tower in France,
I'm hanging round the gardens of Babylon

I still don't have the foggiest idea why life is a minestrone or death a cold lasagne, but who cares? I fully accept that they are.

I could draw comparisons between my mellowing of attitude towards 10cc and their own recorded mellowing towards the subject of love. Take their 1974 hit 'Silly Love' – a sneeringly bitter little song, in which they laugh at all the clichéd little things that lovers say and the cute names that they call each other. Wind forward three years and take a listen to how they embrace these very same things on 'The Things We Do For Love'.

And so one day, a few years back, a day when Colin (the bastard) was getting me to hanker after my lost youth once again, I found myself browsing the bargain pages of Amazon.co.uk and there they were – every 10cc album I had ever owned now repackaged on shiny remastered CDs. I hardly had time to blink. At £3.49 a pop, what was there to think about anyway? And before you could say 'old fart for art's sake', I'd bought the lot. Well, not *Look Hear?,* obviously – I do have some self-control – but every album from *10cc* to *Bloody Tourists* was now winging its way to its new home.

When they arrived, and as I cut loose the cardboard packaging, I felt a degree of sheepishness descend upon me, consuming me as 10cc and me were reunited once again. I started justifying this irrational purchase by convincing myself that I had only ever heard these albums on my dilapidated old Bush Music Centre and how fantastic these albums would now sound on my expensive hi-fi, remastered and polished up for the digital age.

So did they sound any better? I have no idea, because I've never played them. I zapped them straight onto my iPod and never looked at them again. Occasionally, when I'm listening on shuffle (not the Wall Street kind), the odd track pops up randomly, but otherwise we are still worlds apart. Or at least I thought we were.

Fast-forward to the back end of 2011 and there it was, hidden away towards the back pages of that month's *Mojo* magazine – hidden away from everyone else that is, but blatantly shining at me like a full moon on a clear night, teasing me, beckoning me, tempting me.

10cc 40th ANNIVERSARY TOUR – APRIL/MAY 2012
Purveyors of the finest in popular music since 1972

I quickly turned the page and pretended that I'd never clapped eyes on it. And then just as quickly, turned back to read it more attentively. It was all there; the logo, the list of hits and most importantly the dates.

I admit, I felt a little pang of excitement and Tsunami-sized wave of nostalgia sweep over me. I started to wonder whether it would be the original line-up with Lol Creme and Kevin Godley – the line-up that I was too late to catch live first time around. That would be worth a look surely, I thought. Would they play all the hits or impose some ghastly new album on me if I should turn up on the night, just like Gilbert O' Sullivan had done a few years previously? I stared at it for a couple of minutes longer and thought long and hard. Then it suddenly hit me – 'Purveyors of the finest in popular music?' Purveyors? Purveyors? What sort of word was that for a pop group to be using? It seemed that 10cc had learned absolutely nothing over the years and that they were just as insufferably pompous as they had ever been.

But even this still didn't completely put me off. I took my very first peek at their website and learned that for this 40th Anniversary Tour only one member of the band, Graham Gouldman, was actually doing it. This was more than just a little bit cheeky and enough to put me off. I wondered if it was even legal for him to go out on tour alone and claim that he was 10cc. I suppose to expect the original line-up would have been too much to ask, but it's quite surprising that not even the Johnny-come-latelys of the post-Godley and Creme era line-up could be prised away from their day-jobs to trot out 'I'm Not in Love' just one more time for old times' sake. More realistically, nay, mathematically, it should really have been billed as 2.5cc 40th Anniversary Tour.

So that was that. That was where my interest in re-kindling our relationship ended. But the sorry fact is that I considered it. I actually considered it. I can't really explain this fleeting moment of full circleness, nor can I defend it. My love for 10cc was certainly s-s-s-silly, and the only excuse I can offer is that this is what happens when a romance depends on clichés and toupees and threepees.

Ziggy Played (Air) Guitar

A teenage boy's spiritual home is his bedroom. His very own isolated domain, hidden away from parental guidance and sensible telly. This is where it all happens – where he serves his apprenticeship – although an apprenticeship in *what* remains unclear.

As far as fixtures and fittings went, my bedroom was a pretty sparse affair. Minimalist, they might call it today. A single bed, a single wardrobe and my Bush Music Centre. That was about it. Just like my ever-expanding hair, the colour scheme was mainly orange. Orange bedspread (the exotica of the duvet – or continental quilt as they were more grandly known in the early days, had not yet made its way over the threshold of our house), wallpaper and curtains that had a kind of orange and brown swirly pattern going on, and the floor was covered in an orange shag pile carpet. It was all very orange.

My football programmes lived under the bed – piled up high to form a barrier that denied the very existence of the things hidden behind it – those once essential things that I no longer wanted to be associated with, like my *Beezer* Annuals (1970 & 1971) and my Scooby-Doo pyjama case and slippers.

My music centre sat on a fake teak hi-fi stand that also housed my growing collection of LPs and singles. It was already starting to make me anxious that I didn't have enough albums yet to fill the space provided, and because of this, they sat there at an untidy angle. I needed to fill that void so they could stand upright and proud. Not packed in too tight mind, they had to be loose enough that they could be flicked through comfortably and admired by any visitors to my bedroom.

The whole record-collecting thing was starting to become an obsession. Not only did these pieces of plastic have to sound good, but they had to look good too. I began to worry about scratches and blemishes and concerned myself unnecessarily about those untidy angles and how the way the records were sitting might induce unsightly bends and creases in the sleeves. I had one of those Ronco record-cleaning tools that looked a bit like a shoe-polishing brush and would collect all the dust from the record as I placed it gently on the spinning vinyl. I would clean a record before playing it; when it had finished playing, I'd clean it again before I put the record back into its sleeve. I even cleaned records that I had no intention of playing, just because I hadn't cleaned them for a while.

I started buying PVC sleeves for my albums in an attempt to keep their covers in tip-top condition and filed them in alphabetical order of artist. As the collection grew and I found myself owning more than one album by certain artists, they would be filed chronologically within artist.

I fretted pitifully as to whether I should be filing my 10cc albums under '10', 'C' or 'T'. I think I may have had some sort of embryonic form of OCD as far as my record collection was concerned, and looking back on it now, I'm not totally convinced that this is how a teenage pop fan was supposed to behave. This was the 1970s after all wasn't it? Weren't these supposed to be my renegade years? So where was my free love and sexual revolution? Where were my drugs? Where was my free abandon attitude from those anything-goes wildness years? Not in my bedroom, that's for sure.

I blame this whole neat and tidiness phase that briefly swept its way through my bedroom years on those horrible little label-making tools that I think were called Dymos. They were readily available to buy or nick from W.H. Smiths at Gants Hill on any Saturday morning you liked. These things, in which you rotated the disc to point at your chosen letter, and then pressed the handle hard to impregnate that letter onto a hard, sticky coloured label, were considered in 1970s label-making circles as being pretty high-tech. This resulted in an epidemic of gratuitous label making amongst the young and we would stick them on anything that you could stick a label to. But the main flaw with this tool was that there was no going back if you made a mistake. For many years, the two drawers in my wardrobe were labelled up 'PANTS' and 'T-SHITS'. And so it seemed while the rest of the world was delighting in the best the seventies had to offer, I was in my bedroom devising filing systems for my records and pants, blissfully unaware that I was turning into Emily Bishop's more sensible sister.

But it was in that bedroom that I really started to cut my teeth as a pop fan, and I discovered some great music during this mid-seventies period. Ray introduced me to his own personal favourite, David Bowie. *The Rise and Fall of Ziggy Stardust and the Spiders from Mars* was the first slice of Bowie that I acquainted myself with. I was totally enamoured by the characters that Bowie transforms himself into on that album – Ziggy, Lady Stardust, The Starman, and I squawked along like a pink monkey bird accordingly. The song 'Five Years' was probably the first in which I really started to take notice of lyrics and be charmed by them. I didn't have a clue what Bowie was going on about in that song, but it sounded really important.

The album was already three years old by the time I got to it, but even now, firmly in its middle-aged years, it still sounds as fresh to me today as it did back then. It was the first album where I loved every track. The sound of Bowie's warm acoustic guitar passages underpinning the rough, yet subtle riffing of Mick Ronson's electric worked perfectly, complementing songs that had more hooks than a coach full of pirates on their way to a prosthetic hand exhibition. From that kick and snare drum fade-in intro of 'Five Years', to the violins that whisper out that final chord on the closing track 'Rock'n'Roll Suicide', Bowie didn't waste a single second of *Ziggy* – the whole album hung together beautifully and I played it relentlessly. It remains one of my favourite albums of all time.

By the time I discovered Bowie, Ziggy was no more and he was shuffling around the stage under the guise of 'The Thin White Duke' in support of his latest album *Station to Station*. The Ziggy years had been Bowie's purple patch in which he'd delivered albums either side of *Ziggy Stardust* – *Hunky Dory* (before) and *Aladdin Sane* (after) – that add up to a trio of records on the bounce, that you would be hard-pressed to find equalled in pop. The next batch of Bowie songs that appeared on the album *Diamond Dogs*, whilst not quite reaching the glories of those three beauties, can shake its fist fairly vigorously at a lot of other records released in 1974.

I liked David Bowie, not to the point where I needed to paint bolts of lightning across my face in my mum's make up, but enough to buy most of the records he made during the seventies. Bowie broke the rules, reinvented them, and then broke them again just for the hell of it. I admire that. No matter how successful he became, he never reduced himself to 'winning formula'-based pop. He was a risk taker – forever striving forward with something new, changing it around, mixing it up, giving his fans something different each time and forcing them to fall in love with him all over again. Sometimes it worked, sometimes it didn't, but that's what happens when you don't play it safe. I liked the way he could change the way his voice sounded to suit the style of song he was singing, yet always managed to still sound like David Bowie: the deadpan, depressive delivery of 'Five Years', the soulful strains of 'Young Americans' and the shouty exuberance of 'Hang on to Yourself'.

I liked Bowie the man too. He seemed like a good egg. I find it much easier to like the work of a pop star if I like them as a person too. I rarely make an exception to this rule. I dismiss the work of Eric Clapton purely on the basis of it.

Bowie meant so much to so many people for so many different reasons. Even for a casual fan like me, it was a huge shock and very sad when he died. It felt very personal because Bowie belonged to the kids of the seventies and it felt like a little bit of our youth had died with him.

To be honest, I had rarely troubled his catalogue after the *Let's Dance* album in 1983, but I did catch up with him twenty years later when I popped along to see him play Wembley Arena on the *A Reality* tour in 2003. During that gig he played almost everything you could ever wish for from his heady seventies peak, but from our vantage point overlooking the arena, it was cruel to watch his announcement of 'this is one off the new album' greeted as a cue for hundreds of full-bladdered rock fans to scamper out like a pack of turbo-charged Jack Russells eager to relieve themselves against the nearest lamp post.

Back in the day, it was considered cool to be a David Bowie fan, even if it meant you had to wear black lipstick and knee-length leg warmers. Bowie's hardcore fans – 'The Ziganomatrists' (if you like) – can be a difficult bunch to please, though. Their cool aloofness about his work dominates, and they would find it hard to nominate *Ziggy* as their favourite album – it's far too mainstream. They would probably plump for something a little more obscure, like *Low* or *"Heroes"*, simply because these albums are less-accessible beasts. They're a funny lot.

Take my friend Colin (not the bastard, or the one that could turn his eyelids inside out, but another one), for instance. He was into David Bowie when he was still plain old David Jones, but came away from that gig at the Wembley Arena, having just witnessed an immaculate Bowie roll back the years effortlessly for the best part of three hours, complaining that he was sick to death of seeing his hero play 'Life on Mars?' and demanding to know why didn't he play anything off *Tin Machine II*?

I mentioned that it was probably because that album was unlistenable tosh and only about three people owned it. As a member of that elite trio, this reasoning didn't seem to cut much ice with him. He just shook his head, took an agitated bite from his home-time hot dog and angrily spat out some chewed up sausage and bread as he grumbled something about Bowie's refusal to ever play 'Warszawa' (a six-and-a-half-minute instrumental from *Low*).

So that's your Ziganomatrist for you. Less snobbish are the fans of Stevie Wonder. Wonder has failed to produce anything of any substance since the early eighties. So dire are his albums since *Hotter Than July* that Stevie's fans are only too happy to hear him trot out all the hits whenever he plays live these days.

Again, Ray was the catalyst for my interest in Stevie Wonder. He got the *Songs in the Key of Life* album towards the back end of 1976. I'd never seen an LP so elaborately packaged. A double album with a lavish LP-sized lyric book, and as if two records weren't enough, there was a bonus EP with four extra tracks included too. Even before I heard a note of this record I was drawn in.

Reserved usually for contract-fulfilling obligations such as live albums or greatest hits compilations, the double album is a much-maligned beast. These days, few artists are brave enough to chance their arm at delivering the CD equivalent of four sides of vinyl crammed full of bone fide studio material. But back in the over-blown seventies, when unnecessary excesses were second nature, the double album was a big deal. The format now seems like a bit of a dinosaur, but it brought us many a major artistic statement and stamped its feet demanding to be taken seriously. Unfortunately, few could be, and the format became a dumping ground for a core of a few good songs padded out with a whole bunch of filler tracks. But pop history tells us that there are a handful of extraordinary double albums that can be truly celebrated – The Beatles' *White Album, Exile on Main Street, London Calling, Tommy, Quadrophenia, Goodbye Yellow Brick Road, Blonde on Blonde* (pop's very first double album) and, without question, Stevie Wonder's masterwork, *Songs in the Key of Life.*

It took me a while to fully appreciate the brilliance of this twenty-one-song marathon. Half of the problem was the length of the thing. Clocking in at the best part of an hour and three-quarters, and factoring in loo breaks, snack attacks and several journeys from listening position to record player just to flip over its four sides and additional EP, *Songs in the Key of Life* was an exhausting experience, and one for which time needed to be set aside. At first I didn't have the patience for it, but eventually I grew to love it.

Wonder seems to have an instinctive ear for beautiful melody that could only come from someone that writes primarily on the piano, and this album is chock-a-block with flawlessly concise melodies, sung with a voice that explores so many beautiful nooks and untraditional crannies that it makes you feel jubilant to discover that they even exist. Head-jerking rhythms too – Wonder plays drums on most of these tracks, and he nails down beats so fluently that you could almost mistake what he does for sloppiness, but his rhythms get right under you to the point that they carry you along with what feels like effortless exertion.

The album sprawls across a number of musical genres with a collection funky jams, quirky pop songs, soulful ballads and densely orchestrated soul. If I've got a complaint, then it would probably be that a few of the tracks are a little over-blown. I'm not sure that we really needed almost seven minutes of 'Isn't She Lovely' or the classroom chanting history lesson that stretches 'Black Man' to eight and a half minutes, but this doesn't really detract from the fact that if there's another collection of songs that satisfies every mood, then I've yet to hear it. When I used to play new albums, it seemed important at the time to pick a favourite track and run with it for a bit, and usually this wasn't too hard a task, but with this album, it's impossible. It reflects so many different emotions that it just depends on how I'm feeling at the time. As soon as I'd worked out that Stevie wasn't actually singing 'baking Philip all over', on 'Sir Duke', I was ready to commit to it as my happy song forever. This is the one that makes me bounce and has been known to induce a skip in my step. Anyone that listens to this song and doesn't immediately feel the need to blow hard into an air-trombone either has no arms, or a bad case of asthma. Stevie actually sings 'you can feel it all over', and with that one line, summed up exactly how this humongous album touched me. So yes, yes, Stevie I can, and I'd be inclined to check for a pulse of anyone that can't.

But despite such fondness for *Songs in the Key of Life*, I didn't pursue Stevie much further – well not until many years later anyway. Stevie's next album was also a double, the largely instrumental *Journey Through The Secret Life of Plants* – the secret being, it had no good songs on it. *Hotter Than July* had some fleetingly brilliant moments, but after that I promptly forgot about Stevie Wonder. In 1984, he called to say he loved me – I slammed the phone down in disgust.

I came back to *Songs in the Key of Life* some years later when, in an inspirational moment of present buying, my parents bought me the album on CD for Christmas. Having not touched the album for a decade or two, it was like a breath of fresh air to hear it again and be reminded why I liked it so much in the first place. I felt a pang of guilt, and confessed to myself that I had let Stevie go too easily. I slammed myself back into reverse and promptly bought two of his earlier albums *Innervisions* and *Talking Book* – both joyously magnificent. I really should have got to know them sooner.

In the mid-seventies there were three musical formats: records, cassette tapes and 8-track cartridges. I still don't really know what an 8-track cartridge is. I mean, I know what one looks like (a big fat cassette), but I have no idea how they worked or how you played one. I only ever knew one person that owned a machine that played them – Neil, my mum's hairdresser. He drove a Mark III Cortina Estate and hanging clumsily out of the centre console was the monstrosity that was the 8-track cartridge player. He would come to our house and wake me up every Saturday morning with his incessant doorbell ringing. I once asked my mum why she had to have her hair cut every week, when I only needed a haircut on an annual basis, and she looked at my ginger mop, paused for a moment and said 'yes, exactly'.

Neil the hairdresser was what I imagined to be 'a bit of a boy'. He would clip-clop his way into our kitchen in his platform boots, and demand that the kettle was put on before any hair styling was going to take place. He also had certain bow-leggedness about his swagger, which I put down to a combination of the tightness of his jeans and those platform boots. Every week, without fail, he would wink at me and make the sort of clicking sound out of the side of his mouth that I imagined would be a handy skill to have if you regularly needed to round up a herd of goats. 'Alright Tone, 'ow's yer lady luck,' he'd say. I was never really sure whether he was asking if I had been lucky, or if I'd had any luck with the ladies, so I just shrugged my shoulders teenage fashion and walked off, bemused. He stank of Hai Karate, had shoulder-length hair with a centre parting, and a perfectly groomed drop moustache. He dressed exactly how you would expect a man with a perfectly groomed drop moustache in the seventies to dress – as if hairdressing was just a cover-up for his real job as a DJ at Tiffany's. He got on my tits and I assumed all 8-track cartridge owners were like Neil.

So for us teenagers, the 8-track was never a desirable medium for music. However, cassette tapes very much were. Not so much as an alternative to records – more as a supplement.

These days there is a huge fuss made about sharing music via the Internet. I don't understand this at all. Isn't sharing the way that kids have always discovered pop? Unless you turned up at school first thing in the morning with an LP tucked under an armpit, to pass on to friends, you were more or less treated as an outcast. 'Both a borrower and a lender be' was the code of conduct, although in these early stages I was much more of a borrower. For reasons that somehow eluded me at the time, there didn't seem to be a queue of people clamouring anxiously to get their hands on my Sparks and 10cc albums.

But this was how we got to hear a whole range of pop that we couldn't afford to buy. This was our Spotify or Youtube. More primitive, a little more labour-intensive, but the outcome was just the same. Before Spotify, I will admit to illegally downloading my fair share of music from the Internet as a way of sampling music that I hadn't really made up my mind up about yet. But the consequence was, if I found something that I really liked I would go out and buy the album. Having a song in digital form is not sufficient as far as I'm concerned. I have to have something that I can hold and look at and a sleeve that I can refer back to. So rather than stealing music, I consider the downloading of music more as auditioning it. It can't be considered part of your collection unless you can actually pick it up and put it on your shelf with all your other albums (filed in strict alpha/chronological order, of course).

And I employed exactly the same thinking to borrowing music in the seventies. So yes, we would swap albums with each other, slap them on to a cassette and hand them back. I would then listen to them and if I liked an album enough I would go out and get the real thing. But despite this, record companies were just as paranoid back then as they are today, and packets of blank cassettes would come with a silhouetted skull and crossbones logo on them with the warning: 'Home taping is killing music – and it's illegal.' It was, of course, impossible to police and duly ignored.

One enormous avenue that blank cassettes did open up was the world of the homemade compilation tape. This was a hugely entertaining way of whiling away several hours alone – meticulously planning running orders, sitting on the floor surrounded by a pile of records. This labour-intensive way of creating the 'super album' was how we did it while we waited for the iPod playlist to be invented. The great thing about cassettes was the ability to erase and re-record. So if a couple of tracks didn't quite sit right next to each other you could just change them and do it all over again. And then, once I had the perfect mix, I could waste another hour, trying to come up with that killer title for my perfect album. This, I thought, was a little insight into the real world of pop, where I imagined proper bands sitting around the mixing desk in the studio, throwing ideas around at each other. The names I came up with for the first few compilations tended to be based roughly on the music contained within – *Rock'n'Roll Doldrums, Bouncy Songs Volume 3, Sunny Day Music*. I soon grew tired of this sensible naming convention and silliness ensued – *The Fart That I Breathe, Roll Over John Motson, It's Only Cheese on Toast (but I like it), Shirley Bassey's Bosoms* and so forth.

Proper albums could also be bought on cassette. These, in my opinion, legitimately counted towards your collection total. There was a wave of support for them but generally one was either firmly in the record or cassette camp. For me there was no contest.

Pre-recorded cassettes were small and more portable than records, but lacked the majesty of cover art like the full twelve-inch sleeve. There were rarely lyric sheets or poster inserts that you sometimes got with records, just a tiny little cardboard insert with the sleeve on the front and a track listing on the back. This was a huge price to pay for handiness by my reckoning. Cassettes also couldn't hold a candle to records in terms of sound reproduction either. Worse than the sound quality, pre-recorded cassettes often messed around with the running order of albums. Tracks would be shifted around on a pre-recorded cassette to make both sides of the tape of equal length, so you wouldn't have to fast-forward the tape for ages before turning it over. This was totally unacceptable to me and I would often browse the cassette versions of albums that I was familiar with to check which tracks had been switched out of order, purely so I could get all uppity about it. Tracks were placed in the order they appeared on the record for a reason. That was how they flowed best. You can't muck around with stuff like that. Records are not there to be convenient – that's not what they're for. Imagine for a second what would happen if *Who's Next* didn't start with 'Baba O'Riley' and it showed up as track three on side two – yes, all hell would break loose. You can stop imagining it now, perish the thought and go and get yourself a tissue. Whatever next, 'The End' segueing into 'Octopus's Garden' on *Abbey Road*?

And another thing: cassettes were unreliable. With records you knew how to ruin them. We knew that if we played them when they were full of dust or with a fluffy stylus, they were going to crackle for evermore. We knew that jumping around the bedroom practicing a Pete Townshend windmill power chord was going to make the records jump the second your slippers hit the shag pile. But with cassettes I never knew when the cassette deck on my music centre was going to get a bit peckish and start eating its way through my tapes. There were no warning signs. You see, tape, when it's been played a few times, stretches, and starts to speed up and slow down and before you know it, you have reams of tangled magnetic brown spaghetti spewing out all over the shop.

Then the long-winded rescue operation would take place. The first stage was to gently free the tape that was trapped in the tape heads of the machine. This was no mean feat in itself, and involved prising the tape heads open with one hand while gingerly trying to wiggle the tape free with the other, hoping that it wouldn't snap. If stage one of the resuscitation process resulted in success, I could then wave goodbye to the next couple of hours, as I sat on the bed with a huge pile of twisted tape in my lap, painstakingly untwisting it, smoothing it out and rehousing the whole sorry mess back inside the cassette by twiddling a pencil through one of its spools. Have you any idea how much tape there is inside a C90? Well I have (I looked it up), and apparently it's 132 metres (that's 433 feet in seventies speak) and that equates to a lot of pencil twiddling.

It wasn't always possible to untwist all the displaced tape. On one such occasion, a few years later, I benefitted from an episode in which my car cassette player had a little chew on one of my compilation tapes (*The Sacred Biscuits of Steve McQueen*). I ejected the tape as soon as it started going funny and rewound the twisted tape back into the cassette with my finger. I really should have got my passenger to do this for me but anyway, the result was that the bit that was still twisted made the guitar riff from 'Rebel Rebel' on side one, form a psychedelic sounding backwards guitar intro for 'Rain' by The Beatles on side two. It was perfect, and fitted like it was supposed to have been there all along.

Successes such as this were rare; Fraser came up with a novel idea for tapes that didn't make it through the rescue operation. We would undo all the tiny screws, prise open the cassette and take the tape out on its spool to his garden. By holding onto one end of the tape between thumb and forefinger and hurling the spool as hard as we could, the unravelling tape made a fantastic streamer that would stretch across three or four neighbours' gardens. I'm not sure how the neighbours felt about this though – they never said.

But I will say this as the final word on cassettes. It was via a cassette that was lent to me, sometime towards the end of the summer of 1975, that I discovered Queen. The tape had The Who's *Meaty, Beaty, Big & Bouncy* on one side and *Queen II* on the other. This was supposed to be my little taster intro into the world of The Who and Queen. The lad that lent me it was so precious about lending his records that he just didn't. He would record the albums that I wanted to hear on to a tape and lend me that. This was both mean and completely rubbish as I had no means of recording tape-to-tape.

Nevertheless, I got on brilliantly with them both and, in the case of

Queen, the timing of this introduction couldn't have been better. A few months later, Queen would release what I would consider to be the greatest single of all time – 'Bohemian Rhapsody'.

Of course for those in the know, Queen's meteoric rise from college rock favourites to the biggest band on the planet came as no surprise. Queen had famously come to the attention of pop's glitterati a couple of years earlier, when as the support band for Mott the Hoople, they had stolen their thunder. But even with this knowledge and a thumbs-up for their previous hits 'Seven Seas of Rhye' and 'Killer Queen', nothing could have prepared us for what Queen were about to unleash on the world.

I really feel that I should know exactly where I was and what I was doing when I heard Bohemian Rhapsody for the very first time, but the truth is, I can't remember. What I can remember is half the class crowding around a transistor radio on several Tuesday lunchtimes in December 1975, and us all tossing our hair about in unison during the heavy bit as we communally celebrated 'Bo Rap' staying at number one in the charts for yet another week. We broke up for Christmas and it was still there in top spot when we came back in the New Year.

'Bohemian Rhapsody' is just one of those songs that, if you're lucky enough, will arrive when you're young and impressionable enough to be astounded by it. We'd never heard anything quite like it before and there certainly hasn't been anything since. It was our 'Strawberry Fields Forever'.

Sometimes, if I think too hard about it, I can mesmerise myself with the genius of some of our greatest songwriters. I wonder how the hell they can possibly plan all this great weirdness in their minds and actually believe that it's going to work. Take the Who's rock opera *Tommy* for instance: a young boy's pilot father is presumed dead in a wartime air raid. His mother takes up with a new man, they are having sex and suddenly daddy, who actually isn't in the slightest bit dead at all, comes home and catches them at it. New man coshes dad over the head and kills him properly this time. Young boy witnesses it, and goes deaf, dumb and blind as a result. Mother and boyfriend try to get him cured but nothing works. He gets sexually abused by his uncle and physically abused by his bullying cousin. He becomes pinball champion of the world, gets pushed through a mirror and miraculously gets his eyesight, hearing and speech back. He opens a holiday camp and is accepted as the new messiah. Everyone shouts 'hoorah!'.

Now I can't legislate for whatever drugs Pete Townshend was taking at the time when he formulated that idea, but something must have given him an inkling that this highly unlikely tale was a winner. The mind boggles at the thought of Keith Moon's reaction when Townshend turned up at the studio to explain the story of their new album to the rest of the band; it must have been a similar situation when Freddie Mercury first played 'Bo Rap' to the other members of Queen and famously announced '… and yes darlings, this is where the opera bit comes in.'

Now if a mere mortal suggested that the band record a six-minute song that combined an a cappella section, a slick piano ballad, a heavy rock interlude, 180 vocal tracks, a mini aria and a gong, and put it out as a single, you would think he would be laughed out of the studio as if he was Dennis Thatcher riding a unicycle. But Freddie had the vision of what this song was supposed to sound like, and the results were breathtaking. I loved the way he caressed the piano keys in the video for the song. Bong-bong-bong-bing-bong – crossing over his hands, his fingers thick with black nail polish as he made his way up to the higher bings and bongs. It annoys me when people label Freddie simply as a great showman. He was that of course, but he was also a very fine singer, musician and an excellent songwriter.

I'd prepared myself well for the oncoming coronation of Queen as the champions of the world. I could claim to have been a fan before 'Bohemian Rhapsody' etched its willowy melodies into the brains of every milkman, barrister and schoolboy in the country – but only by a week or two. After taking a shine to *Queen II* from that cassette, I brought myself up to date and bought the two Queen albums that bookended it – *Queen* and *Sheer Heart Attack*. Neither were quite as good as *Queen II*, but all three were brash and purposeful and full of the wonders of their own limitless possibilities – a mix of pop and pomp, with a large dollop of hard rock and high camp thrown in just for the hell of it.

When 'Bohemian Rhapsody' hit the number one spot I celebrated as if I'd just got an A in physics, which was actually a more unlikely scenario than a song with the words 'Scaramouche' and 'Bismillah' in its lyrics being top of the charts. 'Bo Rap' as a lead-off single had done its job of whetting the appetite of a nation, and I became hugely excited about the imminent arrival of the main course – Queen's next album *A Night at the Opera*. As it turned out, this six-minute epic merely hinted at how the band could lay themselves open to experiment with all sorts of musical genres and influences. Pop, rock, music hall, opera, folk – all make their mark on *A Night at The Opera*, and, to be honest, at first I didn't get it. I was disappointed with the album when it first came out and it wasn't until later that I realised what a brilliant record it was.

There was far too much messing about, if you asked me. It was tracks like the vaudeville pastiches 'Lazing on a Sunday Afternoon' and 'Seaside Rendezvous' that I objected to the most. Both of these songs owed far more to Noel Coward than they ever did to Chuck Berry. It just wasn't rock'n'roll, and I didn't like it.

But there was plenty on *A Night at the Opera* to enjoy. The bitter

'Death on Two Legs' that oozed nastiness, the extravagant vocal gymnastics of 'The Prophet Song' and the folksy '39' became instant favourites. The album was definitely a grower and I even got to like the silliness of 'Seaside Rendezvous' after a while. But the thing that really appeals to me on this album is not necessarily song-specific, its more the whole Queen sound, the way the voices of Freddie Mercury, Brian May and Roger Taylor blend together so perfectly on almost every track.

I lost interest in Queen after this album. The follow up, *A Day at the Races,* was hugely disappointing and my brief fling with Queen was more or less over. I did dip back in once or twice, and saw them live on the *News of the World* tour. They were, of course, fantastic live, but on record I never felt there was any sort of connection between us. I think that maybe they lacked soul at the heart of their songwriting, and although it was fine to admire these songs for what they were, it was hard to form an emotional attachment to them. Queen were mostly surface gloss with little inner feeling – I never felt their writing was specifically directed at anything that was relevant to me.

I was sad when Freddie died in 1991 and even though I hadn't been a fan for many years, I thought about going to the tribute concert held at Wembley Stadium the following year, but in the end decided against it. I would have felt a fraud amongst all the other candle burners – as if I had no right to be there, and as I watched the thing on TV, I knew I'd made the right decision. Watching the likes of Axl Rose, Paul Young and Liza Minnelli (for fuck's sake), limping their way through Freddie's finest moments was not pleasant. The same goes for the ridiculous *We Will Rock You* West End musical and, for that matter, the reincarnation of half of Queen with Bad Company vocalist Paul Rodgers, which, to me, is akin to the moment they replaced Bruce Forsyth on *The Generation Game* with Larry Grayson. The point being, that Freddie defined Queen, and without his vocals and stage presence, who the hell is interested? We wouldn't accept The Rolling Stones without Mick Jagger, would we?

That's not to say that the other members of Queen were inconsequential – far from it. They all contributed to the Queen sound and were fine musicians. Roger Taylor, the drummer, was the first instrumentalist who inspired me to play music. His playing, especially on their first album *Queen I* (as we called it), was flamboyantly impressive. It was the drum solo interlude in 'Keep Yourself Alive' that made me suddenly sit up and point to the record spinning round in front of me and yelp in a moment of self-realisation 'Now, that's what I wanna do!'. I would listen closely to what he was doing, and make mental notes, and then play along with the record, trying desperately hard to replicate his more basic rhythms on my thighs with the palms of my hands.

And then there were the fills. Roger Taylor performed some beauties. These were too complex for thigh-slapping, and for these I gripped imaginary drumsticks and, with a few flicks of the wrist, worked my way around my incredibly expansive imaginary drum kit in a semi-circular direction, air-drumming my way through the trickiest of his drum fills.

It's alright for us wannabe drummers and guitarists; strapping on an air guitar and miming extravagantly to pop is almost as second nature to us as pulling on a pair of familiar pants. But what about those would-be keyboard players? It's very hard to look cool playing air keyboards, and difficult to distinguish it from nervous typing. As fabulous as Stevie Wonder is, it would be stretching the boundaries a bit to say that he looks cool when he's playing. So who were the other role models available for those whose instrument of choice was the keys? Tony Banks of Genesis? Rick Wakeman out of Yes? They didn't exactly ooze charisma and looked so serious as they glumly sat behind their mountainous banks of kit. And in the case of Banks (Tony, not mountainous), we are possibly talking about the dullest man in rock.

There was Elton John I suppose. He always seemed to be having quite a nice time – well, when he wasn't singing songs about his friends dying, he did. The trouble with Elton was that his slow songs were his best. When he rocked it up, it all felt a little unconvincing. Take 'Saturday Night's Alright for Fighting', for example – it's all very well prancing about on top of a piano, but nobody is really going to believe that a stumpy little bloke in a spangly top and pink glasses is up for a ruck, are they?

A keyboard player can't satisfactorily pose and pout in the way that a guitarist can. He can't drag his piano with him on to those extensions of stage that reach out well into row M of the stalls, rest his foot on a fold back, and wink knowingly at the adoring chicks below. He can't pull those faces of excruciating pain that a guitarist is at liberty to pull when he bends a note so high that it comes down with Gerry Garcia on it. Keyboard heroes were a little thin on the ground in the seventies (although you couldn't move for the blighters in the eighties), and I'm convinced that this is the reason that there were never any school bands that could boast a keyboard player. What was in it for them?

The behind-closed-doors miming to records in front of the mirror was one of the worst-kept secrets of the teenager's bedroom. Everybody did it, everybody knew that everybody else did it, but no one would ever admit to doing it. A bit like masturbation, but with better facial expressions. I did it. Sometimes several times a week, I'll admit. I considered it to be training for what was certain to be my future career. You had to be prepared, didn't you? Put in the hours. I mean you wouldn't want to turn up at the *Top of the Pops* studios to record a performance of your latest chart-topper in front of all the gawping shuffle-dancers, only to be ridiculed by David 'Diddy' Hamilton afterwards for not being able to mime properly.

I didn't have any specific role cast in stone yet; it depended on the record I was miming to – sometimes I was the guitarist, sometimes the drummer, and quite often the bass player. And having a hairstyle that could be best described as an unusual hybrid – part Mungo Jerry, part Barry Sheen – meant that I didn't own a hairbrush to use as a microphone, so I was never the stand-alone singer. Playing air bass was fun. I liked the way I could look cool and standoffish playing the bass, with my arm half-cocked and up high and my fingers walking quickly against my rib cage, jolting my neck back and forth as I mouthed the lyrics at my pouty reflection. Sometimes there would be a nonchalant sideways glance – a smile, or maybe an approving nod at the soloing of my imaginary lead guitarist beside me.

Sometimes things could get more extravagant with the introduction of props. Occasionally my usually unemployed tennis racquet would double up as a guitar – its handle flowered with my fingers, as I contorted them into what I imagined to be legitimate chord shapes. And my bed made a perfect drum riser for me to jump off and attempt to slide across the stage on my knees whilst the tennis racquet was gripped firmly to my lap. However, the perfect execution of this traditional rock move only ever worked in my head. In reality, the orange shag pile didn't lend itself well to being a stage or to the sliding, and I would usually end up flat on my face.

Whilst lost in this fantasy world with the music up loud, I could never hear my mum's footsteps coming up the stairs and inevitably, and to my utmost embarrassment, I was caught in the act on several occasions. When this happened, I would quickly drop my pose and disguise my shame by examining the gut meshing of the tennis racquet as if I was counting the holes, and for the want of something better to do, coolly run my fingers through my centre parting. I don't know why I did that – I didn't even have a centre parting.

I don't suppose I was the only teenager to be caught doing embarrassing things in the bedroom. In fact, I know I wasn't. Ray once told us that he had been hiding under the bed when his brother came into the bedroom they shared, stripped down to his pants, and proceeded to carry out a series of Kung Fu moves in front of the mirror. This was at a time when Kung Fu was the biggest teenage craze to hit the country since … well, the last really big teenage craze. Ray remained silent in his hidey-hole throughout the whole charade, stifling his laughter, probably with his brother's discarded socks. We wet ourselves laughing at this story when Ray re-told it at school the next day, each of us knowing that we all had our own guilty bedroom secrets, and without ever questioning him on what the hell he was doing hiding under the bed in the first place.

Listening to pop music is the second most pleasurable activity a teenager can carry out in a bedroom and, all in all, I suppose I spent an unhealthy amount of time alone in that room. But, then again, with pop you are never truly alone, are you? But away from that bedroom, on a casual walk to school, a face from the past was about to turn my world on its head and things would never be quite the same again.

Here Comes the Sun

I remember it like it was yesterday. It was the spring of 1976, and the weather had just started to warm up, easing us gently into what was going to be the hottest summer of our lives.

You probably don't remember David Freed from the 'Waterloo Sunset' chapter, but he was the kid that caused havoc at my sixth birthday party and demanded that my mum serve him Ribena because orange squash made him do funny-coloured poos, or something equally precocious. Dave, as he was now known, also went to Beal, but being in the year above, didn't associate himself with the likes of me and we weren't really friends anymore. Our acknowledgement of each other these days was generally limited to the occasional nod in the corridor on the way to our respective lessons. But then he started turning up at Ilford football matches and we began to talk. I would occasionally catch up with him at the drinks machine during break time at school; no doubt topping up his Ribena levels, although I never bothered to check.

He still lived a few doors down the road from me and we would sometimes bump into each other on our way to school. This became more and more of a regular occurrence, and eventually I found myself knocking for him every morning. We had music and football in common, and they were our main talking points on the daily journey.

He was a very intelligent boy – what we might refer to today as a 'straight A student'. But, as is so often the case, his extreme intelligence was accompanied by a certain eccentricity that tiptoed its way around the edge of lunacy. He would often come up with random statements that seemed to come from out of nowhere. A recurring theme to these was an announcement of abstinence of one kind or another. He would speak half-completed sentences that would be punctuated by lots of 'mmmm's. So I would question him on what the hell the humming was about, which of course was the reaction that he wanted.

'I've given up saying fuck.'

'Oh, ok,' I would respond.

'Or any derivative of the word fuck,' he would further qualify. This abstinence would usually only last a few days, although he once gave up using the word 'penguin' for three months, but that didn't leave nearly as many holes in his sentences. On another occasion, he declared that he was giving up eating anything that was yellow. I said 'Bananas, Lemons ... chips?' He paused for thought for a moment and came back with 'chips are brown'.

But the one thing that he did more often than giving things up was singing out loud. Just one line from a song, as we walked along. He would never go any further than the tease of the one line that he wanted to sing.

And that's when it all happened.

'Here comes the sun, do, do, do, do' – over and over and over again, relentlessly. 'It's The Beatles,' he said, anticipating my next question. He then started waxing lyrical about a pair of double albums that his dad had brought home some time ago, one of which contained the song that he had been singing out loud. He spoke of them so warmly, in a way that I had never heard him speak before – it was if someone had flipped a magic switch in him and he'd suddenly taken that return flight home from Strangeville. On the basis of this, I asked to borrow them. The two albums in question were what were known as the 'Red' and 'Blue' albums, but officially called *The Beatles 1962-66* and *The Beatles 1967-70*, respectively.

These two compilation albums contained every single The Beatles ever made, plus a number of key album tracks. They still are, just as they were then, your ultimate Beatles starter packs. Pawing over the track list on these albums, I knew I was a little familiar with some of these songs. Perhaps I had even owned some of them as part of that record collection that I had as a kid. I certainly knew 'Yellow Submarine' and 'She Loves You', but I just hadn't realised they were by The Beatles.

I started with the Blue album. It seemed like a logical choice. That was the one with The Beatles looking all hairy on the cover. It looked more modern and I suppose that's because it was. The first track, 'Strawberry Fields Forever', hit me like a sledgehammer and filled my room with colour – there was so much going on, it was hard to take it all in. I was transfixed by the word play in the lyrics sung by a lone nasal voice and the unfamiliarity of the instrumentation that splintered from speaker to speaker all around me. The verse that really hooked me was that one that makes no sense at all:

Always, no sometimes, think it's me,
But you know I know when it's a dream,
I think a no, I mean, a yes, but it's all wrong
That is, I think I disagree.

Had I been an ancient Greek I might have yelled 'Eureka!' at this point. Zip me forward three or four decades and I would probably have typed 'OMG!' onto my Facebook page. In the mid-seventies, there was nowhere to type 'FMS!' but this was most definitely a life-changing, 'fuck-me-sideways' moment.

My first thought was what the hell did he mean? It was like nasal man was having a little argument with himself or just pouring out his thoughts as they popped into his head, without any regard for whether they made sense or not. But more than that, he was sharing them with me and in such a matter-of-fact manner too, as if we'd known each other forever. It suddenly didn't seem to matter that I didn't understand it. I thought it was brilliant, regardless.

Rather than letting the LP carry on, I had to stop it right there and listen to this song again ... and again and, to be quite honest, again and again and again, as if I didn't quite believe how good it was the first four or five times.

Eventually I moved on from 'Strawberry Fields Forever' and journeyed through the rest of the LP, becoming more and more astounded as wondrous song followed wondrous song, each one having something special about it that drew me in and engaged me totally. The melody of 'Penny Lane', the sadness of 'The Fool on the Hill', the musicality of 'While my Guitar Gently Weeps', the poetic genius of 'Across the Universe' and the raucous, shouty, crazy-going-bonkers-at-the-endness of 'Hey Jude'. My personal Beatles magical mystery tour bus was only just pulling out of the car park, and it was a ride that, to this day, I still haven't been able to stop.

I hurriedly recorded both the Red and the Blue album onto a couple of cheap C90 cassettes, but delayed returning the LPs back to Dave in the vain hope that he might have decided to give up bands whose names began with the letter 'B'. He hadn't, and so with regret, I handed them back and bought them for myself. They were both on heavy rotation in my bedroom for the next few weeks. In fact, I played nothing but these records. I adored them both, but after such total saturation it soon became clear that these albums alone weren't going to be enough to quench my thirst for Beatles music.

It was a funny situation; up to this point I hadn't considered the possibility of exploring the music of a band that no longer existed – a band that wasn't going to be in the charts, and allow me to get excited about them getting their records to number one or seeing them appear on *Top of the Pops* on a Thursday night – a band that was not of my generation.

I went for *Abbey Road* next. Not the most logical of choices on the face of it, seeing as it was the last album that The Beatles made, but it was the one with 'Here Comes the Sun' on it so it made complete sense to me. The album was already seven years old, which made it the oldest album that I'd ever heard and it felt a bit naughty, as if I wasn't really supposed to like this sort of stuff. It felt like I was making a secret journey back to the past that none of my peers knew about, and I wasn't sure that I wanted to share my sordid secret just yet. But the truth was that I loved this record from start to finish. Paul McCartney's throaty vocal on 'Oh Darling' and the quirkiness of his storytelling on 'Maxwell's Silver Hammer' impressed me. I adored the blend of exquisite harmonies on 'Because' and sniggered childishly at John Lennon's less-than-subtle references to breasts and drugs.

The medley that took up most of side two sounded like the most perfectly constructed piece of pop extravaganza I'd ever heard: little snippets of songs, some funny, some serious, some just downright catchy, which with their recurring instrumental phrases seemed to fit together immaculately, as if they were written to hang together in such a way. I'm still not sure that pop has ever managed to come up with better track sequencing than that employed on side two of *Abbey Road*.

My favourite moments on the album were the extravagant 'I Want You (she's so heavy)' and 'The End'. The former, with its swirling keyboards and rampant bass runs, is not lyrically the best thing that John Lennon ever came up with, but I loved how he manages to make those three lines sound different each time he sang them. And then there was that abrupt ending, that no matter how many times I have heard it since, I still can't predict exactly when it's about to happen. I gave up counting how many times they go around the riff before it finally cuts off mid-way through long ago, but sometimes pop is just too good for clinical analysis, and so now I just let them get on with it. I think it's best.

'The End' is a bit of a forgotten gem, I think. It's never appeared on any of the many Beatles compilation albums, so you would only know it if you know *Abbey Road*. A simple song, which mainly acts as a vehicle for John, Paul and George to trade guitar solos, but then (and this is the important bit), McCartney hits you with the killer punch: the final line, of the final song, on the final album that The Beatles ever recorded:

And in the end, the love you take,
Is equal to the love you make'.

It's completely obvious, yet genius at the same time and, above all, bloody well right. This line still resonates with me now. How could we not have known this fact until The Beatles told us?

It was at this point that I realised that The Beatles weren't just in my life – they were my life. I decided there and then that I was going to collect every single record that this band had ever made. Now all I had to do was work out how I was going to make that happen.

There were thirteen proper albums, of which I owned just one. Twelve to go then. Except it wasn't just those thirteen albums, was it. There were a whole bunch of songs that had been thrown away as B-sides that never appeared on any albums, and also the *Long Tall Sally* EP – another four non-album tracks. And to cap it all in really annoying fashion, there was 'Bad Boy'– a cover of the Larry Williams song that was recorded in 1966 when The Beatles didn't do covers anymore, which was plonked as the only otherwise unavailable track on the compilation *A Collection of Oldies ... But Goldies*. I was going to have to buy that album too, just to get that one song; I already owned every other track on the LP, which seemed very unfair, but a commitment is a commitment.

Whilst the albums were going to be easy to find, I had no idea how I was going to get all these extra tracks, but I wasn't going to worry about that for now. I thought maybe once I started buying up the albums, I would probably get bored and then not bother following it through to the bitter end. This was the most likely scenario. I did after all have the reputation of starting projects, thrashing them relentlessly until I'd squeezed the last drop of life out of them, and then moving on to 'the next big fling' without having the common decency to finish them. That was me all over, and so I had no doubt my 'Beatles phase' would end in the same abrupt way. And anyway, all these albums couldn't possibly be as good as *Abbey Road,* could they?

Still, this project had to be funded, and for this I turned to my parents – scrounging a few shifts on a Saturday in their TV shop for a fiver a time. Looking back now, I can't think for a second that they actually needed me working in their shop; there was barely enough work to keep the pair of them occupied, and I honestly can't remember exactly what I actually did while I was there. All I do remember is watching the hands of my watch dawdle their way around to 5 o'clock, at which point I would be handed my fiver and sent on my way. I would then walk up Ilford Lane to Penny Farthing Records at the top of Ilford Hill, and have that fiver spent before it even had time to formally introduce itself to the inside of my pocket.

My normal procedure when buying records in Ilford would be to check the prices in Penny Farthing and then nip over to Downtown Records, five minutes down the road in Ilford High Road, and whichever shop had an album at the cheapest price got the sale. I had no preference between the two shops; my loyalty was purely based on price. If I was pushed into a corner, I would plump for Penny Farthing because Downtown had this very irritating habit of placing a Downtown Records sticker directly onto the sleeve, which could sometimes prove a bit tricky to remove. The process of gently easing the sticker off could sometimes send me into a state of irrational panic, fearing that one false move and I could be peeling off a little section of sleeve with it, which would have been in direct conflict with my obsession of keeping my record sleeves in perfect condition.

Records that were in the album charts around this time cost £1.99; old records were more expensive at £2.49, which didn't really make sense to me then, although it does now. This meant that I could buy two Beatles albums for my fiver. I would arrive at Penny Farthing at around 5:15 and have fifteen minutes to make my choices before they closed. At this rate, I would have them all within a couple of months.

I discussed my new obsession with Monty. He, of course, had discovered The Beatles a few years ago, devoured them and moved on, but gave the thumbs up to my newly formed plan anyway. In fact, he could help out if I was interested in a second- or possibly third-hand Beatles album. He had a copy of the *Yellow Submarine* album that he was prepared to let me have for fifty pence on the proviso that I never had the urge to play side two. This was the side that contained the classical incidental score used in the cartoon film and wasn't really Beatles music at all as it was played by the George Martin Orchestra. For an album that was going to cost fifty pence, that seemed like a fair enough caveat. I did ask him why he wasn't keen on me playing side two. He explained that it could no longer be played even if I had wanted to, because the first time he played it he was so appalled by it that he ran a fork all over the vinyl so he was never tempted into such foolishness again. I bought the album from him and played the fool.

Discovering the music of The Beatles was the most exciting thing that had happened in my life so far. As my collection grew, I was no longer waiting for Saturday to come for the football; it was eagerly anticipated as the day when I could get the next two Beatles albums.

As the summer of 1976 drew nearer, the weather was getting warmer and warmer, but I didn't care – I was spending an increasing amount of time in my bedroom listening to this stuff. I was enchanted by this world that had been and gone and I had known nothing about. And the more I listened, the more captured I became. The nicest sort of capture. In my little world, there were just the five of us.

The Beatles career can be split easily into three bits – the 'cute' years, the 'off-their-tits' years and the 'not-liking-each-other-very-much-at-all' years; all equally interesting, but for very different reasons. In terms of albums this split can be defined as *Please, Please Me* to *Help!*, *Rubber Soul* to *Magical Mystery Tour*, and *The White Album* to *Let It Be*. I was keen to spread my weekly buying fairly evenly across all three periods, but I definitely favoured the latter two. I also discovered that I was right: not all the albums were as good as *Abbey Road*, but the good news was, that there was one that was even better.

The Beatles' *White Album* was off its head, as you would expect from any album that boasted song titles such as 'The Continuing Story of Bungalow Bill', 'Why Don't We Do It in The Road' and 'Everybody's Got Something to Hide Except for Me and My Monkey'. A colossal opus of thirty tracks spread across its four sides. Unquestionably, these are not the thirty best songs that The Beatles ever recorded – in fact, some of them are downright silly – but put them together and they make what is, in my opinion, the most eclectic collection of songs ever compiled under one sleeve. This is what I love so much about this album. Almost every invented genre of music is here, and one or two that hadn't even been thought of yet. It takes you on a journey from the sublime ('While My Guitar Gently Weeps', 'Dear Prudence', 'Cry Baby Cry') to the ridiculous ('Wild Honey Pie', 'Revolution #9'); there's good old no-nonsense rock'n'roll ('Back in the USSR', 'Birthday'); pure unadulterated pop (Ob-la-di, Ob-la-da', 'Martha My Dear', 'I Will'); a little Country ('Don't Pass

Me By', 'Mother Nature's Son'); songs that made me think ('Glass Onion', 'Happiness Is a Warm Gun' and 'Blackbird'); and songs that just made me smile ('Piggies', 'Honey Pie', 'Rocky Raccoon' and 'I'm So Tired'). The album has divinely gorgeous acoustic ballads such as 'Julia' and the ridiculously under-rated 'Long, Long, Long' and then, on the other hand, 'Helter Skelter' and 'Yer Blues'– songs so dirty that if they were cars parked in your garage, they would be only too pleased to leave you a filthy great dollop of oil on the floor as they drove away.

It's a fairly common conception amongst Beatles fans that many of the tracks on the *White Album* could be disregarded as filler and the album could have been whittled down to around fifteen songs to make one fantastic single album. Log on to any Beatles fan forum and you'll almost certainly find hundreds of posts, each arguing passionately on behalf of the poster's preferred fifteen songs in this imaginary scenario. Unless you have a couple of weeks with nothing to do, it's an argument that's best steered clear of. I, of course, have tried to come up with my perfect slimmed-down version of the *White Album* but some decisions in life are just too hard to make and, for me, ostracising songs from the *White Album* is an impossible call – it's a bit like asking me to choose a least favourite testicle. The truth is, that I wouldn't want to be without any of these songs – even 'Revolution #9'. This is the bloody *White Album* for Christ sakes, it's supposed to be like this, perfect in its imperfection, that's the whole point, so let's just leave it alone!

There's something about this album that just makes me go a bit gooey and I can't quite put my finger on what it is. Back in 1976, I can remember lying on my bed listening to it and just adoring the whole package that came with the album. Those iconic Apple logos on the record labels, the slick white gatefold sleeve, adorned on the inside with just the black and white portraits of the four Beatles and the track listing. The front cover with just 'The Beatles' embossed onto the cardboard, and stamped with the number of my own personal copy. Inside the sleeve were those four photos from the inside cover, blown up and in glossy colour, and a huge poster that was a collage of hundreds of pictures of the band, where you could find something new every time you looked closely enough. Printed on the back of the poster were the lyrics to all the songs. As I held the sleeve in my hand I wondered how on earth something this beautiful, containing all this fantastic music, could cost only £6.99.

In 1982, I bought the whole thing again. That was the year that I left home. Two years earlier, in a fit of pop-orientated decoration, I had foolishly glued the four Beatles photographs and the collage poster, to my bedroom wall. I had no intention of leaving home without them, but they were stuck good and proper, and so to keep my package intact I bought *White Album* number two.

In 1987, the *White Album* came out on compact disc – of course I bought it. The HMV special edition box set actually. It set me back the best part of thirty quid.

In 2009, all the Beatles albums were finally re-mastered in glorious stereo and issued in a fabulous box set. Two hundred and fifty quid lighter of wallet, I owned *White Album* number four.

Now, how was I supposed to know that Apple were going to release all the albums again in 2014 – this time on super high quality vinyl and in mono as well, if you don't mind. I'd never heard all the albums in mono, with all their miniscule differences to the stereo versions that only I care about, so once again I was shelling out and that made *White Album* number five.

In all the years that have passed between *White Album* number one and *White Album* number five, I haven't heard an album by anyone that I have loved quite as much. I doubt I ever will. It's now forty years since me and the *White Album* first got it together, that's a hell of a long time and we could be forgiven for drifting apart and growing bored with each other. During that time there are a whole host of things that I once loved the life out of but later metaphorically boxed up and banished to the back of the wardrobe with the 'Buckaroo': snooker, Mike Yarwood, Curly Wurlys, Oasis, cheesecloth shirts, 10cc and *Fawlty Towers* – but not the *White Album*. Never the *White Album*.

The early Beatles albums were easy to get on with but I had no concept for the time in which they were made and didn't like them as much as the later stuff. I considered these early albums to belong to the knicker-wetting, screaming teenage girls that loved them so much and I wasn't quite so ready to commit to them. Much later I appreciated how good they really were, (notably *A Hard Day's Night*) and the quality of the developing songwriting skills of Lennon and McCartney.

Making a connection with a new album has its parallels with starting any other sort of relationship, and my relationship with *Revolver* was not an easy one to begin with. Some albums are at their most tantalising the first few times you hear them – the initial seduction, if you like, and pop knows how to seduce – it's one of the things it's really good at. Once you've fallen for their charm, you play them to death and then after a while, over-familiarity creeps in (the farting in front of each other stage), and eventually they fall from grace. But there are certain albums that play hard to get on those first few plays – what you might call a grower rather than a shower. This is where the relationship has to be nurtured and developed. But if an album is worth getting to know, it's worth allowing it to flirt with you, tease and touch you, until you fall for it completely, and before you know it, you're writing its name in felt tip on your history folder.

That's how it was for *Revolver* and me. We went through the small-talk stage – the awkwardness of trying to find a common bond. Songs like

'Taxman' and 'Eleanor Rigby' didn't strike a chord with me at first, probably because I wasn't a taxpayer and didn't tend to keep my face in a jar by the door (I kept my house keys there instead). I totally detested the acid-drenched final track 'Tomorrow Never Knows', with its single droning C chord, seagull squawks, assortment of backwards loops, and a vocal from Lennon that sounded as if he was singing it from the bottom of a mineshaft. It sounded like a tuneless mess to me.

I also had a big problem with 'Yellow Submarine' – I still do. Whilst I still can't find it within myself to totally disregard anything The Beatles have put their name to, standing shoulder-to-shoulder with 'Yellow Submarine' is difficult. It still galls me today that *Revolver* is blighted with this song. I had been acutely aware of it as a kid – who hadn't – it's a song aimed at kiddies, and as much a part of everyone's childhood as 'The Wheels on the Bus' and grazed knees, but why did it have to be track six, side one on one of the finest pop records ever made. Why? There was no need, it could have just remained as a standalone single and had its place on the album taken by the wonderfully psychedelic 'Rain', which had been criminally subjected to a lifetime of anonymity tucked away secretly on the B-side of 'Paperback Writer' two months earlier. 'Rain', with its caustic guitar phrase and Ringo's energetic drumming, would have fitted perfectly into 'Submarine's slot on *Revolver,* where it could have served as the perfect antidote to the tenderness of the preceding track, 'Here, There and Everywhere'. I don't think anyone would have minded.

Even if we put the childishness of the thing aside for a second, the other bone that I have to pick with 'Yellow Submarine' is its notoriety. Hand a copy of *Revolver* to a Martian, and the chances are that the only song he will recognise on the album is that one. It is unquestionably the most famous song on there, and I resent it for that. Walk into any bar in China with a Beatles t-shirt on, and you will be instantly approached by someone who generally doesn't speak a word of English, but will greet you with 'ahhh Beatles – we all live in a…'.

So yes, *Revolver* was tricky, but this, I had read, was The Beatles at the peak of their power – there had to be more to this album than it appeared to be delivering. I thought it was me, and wondered why I wasn't quite getting it. It wasn't all bad though; I was a teenager so I could totally relate to the laying-in-bed-all-day dreamy philosophies of 'I'm Only Sleeping', and I adored the rough-house riffing and thrusting harmonies of 'And Your Bird Can Sing' and 'She Said, She Said'. I was just disappointed that *Revolver* was only saying 'ok album', rather than screaming 'classic' at me.

Luckily, we both had the desire to get to know each other on a more intimate level, and we persevered. I felt I needed to love this album and I had no intention of giving up on it, nor it on me. I played it relentlessly and in the end we were doing it four or five times a night – occasionally, we'd leave the lights on – and it was only a matter of time before everything slipped into place and we fell for each other.

Of course, these were still the early days for The Beatles and me and I didn't understand pop or its power in the way that I do today. The track 'For No One' I considered back then to be a fairly decent love song, but I'd never been in love so the emotion of the song didn't resonate with me. I must have heard the song thousands of times, yet one day, a few years ago, for no apparent reason and without warning, 'For No One' seduced me like it was our first time. As I listened to the lyrics, I suddenly felt a strong wave of emotion and the uneasy feeling of tears filling my eyes. I had no idea why. The story that is depicted in the song was not something that was relevant to my life at that moment – I couldn't explain it. I was literally crying for no one. I wondered if Colin (the bastard) was responsible – he was adept at making me feel like that – it's part of his job description. And then … I got it. After over a quarter of a century of taking the song for granted, it finally hit home – the genius in which McCartney so beautifully describes how we retread old conversations and feelings of a relationship when love breaks down. McCartney was just 24 years old when he wrote that song – and there was me, a 46-year-old man crying tears of joy because I'd finally understood just how spot-on he'd got it.

My introduction to *Sgt. Pepper's Lonely Hearts Club Band* couldn't have been more different to that of *Revolver*. I was already familiar with four of its tracks, having spent so much time with the *1967-70* compilation, and it didn't take long to get acquainted with the rest of the gang. The album was instantly likeable and I felt comfortable enough with it to call it *Pepper* right from the outset. I've never really got the whole concept idea, the songs seem completely unrelated to me, but what I did get from it straight away was that this was a complete album, rather than just a bunch of songs gathered randomly – the whole thing seemed to hang together beautifully. Even 'Within You Without You', the gorgeous classical Indian piece written by George Harrison, didn't seem out of place.

The druggy aspects intrigued me and I assumed from what I'd read about the LP that the whole album would be littered with hidden references for me to discover, but in terms of the lyrics they are surprisingly limited to a mere smattering. I longed to drop some acid and allow myself to be transported back to the 'Summer of Love'. A ridiculous notion – I was still struggling to hold down a couple of glasses of sweet cider, let alone LSD – but that's what I assumed was required to feel the full benefit of the album. It's still really difficult for someone of my age to put myself back in the time to try and understand exactly what all the fuss was about. Even back in 1976 it seemed a little primitive in places, but I really wanted to feel, what first-generation Beatles fans felt when they first heard *Sgt. Pepper*.

The best I could do was listen in the dark, preferably through headphones. That's what I was told – 'you have to listen to *Pepper* with the lights off and headphones on man, to get the full effect – no one listens to *Pepper* in broad daylight'. But of course they did. How else could you gaze endlessly at the lavish busyness on the gatefold sleeve or paw over the lyrics on the back cover? Inside the sleeve there were some cardboard cutouts, which to this day remain tucked away safely inside all my copies. I haven't yet felt the urge to actually cut them out, if that's what the cutouts are really for, but if ever the day should come when I desperately need to get my hands on a cardboard moustache and Sergeant stripes at short notice, I'll know exactly where to go.

I think that, over the years, *Pepper*'s stock has devalued slightly. It's still hugely admired but it's certainly been knocked from its lofty perch somewhat, and that is completely understandable bearing in mind the number of years that pop has had to catch up.

Although there's nothing horrid like 'Yellow Submarine' on *Pepper*, if I was making a compilation CD of the best-ever Beatles tracks (and with no pun intended – the acid test) only one song – 'A Day in the Life' – would make it. Maybe that's a testament to the fact that all the songs work brilliantly within the confines of the complete album, but take them out of their natural environment and maybe they start to show their vulnerability a little.

'A Day in the Life' is different. It's an astonishing piece of music and stands out on this album like a pair of Chippendale pecs at a moob convention. It's quite simply my favourite song by anyone, ever. When I actually sit down and think about this song and listen to it properly without any distractions, it's quite overwhelming what has been achieved here. I'm not sure that pop has anything in its locker that can compare with 'A Day in the Life'. It is completely original and, to these ears, unequalled. The only song that I think can come remotely close in terms of originality, structure and the segueing of several completely different parts within the same song is 'Bohemian Rhapsody' by Queen, and I'm sure that Freddie Mercury had a cheeky eye on 'A Day in the Life' as he and his chums put together their career masterpiece.

I like the way that the crowd noise fades at the start of 'A Day in the Life', leaving us with the sound stripped down to the simple acoustic guitar and piano, allowing us to get the full impact of that opening line: 'I read the news today, oh boy'. I find myself immediately covered in goose bumps. Never before or since had Lennon's voice sounded so crisp and lean and so hauntingly beautiful. I always thought 'oh boy' was a funny expression for a pop star to use in a song. It's more boys' comic book speak than something a pop star would say – although Buddy Holly would probably argue with that.

I love story songs, and the imagery in this one is so vivid that I never have any problems seeing the pictures in my mind as the story unfolds. I know exactly what the car crash looks like in that first verse, and can envisage the crowd of people gathering around straining to see whether or not they recognise the victim. The second verse has equal impact but in a different way. In this verse where John is talking about war, the 'crowd of people turned away' whereas in the first verse they 'stood and stared'. I think he's being very cute here by comparing how people are sickened by the sight of bloodshed in war, to how people bustle with each other to get a decent view of the blood spilled in a celebrity car crash. The killer line, of course, is 'but I just had to look' – it's very, very clever. The craziness of the last verse just makes me smile. They had to count all the holes to know exactly how many would fill the Albert Hall. This seems over-zealous to me. Surely a rough estimate would have been ok, and poses the question, 'did they firstly have to remove Hitler's 'other' ball, which had been in residence there for several decades, in order to squeeze all 4,000 in?'.

When there are certain stories that pertain to the recording of a song they can add to its legend, make them more enjoyable, and 'A Day in the Life' has such stories in abundance: the orchestral crescendo interlude is used as a way of connecting Paul's 'woke up, got out of bed' sequence to the rest of the song, and I find it highly amusing that to achieve that cacophony of noise, George Martin had to explain to a classically trained orchestra how to ad-lib! There's also the delightful story of the orchestra being made to wear false noses whilst recording their part. The thought of George Martin (presumably un-nosed) conducting these musicians is a delicious image too. Then there's the alarm clock – originally set off to mark the exact point where the orchestral part would end and Paul's verse would begin and thus enabling the band to record the rest of the song around that 32 bar gap, while they waited for the orchestra to come in to the studio to record their part. It needn't have been an alarm clock – it could have been a drum beat or something else that could have marked that point, but it was an alarm clock, and the realisation that an alarm clock going off preceding the line 'woke up, got out of bed' fitted so brilliantly, it was left in the released version. A complete fluke, but it's things like that which make the song even more special for me.

I've always thought that the 'I'd love to turn you on' refrain coupled with the often mimicked, dreamy 'aaah's', made this the ultimate hippy stoner song, absolutely perfect I would imagine, for summer of 1967. And as that final E chord that never seems to end pales away into the distance, you can almost feel the last knockings of the Summer of Love fading away into autumn with it.

I find it quite interesting that despite '*Pepper*' being lauded as the soundtrack for the Summer of Love, it never mentions any hippy ideals, never talks of peace and love or plays host to a single love song. And so as far as trying to understand what it was like to be hearing *Sgt. Pepper* in

1967, I'm none the wiser, and can only assume that *Sgt. Pepper*, with all its weird and wonderful characters and trippy references, was just one of those albums that showed up at the right time with all the right songs.

If ever there was a perfect time to discover The Beatles as a second-generation fan, then it was the summer of 1976. The Beatles' contract with Apple was about to expire, and EMI, in an attempt to drain some extra revenue out of it, re-released all their singles in their original formats. All of a sudden The Beatles were back in fashion and 'Yesterday', 'Hey Jude' and 'Paperback Writer' were back in the charts. I'm sure someone, somewhere was screaming 'rip-off', but I was delighted. It meant that I could buy up all the singles that had those non-album B-sides that I needed. And then, as if there really was a God, they then brought out a compilation album called *Rock'n'Roll Music*, which contained those four tracks from the *Long Tall Sally* EP that I was still missing. I was complete. I was a Beatles completist.

The problem with owning everything by a band that no longer existed was: where do I go from there? Easy – you start collecting the Beatles' solo albums. Whilst I was aware that everybody else was a bit miffed about The Beatles breaking up, I couldn't have been happier about it. The break-up meant that there were now around twenty more albums for me to devour and collect, whereas had they stayed together, by 1976 we might only have had five or six. I started off with *John Lennon/Plastic Ono Band* and *Imagine,* unsurprisingly by John Lennon, which turned out to be very good choices for a first crack. I followed them up with George Harrison's *Dark Horse,* for reasons I can't really remember, but can only think that Penny Farthing must have had it on special offer.

The BBC, as if they had some sort of clue about the sort of commotion that was going on in both my head and my bedroom, chose this exact time to re-run all the Beatles films (except *Magical Mystery Tour*) over four weeks on a Tuesday evening. These were of course the days before we owned a video recorder, but I needed some sort of souvenir and so I recorded the sound on my Sony cassette deck. Lord knows why – I don't think I ever played those recordings, but the point is, that I now recognise this act of ridiculousness as the beginnings of what I refer to as my 'Quick!, Macca's on *Wogan*' phase. This is where later, I would video every single fleeting TV appearance by a Beatle – recordings that I still have.

As if all this wonderment wasn't enough to be getting on with, Beat Publications, who published a monthly fan magazine called *The Beatles Book* throughout the sixties, decided that this was the perfect time to start re-printing the original magazines. Too right it was. I was a regular subscriber until they finally gave up the ghost sometime in 1997, by which time I had collected every issue.

I was well and truly hooked and I hadn't even scratched the surface of this obsession yet. It's fair to say that I played very little other music during this period, as I got more and more dedicated to this band from a bygone age. I wanted to shout from the rooftops and tell everyone I knew about this wonderful new world that I'd discovered. I felt sorry for them, as if they were missing out on something magnificent.

I took Abbey Road round to Fraser's house – it was time. We sat in the dark on his bed and listened, sucking on a couple of Silk Cut ciggies that he had pilfered from his mum's handbag. I didn't really smoke, or even refer to them as ciggies, but The Beatles did, which made it ok. We didn't talk, we just listened. I may have interrupted our silence a couple of times to tell him to listen closely to this bit or that bit, hoping that he would be as enchanted as I was. I could tell he was totally captivated – he didn't break wind. Not once.

He agreed that the album was fantastic, but his candle for Slade still burnt brightly. It wouldn't be hard to talk him down – at the end of the day, you're either behind the band that had written the greatest songs of their generation, or you were behind the band that had written 'My Friend Stan', right? By the time I'd tried him on some of the other albums, he was ready to commit.

We felt that such a monumental decision needed a proper ceremony befitting the occasion, and so we took his copy of *Slayed?* – the one where the band have 'Slade' written on their knuckles and Dave Hill is bare-chested on the cover – down to the far end of his back garden and burnt the bloody thing. Now, I'm not really down with denying your pop past, and as an erstwhile Slade fan myself, I did feel a little pang of guilt about such an act of extreme destruction, but there was something acutely satisfying about watching the black plastic shrivelling around the red Polydor label under the heat. There didn't seem to be any logical reason why Dave Hill had his shirt off on that cover – maybe there was a need to prove that oven-ready beavers had nipples too, but it felt good to give them a good old scorching. He was asking for it.

So Fraser was in. He recorded all my Beatles records on to cassette while he gradually built up his own collection of the real thing. I can remember being extremely jealous of his copy of *Let It Be*. Somehow, he had managed to get a copy that had a red Apple label. I'd never seen one before. The vinyl was warped out of all proportion – ridiculously so. I've never seen a record so bent and out of shape, but it still played perfectly. He thought about returning it to the shop, but there seemed to be no good reason to do so, and the risk of getting a replacement without the red Apple was too big as far as I was concerned, and so I persuaded him to keep it. I wonder if he still has it. I do hope so, I must ask him.

The school summer holidays of 1976 seemed to last forever. They were to be my last. People of my age still reminisce about the summer of '76.

We'd never had one like it. It started getting hot around mid-April and we didn't see a drop of rain until we were back at school in September. Britain was officially in a state of drought and it was bloody marvellous.

I spent most of that summer either relentlessly playing Beatles music in my bedroom or over at Valentines Park with Fraser and his neighbour Mark, playing pitch and putt or cricket, or swimming in its lido. Mark wasn't really a music fan, but we found common ground in sport. He was one of those lads that was pretty good at most sports that he turned his hand or leg to. He had also joined Fraser and me at scouts and his record as a mischief-maker there appealed to me, so we soon became close.

Valentines Park's lido had the reputation of having the coldest water this side of the North Atlantic. An outdoor pool in temperatures that very often during that summer topped ninety degrees proved, as you would expect, very popular. If it had had any rafters, it would have been packed full to them. On some days we could queue in the blistering heat for over an hour just to get in. It would all be worthwhile when we could finally plunge our steaming bodies into the sub-zero temperatures of the pool. It had a water chute, a couple of diving boards and a fountain that we weren't allowed to climb into, but did anyway, and we sat under its huge lips and let the freezing water cascade through our hairy teenage heads. The pool was surrounded by hard grey concrete, which was not attractive to look at, but the outlook was softened by the hundreds of bronzing bodies spread out on towels around it. Unattractive it may have been, but for two months during the summer of '76, Valentines Park lido represented a little piece of heaven on earth.

That summer I also got myself on to TV. Not just a fleeting appearance either; it was at the England v West Indies test match at the Oval. I managed to position myself right underneath the scoreboard so that at the end of every over, when the cameras focused on the board, there was I, surrounded by all the West Indian fans slapping two tin cans together, like some sort of demented sea lion (not that sea lions usually have access to cans of fizzy drinks, but you get the picture). Unfortunately, I hadn't really thought this through beforehand, and so in my TV debut the world saw me wearing a light blue Wrigley's Spearmint Gum cap-sleeved t-shirt that bore the words 'chew me' on the back.

Fraser, Mark and I spent a week away from Gants Hill during that summer too – camping with the scouts in Meopham in Kent. I wasn't really too keen on the prospect of spending a week away from my Beatles records, but it was only for a week – I would probably be able to cope. To help pass the time on a particularly irksome ten-mile hike through the Kent countryside in the searing heat, the three of us devised a game to amuse ourselves, which we unimaginatively called 'Fart Cricket'. The rules were simple: every time one of us could muster a fart, that would count as five runs, and an accidental burp would signify the loss of a wicket. When you're fifteen, it's surprisingly difficult to suppress a burp rather than letting it out into the public domain of your peers for all to enjoy. The game kept us amused for most of that week, but we didn't feel the need to patent it later.

The other major source of amusement during that camp was the unusual addition to our number of the local Girl Guide troop, or pack, or whatever the collective noun for Girl Guides is. If memory serves me right, I think all three of us managed to bag ourselves a Girl Guide of our own (or whatever the collective verb for getting a snog off a Girl Guide is). Fraser's was a rather spotty girl called Susan but I can't remember what Mark's was called, nor anything about her skin complexion. Mine was called One-Titted Claire, and as a couple we almost made it to the end of the week.

I would just like to point out at this stage that, despite the handle, Claire was the proud owner of two breasts. It wasn't until we returned to school after the holidays and discussed our summer adventures that Milly and Billy decided that she had just the one and named her accordingly. It was usual behaviour amongst the three of us to greet any of our dalliances with the fairer sex with ridicule and a devaluing of importance, culminating in the award of a derogatory name. I can point to a smallish list of previous victims of the naming convention – 'Smelly-hole Malina' springs to mind, as does Bill's short-term beau 'Glynis the Pimp' – who obviously was not an actual pimp and come to think of it, might not have even been called Glynis. So a name for Claire wasn't completely unexpected and the hapless uni-breaster was also awarded the dubious distinction of the traditional drawing on the front page of Milly's new-term rough book, complete with single boob placed centrally. I dread to think what poor old Claire might have thought if she had known about her single-breastedness, and what's more, that it is still being discussed forty years later.

It felt a bit lame to have spent some of my summer holiday camping with the scouts. I didn't see much of the lads from school during the holidays. Ray had spent some time in Scotland visiting his mum, while Milly and Billy had been camping up in the Lake District, chasing girls, drinking beer and occasionally getting served in pubs. They brought me home a red Younger's Tartan Bitter ashtray that they had stolen from one of them as proof. I can't really remember what Monty did during that summer but he probably spent it attending various pop festivals or hitchhiking his way across southern Scandinavia. Whatever it was, it would have been something far cooler than camping with the scouts, and any girls that he may have encountered would no doubt have had the requisite number of breasts.

Billy and Milly were also coming along with me on my Beatles odyssey. Not in quite the same obsessive way, but they bought into it to a certain degree for sure. While on their camping trip, Bill was reading *The*

Man Who Gave The Beatles Away – a brilliantly funny memoir, written by Allan Williams, a bluff Scouser who had managed the band before they became famous. In the book, Williams tells of how the band drank so much during their early days as a club band in Hamburg that they even had beer with their breakfast cereal. Bill, in a kind of 'well if it's good enough for The Beatles …' stance, thought that this was an experience that might be worth a try. Misinterpreting Williams' tale, they both duly poured a can of lager over their morning cornflakes as a milk replacement and tucked in. Very rock'n'roll, I have to admit, but a classic schoolboy error, which is ok I suppose, on account of them being classic schoolboys. The thought of them trying to save face by struggling on to the end of the bowl is something that still delights me.

Meopham would be my last with the scouts. I didn't exactly engineer the end of my scouting life, but in the end, I took a convenient exit route. The 'fairly average stink-bomb incident of 1976' happened just at the right time. It was during a game of Barricades shortly after we returned from Meopham. Barricades was a game that was played in the dark, with all the scout hut tables and chairs piled up in a huge heap in the middle of the room – the idea being that you wriggled and wormed your way through the barricade without the whole lot crashing down on to your head. There didn't seem to be any particular reason why Fraser had taken his life's collection of stink bombs to scouts that night, but he seized the moment and crushed them as twenty or so boys fumbled about in the pitched darkness.

The reaction was, as you would expect, a lot of wailing and clasping of hands over mouths and noses. The lights came on and the scout leader demanded to know who the culprit was. After a little bit of sniggering and elbow-nudging, Fraser eventually came clean and was told in no uncertain terms to collect his things and go home. In an act of unrivalled solidarity, Mark and I declared that if he was going then so were we, thinking that this would force a re-think. The leader just said, 'Ok then, off you go'. And so the three of us walked, and we never went back. It was time.

Back in my little Beatle world, I was starting to get more and more inquisitive about the music and about the four men that made it. I hadn't really felt the need to delve too deeply into the background information of the music I had liked previously, but this was something so very different to anything I had ever felt about music before.

The music on those LPs was so good and ever-evolving that it warranted further explanation. How did 'She Loves You' come from the same band that made 'Come Together'? How did they get from being lovable mop-tops that wanted to hold your hand to hairy hippies singing about semolina pilchards climbing up the Eiffel Tower? I wanted to find out.

171

For this, I turned once again to Monty. He lent me a few books that he considered important reading for my education on this band. One of the books that he lent me, *Lennon Remembers,* was key. This book was a lengthy interview that *Rolling Stone* conducted with John Lennon in the autumn of 1970, a few months after The Beatles had split up and a few weeks after the release of his first proper solo album *John Lennon/Plastic Ono Band*. It caught Lennon in what I was about to discover was his most caustic of moods, in which he discusses his childhood, fame, his music and being a Beatle. It was fascinating throughout, brutally honest almost to the point of cruelty, and full of vitriol. I felt like I'd met him at his most vile, yet I still warmed greatly to the man and wanted to learn more.

I started buying lots of books about The Beatles; I read everything I could lay my hands on until I built up a decent-sized knowledge of the band. The more I read about Lennon, the more I loved him. Although we were nothing like each other and had completely different upbringings, he was the one of the four that I could relate to the best. I learned of his schooldays and how he considered his sole purpose of being at school was to be the class jester and make his friends laugh by shouting out stupid things in class – I thought that was pretty much how I behaved at school, too. How he was told by his teachers that he would never amount to much because he was stupid – snap!

I loved his wit. The press conferences played such a huge part in how popular The Beatles became, especially in America. Although they all played their part in piping up with the funnies, John's always seemed to be a little more thought-out and clever. Of course they couldn't have been, they were spur of the moment things, but the cogs just seemed to turn that little bit faster in John's head.

'Don't you care that you can't hear yourselves sing at your concerts?'

'No we don't care, we've got all the records at home.'

'How did you find America?'

'We turned left at Greenland'

And bam! Thousands of teenagers suddenly knew where Greenland was. Educational.

Obviously, the music was the biggest draw. He could write the tenderest of love songs like 'Julia', 'Oh My Love' or 'In My Life', but also heart-wrenching pieces like 'Mother' and 'Isolation'; angry songs such as 'How Do You Sleep?', or political songs like 'Give Peace a Chance', 'Give Me Some Truth' or 'Power to the People'. And then there was the word play. Songs such as 'Across the Universe', 'I am the Walrus', 'Strawberry Fields Forever', where he wove exquisite tapestries with words and somehow made them fit into songs. Not easy to do and impressed me no end – but John wasn't just about the clever, clever stuff; he had an ear for writing damn good pop songs too: 'If I Fell', 'This Boy', 'Please Please Me'... I could go on, but I can tell you're getting fidgety and

I haven't even mentioned the voice – a voice that at times can send shivers up and down my spine, like nobody else can. A voice that felt that it was coming into my bedroom specifically to speak to me. When he sings with such emotion and honesty it's hard not to be moved in some way, unless your heart is made of stone.

I also loved how his character was so complicated and complex – so many different sides to the same coin, not all of them adorable, but all of them as honest as the day is long. My seven-year-old daughter Sarah once asked me, 'Daddy, are The Beatles as nice as The Spice Girls?'. It was quite possibly the cutest thing I'd ever heard, but I do worry about the kids of today and where all of pop's heroes have gone. Who have they got worthy of hero status? One Direction? Justin Bieber? Ed Sheeran? You see, when you're a teenager you tend to fall into one of two categories: either you're all twisted up with raging angst and riddled with hormones that you don't know what to do with, or you have no idea what you're supposed to feel because you don't feel or care about anything at all. I fell into the latter category. I needed a hero and in Lennon, I found one; he forced me to care. And once I found him, I started to think like him. If he was a jealous guy, then so was I. If he thought that all you needed was love, I believed him. If he said instant karma was gonna get you, then it bloody well was. If he was a walrus, then I was one too. All my best ideas came from him; with hindsight, not all of them were sound ones, but they were his ideals all the same. If he said it, I thought it too – at least up until the point when I knew better, by which time he'd probably had a re-think too.

John Lennon was one of the four biggest pop stars in the world but that didn't stop him getting down on the streets and marching with the people if it was a cause he believed in. It also didn't stop him from making an arse of himself – staying in bed for a week or holding press conferences from inside a white bag to give publicity to the peace movement. He didn't care if the world laughed at him, if it meant he got what he wanted. It's just a pity that everybody else didn't want it quite as much as he did. But my point is that he used his celebrity to try and do something worthwhile, not just to get into movie premieres or jump the queue at Waitrose, and now it's up to you, Harry Styles. What have you got?

As I delved deeper and deeper into my Beatles obsession, I decided that owning just the essential Beatles solo records was simply not enough, I needed them all. A few days before my sixteenth birthday, my parents asked me what I would like as my present. I predictably said 'records'. I wasn't given a budget but dad insisted that he was coming with me to oversee my purchases. When you're sixteen, it's never ideal dragging your dad around record shops, but he was about to suffer open-wallet surgery, and I was about to be relegated to Credibility League Division Two. It was something we were both going to have to swallow.

I made intelligent choices, going for the triple and double albums that would be much harder for me to save for: George's *All Things Must Pass* and *The Concert for Bangla Desh* and John's *Sometime In New York City*. When I had a bundle of empty sleeves in my arms that totalled fifty pounds I was told to stop. I'd had a huge leg-up in collecting the solos, which made it the most precious of birthday presents.

The solo albums of the four Beatles, to be honest, are a bit of a minefield. You have to tread carefully and know what you're doing. If you thought the *White Album* was a bit whacky in places, then step back and take a deep breath before you tackle *Electronic Sound* by George Harrison or *Life with The Lions* by John and Yoko. Of course it's quite possible that you may want to listen to the heartbeat of the last five minutes of John and Yoko's miscarried baby's life, followed by two minutes of silence and then thirteen minutes of John Lennon playing with the dial of a radio, but the chances are that you probably won't.

Having said that, even by the time that I had started investigating the solos there had already been several utterly brilliant albums made by the individual Beatles: *John Lennon/Plastic Ono Band*, *Imagine* and *Walls & Bridges*, by John; *Ram*, *Band On the Run* and *Venus & Mars* by Paul McCartney & Wings; and the finest of all the solos, George Harrison's magnificent *All Things Must Pass*.

I had no idea that such a commitment made back in 1976 would still be keeping me busy today. Paul McCartney and Ringo Starr still make records and therefore I am still buying them. But when you make such a commitment there are certain questions that you have to ask yourself and put in a little soul searching. Do I really need *Two Virgins* (the one with John and Yoko stark-bollock-naked on the cover)? Is it essential that I own Wings' version of 'Mary Had A Little Lamb'? Do I really need *Old Wave* by Ringo Starr – an album so poor that it was only released in Germany – the country responsible for spawning Boney M and Milli Vanilli? Is it really necessary to own both the seven-inch and the twelve-inch remixes of 'We All Stand Together'? And the biggest tester of all – do I have to get all the albums made by Yoko Ono just because John Lennon plays guitar on them? When you're in it for the long haul, and you're me, the answer to all these questions is yes. I'd like to say that I draw the line at buying albums by Beatle children, but if I did, it would be a lie, the truth being that if Apple released a souvenir turd that had the name Beatles running all the way through it, I would probably buy that too. Even more so if it was a previously unreleased, remastered turd.

There were singles by all four of them backed with non-album B-sides that also had to be sought out. Most of these were easy to get if you could suffer the indignity of asking for them at Penny Farthing. They kept a big fat book behind the counter that listed every single ever released on any label – a huge tome to pop's past. You had to order them though; they didn't have them in stock just on the off-chance that a ginger Beatle-head might pop in one day and want to buy 'Give Ireland Back to the Irish'.

The bluff bloke behind the counter in Penny Farthing didn't take kindly to being asked to get out his big fat book and would slam it on the counter with a big huff and slightly more audible puff. He would groan further as he fingered his way around the wafer-thin pages searching for the catalogue number. It was just too much trouble for him, and he spoke to me in a tone that suggested that I was really putting him out and that I was just being lazy for not buying it in 1972 when the thing was first released.

There are other indignities too. I'm not sure why so many people take such great delight in running down the work of Paul McCartney. Surely the man is a national treasure and should be cherished as the greatest songwriter this country has ever produced? Yes, there have been moments, bad, bad moments, very bad, cringeworthy moments – the aforementioned 'Mary Had A Little Lamb' and 'Frog Song' debacles – but these are just a couple of misdemeanours in a career that has spanned half a century. I suppose there was the *Give my Regards to Broad Street* project, and the *Pipes of Peace* album left a lot to be desired too, so ok, there have been a few low points, but if I had a penny for every time I have had to defend his work down the years, I'd have … £8.97 by now. I don't bother with the defending too much these days, but all I will say is this – when you have songs like 'Hey Jude', 'Yesterday', Let it Be', 'Maybe I'm Amazed', 'Band on the Run' and so, so many more in your locker, surely you've earned the right to do what you fucking well like mate – even if it entails songs about frogs.

So yes, the solos are a minefield, but a delightful one to wade through whilst sorting out the wheat from the chaff. Always full of intrigue, if not always full of great music, and so they're not for everyone, but for me they are essential.

Kids today have so much free music at their fingertips, available on the likes of *YouTube* and *Spotify,* that they can afford to experiment with the old stuff – not quite in the same way that I did in the seventies, but the outcome is just the same.

It makes me very happy these days to see that The Beatles and their music are still relevant to young people. I think this may hark back to the point that I made earlier about the lack of heroes in today's pop music. Beatles Internet forums are full of young people singing the praises of albums such as *Abbey Road* and *Sgt. Pepper*, having only discovered them yesterday. And there will be new fans discovering Beatles music tomorrow, and the day after that. I find this very exciting and it makes me feel proud of the band and of the young people that are open-eared enough to listen to beyond what is current. I have spoken to many of these people, and it is thrilling to watch them slowly discover the same things that I did all those years ago. They want to know all about the band, about the songs, why they did this, why they said that, just like I did. It's fascinating to hear their opinions – how this music is perceived through young ears as their journeys unfold. Of course, for some, this will just be their Beatles phase and they will move on, but for others – they will be teaching the words to 'All My Loving' to their children.

I've often been asked 'why?'. Why The Beatles? What's so special about them? Why are they so important? It's almost impossible to put down the words that sufficiently describe the answer. I don't really feel the need to convince the unconvinced, but if they insist, I'll tell them to go away and have a listen to 'Long, Long, Long' or 'While My Guitar Gently Weeps' from the *White Album* and inform them that the author of these songs was the THIRD best songwriter in that band. That probably tells them all they need to know. If that doesn't hold any water, I'll just say it's because they were as nice as The Spice Girls.

Did The Beatles change the world? Probably not, but they changed my world. They really did.

And, of course, just as young people spend time discovering music from the past, a reciprocal arrangement exists in which I am free to investigate some of today's music. Searching for something new and exciting is important, because if I don't, there will come a point where I have nowhere else to go – nothing new to listen to, and I'll just end up drowning my sorrows with several pints of bitter and twisted, and moan about how the charts are so full of crap these days. So me and Ed Sheeran? Oh, go on then.

The Boys Are Back In Town

There was never any doubt when we went back to school in September 1976 that this would be the last year of my education, and I could hardly wait for it all to be over. I had absolutely no idea what I was going to do come next summer, but two things were certain: the first being that I was not going to achieve the results I needed to buy myself another couple of years of delaying career decisions in the sixth form, and the second being that there was no way my mother was going to allow me to laze away my life on the dole.

Certainly everything started off a little more serious that term. John and Laurence came back to school declaring that they no longer wanted to be known as Billy and Milly. And so Monty also insisted that his name was now Ian and not Monty, as Monty was another name altogether and a silly one at that.

Nicknames were common stock at Beal and I don't suppose that is particularly unusual. I had a couple. I started off being known as 'Bell-Head', mainly because my hair tended to be bell-shaped. It wasn't my fault, it just went like that and I couldn't do a thing with it. The bell could be seen at its most bell-like when cast as a shadow on the playground tarmac. Later I became 'The Bear' or sometimes 'Shelley Bear', but usually just 'The Bear'. This name came about when Drew decided that I bore an uncanny resemblance to Bungle, the bear from *Rainbow*.

To most, though, I was still known as Anthony (pronounced in finest cockney by most of my friends as Ant-knee) and usually shortened to just 'Ant'. This was fine and I quite liked it, although it once led to an uncomfortable moment on the phone when I caught John in an unusually facetious mood, and forgot that he was no longer responding to the Billy moniker.

'Alright Bill, it's Ant.'

'What the fuck's an ant phoning me up for?'

Followed by an abrupt slamming down of the phone. A far more pertinent question would have been: 'How the fuck is an ant phoning me up?'.

My geography teacher Mr Curry thought it hilarious to call me 'Perce', as in the nineteenth-century Romantic poet Percy Bysshe Shelley. That was ok; I thought it hilarious to call him Big Jim Curry like he was a centre back for Stockport County.

By now, I had totally given up the ghost as far as my schoolwork was concerned. Previously, I'd always started each new school year full of hope and determination, confident that this year it was going to be different – I was going to try harder, I was going to be attentive in class and I was actually going to do some homework. The new resolve usually lasted about two or three weeks and then I would just lapse into my old habits.

At the start of the fifth form, I didn't even pretend to myself it was going to be any different – not even renewed vigour and a W.H. Smiths 'Back to School' kit could help me now. As far as I was concerned, school was about spending poor-quality time with my friends, cheeking teachers and generally making a nuisance of myself by being as disruptive as possible in class. At least I'd found something I was good at.

It seemed like most of the gang had woken up to the fact that unless we stopped treating school like some sort of apprenticeship in comedy heckling, we were going to be thrust out onto the streets next June, with no particular place to go. Ray had already pulled his finger well and truly out and had been moved up a class, leaving the rest of us still on Duffer Street.

In class 5D we were split up into sets for each subject, with those that were reasonably equipped brain-wise put in the O Level set and the rest in the CSE set. The long-since replaced O Level qualification stood for Ordinary Level of Education, and passing these exams meant what? That after five years of grammar school education, the best that we could possibly hope to attain was to be classified as ordinary? CSE, the lowest qualification available, stood for Certificate of Secondary Education and in terms of value out in the real world, this certificate stood somewhere between a warranty for an Austin Allegro and 25 yards breaststroke.

I had managed to sneak my way into a few O Level sets but I was mainly to undergo the indignity of taking CSEs. This meant that I was separated from John and Laurence for most of my lessons and, worse still, had to spend most of my lessons in the company of the kids from the lowest class in our year, 5K.

5K contained some of the most vicious thugs in the school. The walls of their form room were decorated with National Front graffiti – which was quite odd really, considering that the main thug was a black lad called Trevor. Trev seemed quite oblivious to the National Front's manifesto and bandied about words like 'Paki', 'Yid' and 'Pooftah' along with his sidekicks Harry and John, with free abandon and without any hint of irony. So well hidden was the irony, rumour had it that Trev had applied to become a fully paid-up member of the National Front. Did he think they wouldn't notice?

He'd grown up in the local children's home Dr. Barnardo's, and with that tough upbringing came an in-built hardness; because of this, the others in his gang were totally in awe of him. He was more of a silent assassin type, who only called on his hardness when it was absolutely vital. He preferred to bark out his commandments for his henchmen to carry out, thus keeping his own nose clean. What he said went, and the other two were only too happy to carry out his wishes.

John was a bully, nasty through and through, a vindictive sort who didn't really need a decent reason to cause pain. I certainly can't recall any redeeming features to credit him with.

Harry was different to the other two. Not vastly different, but he did at least occasionally display some humour. I always thought he was a little smarter than Trevor and John, and probably understood the ridiculousness of a National Front-supporting gang headed up by a black person, but chose to keep it from the other two simply because it amused him.

He had a nose that had been so severely broken that the end of it almost sat at right angles to the rest of his face. This didn't make him the handsomest of chaps, and his speech was clearly affected by the difficulty he had breathing through such a hacked hooter. On the upside, he was really good at smelling around corners.

I caught him in a good mood one day and plucked up the courage to ask him what had happened to his nose. He calmly explained that it was his dad that had given him the broken nose. I thought this was appalling, and I almost started to feel sorry for him. Well, it kind of made sense, and to some extent excused him. No wonder he had turned out to be such a violent individual when he was suffering physical abuse at home at the hands of his own father. However, as he further qualified the broken schnoz, it transpired that Harry wasn't a victim of domestic violence at all, and the reason his dad had broken his nose was because Harry had shaken a ladder that his dad was at the top of, whilst innocently painting the window frames of the family home. The helpless Harry Senior came tumbling down and landed on his son's face. I asked him why he had shaken the ladder, to which he replied 'had to be done Bear – the man's a menace'.

The three of them went about their business of making the lives of their targets a misery and as a trio they were pretty good at this. They terrorised the weak and exerted their authority over the strong. Demanding money with menace was their favourite form of abuse and they never encountered much resistance to this. On the rare occasions when someone was brave enough to refuse, they would administer what they called 'Beatings'. This involved Harry and John standing either side of their victim's desk, each holding a rolled-up atlas above their heads, which they would then bring down alternately and with full force on the poor lad's head, with the precision and timing of the clockwork hammer and anvil men from a Swiss cuckoo clock. 'Beatings' usually had the desired effect and money was usually begrudgingly handed over. When it wasn't, plan B, a good old-fashioned kicking, usually did the trick.

I have to admit that in all my years of schooling I was never really a target for bullying. This is quite odd really seeing that I was ginger, a Jew and becoming slightly more rotund with each passing month. Lord knows I was asking for it. Unfortunately, the same couldn't be said for my new mate Ross Landau. He was just about the only lad from 5K who seemed to be worth getting to know. Ross was a big rock fan with an encyclopedic knowledge of music that could rival Ian's. He had a Saturday job working in a record shop somewhere in West London and was on a promise of a full-time job there once this final year of school was over. I very much liked the idea of working in a record shop, it seemed like the perfect job to me; what could be better than sitting around playing pop music all day long?

From that point of view Ross was more sorted than any of us. He had his immediate future mapped out and it was just as well – he was a terrible student. He was so bad a student that he had to rely on copying my homework. That's what you call a desperado. We sat together in most classes and became good friends. His schoolbooks were covered with the names of pop groups, which wasn't really that unusual – mine were too – but he used to draw the proper band logos on his and colour them in, usually during lessons. His favourite band at this time was Thin Lizzy. He insisted that the riff from 'Jailbreak' was the greatest riff that rock had to offer and would constantly run through it over and over again from behind his hand-cupped mouth during lessons, making that guitar sound that you can make by pouting and 'der-derring' through tightly pushed-together teeth.

I remembered Thin Lizzy having a hit back in 1973 with 'Whiskey in the Jar'. It was in that very first chart rundown that I recorded off the radio on that old reel-to-reel tape recorder. I had really liked the song but had always assumed they were a bit of a one-hit-wonder band. I had no idea that they were still making records until 'The Boys Are Back In Town' made the charts back in the summer.

Ross lent me their latest album, *Jailbreak*, and I loved it. Not on the same scale as I was loving all my Beatles albums, but suffice to say I had a new band name to write on my exercise books.

Ross played bass guitar in a band of older lads that didn't go to school anymore – friends of his elder brother, I think. He had the coolest of bass guitars: a Rickenbacker just like the one McCartney had played on *Magical Mystery Tour*. He also smoked pot. He smoked pot a lot. He smoked it a lot, and talked about smoking it a lot. He even knew where to buy it. Along with my growing love for all things Beatley came a fascination for the hippy counterculture, with particular reference to the music that the Beatles had made under the influence of pot and acid. The fact that I now knew someone that actually took drugs pretty much made me hippy by proxy and made me inquisitive to find out what all the fuss was about for myself. I nagged him to get me some, but it would be a long while before he did.

He was very fussy about the bands that he thought it was ok to like, very much like Ian in that way. He absolutely hated seventies schoolboy favourites Black Sabbath and Status Quo. He dismissed them as talentless riff-peddlers and poured scorn on anyone that dared to like them. He had this habit of insisting that you liked them even if you didn't. If you looked away for ten seconds he would adorn your exercise book with 'Quo' or 'Sabbath' and then accuse you of being a fan because you had it written on your book. If he was in a particularly playful mood, he would invent scenarios that went something like this;

'You know how that time you said that *Sabbath Bloody Sabbath* was the greatest album ever made?'.

'I've never said that, I don't own any Sabbath albums.'

'Yeah you do. Remember that time you came in to my shop and bought a new copy of *Sabbath Bloody Sabbath* because you loved your old one so much and played it so many times that you wore it out and all the music fell off?'.

'No, I've never owned a Black Sabbath album in my life.'

'Oh wait a minute, no, I'm thinking of the Quo. You love the Quo don't you? Down, down deeper and down, down, down deeper and down.'

He would sing this right in my face, head-banging as he sang, with his long hair flying all over the place in a million different directions, but mostly in my eyes.

'No Ross, it's you that loves the Quo. In fact, it's not only you that loves them – your mum loves them. Your mum loves them even more than you do. Your mum loves the Quo so much that she named you after their lead singer.'

And so it went on. These were our tender, more grown-up moments.

Ross had been saddled with Trev's boys for most of his time at Beal, and had been bullied and beaten by them many times. He wasn't really the sort of person that you would expect to be bullied. Yes, he was quite overweight, but as I've mentioned he wasn't a swot. He had long hair just like everyone else, so it wasn't his haircut. He wore a pair of blue-tinted Aviator style glasses that he constantly pushed up the bridge of his nose. In truth, he looked a bit like a rock star, albeit a somewhat portly one. His glasses gave off an aura of coolness rather than hanging out a sign that said 'bully me' like those 'speccy' National Health glasses of the time tended to do. So I'm not really sure what it was about him that flagged him up as a target for bullying, but he had it rough.

There had been lots of Ross-bullying sessions down the years, but the most severe episode was the occasion when Harry dangled him out of a third-story classroom window by his ankles just for a laugh. For that little escapade Harry received a one-week suspension from school, which even by seventies standards seems a little bit on the light side. These days he would probably be beheaded.

During a maths lesson towards the end of our final term, as we prepared for our exam, our maths teacher, the droopy-moustachioed 'Ed' Bevan, was explaining a particularly tiresome equation on the blackboard. He suddenly spotted Ross writing something (probably 'Tony Iommi is God') on my maths book as I stared gormlessly at the blackboard.

'And so Landau, as you seem to know how to solve this so well that you can afford to interfere with Shelley (a bit of homoerotic innuendo was never too far from the lips of teachers with droopy moustaches in the seventies), would you care to explain to the rest of the class how it's done?'.

With that, Ross rose like a one-man Mexican wave and spoke;

'Sir ... Ed ... can I call you Sir Ed? In two months' time I'm going to be working a record shop. Why the fuck would I want to know, or even care what 'x' is? How will knowing what 'x' is improve my life? The only 'x's that I'm interested in are the ex-members of Deep Purple.' And with that he sat down.

With those couple of sentences, he summed up what most of the class were feeling about algebra and his statement was greeted with much cheering, whistles and a round of applause. Even Harry shouted out, 'Ooh gud fungs,' and rubbed his hands together with glee. This was one of his catch-phrases. We assumed he was saying, 'Oh good things,' and it just came out like that because of his broken nose – but he always said it and rubbed his hands together whenever he got excited. It made us laugh inwardly, but we were too scared to openly enjoy it, just in case he couldn't help it and thought we were taking the piss. Five years too late, Ross had finally earned the respect of his tormentors.

He had already earned my respect by introducing me to Thin Lizzy. In the autumn of 1976, Lizzy released their follow up album to *Jailbreak* called *Johnny the Fox,* and to promote the album they were touring the UK. I thought it was about time that I lost my gig virginity and so along with John, Ray and Ross we bought tickets for their November 13 gig at the Kursaal Ballroom in Southend-On-Sea.

By the time we had decided to take the plunge there were only a couple of weeks to wait until the day of the gig arrived. I felt the excitement of anticipation of my very first gig in the same way that I had for my first football match. The days dragged slowly and break and dinner times were spent discussing what we should wear, speculation about which songs the band might play, and how we should behave so as not to look like rock gig novices.

Your first gig has the same place of importance in your pop history as the purchase of your first record. And with it comes that same dollop of kudos that is afforded to those that manage to pick a good'un.

With gigs there is even more potential to flex your pop muscles, because if you're really quick out of the starting blocks you could be seeing a band that are so fresh and so 'now' that they don't even have a record deal. There will always be a nod of recognition coupled with a suitcase-sized pang of jealousy from me for those fortunates that managed to have the foresight to check out The Beatles at the Cavern, The Stones at the Crawdaddy or The Sex Pistols at the Screen on the Green.

Just like the purchase of your first record, the first gig you attended presents another opportunity to bend the truth a little. You have to be careful with this one though. Gigs are far more of a one-off than records. A time, a place, with no variables. It's no good claiming you were at Knebworth when everybody knows you were really at Woolworths. But for me there was no need to change a thing. To have Thin Lizzy at the all-standing Kursaal Ballroom, when they were at that point just before they exploded and went global, as my first-ever gig is a fabulous entry on my pop CV.

The excitement was reaching fever pitch by the time the day of the gig arrived. Clothes-wise, I went with jeans and trainers, complemented by my yellow *Magical Mystery Tour* t-shirt and a jean-jacket that I was never completely happy with. The jean-jacket was a real dilemma. I always felt it was way too long and not faded enough – to me it screamed 'bought by your mum from C&A' which, to be fair was exactly what it was. And then there was the issue of what to do with the jacket once you got inside the venue. Do you tie it around your waist? Simple and efficient, but it does tend to make you look like a cricket umpire. Do you dump it on the floor and risk having to go home wearing not only a jacket that you'll never grow into, but also the seventeen pints of Double Diamond that it's been doused in? Or do you hand it in at the cloakroom, which is probably the most sensible solution, but only if you have two or three spare days to stand in the queue waiting to get it back after the gig? The steaming sweatiness of the gig to the contrasting freezing cold outside is an age-old problem for British jacket-wearing gig-goers that has never been satisfactorily resolved.

On gig day, we boarded the train from Ilford to Southend-On-Sea late that afternoon, each of us sipping from a communal bottle of Woodpecker Cider en-route, assuming that, in the absence of soft drugs, that's what rock fans did pre-gig. On entering the venue I bought a mirror badge of the Lizzy logo and in we went to soak up the atmosphere. The venue was dimly lit but not totally dark and music by bands we'd never heard of was playing over the PA. We weren't early but managed to snake our way through gaps in the crowd to take up a position not too far from the front and dead centre stage.

It wouldn't be long before support band Clover, who were a sort of Irish folk/rock group, took to the stage. We applauded politely at the end of each song of their forty-minute set despite spending most of the time during their set talking/shouting through cupped hands. The role of the support band is a tough one. No one really wants to watch them, but it's necessary if you want to take up a good position for the main event. However, almost the second that Clover left the stage, the crowd swelled to ridiculous levels of uncomfortableness, as the bar emptied and hundreds of Lizzy fans, wearing much shorter and more faded jean-jackets than me, pushed their way to the front. It was highly irritating to be pushed back and we now stood halfway between the stage and the back of the room.

The roadies started to clear Clover's gear from the stage and the tension started to mount once more. After around thirty minutes the house lights went down, a huge cheer from the crowd went up and we stood for a few seconds in complete darkness save for the red power lights on the huge stacks of Marshall amplifiers and speakers on the stage. And then a single searchlight started up, skimming across the hundreds of heads in the audience, the sound of a siren rang out and the band invisibly strode on to the stage. The familiar opening single chord from 'Jailbreak' rang out from the combined Les Pauls of Scott Gorham and Brian Robertson. I'd never heard anything quite as loud as that chord in my life. And with a thud of Brian Downey's snare they were away, and we were suddenly ensconced in a sea of bounciness. We were still stood centre stage, directly in line with Phil Lynott, and he looked commanding, clad in red leather jacket, black Levi's and with his Afro shaped into a partial fringe that covered one eye. Lynott had the power to mesmerise. It was difficult to take your eyes off him, he was that magnetic. His black bass guitar had a shiny mirror scratchplate, and he would purposely catch it in the stage lights, causing a flash of light to be reflected into the faces of the audience. He was menacing, yet playful with the crowd.

'Is there anybody out there with a little Irish in them?'.

Which of course was greeted with cheers from those that were either Irish or had heard him say it before and knew what was coming next.

'Are there any of the girls that would like a little more Irish in them? This is a song called "Emerald".'

The band thundered through their set, tightly and efficiently like they'd done it a million times before – which of course they had – but for me, watching a live band for the first time, it was as fresh as if they'd only written those songs that morning. I was totally enraptured and their set zipped by in no time at all. When it came to the encore Lynott teased once again by asking us which song we wanted to hear. To a man, the yelled response was 'The Rocker'.

'No, no, no, no, no' teased Lynott

'Yeah, yeah, yeah, yeah, yeah' was the defiant reaction.

'No, no, no, no ... NO'

'YES'

'NO'

And so it went on until the smiling Lynott finally announced,

'This is a song that I wanna do ...' emphasising the 'I' as hard as he could. 'It's a song called 'The Rocker'.'

And with that the band launched into the opening riff and we all dug deep for a final bout of bouncing.

As magnificent as Lynott was that night, I managed to find myself somewhat distracted by the energetic drumming of Brian Downey. He was as flamboyant with his instrument as Lynott was with his stage presence. Watching Downey confirmed in my mind that I really did want to become a drummer. That and the incessant ringing in my ears, which lasted for several days afterwards, were the two things that I took away from the Kursaal. I'd loved it and couldn't wait until the next one.

Back at school, our mock O levels and CSEs were fast approaching and if neither Ross nor I cared very much about passing our maths exam, John was a little more concerned. Or rather his parents were. They had decided that he needed a little extra help and had paid for him to have private tuition after school with a new Indian maths teacher called Mr Sharma. He was a strange cove, to say the least; usually a rather quiet and genteel sort of chap, but when riled he had a bit of a vicious streak – which he called 'De Whopper'. 'De Whopper' was a huge slap around the face, which Mr Sharma would administer with great force which apparently hurt quite a lot. He took no shit. It was a nice arrangement though, so polite, he gave you the choice – 'you want De Whopper, boy?'. Most abstained.

Because of my ever-growing interest in The Beatles, and the fact that John was having private lessons with an Indian teacher, I was quick to make the parallel comparison between this and George Harrison having sitar lessons with Ravi Shankar. Laurence and I would insist that it was actually sitar lessons that John was having with Mr Sharma and not maths lessons at all. John hated it, which only encouraged us more.

'What you learning about today John?'.

'Oh some geometry shit,' John would respond, making it clear that these lessons were not his idea of a fun after-school club.

'Geometry my bollocks! You're learning the sitar riff from 'Norwegian Wood' aren't you. Better get it right or you'll get De Whopper.'

I'm not entirely sure why this managed to rile John quite as much as it did, or why we thought for a single second that having private sitar lessons was in any way less cool than having private maths lessons.

Laurence and I had our own little after-school routine. We would get the bus back to Gants Hill and then walk home along the Eastern Avenue together. Along the route there was a house that had a privet hedge that was so trim and perfect that Percy Thrower would have been proud to call it his own. One day, and without warning, I had the sudden urge to push Laurence through it. He wasn't expecting it and it took just the slightest of shoulder barges to set him a little off-balance, and tumbling through it he went. He could barely get up, he was laughing so much, and as I helped him up we observed our destructive handy work – a gaping hole in this most perfect of hedges.

The next day – and how I didn't know it was coming I don't know – he did exactly the same thing to me. And so this became our daily-premeditated routine, so much so that we would argue about whose turn it was to be pushed. There was no resistance, it was accepted that one of us would be going through the hedge and we thought it was hilarious as this perfect hedge became balder and balder and the hole became slightly more gaping than the day before.

Hilarious that was, until the day when there was a knock on my door and an elderly chap asked if my father was there. I didn't connect at all that the caller was Mr Hedge himself and I went to fetch my dad. The man told my dad that he would leave it up to him to punish me, but he was going to inform the school. When my dad had finished tearing a strip or three off me, I rang Laurence to warn him that he was probably about to get a visit but it was too late, the man was already explaining to his parents what a destructive son they had.

Even though we had been busted, we still found potential to laugh about the whole affair. We conjured up scenarios of how the man knew where we lived. We decided that the one that amused us the most was where the man followed us home, creeping like Secret Squirrel on tiptoes and darting to hide behind each lamppost along the way so we wouldn't see him. In this scenario he was wearing a trench coat, dark glasses and a false beard. No wonder we didn't notice him, in such an inconspicuous disguise.

The next morning Manny concluded the after-assembly announcements of inter-school sporting achievements with '... and finally, will Nesbitt and Shelley from 5D come to my office immediately.'. When we arrived at his office we were certain that we were going to get caned, but what we actually got was just the Manny hairdryer and instructions to write a letter of apology to Hedge Man, which didn't seem like too much of a hardship – result!

I'd never had to write a letter of apology before and wasn't really sure how to pitch it. Should I take the gushing, grovelling approach, or should I try and be a little bit cool about it? If the truth be known, we still thought the whole episode utterly hilarious and didn't really feel the slightest tinge of remorse for our act of total demolition.

So I decided that maybe a bit of both might be appropriate. Manny hadn't told us the name of the man and so I began the letter – 'Dear Hedge Owner', which with hindsight, probably wasn't the best of starts. I don't remember everything I wrote, but I do remember the line that went 'I'm really sorry for the damage that I caused to your hedge – I had no idea it meant so much to you'. I wrote this with a sneaky eye on getting a laugh out of Laurence (achieved), and with the other on delivering some sort of decent apology that was going to get me off the hook for what really amounts to horticultural murder.

Needless to say, Manny went ballistic when he read my letter the next morning and screwed it up and threw it on the floor in disgust. I was ordered to spend my lunch hour in his office doing the re-write. We delivered the letters that evening. The man grudgingly accepted them and the verbal apologies that accompanied them, but probably knew deep down that he was only getting them because we had been forced to write them.

That was the last time we pushed each other through the hedge as schoolboys. We still thought about it every time we walked past; we even went through the old routine of asking whose turn it was to go in the hedge, but never followed it through.

A couple of years later, whilst taking that same walk home completely mangled after a night of drinking at the Green Man in Leytonstone, we again played out the 'whose turn to go in the hedge?' routine. But this time, fuelled with several pints of lager, I just said 'yours!' and shoved Laurence as hard as I could straight through the greenery – which had once again been restored to its former glory. He flew through it like a seagull diving for a herring, and in his drunken state had extreme difficulty getting out – his little legs kicking into the thin air and getting him nowhere fast, just like Wile E. Coyote when he runs off the edge of a cliff in pursuit of the Roadrunner.

I grabbed his arm and pulled him out sharply, and we ran off as fast as drunken legs carrying bellies full of beer can run. And then just as sharply we pulled up. What were we running for? There was no more Manny. There were no more parental punishments. There would be no more apology letters. We were free, free, free, and laughed all the way home. We'd missed it. As fully grown men in our early fifties, when Laurence and I get together, 'the hedge' often crops up, and we still find that the whole episode hasn't really lost any of its shine.

But my favourite story from school dates back to a year or so earlier. The aforementioned Big Jim Curry, our geography teacher, played an instrumental part. Mr Curry was one of those teachers that you might describe as being firm but fair. He could certainly take a joke – he could make them too, but he was another teacher that had a vicious temper when pushed to his limit, so you had to keep your eye on him. If there was a seventies teacher's look, he didn't have it; he wore thick black-rimmed glasses, which had lenses like the bottoms of beer bottles. When he stared at you his eyes were scarily huge and bloodshot. He always looked a bit dishevelled when he arrived in class, as if he'd only just remembered a few seconds before that he had a class to teach. He would often arrive with his hair all windswept and his knitted tie draped over his left shoulder. On one occasion we thought it would be amusing to mimic him, and so when he arrived to teach us, the whole class rose as one with our school ties flung over our shoulders. He found that sort of caper amusing, as he did the day that Ray sat in class with a pair of black-rimmed glasses just like his, except these glasses had no lenses in them at all. 'New specs Pearce?' he enquired. 'Yes sir – I wanted ones just like yours,' as Ray rubbed his left eye through the hole where the lens was supposed to be. 'Good-oh lad, but you might want to get some lenses for those. Not much use without lenses.' Not much got past Big Jim.

On the other hand, if you weren't paying attention when he was speaking, or talking to someone else, he would have no hesitation at hurling a wooden blackboard rubber at your head with great force. On one occasion the whole class was making a bit of a racket as we queued up to go into the library following afternoon break. The library was situated next door to the staff room, and Big Jim came out to see what all the commotion was that was disturbing his own break-time ciggie and cuppa. He immediately sent Benjy Fenster down to the gym with instructions to bring back the biggest plimsoll he could find. He then proceeded to slipper the entire class right there and then on the stairs. Thirty-two kids slippered one after the other – that takes a bit of doing.

Big Jim was a good teacher, one of the few that were worth listening to. Despite the general dreariness of his subject, his lessons were never as dull as those taught by other teachers because he forced you to participate. If he asked a question, he would never ask the kids that had their hands up, always the ones that didn't. I always got the impression that he had a soft spot for me despite the fact that I was as bad at geography as I was at everything else. I don't really know why, but if I'm honest, I had one for him too. I particularly liked the fact that he would never mark any homework unless it was coming up to report time – which came around twice a year. This meant that, once we had sussed this out, it was a license to delay doing geography homework, as we knew it wasn't going to be collected in for marking at the next lesson.

One lad who took liberties with this situation was Lesbie Mainwaring. (Real name Leslie, but we called him Lesbie because we were grammar school boys). Big Jim Curry called him Captain. Of course he did.

Lesbie hadn't done a stroke of homework all year, and Big Jim announced that he would be collecting our books for marking after the next lesson. Seeing as the next lesson was just two days away, there was absolutely no chance of Lesbie filling in the gaps. So when it came around, Lesbie mysteriously developed an illness and headed off to the sick bay. Unfortunately for him, he forgot that the next geography lesson was in our form room rather than in the geography room.

So when Big Jim collected in the books he enquired where the Captain was. 'Sick bay, Sir,' was the resounding answer from those that had a thirst for blood. A lone voice belonging to Lesbie's best mate, Johnny 'Hangdog' Fuller (he had one of those tongues that was too big for his mouth) piped up: 'but his geography book is in his desk, Sir'.

'Find it for me,' Big Jim demanded of the hapless Hangdog. Johnny dived into Lesbie's desk and started delving. He eventually emerged to hand over the totally blank exercise book with a big grin on his face – like a Golden Retriever that had just delivered a slobbery ball back to his grateful master. Big Jim took a quick flick through the empty pages and his face turned to thunder. 'If a single one of you tells the Captain that I have this, I will cane the whole lot of you,' he declared, ensuring a solidarity of silence.

When the next lesson came around we trundled off to the geography room, excited with the anticipation of what Big Jim had in store for Lesbie. What he delivered was beyond our wildest dreams. At the start of the lesson, and without saying a word, he beckoned Lesbie to the front of the class with his index finger. Lesbie, without questioning the request, faithfully obeyed the instruction.

'Go and stand in the corner, boy,' Big Jim demanded.

'Why sir?'

Big Jim had fire in his eyes and raised his voice, already irritated at being questioned.

'Go and stand in the fucking corner boy!'

Lesbie trudged off to the right-hand corner at the front of the class and stood facing the wall, surely by now realising the reason he was there.

'Did I say stand in the corner Captain?'.

'Yes sir, I am standing in the corner.'

'Don't be insolent boy, I obviously meant stand on your head in the corner, didn't I?'.

The baying class had tried in vain to stifle its collective laughter during the anticipation period. As Big Jim's moment began to fully unfold, such was the hilarity being expressed across the class that I wouldn't have been surprised to learn that there were several small puddles of wee being produced all over the geography room floor. It was rare for this class to back a teacher against one of its own classmates, but there was an overriding feeling of injustice here that needed to be levelled. Why should we have wasted all that time completing homework assignments whilst Lesbie had not?

There then began a farcical few minutes as Lesbie failed in attempts to swing his legs up so that they were leaning against the classroom wall. As he pursed his bum towards the class, a small, sheepish fart escaped, leading to the further merriment of his classmates. Eventually he arrived at the correct headstand position and as his face got redder and redder, the accumulated sweat from his face forced his glasses to slip down his nose and numerous coins trickled out of his pockets and on to the floor.

At this point, Big Jim attempted to begin the lesson by trying to teach us something about the industrial wastelands of the Northern England. It was impossible to concentrate on anything that he said, as all eyes were now fixed on how Lesbie was doing in the corner. The whole lesson was just a constant stream of laughing as the wretched Mainwaring kept losing his balance and collapsing in a flustered heap in the corner. From time to time Big Jim would ask a question relating to the topic and say 'You can answer this one Captain – no need to raise your hand boy'. More hilarity followed as Lesbie attempted to give serious answers whilst standing on his head.

About halfway through the lesson there was a knock on the door and in walked a third-former who asked whether he could retrieve a book from his desk. As he entered he did a double-take and burst out laughing as he spotted the fiasco going on in the corner of the room. He gathered his book and left in a hurry without questioning what he had just seen.

Lesbie remained in that corner for the entire lesson and at the end of it he was told to complete the missing homework for the entire term over the weekend and deliver it to the staff room on Monday morning or he would face the cane and receive an E grade on his report.

The whole Lesbie-Mainwaring-standing-on-his-head episode is one of those stories that you really had to be there to fully enjoy in its glory. It's a very visual tale that is hard to translate to the written word whilst keeping its true splendour intact. The story has stood countless re-runs over the years when we have all got together and chewed over the fat of old memories. It remains my favourite memory of school, but a couple of years ago part of the story took an unusual twist.

Whenever I had repeated this anecdote, I had always included the bit about the third-former coming in halfway through the lesson and doing the double take, as I considered it to be an integral part in the comedy of the tale.

My brother-in-law Glen also went to Beal, but he was in the year below me, and so we never knew each other back then. I have now known Glen for over thirty years, but amazingly we had never really talked about old school stories before – on one occasion, however, we did. As we swapped episodes, I was just lining up my Lesbie Mainwaring story as my jewel in the crown when Glen began to speak:

'There was this time, I went back to my form room, the geography room, to get a book out of my desk, and Big Jim Curry was teaching a class in there and he had some poor kid standing on his head in the corner.'

All those years that I have known Glen – all those years that I had been relaying the story, and to suddenly find out that my brother-in-law was THAT third-former in the story! I found that quite astounding, and a beautiful twist.

When we reflect back on tales of schooldays there is usually a story to be told about school discos. These were rare treats at our school – a one-off night every year where pop would be allowed to strut around the school hall and use its facilities as if it owned the place. I would always say that Thin Lizzy at the Kursaal was my first proper gig, but prior to that I had seen Ian's band, The Thin Yoghurts, play a gig in the school hall at the school disco. For this annual event, the fifth and sixth form lads from Beal Grammar School for Boys were joined by the girls from Beal Grammar School for Girls for a night of awkward dancing, awkward conversation and some awkward-looking boys on the stage playing pop music.

There were three bands on – a sort of mini Woodstock of grammar school rock. We were there to support The Yoghurts. First on the bill was a band whose real name escapes me now. I'm not sure if I ever knew it – we just referred to them as 'The Meemos' – mainly because Ian called their lead guitarist 'The Meemo'. I have no idea why, or even know what a meemo is, but they played the usual fifth form fare of Quo and Sabbath covers and would have therefore have been really popular with Ross. Another band, Sandy Richardson & The Wheelchairs, featured brilliant young guitarist Steve Ricard. We had become friends with Steve recently and although he wasn't in our class, he was spending an increasing amount of time hanging out in our classroom during breaks and lunchtimes.

His band played mainly self-penned stuff, which consisted of songs about the end of the universe, committing suicide and whether or not it was possible to walk normally on the moon. If I didn't know better, I would swear that Sting based the early work of The Police on the songwriting of this band. Despite being quite talented, they were a very dull band to watch and were currently peddling their wares under a suitably dreadful name that was something like 'Curriculum Vitae' or 'Resumé'. I dared Steve to go on stage that night as Sandy Richardson & The Wheelchairs. I considered that what they needed to liven up some very insipid songs was some political incorrectness and a tribute to *Crossroads* all rolled into one. He didn't disappoint.

The Thin Yoghurts (so called because of the Prize Yoghurt TV ad campaign of the time in which a battle of the bands takes place between the thick and fruity 'Prize Guys' and their arch enemies, the runny, wimpy 'Thin Yoghurts'), comprised Ian Montague (lead vocals/guitar), Mark Anderson (lead guitar), Steve Anderson (bass), Drew Adamson (rhythm guitar) and a kid called Mike, who didn't go to our school, on drums. The only thing I can remember about Mike the drummer was that he was quite good on the drums and had a girlfriend called Pillah Salmon, which obviously is not a name that you tend to forget in a hurry. There may well have been some comments bandied about relating to what exactly it was that Mike the Drummer posted in Pillah's box – sophisticated humour was our calling card. The Thin Yoghurts' influences? Zeppelin, Floyd, Yes, Genesis, Free – anything really, as long as they didn't have a record in the charts and the songs were at least eight minutes long – and if they weren't originally, The Yoghurts would make sure that they were now.

Ray and I were invited one Sunday morning to go and watch The Yoghurts rehearse at Bell Studios in York Road, Ilford. Bell Studios should not by any stretch of the imagination be confused with studios that belonged to Bell Records – the record label on which Gary Glitter, The Bay City Rollers, David Cassidy and the mighty Showaddywaddy released records. The Bell Studios that I'm talking about was a shabby old room opposite where all the buses stopped and was owned by a bloke called Bob Bell. Anyway, despite these less-than-salubrious surroundings it was enjoyable watching the Yoghurts putting their set through its ploddy-prog paces. I was surprised at how good they were. Mark Anderson in particular was an incredible guitarist for his age. Actually, he was an incredible guitarist full stop. Reminiscing about his time in this band many years later, Ian the still-strumming former singer, remarked that Mark was a better guitarist back then, aged fifteen, than he (Ian) was now!

The Yoghurts were far and away the best band on show in the school hall that night. They delivered a set full of technical majesty – 'Stairway to Heaven', 'Black Dog' and 'Rock'n' Roll' by Led Zeppelin, 'Money' by Pink Floyd and 'Lady Eleanor' by Lindisfarne. This was the sort of stuff that delighted the on-looking gaggle of grammar school boys, but was less appealing to the girls in the audience and so The Yoghurts received a mixed reception. Although most of the band had top-class equipment – Les Pauls, Fender Stratocasters and Marshall amps – Ian was the exception; he didn't have posh gear like the others. He played a white Vox Stroller guitar and his amp was connected to a huge speaker that had been covered (presumably to hide its state of disrepair) in what looked very much like my orange bedspread (but actually wasn't). The guitars were magnificent, but louder than they needed to be, and this meant that Ian could barely hear what he was singing and consequently, spent the entire gig singing with one finger stuck in his ear – an action aimed at partially rectifying this problem. Having a finger hanging out of your ear is not a good rock look, and it came back to haunt him a couple of weeks later whilst walking around Sainsbury's. He was approached by a rather nice-looking girl who enquired, 'Didn't I see you singing at Beal school a couple of weeks ago?'

'Yep, that was me', responded Ian, rather pleased with himself for being recognised in public for rockular activities.

'Yeah, you had yer finger stuck in yer ear didn't ya'. A unique icebreaker, I always thought.

It felt a bit naughty being in the school hall listening to pop music after hours. From our vantage point I could see all the classrooms that surrounded it, which only a couple of hours earlier had been vibrant hives of activity, but were now plunged into darkened silence. The school hall was the hub of everything that happened at Beal. It was where the whole school gathered for assembly, and where the walls were decorated with outstanding pieces of schoolboy art, photographs of the entire school population from previous eras, and a wooden board etched in gold print with the names of former pupils that had gone on to achieve great things. The stage was usually reserved exclusively for Mr Shaw's drama department's end-of-year productions such as *Guys and Dolls* or *Hello, Dolly!*, however tonight pop was taking over, and Ian was up there, doing it – playing pop music, playing it loudly and playing it with a finger in his ear. They looked great up there, legs defiantly astride, tightly clasping their low-hung guitars as if they were their very own penises. Clad in velvet jackets, their long hair nestling wispily on their shoulders, disguising the merest hint of dandruff, and every one of them sporting a floppy, sweat-drenched centre parting that said a collective 'fuck off' to *Hello, Dolly!* and the high achievers on behalf of us all. This was pop being as naughty as you like.

They all seemed slightly nervous – boys sent to do men's work – but they pulled it off. Ian didn't engage with the audience in very much in-between song banter (something that he would become very astute at much later), but he was still in command. He thrust at his Vox Stroller with authority when needed, and ended each song with a mumbled 'thanks very much'.

I longed to be up there with him. Not that I could contribute anything musically, but this looked like living the dream to me and, as I watched, I played out imaginary scenarios in my head. Any moment now, Ian was going to announce 'This next one's a song by Wings and I wanna bring on a friend of us all ... Mister Ant-knee Shelley' – in almost word-for-word mimicry of how George Harrison introduces Bob Dylan on *The Concert For Bangladesh*. The 'Mister' bit would be essential. He would have to say the Mister – it's pop's most irritating law.

As Ian announced my name, there would be cheers of excited anticipation from the crowd. My back would be slapped by all around me as I bustled my way through the thronging masses and made my way to the stage. Might it be a little too extravagant to expect the distant echoes of my name being chanted from the back of the room? Ian would offer an outstretched hand and help me climb on board the stage (this would be a much cooler entrance than the traditional method of simply using the steps). We'd hug – nothing too emotional because Ian didn't do 'too emotional'. And not a 'I haven't seen you in forever' type hug either, as that would be inappropriate having sat next to each other in physics not three hours earlier – just a warm, 'great to have you up here with the band, man' hug. Anyway, the hug is not important. He would usher me to the drum kit, happily vacated by Pillah Salmon's boyfriend, the opening riff to 'Junior's Farm' would ring out from Mark's Les Paul, and we'd be off.

There are so many reasons why this little scenario could never have really happened. Firstly, I had no more idea of how to play the drums than I did of how to play backgammon, and secondly, a drummer would never happily vacate the drum stool to let a novice have a bash. A drummer thinks of his kit as an extension of his own family – each component routinely positioned and tuned to perfection. Tamper with it at your peril – but trying to shag his sister might be a safer option.

Seeing The Yoghurts on stage served as just another little reminder that I wanted to play pop music as well as listen to it.

Ian, Mark and Drew weren't the only musicians in our class. There was Benjy Fenster, mouth organ specialist with Doctor's Wotsits, for a start. I have no idea why he was called Benjy when his name was Jonathan. In fact, the entire line-up of Doctor's Wotsits were called Jonathan, which in itself is a little freaky. Jonathan Beech owned a Chad Valley drum kit and the line-up was completed by Jonathan Crego (Bontempi organ). It's quite incredible that they didn't call themselves the Three Jonathans or the Three Johnnies, and it is to their eternal credit that they didn't allow the Three Johnnies concept to manifest itself into calling the band Packet of Three.

The only real mistake that Benjy made was telling me that this group, playing what basically amounted to toy instruments,

a) existed at all, and

b) had somehow with this ridiculous set of instruments managed to perform 'The Sun Has Got Its Hat On' and some sort of reworking of Sweet Sensation's 'Sad Sweet Dreamer'.

I took this hilarious information straight to John and during the next break we started to write the words for what was to become our first song.

Went to a Party at the county jail
Doctor's Wotsits began to wail
Johnny Beech on the Chad Valley drum kit
Benjy on the mouth organ, stupid little git

Let's Bop, everybody let's rock
Rock, rock
Do the Wotsit's Bop

'The Wotsits Bop' was never meant to be anything more than a gentle piss-take and to that end, it fulfilled all its requirements. I don't think at this stage it got past this first verse and chorus, but it was wrapped up in mothballs and saved for later ... although saved for what, we weren't really sure yet.

In the real music world, where people played proper instruments, something new was afoot. One Sunday lunchtime towards the end of 1976, I watched an edition of the *London Weekend Show* with Janet Street-Porter. The whole episode was dedicated to a new genre of music that had started to emerge out of the underground: punk rock.

The show was mostly about a band that called themselves the Sex Pistols; it showed footage of one of their early gigs and a very awkward interview with the band that Street-Porter handled brilliantly. The spokesman was a bloke with bright orange hair who called himself Johnny Rotten, although for a spokesman he didn't really have much to say for himself. Street-Porter managed to coax a few words out of him that were mainly delivered in helpings of one or two word sentences. It seemed that these punk rocker types were bored, bored, bored but had difficulty getting over just how bored they really were without sounding really boring. They were outraged that kids had to pay as much as five pounds to get in to see bands that only played in stadiums and arenas. They didn't like music that had nice tunes, strings and orchestras playing on them, but mostly they didn't like the fact that the music industry was dead.

And they were right. The British music scene hadn't produced any new acts of any substance since the early seventies. All the big bands of the time were either bands like The Stones and The Who, who were a hangover from the sixties, or the prog rock lot who were still plundering hippy ideals in a time and to a country that just wasn't interested anymore. Britain was there for the taking.

The fans of punk were fed up with being on the dole, and fed up with their parents and their government. Punk rock was something new and exciting in their lives. They wore clothes that were ripped up and then put back together again with safety pins, or dresses made of bin liners, and their hair was short and spiky, and dyed colours that hair just wasn't supposed to be dyed. The whole ethos of punk was giving music back to the kids, where they could afford to go to gigs and anyone could pick up a guitar and be in a band regardless of talent. They didn't have time to wait for their lucky break from a big record label, this had to happen here and now.

Punk was supposedly about to take over and blow the old guard such as Genesis, Yes and all the other prog acts out of the water. As much as I welcomed the notion that we would all be waving goodbye to the likes of Rick Wakeman and his silly cloak and pointy hat forever, I'd never heard anything quite so ridiculous in my life. These guys couldn't play, they couldn't sing and ok, yes, that was the whole point, but who the hell was going to buy this shit?

I saw Fraser that afternoon and he had seen the programme too. We both agreed it was horrible and best ignored and it would go away. We shut the door, drew the curtains, shook our heads and listened to *Wings at the Speed of Sound*.

A few days later on the *Today* show – a show that we always had on in our house whilst we ate our dinner – The Sex Pistols appeared again. This time they were accompanied by a gang of punk fans and were being interviewed live by the show's host Bill Grundy. Grundy asked the band what they had done with the money that they had been given by their record label. He was so drunk that he didn't even notice when the equally drunk guitarist Steve Jones had answered, 'we fuckin' spent it'. The interview descended into further chaos following a flirtatious comment from a teenage Siouxsie Sioux in which she told Grundy that she had always wanted to meet him. The middle-aged Grundy took the bait, and retorted, 'Well, let's meet after the show shall we?' This prompted Jones to call Grundy a 'dirty fucker' and a 'fucking rotter' right there live on my telly! Jones' torrent of abuse was hilarious and I spurted out a mouthful of peas in delight. My parents sat there open-mouthed and their peas dropped out freely. Although I may not have been convinced about the music, this was TV gold happening right in front of my eyes. This historic couple of minutes of TV kick-started The Pistols' career and Bill Grundy never worked again. Punk 1, Establishment 0.

All the talk at school the next day was about this interview. It was spread across the front page of every newspaper that morning. Tales of middle-aged men kicking in their television sets because they were offended by the swearing at tea time seemed utterly ludicrous to us – had they lost the plot as well as the ability to switch the TV off? In my eyes, this was the day that punk was born, even though it had been gathering momentum for some time. Trousers were tapered, hair was shorn and several kids at school started walking around declaring that they were punks. It would take me a little more time to fully embrace the punk movement, but embrace it I eventually would.

As 1976 rolled into 1977, I awaited the results of my mock O levels and CSEs. I wasn't expecting any academic gratification, but the results were important because my mum had encouraged revision for these exams with the promise that if I passed seven, then she would buy me the new Wings triple live album *Wings Over America.* I needed this record but at £10.99 it was outside of my saving capacity and was definitely present material.

Needless to say, I never got anywhere near the seven required passes, but I told my mum that I had anyway and claimed my prize. I still had no idea what I was going to do when I left school in a few months and it was beginning to worry me. It was also worrying my parents, so much so that my mum was actively seeking out employment for me. This felt a bit strange, but if she was happy to do the legwork then I was happy for her to do it, too.

She came across an advert in the *Ilford Recorder* for a merchant bank in the city of London that were looking for school leavers to join as trainee bank clerks in the summer. I was almost at the point of despair when she suggested that I write them a nice letter of application – that's the second letter I've had to write in this chapter! I didn't want to work in a bank; I didn't even think I was capable of working in a bank. Didn't you have to be good at maths for that sort of thing? I felt obliged to write the letter as she requested, thinking that whoever read it would piss themselves laughing and throw it in the bin, but surprisingly I got a letter back asking me to come to their office in Cannon Street for an interview.

My mum said that I needed to buy a suit for the interview and apparently my purple crushed velvet dinner jacket from my Bar Mitzvah was not going to fit the bill. So off we went to C&A's in Ilford, to buy me a suit and matching tie. I was about to cross the line.

I was nervous as hell waiting for my interviewer to arrive. I don't know why – I didn't want the job anyway. When he arrived he was a stuffy-looking businessman in his mid-fifties called Ken Willingale. In the half an hour or so that I spent in his company, he didn't really convince me that banking was the new rock'n'roll, but I came out of there thinking that I had to do something when I left school, and this might not be quite as bad as it seemed after all. He explained that many years ago he had also been brought up in Redbridge and asked me about whether certain places were still where he'd left them. He also told me that he had attended Beal and so knew about the qualities of the school and made it clear that this was a good enough recommendation for him. It was in the bag.

When the letter arrived saying that I was being offered the job, I was relieved. I now seemed to have something to do after school finished and it had been achieved with the minimum of effort. I was to be paid £1,750 per annum. That's a lot of records, I thought. Of course having a job in the bag before I did my final exams was excuse enough for me to be totally complacent about them. I had a job, so what was there to worry about? I stepped down my revision programme from bugger all, to something considerably less than that.

The last day of school came around very quickly. It was a Friday and after this day there would be no more lessons and we only had to go into the wretched place on the days we had exams to sit. That lunchtime, John, Laurence, Ian and I went back to Ross's house and piled into his parents' drinks cabinet, relieving it of all the Dubonnet and Cinzano that it had to offer. I'd never been drunk before and I liked it.

When we got back to school there was a leaving ceremony in the school hall, at which we had to go up and collect some sort of certificate from Manny. We were called up in alphabetical order and as I walked down the stairs from the stage after collecting mine, despite my best efforts to appear sober I lost my footing and fell. It was good that my final exit was a memorable one and I got that one last laugh.

At the bus stop Laurence and I were set upon by Trev's boys – not in a violent way, but they ripped our blazers to shreds, leaving me to go home clutching just the breast-pocket that the school crest was sewn to. My souvenir.

Physically that was all I was left with from my time at Beal. I went back to sit my exams and came away with a small collection of poor results – not a lot to show for five years of education. However, I may not have come away with the qualifications that I expected to achieve when I started the school back in the Autumn of 1972, but what I did take away from Beal are the hundreds of memories and the fantastic friendships – good, strong, lasting friendships that still exist today. And to me, both of these things are worth more than a million certificates. Thank you.

Welcome to the Working Week

Today is 27 June 1977. Six days ago I was wasting words on an essay about the Canadian Prairies during my geography O level. Yesterday, I was wondering what the hell I was about to let myself in for. Today, I'm going to find out.

It was early. Elsewhere, my friends would still be sleeping. Later, they would be enjoying yet another carefree day of their summer holidays. As I laid on my back in my bed, I stared at the huge poster of John Lennon on my wall – the one from the *Imagine* album where he's sitting in the white room playing the white grand piano. I don't know why I was staring at him quite so intensely, maybe I was hoping for divine intervention. He seemed to be ignoring me, and so I nervously put on my navy blue suit, crisp white shirt and a plain dark blue tie, and prepared myself for the first day of my working life. My mother made me some breakfast, which I tried my best to hold down.

Once again, my hair had been slightly tamed at her request, which on this occasion seemed reasonable as this was a job with a bank in the city after all, and jobs with banks in the city very rarely required people to sport large ginger afros that had been fashioned into the shape of a bell. Jobs for people with those sorts of hairstyles could be found in discotheques or Mr Byrite. As I prepared to leave for work, my mum brushed imaginary fluff from the shoulders of my jacket and sent me on my way with a kiss. I hoped that every morning from now on wasn't going to feel like this.

I trudged my way along the Eastern Avenue just like I had every morning for the past five years, but there was to be no more knocking for Dave Freed or random conversations about penguins. I headed down into Gants Hill tube station and onto the westbound platform.

The platform was packed with people, some reading big newspapers whilst they waited for their train, others bustling their way down the platform to find their favourite spot. When the train came in, it was even more crowded than the platform. I managed to bundle my way on to a train that barely had enough spare room to house a slightly hairy chest, let alone a whole person, and of course there was nowhere to sit. I squeezed into an area the size of an Opal Fruit, next to a lady reading the *Daily Express* who thought it was ok to brush my face with her paper as she turned the pages. Looking around the carriage everyone seemed so miserable staring at their books or papers or just into space. The thought of doing this every day for the next fifty years filled me with panic. I thought to myself 'I'll give it till the end of the week'.

I got off the Central Line train at Mile End station and crossed the platform to take the District Line. Mile End station was one of the most depressing places on earth: run-down and filthy, the 19th-century brick walls thick with black soot from a long-gone era. It stank of the still-moist patches of vomit that littered its platform, which told the story of its weekend visitors. I boarded the first train out and concluded the final part of my tube journey to Mansion House station. As I made the short walk from the station along Cannon Street to the offices of Singer & Friedlander Ltd, the nerves kicked in again and my stomach felt like it had a small gathering of Hawkwind fans acing inside it.

On arrival, I was collected by a man in his late thirties called Dave Elms, who sported a neatly trimmed beard and a waistcoat. He explained that he was the Assistant Manager of the cash department, and that was where I was going to be working.

Dave took me to my new office and introduced me to the rest of the department: Malcolm Duckworth, a chap who spoke with a very posh English accent and whom everyone called 'Ducky', a secretary called Linda and a young lad that was only a year older than me called Dave Hewitt. They all called him 'Huey'.

'This is Tony, who is joining us as a trainee today. I expect everybody calls you Tony, don't they?', he said, looking down on me from his six-foot-plus vantage point.

I was too scared to say, 'well actually, no, they don't. In fact, nobody calls me Tony, ever.' It suddenly seemed childish and inappropriate to tell him that everybody calls me 'Ant' or 'The Bear' or 'Bell-Head'. And so from that moment I became known as Tony. I'd only been in banking five minutes and I already had a new identity. Within a couple of days I had got used to my new moniker and started to like it. Especially when it was abbreviated to 'Tone'. That sounded friendly and made me sound like I was one of the gang.

I took my new name back to the boys. I felt a bit sheepish telling them that I now wanted to be known as Tony, but then, John, Laurence and Ian had all rejected their nicknames in recent months so why not me too? They all took to it fairly easily – even my sister embraced it – but my parents were having none of it – to them, I would always be Anthony and that, it seemed, was non-negotiable.

My colleagues were all good people and fun to work with. There was a lot of mickey-taking and messing about during quiet periods. It was actually a little bit like school. They tried to scare me with tales (mostly untrue) about John Looker, the Manager, who was on holiday during my first week. John was gay, and they playfully told me that he painted his nails pink, came to work wearing floral kaftans and liked to be called Tarquin, but most of all I would have to watch myself when he came back, because he liked little ginger boys.

I'd never met a real gay person, (unless you count 'Bender' Burns from school, but that rumour was never fully substantiated), however, I had seen *The Naked Civil Servant* with John Hurt twice, so that would stand me in good stead.

When Mr Looker did turn up for work the following Monday, there was no kaftan or painted nails, but there was no doubt that he had spent many years studying at the John Inman School of Camp. He was a man in his late fifties, who lived with his boyfriend Edgar. They were forever hissing at each other down the phone, and it was hard not to listen in and be intrigued by these calls. I now understood what Rod Stewart meant by the line 'old queens blowing a fuse' in his song 'The Killing of Georgie'.

As bosses went, he was ok. He turned out not to be nearly as scary as the others had made out, but I learned it was sometimes wise to let him think he was. Huey was really cheeky and playful with him. He once left the office on a Friday night with a cheery 'have a good weekend John – I hope Edgar gets piles'. Mr Looker seemed to take it quite well.

There was a pub at the back of the office in Cannon Street called The Sea Horse. There would be a crowd from the bank in there every lunchtime and after work too. Huey took me down there on my first day but they wouldn't serve me. Dressed like my dad, I still didn't look over eighteen.

In time, I got to really like Huey, we hit it off. He lived in Redbridge so we used to travel home on the tube together. He even started coming to the Green Man at Leytonstone with the gang on Friday nights, where they were much more laid-back about under-age drinking, and where we would drink stupid amounts of lager and watch the resident house cover band Deep Feeling.

My job wasn't a difficult one. I was responsible for preparing all the cheques that came into the bank for paying into the bank's account. I also had to deal with chequebook requests from customers, which involved stamping up blank chequebooks with the customer's name, and delivering cash on request to the Directors of the bank. They would phone down and say 'Bring me up £100, boy'. I hated having to do this. They would look down on me like I was a piece of shit that had accidentally found its way onto their nice clean brogues.

When 5:30 arrived on my first day, I was hugely relieved to get it under my belt and it seemed totally incomprehensible that at the end of the day you could just go home without anyone saying that you could, or a bell ringing.

Whilst the others spent theirs in The Sea Horse, lunchtimes for me were a bit tricky. As part of my salary I used to receive 25p a day in Luncheon Vouchers. Even back in 1977, 25p only bought you about a third of a sandwich in London, so I used to run out quite quickly after payday. While the vouchers lasted, I would sit alone in The Luncheonette on Cannon Street and make a sandwich and a can of Pepsi last an hour before drifting back to the office. When they ran out, I had to find my own entertainment to get me through the lunch hour.

Sometimes I would meet Ray for lunch. He had started working for a shipping company in Upper Thames Street a few weeks after I started at Singer's. The rest of the time I would spend my lunchtimes in James Asman's Records, which was situated on the stretch of Cannon Street that headed down towards the Monument. It took me a while to discover it, but once I had it became my lunchtime haven.

Oddly, I discovered the existence of Asman's through another record shop – Farringdon Records on Cheapside. Farringdon Records was a peculiar record shop. They had a whole basement dedicated to classical music, which left them a bit light in the pop department. But still, it was a record shop so I hung out there during my first few weeks of working in the city. I had a feeling, however, that this was not going to be the shop to buy my first proper punk rock record.

My life was starting to feel like one great big contradiction after another. I was almost ready to commit to punk rock, but how could I, when I was a huge Beatles fan, and punk had made no bones about being essentially anti-Beatles. On top of that, we had only a few weeks ago witnessed the Queen's Silver Jubilee and what had I done to rebel against such an outrageous waste of money? My heart was telling me that I should really have been pogoing to 'God Save the Queen' by the Sex Pistols, preferably on Her Majesty's private yacht, or at least trying to see how far I could flob a monstrous 'greeney' down the Mall. But no, I was at a Jubilee street party in Albermarle Gardens just around the corner from my house, with Fraser and his sister Donna, joining in the fun with the other flag-wavers and patriotic chest-beaters. In reality I had opted to let the proper punks gob and pogo their way to rebellion, whilst I quietly applauded from afar.

The truth is that punk rock was a slow burner for me. I'd really love to be able to tell you that the second that I heard 'White Riot' by The Clash I dyed my hair luminous green, discarded my flares for a pair of bondage trousers and thrust a safety-pin through my lip. But it didn't happen like that. It should have, because this was my time, my chance to be involved with a pop music movement that was actually happening right now, but I elected to sit tight with my Wings and 10cc records and allowed the first knockings of punk rock to pass me by.

For this I lay the blame squarely on the shoulders of Gants Hill. It was hardly a hotbed of punk rock. When Paul Weller wrote 'Sounds from the Street', I doubt it was the streets of Gants Hill that he had in mind. If he had decided to walk the streets of 'the Hill', the sounds that he would have heard would probably have been the squeaking of T-cut being massaged into the bodywork of Mark III Cortinas and taxi cabs, rather than the thrashing noise of cheap guitars emanating from open teenage bedroom windows.

But, like everywhere else, punk rock did eventually come to town, albeit in dribs and drabs rather than the epidemic that was sweeping inner-city London. Hair was dyed (not mine, obviously – it was already a silly colour), cut and fashioned into spikes, and cheap replica punk t-shirts began to appear in the shop windows of Ilford town centre. Flares were finally thrust aside and replaced with tight skinny drainpipe jeans, which had such a narrow hole at the bottom of the leg that forcing your foot through took a similar amount of effort as pushing a baby out of a vagina. An alternative to the skinny jean was a pair of bondage trousers. These were usually made of PVC or leather and were covered in zips of all shapes and sizes. All very well until you needed to go to the toilet, and then the search for the zip that your winkle was behind began.

But the strangest of punk fashions was the piece of material that was sewn between the two legs of jeans or bondage trousers, which hung below the buttocks. This would more often than not be tartan in pattern, although I have no idea why. A cheap do-it-yourself version of this would be to steal a beer towel from your local pub and use that. It worked a treat, as long as you had no objection to 'Worthington E' taking out a double-cheek advertisement across your bum.

My purchase of 'Pretty Vacant' was the first real sign of a submission to the punk movement. It followed The Sex Pistols' exciting appearance on *Top of the Pops* in which Johnny Rotten wore a cashmere jumper that was thirteen sizes too big for him and Steve Jones celebrated summer by sporting a knotted hanky on his head. The Pistols that I was seeing and hearing on *Top of the Pops* didn't much resemble the shambolic noisy bunch of misfits that I had witnessed a few months earlier on *The London Weekend Show*. They were still full of energy and venom, but a more polished version. This record was good and I wanted to buy it.

The next day I took my contradictory self to Farringdon records, and in my suit, as a bank clerk, asked the stuffy man behind the counter for 'Pretty Vacant' by The Sex Pistols.

'I'm sorry sir we don't stock '45 singles here. Try James Asman's in Cannon Street'.

Don't sell singles? A record shop that didn't sell singles? What kind of record shop didn't sell singles? The kind that has a whole floor dedicated to classical records, that's what kind.

And so I went in search of Asman's. When I found it, it didn't look much like any record shop I had ever come across before. The windows were painted black save for the words 'James Asman Records' written in drippy white emulsion across them. I could tell that this was no ordinary city establishment and no ordinary record shop.

The interior was decorated from floor to ceiling with pop posters, but not your usual record shop promotional stuff – these were posters for all the new punk rock bands. The poster for *Damned, Damned, Damned* had all four members of that band covered from head to foot in what looked to be custard pies; there was an orange and black poster that just had a picture of a rat on it, and the words 'The Stranglers: Rattus Norvegicus'; and another with the familiar image of the Queen with a safety pin through her nose that I did, of course, recognise. Behind the counter was a young man with black hair that had been gelled into several spikes, wearing a black Ramones t-shirt and a pair of black Levi's.

I tried again. 'Do you have "Pretty Vacant" by the Sex Pistols, please?'

I'm not sure why I asked; it was clear that he had the record as it was bellowing out from the huge speakers hung on the wall behind the counter.

'Have it mate? Got hundreds of 'em. 'Ow many do you want?'

'Just the one please,' I said, sheepishly.

'60p mate. I don't get many of your sort in here buying the Pistols.'

What did he mean by that? Many ginger people? Many Beatles fans? Many under-55s? Reflectively, I guess he meant people in suits. He'd spotted the contradiction straight away.

And so that was it. My first toe into punk's dark and murky water dipped. 'Pretty Vacant' bought the week it was in the charts – picture sleeve, the lot.

The bloke behind the counter intrigued me, my first real life encounter with a proper punk, and I had found myself a new lunchtime hang-out where I could browse the racks of records and, more importantly, listen to pop music in the middle of the day. If you're not getting the novelty value of this, remember that the Sony Walkman hadn't even been invented yet, let alone the ability to carry around your entire record collection on a device the size of a fag packet.

From my next visit to Asman's, it became apparent that there was a third reason for hanging out there – a little bonus item that would draw me back to this place day after day for the next few months, and that was to watch this man behind the counter in his natural habitat, loving his work while I was loving watching him loving it. He was a cool guy, and it was refreshing to come across someone that worked in a record shop who wasn't a cock. Previously, there had been record shop rules – number one being that under no circumstances do you ever, ever approach record shop staff, with any sort of question, or enter into casual pop-based chit-chat with them, because they will make you feel inadequate and unknowledgeable by exercising their right to mock and their gift for smart-arsery, and you'll end up fleeing the shop empty-handed and probably in tears. Up to this point I would have preferred to search the racks blindfolded, looking for a record that I neither knew the name of, nor the artist that performed it, rather than having to face the indignity of approaching the counter of ridicule and mumble guardedly 'you know the one – it goes: doo-doo-chugga-wugga, diddly-doo-doo'. This man, I felt, was not like them – well not to me, anyway.

I was often the only other person in the shop and he got used to seeing me in there every day. Eventually he trusted me enough to engage me in conversation. He told me that his name was Dave and that he used to work in an office too, and when I introduced myself, I remembered that my name was now Tony, which I was starting to concede sounded a little bit cooler than Anthony.

Dave spent all day playing records very loudly and drumming along to them furiously with two Bic biros, which he used as drumsticks as he beat out frantic rhythms on the ink blotter that rested on the counter. Another frustrated drummer, I thought. When he wasn't drumming, he was pogoing around behind the counter to whatever it was playing on his turntable at that particular time. On one occasion, during some very frantic pogoing to the first Boomtown Rats album, a Bowler-hatted and suited gentleman had the audacity to approach him and ask if he had anything in stock by Manhattan Transfer. Dave continued to pogo as the question was being asked and, without saying a word, pogoed his way from behind the counter over to the 'M' rack singing 'Chanson D'Amour' as loud as he could to get his voice above that of Geldof's. On arrival at the Manhattan Transfer LPs, he bowed, waved his arms in a displaying gesture as if he'd just laid down his cloak over a puddle before a member of the royal family, pointed at the rodent on the Stranglers poster on the wall and yelled 'Rat-a-tat-a-tat!', and without flinching, pogoed his way back behind the counter. I, meanwhile, quietly wet myself by the George Harrison albums.

To watch him at work was pure joy. On another occasion, a middle-aged lady came in and after half-heartedly browsing for all of 30 seconds claimed, 'I can't see Roy Orbison'. To which Dave replied, 'and he can't see you either, love'.

I've never really understood why someone would go into a record shop and ask where the records of a particular artist were located without looking properly. Is it not completely obvious that records are filed in alphabetical order by artist? Everybody knows that, don't they? I suppose I got to understand this cavalier approach to searching much better in later life. These days I tend to ask my wife where certain items are located in the fridge before I've bothered to look for them myself – but then again food isn't filed in the fridge in alphabetical order. More's the pity really – maybe it should be, and if you're going to start stacking fridge food alphabetically, you may as well apply the chronological order rule to the food too, with nearest to sell-by-date stuff at the front and the freshest food at the back. Fridge stacking has a lot to learn from record-collection curation.

A police officer once came in whilst I was browsing. The minute he walked through the door, he asked, 'Got any Poxy (sic) Music?'. I knew there was going to be trouble. He was asking for it. The copper was quite clearly on an errand to buy a record by Bryan Ferry's art-popsters for an offspring or some other younger person and was on a hiding to nothing.

'Poxy Music? Yeah mate, it's all poxy here', retorted Dave the Punk, facetiously. And I must admit, I didn't see this coming at all. 'You'll find most of it under P … for pig,' Dave continued.

I stood, open-mouthed. You could almost see his words hang in the air and flutter to the floor as they withered and died with a little 'pop!' in the very little space between the two of them.

Dave the Punk and the policeman stood staring at each other, noses almost touching and without flinching for a good ten seconds, which must have seemed like a lifetime for them both, each wondering who was going to crack first.

The fury in the copper's eyes left no further words necessary, and so he purposefully marched out of the shop. Dave cracked up – almost uncontrollably. 'I thought he was gonna nick me there for a minute' he said – 'I was about to leave you in charge'.

'Nick you?', I said, 'What for – knowing your alphabet?'.

I am without doubt that placed within his comfort zone, the copper would be pretty adept at wrestling a fleeing mugger to the ground with a perfectly timed rugby tackle, or could bring down his truncheon with the thunder of Thor if absolutely necessary, but cheeky punk rockers – they are a very different prospect.

As much as watching Dave the Punk in action with his customers was reason enough to spend my lunchtimes in James Asman's Records, the real reason that I spent so much time in his shop was to listen to the great stuff he played. So many albums from around this time made their way into my collection thanks to hearing them played first by Dave the Punk. The first Clash Album, *In the City* by The Jam, *My Aim is True* by Elvis Costello, The Boomtown Rats debut, *New Boots & Panties* by Ian Dury and The Blockheads and, of course, *Rattus Norvegicus* by The Stranglers.

One record that I didn't need to hear first before buying was the biggie. I was going to buy it whatever it sounded like, with no prior approval necessary. *Never Mind the Bollocks, Here's the Sex Pistols* took forever to arrive in the shops. By the time it was actually released, punk rock was almost done and dusted and the Pistols had already released four singles, all of which were included on the album. To already own four out of the twelve tracks was the only disappointing element about it though – in all other departments, it completely satisfied. From the sound of the marching jackboots at the start of 'Holidays in the Sun' to the big fat raspberry that brought 'EMI' to a close, the music in between was everything that a punk rock record should be. Every song laden with thrashy, multi-layered guitars and the snarling rasp of Johnny Rotten's astonishing vocals. *Bollocks* might not have been where punk started, but it was pretty much where it ended.

By this time, I had indoctrinated Huey into the glories of punk, and on the day that *Never Mind the Bollocks* came out we went to James Asman's together and both bought a copy during the lunch hour. Huey knew that the very sight of the album sleeve would be enough to send Mr Looker into a purple fit of disapproval, and so we decided to make the most of it.

The sleeve was mostly bright yellow with the words 'Never Mind the Bollocks Here's the' written in black type face, and the words 'Sex Pistols' diagonally posted in shocking pink across the bottom. It was a simple but very powerful piece of cover art that many have tried to copy since, but with little success of emulating the impact. There were no pictures, no photos of the band and just a plain white paper inner sleeve. On the back were the song titles written in random letters that you might cut out of a newspaper if you were a kidnapper writing a ransom note.

We strode back into the office, holding our copies of the album aloft as if we were parading some sort of sporting trophy (probably the Wimbledon Ladies singles shield is closest in size and shape).

Ducky Duckworth and Dave Elms were already laughing, anticipating what was about to happen. Mr Looker momentarily looked up from his *Financial Times*, looked back down again and then quickly did a double-take, looking up again sharply, partially choking a little on his sandwich and spluttering a little of it over his pink newspaper.

'Bring it here, Tony,' he commanded. I don't know why he asked me and not Huey – maybe he thought that I would be more intimidated. He beckoned me over with his index finger. For a panicky moment, I thought he was going to confiscate the album, and then I remembered that I wasn't at school anymore and he couldn't actually do that.

Mr Looker wore those glasses that were secured on a chain that hung around his neck, made popular in the eighties by perennial door-shutter Larry Grayson. I always thought that glasses on a chain was an odd fashion for the middle-aged. A bit childish, like the gloves you had sown into the sleeves of your coat when you were a kid, but for glasses. Surely a man of his age could be trusted to not lose his glasses. If you need to wear glasses, you're going to know they are missing straight away, aren't you?

He peered at the sleeve over the top of these glasses, examined it and asked whether it was actually legal to have 'that word' blazoned across the front. 'And I suppose Sex Pistol means penis, does it? I'll have to tell Edgar that one later,' he added.

He then instructed us to put them away in the safe until it was time to go home. 'I don't want you frightening the customers – well no more than usual, anyway'.

I suppose out of all the gang, John and I were the biggest Pistols fans. There was a lot of humour in Rotten's lyrics and we had a lot of fun discovering them. We always loved that bit in 'Bodies' where he is trying to comment on a serious subject (abortion) and makes pop's most ridiculously childish rhyme ever;

She was a girl from Birmingham
She's just had an abortion
She was a case of insanity
Her name was Pauline, and she lived in a tree

John once called me and said 'Let's go down to Heathrow Airport now'. When I asked him why, he said: 'I've just heard on the radio that the Pistols are down there, puking up over passengers in the arrivals lounge. Come on, it'll be a laugh'.

Never Mind the Bollocks was huge; it sold millions despite major record retailers like Boots, W.H. Smiths and Woolworths refusing to stock it because of the sleeve. It's still revered as one the best albums of the seventies, and a groundbreaking monument to the times.

It was to prove to be the Sex Pistols epitaph as a few months later Johnny Rotten left the band, signing off with one last great quote as he crouched despondent on the edge of the stage at the end of the Pistols' final gig of an American tour. 'Ever get the feeling you've been cheated?' he tormented after another typically shabby performance. The band limped on without him, indulging themselves in several silly projects that included making *The Great Rock 'n' Roll Swindle* film and allowing Great Train Robber Ronnie Biggs to sing lead vocals on 'No One Is Innocent', but it was never the same without Johnny. How could it be?

It's also with some irony that a few days after Johnny Rotten left the Pistols, I went on one of my usual lunchtime visits to James Asman Records to find the shop closed. Same story the next day, and the day after that. After a couple of weeks, it became obvious that the shop was closed for good. I was convinced it was no coincidence that the shop's closure coincided with the break up of the Pistols. It crossed my mind that maybe without the Pistols, Dave the Punk had decided that punk rock was dead, and he could go on no longer, and had retreated to south Norfolk to become a Morris Dancer.

I often wondered what happened to Dave the Punk in the months immediately after the closing of the shop. I'm sure that I thought about Dave the Punk far more often then he thought about Tony the bank clerk.

It was some time in 1979 that my curiosity was finally quelled. There I was, watching *Top of the Pops*, and there, right in front of my very eyes, right there on my telly, was Dave the Punk, playing drums on 'Babylon's Burning' with The Ruts. All that ink-blotter drumming with the Bic biros had finally paid off, as Dave the Punk turned out to be none other than Dave Ruffy out of The Ruts. Damn fine record, too. So fine, that I bought it, and the album *The Crack*. Well, I had to really, out of loyalty to Dave – we had history and were virtually mates, weren't we?

Welcome To The Working Week

I suppose I have dined out fairly frequently on my early connection with Dave Ruffy out of The Ruts. Well, there are some stories that you just can't hear often enough, aren't there. At the end of the day, buying a few records from Dave Ruffy out The Ruts is not quite the same as, say, going to art college with John Lennon, but if I ever meet anyone that did actually go to art college with John Lennon, at least I'll have a similar 'rubbing shoulders with pop' story to come back at them with.

Pump It Up

Punk rock groups sprouted up all over the country; hundreds of them. That was the thing with punk – you didn't have to be particularly talented to be in a punk band and record companies, desperate not to miss the boat, signed up every Tom, Dick and Sputum as if they were going out of fashion – which was exactly what they were going out of. In the end, the only punk bands that really mattered were The Sex Pistols and The Clash.

Not that there weren't lots of other great bands that popped up under the punk umbrella around 1977 and 1978 – The Stranglers, The Jam, Elvis Costello & The Attractions, and countless others who were all part of the punk movement but, as it turned out, weren't the real punk rock deal after all.

It was a kind of punk rock. It had punk's attitude but with better tunes. The songs were not about mythical beasts or airy-fairy love stories but about real things that mattered, things that were actually happening to you and your mates – things that affected us all. Songs about love, sure, but not about romantic gesturing, these were songs about getting dumped for the bloke that works in the chippy, songs about being thrown out of school or, even worse, having to go to school. Songs about being out of work, or working in a factory or a shop or in a fucking bank. Songs about the street that you lived in and even if it wasn't about the actual street that you lived in, it was about a street that you knew and wouldn't want to live in for all the tea in Sainsbury's. Songs about being in bands, or wanting to be in bands. Songs about being gay, or black or even both. Songs about anything really, as long as it was real and mattered to the young.

The label that music press coined for these bands was 'new wave' or 'post-punk', as if it was some sort of watered-down version of the real thing, which I suppose it was, but watered-down in a good way. When you look at the musicians that emerged from this period: Paul Weller of the Jam, Glen Tilbrook and Chris Difford from Squeeze, Ian Dury, Elvis Costello, Joe Jackson, Hugh Cornwell, Graham Parker, and even Sting from The Police, this was no wishy-washy collection of post-punk wasters, what this lot actually represent is the last great wave of British songwriters. A great big fat influx of talent that arrived all at the same time, just like the first great 'coming' in the sixties when Lennon and McCartney, Jagger & Richards, Ray Davies, Steve Marriott, Ronnie Lane and Pete Townshend showed up.

Rattus Norvegicus by The Stranglers was the first punk album that I bought. Vocally and lyrically The Stranglers sounded like a punk band but musically they didn't. If anything, they sounded like a much more fun version of The Doors, with swirling keyboards and throbbing baselines dominating their sound. Musically, they defied punk's number one rule –

210

they could play their instruments! They had somehow managed to get their single 'Peaches' into the charts during the summer despite the BBC banning it in their usual stuffy manner; objecting to the word 'shit', 'clitoris' and even 'bummer'. 'Clitoris' – fair-dos, 'shit' – maybe at a push, but 'bummer'? Really? In 1977? The Beeb insisted on a newly recorded version with those words replaced before they would play it; amazingly, The Stranglers agreed and into the charts it jolly well went.

The BBC, had they just given it a chance, could have found lots of genuine reasons to ban records by The Stranglers, who were not exactly the most politically correct of bands. Their second LP, *No More Heroes,* opens with a song called 'I Feel Like A Wog' and featured another called 'Bring On The Nubiles', which included a verse in which singer Hugh Cornwell informs one of these nubile types that there's plenty for him to explore in her erogenous zones, and that he's 'gonna lick her little puss' before heading, nob-first, to the song's main refrain – the bit that goes 'Let me, let me, fuck ya, fuck ya'. For those of us that thought that the erogenous zones were places where you weren't allowed to park your bike (which technically is true), it was nice to finally learn the truth and somewhat comforting to know that even punk rockers were great believers in foreplay.

Gigs by The Stranglers were exciting but dangerous affairs. There always seemed to be some sort of ruckus going on at their shows, whether it be punks versus skins, punks versus punks or sometimes the band just getting pissed off with being spat at by the punks that were supposed to be fans. Oh yes, I haven't mentioned that have I – the spitting thing. One of the hazards of going to punk gigs in the early days was that if you got anywhere near the front of the stage, then the chances were you were going home covered from head to foot in phlegm. I'm not sure how this most disgusting form of appreciation started, but apparently that was what you were supposed to do if you were a proper punk – if you liked the band, the best way you could show them just how much you liked them was to hurl a ball of green saliva at them.

As I mentioned, the gobbing thing was more prevalent in the very early days of punk, amongst the proper green haired, spiky-headed, bondage-trousered, studded dog-collar-clad punks. That wasn't me and I'm not going to pretend it was. So I wasn't there when the gob was flying through the air, but if I had been, I'd probably have been standing somewhere near the back and wearing a Pac A Mac with the hood up, just to have been on the safe side.

Missing the early gigs wasn't generally a problem with punk bands. Even if you got in a bit later, as I did, there was still plenty of fun to be had. Not with The Stranglers, though; because of the violence that followed the band around at their gigs, and the fact that venues tended to end up slightly worse for wear after The Stranglers had played there, the

GLC decided to ban them from playing gigs in London, so if you missed them in the early days you were pretty much out of luck. Of course this was a movement about rebellion, and The Stranglers would play secret gigs under easy-to-identify pseudonyms such as The Old Codgers. Not that I ever easily identified them; the secret gigs eluded me too. I had to wait until the GLC decided to lift the ban and allowed The Stranglers to play a gig in Battersea Park in September 1978 before I got to see them.

By this time, their third album *Black And White* was out and in support of their latest single, 'Nice 'n' Sleazy', the band were joined on stage by a plethora of strippers who, much to our approval got their kit off during the song. That seems to be the lasting memory of that gig for most teenage boys who were there. But it's also worth remembering that the Stranglers delivered a great set that day. Another point of note from this gig is that The Stranglers invited former Genesis frontman Peter Gabriel to be the main support act. This most unlikely combination of punk and prog seemed to actually work a treat on the day. At one point Gabriel hopped off the stage and walked amongst the crowd whilst singing into a remote microphone, surprisingly loved by both Stranglers fans and his own alike. The joining of fans in a rousing singalong to 'Solsbury Hill' was a moment to savour.

I only ever saw The Stranglers once more after Battersea. They played a gig at the Rainbow, probably around 1980. The gig was supposed to be an all-standing affair, and there were hopes of pogoing until we were breathless and standing in our own personal puddle of sweat. But when we got to the Rainbow on the evening of the gig, we found that the seats were still in place and had not been removed as promised. As the gig continued, we watched the front row of seats being dismantled by the fans sitting in them, stamping on them until they snapped off their hinges. Then the seats were passed along the rows, person to person, until there was a huge pile of beer-stained dralon in the aisle. Then the second row, and then the third. There were a lot of things that punk rock stood for, but one thing it didn't stand for was sitting down.

I stopped buying Stranglers records after their next album, *The Raven*. They went a bit intellectual and a little bit too French for me after that – a departure that was no doubt influenced by their French and fairly intellectual bass player Jean-Jacques Burnel. Nevertheless, it wasn't punk rock anymore, and the music that they made in its place wasn't enough to keep my interest.

My final words on The Stranglers have a touch of irony about them. After all the bans from the BBC and the GLC, the biggest hit that they ever had was 'Golden Brown', taken from one of those French-sounding albums, *La Folie*. It was a song promoting the glories of heroin. Did the BBC ban it? No they flippin' well didn't. Not only did they not ban it, but Radio 2, who at the time (1982) were pretty much a totally MoR station, only went and made it their record of the week, thus helping a record about smack get played on the radio, *Top of the Pops* and just about everything else since. It got to number two in the charts and Legs & Co. even performed a dance routine to it, in which they busted some long sweeping arm manoeuvres as if they were painting a large fence. Perhaps they interpreted 'Golden Brown' to mean creosote.

Whilst the songs of The Stranglers contained smatterings of what might have been referred to several decades later as political incorrectness, The Clash on the other hand were probably the most political (correct or other-wise) band of their generation. The Clash were well loved, they still are, although if I'm honest there's something about them that doesn't sit quite right with me and I'm not sure exactly what it is, but I'm pretty sure it's the reggae. Not that I have any particular beef with reggae per se – I quite like it, and I can skank to Bob Marley just as well as the next chubby white man, but The Clash's transformation from punk elite into fifth-rate reggae band grates with me a bit. Sure, their first album was exciting. 'White Riot' is as thrilling as a song can get in under two minutes. 'Career Opportunities' was as angry.

The Clash made good singles too, a great big string of them, but it was their 1979 double album, the accomplished *London Calling*, that really consolidated them as a force to be reckoned with. However, the whole thing seemed to go to their heads. Their next album, *Sandinista*, was a triple LP and was a big pile of steaming, self-indulgent plop, and it was all a bit downhill for The Clash from there.

I only saw The Clash once, and that was by accident. When I say 'by accident', I don't mean that I accidentally opened the door to a concert hall and there they were thrashing away at 'Garage Band', when all along I meant to open the door that Queen were playing behind – although, metaphorically, perhaps I do. They were playing at Victoria Park in East London one sunny afternoon in April 1978 as part of the first free Rock Against Racism gig.

The Rock Against Racism movement had been formed following a stomach-churning tirade of racial bile dished out by 'God' himself Eric Clapton, at a gig he'd recently performed in Birmingham. There, the pissed-up erstwhile Cream axe-man, behaving like some sort of musical Eddie Booth, saw fit to deliver a speech to his audience instructing them to vote for Enoch Powell because he was the man to get the 'coons, wogs and bastard blacks' out of 'his Great Britain'. The irony that Clapton had carved out a career for himself on the back of black music seemed to be lost on him.

I find it strange that the only media sources to report this at the time were the likes of the *NME* and *Melody Maker* – it never made the nationals. It's often quite interesting to take something like this and transpose it into the context of today. If Clapton's ill-informed mouth had been let loose at a concert these days, he would no doubt be arrested on the spot, leaving the red-tops free to run at will with 'God nicked by Plod', and 'Wonderful Tonight' never again chosen to be the opening dance at a wedding – neither of which would be a bad thing.

The gig at Vicky Park was the culmination of a march attended by thousands. It started at Trafalgar Square and ended at the park. We didn't go on the march – that seemed like too much effort – but me, John, Laurence, Ray and Ian went to the gig. I was there to see the Tom Robinson Band, who were headlining, but The Clash, along with X-Ray-Spex and Steel Pulse (a proper reggae band) were on too. Not a bad line-up for a free concert by anyone's standards.

Accidental or not, The Clash were on fire that day, at their stomping, shouty best. Belting their way through 'London's Burning', the fantastic 'Complete Control' and of course 'White Riot', they were joined on stage by Jimmy Pursey from Sham 69 – I'm not sure why.

I've always insisted that the most emotionally charged piece of rock audience footage is that moment from Live Aid when the Quo start up the opening riff to 'Rockin' All Over the World'. There couldn't have been a more appropriate song to play at that moment in time and everybody knew it. The second most emotionally charged piece of rock audience footage for my money is from The Clash's film *Rude Boy*. The 'White Riot' sequence was filmed at Vicky Park that very day and as Strummer and Jones spat out the words, thousands inside the park, including me, went mental and pogoed for all our worth. That particular moment of footage, and it's not a long piece, filmed from the band's point of view, looking out from the stage onto the mayhem that was going on in front of them, sums up and captures perfectly the very essence of what punk rock was about.

When you're trying to impress your kids, teaching them about the old days and what a wild young buck you were when you were their age, then look no further than this little two-minute clip of film because that says more about what you did in the seventies than any dewy-eyed tales of Humphreys and klackers ever can. Of course, if you can actually point to yourself amongst the throng of thrusting heads, this can add a bit of weight to the impressing of the sprogs. Recently, whilst searching YouTube for videos of this concert, I came across the clip from *Rude Boy* and spotted what I thought looked something like a ginger head of hair fashioned unkemptly into the shape of a bell. I paused the clip and took a closer look. It couldn't be me, could it? I couldn't remember being that close to the front or anywhere near that bouncy. But on close inspection (I took a screen shot), there is little room for doubt, that it is my bell-head in the footage, as clear as a … well, a bell.

I waited patiently for the Tom Robinson Band to take to the stage. I'd already had a couple of goes at trying to see them live but until now I'd never been close enough to the front of the queue to make it inside the door. Hyped into the limelight by Nicky Horne on his Capital Radio show *Your Mother Wouldn't Like It*, and a healthy showing in the charts for their debut single '2-4-6-8 Motorway', TRB were on the cusp of greatness. They were worthy headliners, yet in terms of record sales were not as big as The Clash. There is something in the back of my memory that's telling me that The Clash had another gig to get to that evening and that's why they weren't on last. But TRB seized the moment, plying us with songs from their forthcoming album *Power in the Darkness*, which turned out to be just brilliant. Tom wasn't a great singer, but you didn't have to be anymore. He was from the Dylan and Jagger school of vocals – that it's the delivery that makes a good singer rather than the tone of the voice itself. TRB were on everyone's case. Songs championing women's rights, songs berating the National Front and the establishment, a song called 'Martin' that was an affectionate tribute to his brother, who may or may not have actually existed – it didn't matter, and most famously his song '(Sing If You're) Glad to be Gay', whose powerfully bitter lyrics described the prejudices that faced the gay community in seventies Britain. When Tom stood up with such conviction and snarled out the song on BBC2's *Sight And Sound* in 1978, it was astounding. Nobody had ever sung lyrics like those in a pop song before – I thought it was the bravest thing I'd ever seen on TV, and I couldn't possibly have had any more respect for a pop star than I had for him at that precise moment.

Tom would introduce this song by saying 'you don't have to be gay to sing along with this song' and as the cheers died down, he would add with a wry smile 'but it sure helps'. Despite this, we sang along. Maybe actually being gay did make the song more enjoyable, but it was a truly great song regardless and deserved to be joined in with. TRB's logo was a clenched fist and most of their songs were greeted with punches into thin air by the audience. The songs were kind of made to accommodate that.

Fraser and me couldn't really get enough of the Tom Robinson Band. The gigs were always fun and sweaty affairs; we ended up seeing them live thirteen times. We even went as far afield as Guildford Town Hall to see them, which was a little bit over-zealous seeing as they were playing at the end of my road, Gants Hill Odeon, the very next night.

The last of those thirteen gigs was in June 1979. It was billed as 'An evening of comedy and song featuring Tom Robinson in aid of Gay Pride'. We'd never heard of Gay Pride but Tom Robinson was in it so we thought we ought to go. I was slightly suspicious that we may not be in for the sort of evening we had hoped for. The mention of comedy and the fact that it was Tom Robinson and not the Tom Robinson Band fed that notion.

We got there early and managed to have a few words with Tom himself as he set up the stage. He seemed like a thoroughly decent bloke and probably assumed that Fraser and me were an item. I asked him where Danny (Kustow, guitarist from TRB) was tonight. 'Let's just say it's not his bag' said Tom sadly. The Tom Robinson Band never played together again.

Things went quiet for Tom for a while. He formed a band called Sector 27, who I thought were rubbish. Then out of nowhere in 1983 he came up with the hit 'War Baby', which turned out to be even bigger than '2-4-6-8'. I bought the album that it came from *Hope and Glory*, which was ok, but nothing special. The eighties had seemed to dry the passion out of Tom, just like they did everybody else.

In 2016, I caught up with Tom after 37 years. It had been way too long. He played a low-key gig in London and me, Kim and about 50 other people who we had never met before popped along. He looked great, and has turned into a marvellous storyteller who is able to laugh at his preposterous self. He talked us through all his greatest songs, in a pre-song preamble – how he wrote them and, more importantly, why he wrote them. These days Tom is married with kids but maintains that he is still a gay man who just happened to fall in love with a woman. On the night, he explained this by saying, 'when I was young, I loved The Beatles. More recently, I love Radiohead ... but, I still REALLY love The Beatles!'. Put like that, it makes perfect sense. He's also a DJ for Radio 6 and runs his YouTube account under the rather appropriate user name of 'Both Ways'. If you send him a message, he answers it.

And then there was Elvis Costello, standing there on *Top of the Pops* in his black horn-rimmed glasses with his feet pointing inwards, looking more like Buddy Holly's geekier brother than a punk, and backed more than ably by The Attractions as they skanked their way through the reggae-tinged 'Watching the Detectives'. Elvis' debut album, *My Aim is True,* was fantastic. The follow-up, *This Year's Model,* was even better. Words seemed to drip from his lips as if there were too many to fit in his mouth all at once. But he was clever, very clever. In his hit '(I Don't Want To Go To) Chelsea' (and let's face it, who did? – they were rubbish), he somehow manages to rhyme the name Elsie with Chelsea as if they should never be apart again.

The album also contained the song 'Pump It Up', which may or may not have had sexual connotations but 'Pump it up, until you can feel it' could just as easily refer to the music with which we were quickly falling in love. These days, 'Pump It Up' serves out its days as staple fodder for cover bands playing pop music in a pub on a Saturday night, which is a shame. It deserves better.

Elvis' 'difficult' third album, *Armed Forces*, turned out to not be very difficult at all – not for Elvis anyway; he was becoming prolific in his writing. The hit from it, 'Oliver's Army', lifted Elvis into the big time, a place that he is yet to vacate. He had delivered three truly great albums in succession that are as good a first three albums as you will find in pop.

They gave him the passport to explore other genres like country, hip-hop and even classical, but Elvis is only truly at his best when he's being all loose-lipped and edgy.

Squeeze, from Deptford in South London, had this great idea of blending the melodic high vocals of Glen Tilbrook with the very deep voice of his songwriting partner Chris Difford, and how perfect the pair of them sounded together. Difford wrote the words and Tilbrook the music, and they came up with tunes so strong that for a time they were bandied about as being the new Lennon & McCartney. That was their undoing, really. Between 1977 and 1982 they had a big string of hits that has kept them going to this very day. They have split up and got back together more times than Ken & Deirdre Barlow, but when they first went their separate ways in 1982, there can't have been a household in the country that didn't own their hits compilation *Singles 45s and Under*. It was the perfect best-of, containing everything you needed – the amusing 'Cool for Cats', the fabulous storytelling of 'Up the Junction', the commentaries on the over-familiar of the marvellous 'Pulling Mussels (From A Shell)', 'Tempted' and 'Is that Love' and the sublime 'Black Coffee in Bed', with its organ riff that is just impossible to get out of your head once its been lodged there.

I always thought of Squeeze as primarily a singles band – their early albums such as *Argy Bargy* and *East Side Story*, despite being very popular, never really resonated with me or offered me anything better than the singles that they spawned. It wasn't until 1989, when Claire, a girl that I worked with, handed me a cassette of their album *Babylon & On* and urged me to listen, that I really liked any of their albums. Claire was beautiful, and if I'm perfectly honest, I only agreed to listen to it because I thought the opportunity to enjoy a little slap and tickle might present itself. It didn't, but don't judge me, there isn't a music fan alive that hasn't been persuaded to listen to some dreary record by a girl in the misguided hope that by doing so, it might result in him familiarising himself with the contents of her sweater. It could have been worse, at least this was Squeeze – she could have been a Hall & Oates fan.

As it happens, *Babylon & On* was a great album, and so this was where I picked up with Squeeze again. It's funny, Squeeze never had another hit record, but every album they made after their peak commercial period was an absolute corker despite being bereft of hits. Not simply a singles band at all, as it turned out.

I've lost count of the number of times I've seen Squeeze play live. They still get together every now and then to deliver their hits to their loyal fans. Sometimes the best gigs are the ones where the band doesn't have a new album to flog. The last time I saw them was in December 2012 – they were superb. What they do these days is record every gig and then half an hour after the show is finished you can buy the CD of the concert you've just seen. That's technology for you. On this occasion, you went to buy your CD, and then the band was sitting all sweaty and triumphant at a table ready to sign it for you and have a bit of a natter.

Meeting pop stars is always a bit of an ordeal. There's a very thin line between being almost standoffish with them and telling them you want to have their babies. I had high hopes for a bit of sparkle from Chris Difford as I sidled up to where he was sitting and handed over my CD for him to sign. When you listen to some of the lyrics that he's written over the years, it's clear that he is a very witty man, yet the extent of his rock'n'roll small talk as he scribbled his name was: 'Have you come far?'.

When Squeeze aren't touring you can go and hear these very same songs being played without the tenor tones of Chris Difford by seeing one of Glen Tilbrook's solo shows. Tilby (as I like to call him in rather over-familiar fashion) makes pretty average solo albums these days (whereas, surprisingly, Chris Difford's are remarkably good), but his solo shows are great. I once went to see him with Ian at a tiny venue in Shepherd's Bush. There were only about 80 of us there, and when it came to performing 'Goodbye Girl' the band, armed only with acoustic instruments, hopped off the stage and sang the song whilst forming a dancing circle around a group of girls. They then made their way out of the doors at the back of the hall and into the foyer. The entire audience of course followed them out and gathered around the stairs where the band were now sitting and running through 'Black Coffee in Bed'. As we all trooped back into the main hall, following the band once more, the lady behind the cloakroom counter said, 'you should have been here last night. They went out the front door and into the pub next door'. I would have liked to have seen that.

Another artist that is still going strong from those heady days of the late seventies is Paul Weller of The Jam. Of all the bands that came out of this period under the so-called punk armoury, The Jam were my absolute favourites. 'In the City' was the song that turned me on to The Jam, and jumping around my bedroom to it in my socks caused more than a little anguish to my parents and the shaking light fittings below.

What Weller was saying in 'In the City' wasn't anything new. Didn't Bob Dylan say something similar in 'The Times They Are A-Changin'' all those years ago? But in this song Weller did manage to encapsulate everything about how young people were feeling about their voice in society.

Paul Weller, a boy from leafy Woking in Surrey, had probably not actually spent too much time in the city, but somehow still managed to get it. The Jam were alienated from the punk rock elite – they wore suits, for a start. They were essentially a mod band hanging out the back of the trousers of punk rock. Weller's heroes were The Beatles, Steve Marriott of the Small Faces and Ray Davies of The Kinks, and The Jam had this brilliant idea of releasing singles that weren't on albums, just like his heroes did in the sixties. They weren't the only ones to do this, but I like the fact that new wave, punk or whatever label you want to hang on it was partially responsible for bringing back the idea of the pop 45 as a legitimate piece of stand-alone art, rather than just a vehicle to launch and sell an album.

Bass player Bruce Foxton was the perfect foil for Weller with his throbbing yet unrepentantly melodic bass lines and tenacious harmonies, which merged perfectly with Weller's vocal shards of venom and splintery guitar thrashes. They both played Rickenbacker guitars to give their sound that authentic sixties feel, and when they played live Weller and Foxton would take off into mid-air simultaneously with their legs neatly tucked in, just like Pete Townshend did in 1965. There was nothing original about The Jam, but for those of us that were too young to have been a part of the sixties, this was sixties nostalgia being delivered directly to our seventies record players.

The band's first album, was a strong and ridiculously exciting debut – full of teenage angst, so much so that you could almost hear the spittle moistening on Weller's lips as he spat out the vocals. Quick to cash in on the excitement generated by the band and punk rock in general, their second album *This Is the Modern World* was clumsy, rushed and mostly full of flimsy, unmemorable tunes that left me full of disappointment. It wasn't until *All Mod Cons* in 1978 that they really nailed it. Songs like 'To Be Someone' – the bit where he sings:

To be someone must be a wonderful thing.
A famous footballer or rock singer or a big film star,
Yes, I think I would like that

Boom! That was the moment I truly connected with Paul Weller. That was exactly how I felt. For me and countless other lads – a footballer or a rock star – was there anything else to be? It felt personal, as if he was talking directly to me. Yes, Paul, I think we would all like that. I don't recall anyone ever writing a song about how great it would be to be a bank clerk.

The album's crowning glory though is its final track, 'Down in A Tube Station at Midnight'. This is storytelling at its very best, accompanied by drummer Rick Buckler's frantic hi-hattery and a bass line from Foxton that was so punchy, it knocked you out cold.

But Weller says things in this song in a way that we hadn't heard before. He involves you in the story to the point where you are actually wondering whether his wife is going to be ok – the 'they took the keys, and she'll think it's me' line is actually quite scary – mainly because it never gets resolved. The descriptions he uses in the song are so vivid that anyone that has used the London Underground system late at night is placed right there in his shoes, familiar with the 'glazed dirty steps' and the British Rail poster. 'They smelt of pubs, and Wormwood Scrubs and too many right-wing meetings' is just genius. We all knew exactly who he was talking about here, even if we didn't know what a right-wing meeting smelt like. 'Tube Station' has now become a bit of a seventies timepiece. The underground isn't that scary anymore and mostly just smells of Nando's.

Weller broke up The Jam at their peak. Everyone including me was a little bit cross with him, but it's because he did it when they still on top of their game that The Jam's legacy is still intact. They are still loved, which is more than can be said for his next band The Style Council, who with their leanings towards free-form jazz, balladry and dance music, didn't have a hope in hell of being accepted by tearful Jam fans, unable to move on. Personally, I quite liked them.

Weller, like one of his mentors Paul McCartney, has been lucky enough to have had success with two bands and as a solo artist. He still plays live but rarely performs Jam songs. He believes that that is the past and the songs are no longer relevant, yet when he does occasionally perform 'Town Called Malice' or 'That's Entertainment' they are greeted with a reception that his latter songs could only dream of. He's a stubborn old Hector and needs to learn, again like McCartney did before him, not to bite the hand that feeds, and play the songs that are the reason that the concert hall is full. And when he has learnt this, he needs to give Gilbert O'Sullivan a call.

All these bands were the big hitters for me. There were others: Ian Dury was a great poet and made some superb records and whatever your view on how Sting turned out, there's no denying that the first Police album was a little belter. Then there was the Boomtown Rats, fronted by resident bigmouth Bob Geldof. Who had an inkling what lay ahead for this young upstart back in the late seventies?

The Undertones had a string of hits starting off with an ode to wanking – 'Teenage Kicks' – in which lead singer Feargal Sharkey's voice was so trembley that you couldn't be entirely sure that he wasn't actually knocking one out as they recorded it. It had the dubious honour of having no guitar solo or any drum fills. In yer face, Emerson, Lake & Palmer.

There should also be a special mention for The Members. I think they only ever had one hit, 'Sound of the Suburbs' – a song that never fails to make me smile. Only a punk rock band would have the audacity to put out a song that repeats the line 'this is the sound of the suburbs' when its lead singer had rock's most ridiculous lisp.

I suppose I think of the period 1977–79 as my peak pop period. This is the time when I was spending most of my wages on records and concert tickets. There seemed to be a gig to go to every single week, and I'm struggling now to think how the hell I afforded it. Of course we shouldn't get too carried away with the wonders of new wave music from this period. As lovely as all this was, let us not forget the atrocities that were also happening around this time. Boney M singing 'Brown Girl in the Ring', which drove me insane to the point that I wanted to extract my own teeth with a claw hammer. Althea & Donna's ting 'Uptown Top Ranking', Brotherhood of Man singing 'Figaro' and for most of the year the charts completely dominated with songs by John Travolta and Olivia Newton John, which always begged the questions: could Travolta really sing and could Neutron-Bomb actually dance? Don't even get me started on 'Matchstalk Men and Matchstalk Cats and Dogs' by Brian & Michael and a bunch of head-swaying school children. What the fuck is a matchstalk anyway? It's matchstick, you pair of pillocks. Go on, Google 'matchstalk' and you will only find references to this dreadful song, which basically means that they made it up. And finally, the song that my friend Darryl will name as the worst record of all time, 'Lucky Stars' by Dean Friedman and some unknown woman that doesn't even get a credit, for which now I'm sure she is thankful.

The song plays out a couple's argument where the bloke has just had lunch with his ex, Lisa, and by the end of the song you are left in no doubt that this trinity of ninnies completely deserve each other. At one point he says 'I know you're dumb, but that's ok, no need to look so glum' – that should be a comfort to the uncredited moron then. In another part of the song, he says: 'We had lunch today, her life's in disarray (great couplet), she goes around as if she's always stumbling off a cliff', which makes you wonder, how many times can a girl fall off a cliff and come up smiling. And the 'Did you see Lisa? Yes, I saw Lisa' part would drive the most saintly of gentlemen to go for the jugular. I've always wanted to have a friend called Lisa so someone will one day ask me if I've seen her. And while all this was going on, West Ham got relegated.

Gud Fungs

Listening to all this great music was one thing, but playing it was another. It was something that I'd wanted to do for a long time and now the time had come.

My first month's pay from Singer and Friedlander furnished me with exactly £120. When your pocket money has been a pound a week, this seemed like an absolute fortune. I knew before I'd even got it how it was going to be spent and so as soon as I had it in my sweaty little mitts, I started scouring the small ads in the *Ilford Recorder* (because that's where we bought anything secondhand in the days before Gumtree and eBay, kids). It didn't take long.

Drum Kit for Sale £60

That's all the ad said, but that was enough to have Dad drive me to a house in Barking to have a look at it. I didn't really know what I was looking at or even how it was supposed to sound. I certainly had no idea how to play it, so there would be no trying it out for size in front of a proper drummer (and a proper drummer's mum, as it turned out). It was yellow – yellow and glittery. I think it was a safe guess that this kit had been made in the early seventies, with the view that it was going to have a six-inch platform boot stomping its weight down on its kick drum pedal.

The kit consisted of a bass drum, a snare and a top tom-tom. The bass drum had a rod coming out of the top of it, which housed a very small cymbal that sounded a bit like a saucepan lid – one of those horrid tin ones, not those posh, see-through Pyrex ones where you can see everything that's going on inside the pan – they hadn't been invented yet. There was also a hi-hat and the aforementioned bass-drum pedal. It looked like it had never been played and there was no guarantee that this was going to change by me owning it, but I was having it anyway. That left me with £60 to last me until next payday, but I didn't care – I had a drum kit.

I watched carefully as the seller dismantled the kit so I would know how all the bits fitted together again. When I got it home I set it up in Mads' bedroom, as there was no room in my little box room. She must have been out. Once the kit was assembled I was ready to go. Or at least I thought I was. What I had overlooked was that a drummer needs something to sit on when perched at the kit, and this kit didn't come with a stool. The solution was sitting there right in front of me: Mads' dressing table stool would double as the perfect drum throne. Well not exactly perfect – for a start the cushiony bit was purple crushed velvet, so not exactly very rock'n'roll. However, it did swivel and that was the main thing. It would do for now, until I could afford to get a proper drum stool at least. Strangely, I got to quite like the purple velvet dressing table stool and used it until I sold the kit a couple of years later.

So now I really was ready to go. In 1977 there were no tuition or YouTube videos to refer to that would teach me what I was supposed to do; I was pretty much on my own. All I could do was listen to the records and try and work out which drum was being hit and generally try and pick out what the drummer was up to. The easiest way to do this was to record the song that I wanted to learn on to a cassette so I could keep rewinding the tape until I got the beat and learnt the fills. Cassette really was the only way to go. You couldn't be learning drumming using records, getting up every few seconds to replace the stylus on the bit you wanted to try again, and anyway the drumming vibrations would just make the record jog and that would never do.

I started with what sounded like an easy song to me – 'Get Back' by The Beatles. It seemed that all that tapping out rhythms with cutlery on dining room chairs had paid off, as I seemed to pretty much be able to drum along with Ringo without too much trouble.

The next song I tried was a little more ambitious – 10cc's 'Second Sitting for the Last Supper'. I'm not sure why I chose this because it was quite a difficult song to drum to – very fast, with lots of fills throughout – which with hindsight was probably the exact reason why I chose it. This took a bit longer to master, but after a while I had it. I must admit that I had surprised myself in that being able to master the basics had come to me very quickly and without too much effort.

I discussed my newly acquired skill with John in a phone call, and he mentioned that coincidently he was buying Ian's old Vox Stroller guitar, with the intention of learning how to play the thing. This was no ordinary call – this was a calling dialled with the seductive fingers of Mistress Rock. It was time to form a band.

I don't recall how Ray got assigned the job of being the bass player, but I suspect we just asked him and he said 's'pose so' in that 'oh very well, if I really must' way that only Ray can. All we needed now was a singer. Laurence wasn't interested in being in the band and certainly wasn't up to the job of singing, and we were rapidly running out of gang members. And so I asked Fraser, who I knew had a decent voice. He didn't really know the others as he had gone to another school, but he agreed anyway and the others grudgingly consented that he would do.

Fraser could sing, and was brilliant at swearing, but he wasn't an ideal fit for this band. Being two years younger, and an unknown quantity to the others, didn't help his cause. They were not kind to him, and made little effort to ingratiate him into the band and were often rude about his trousers, which left me uncomfortably stuck in the middle. This awkward situation didn't do me any favours at all, but it did occur to me that it felt a bit edgy to have some sort of discord within the band. After all, The Who had gone on for years not liking each other very much, hadn't they? However, as time passed and they got to know Fraser better, they began to mellow towards him and things improved.

With all roles now assigned, it was decided that the name of this fledgling band would be Gud Fungs. Not the catchiest of names I'll admit, but we all thought it was hilarious to name a band after a ridiculous expression uttered regularly by Harry the school bully with the broken nose – you'll remember him from a couple of chapters ago. An in-joke that nobody else would get, but probably better than other contenders that were put forward, such as 'Plimsoll' and 'The Winkles'. That is two separate names by the way; being called Plimsoll & the Winkles was never on the cards. Although it would have been very punk rock to have punk rock pseudonyms, like Sid Vicious (real name Simon Richie) or Rat Scabies (real name Christopher Miller), I didn't see Fraser as Plimsoll Cooper and I really didn't fancy being in a band where I was one of the Winkles.

With my house empty on a Sunday afternoon, all that was left now was to make some music. The first song that we had decided to learn was 'Come Together', the old Beatles tune. Not very punk rock, but maybe we could punk it up a bit later. On paper it looked easy enough; the paper in question being the 'Come Together' page of Fraser's *Beatles Complete Songbook for Easy Guitar*. Just four chords, so how hard could it be? Well, quite hard is the answer to that. There were two main problems, the first being that John only knew three chords. That would probably have been ok – after all, Status Quo had had a lengthy career, had thousands of fans and made themselves millions without having to ever trouble themselves with learning that tricky fourth chord, so surely we could muddle through. The second problem being that none of the three chords that John knew featured in this song.

We could add to this the fact that as our bassist, the minimum requirement for Ray, would be to own a bass guitar. Unfortunately, he was lacking this vital component to the tune of one. This he promised would be rectified very shortly, but for now we had to make do. And so a makeshift bass guitar was made – not from scratch obviously – that would have been ridiculous. Fraser had a totally hopeless Spanish guitar that he used for guitar lessons at school. It had nasty nylon strings that were set so far from the neck that they needed to hop on a bus to make contact with the fretboard. We took this and loosened off the top two strings, leaving the lowest four to get that 'authentic' bass guitar sound. We then amplified it by taking the microphone from my Sony Cassette deck, flipping the switch to the amplify setting, and sticking the mic in the hole in the guitar. Bingo, we had a bass guitar of sorts – very loose sorts.

The Beatles Complete Songbook for Easy Guitar kindly provided the fingering for the chords required for the song and after an hour or so of John tinkering about, contorting his fingers clumsily in roughly the right shapes for all the chords, we were ready to start.

'1-2-3 shhhhhhh' … nothing. And again '1-2-3 shhhhhh'… nothing again. So, after two hours of pissing about, we had managed nothing more than 'Come Together's opening word (if 'shhhhhh' counts as an actual word). Where was the riff? *The Beatles Complete Songbook for Easy Guitar* didn't mention anything about the riff, and John didn't have a clue how to play it.

'Just do the drum bit Bear, and we'll join in after that,' suggested John, trying to be helpful yet cleverly deflecting from the absence of his riff at the same time.

So, with a '1-2-3' and a 'shhhhhhh' from Fraser, I was on my own with Ringo's little drum fill from the song, which when broken down goes thud-thud, tsst-tsst-tiddly-tee, dugga-de-dugga-de-dugga-de-dugga round twice, and then we were in the verse.

It didn't sound very good at all. 'All over the place' would have been disrespectful to the place. The only bit that sounded remotely decent was the little bit of chuggy guitar that leads up to the 'come together, right now, over me' bit. Punk rock had insisted that we didn't need to be able to play our instruments and that anyone could be in a band – so we should have been perfectly qualified. However, punk rock is a big fibber, and everyone left my house that evening feeling a little bit disheartened and inadequate.

The following day, John mentioned this whole debacle to Ian. The Thin Yoghurts were in a state of flux. Drew had been sacked for what basically amounted to having a girlfriend and not liking the removal of a couple of Yes songs from their set – 'we've gone too commercial', he laughably protested. What with that and the glue of school no longer there to keep the others together, activity had been quiet. As far as Gud Fungs were concerned, a bit of guidance was what was needed – a helping hand from someone that knew how to do this whole band thing – and Ian thought he was the man to provide it. Still, The Yoghurts loss was The Fungs gain, we thought. Not wanting to get himself lumbered with this ensemble of desperados forever, he made it abundantly clear from the start that this was only a temporary arrangement until we found our rock feet, and when that had been achieved he would be off. He had no idea what he was taking on, and as far as rock feet were concerned Gud Fungs would be perennial amputees. He was there to the bitter end.

The addition of Ian as lead guitarist was a boost for us all, though. We thought it was going to be ok after all. The first session was arranged for the following Saturday. Ray turned up fully embracing the punk ethos, with his new bass guitar in his hand, his hair dyed purple and what could best be described as a small cooking utensil hanging from his left ear. He had raised the bar.

Ian taught the band how to play 'All Right Now' by Free. Standard fare for any cover band, it was easy and Ian knew the guitar solo note for note. The only problem the song presented was that tricky bass riff that leads into the guitar solo and carries on throughout it. Ray sat in the kitchen with Ian, going over it and over it, and over it some more. It was a difficult piece for a beginner by any stretch of the imagination and he tried his best to master it. We could get through the verse and the chorus without too much trouble, my newly acquired cowbell clanging away throughout like an over-zealous dinner-lady mashing potatoes in a tin tray, but as soon as we got to the bass part it would all fall apart. A decent attempt would be around six notes before it fumbled into a mess. The next time five, then four, until he could barely put plectrum to string before we would all fall about laughing in anticipation. The longer it went on the bigger Ray's mental block became.

Ian suggested that cover versions were maybe a bit beyond us at this stage and that we should consider writing our own songs. What a great idea! Paul McCartney had banged out 'Yesterday' in his sleep and it had been played on the radio seventeen squillion times – a song based on a rhyming pattern of 'yesterday … away … stay … play'. How hard could it be? Most importantly, there would be no rules, we could make the songs as easy as they needed to be, and there would be nothing to compare them against. The thought of writing our own stuff was also an exciting proposition. *The Gud Fungs Songbook for Easy Guitar* was about to get its first entries.

Although there were some contributions from me, they were sporadic and limited to the odd line here and there; most of the songwriting was done by John and Ian. The pair of them were wasting their days sitting at the back of their lower sixth classes, just waiting to be told by Manny that there probably wasn't any point in them being at school any longer. By the Christmas of 1977 they were out, but in the three months that preceded their exit, they filled their rough books with lyrics. They were as prolific as Lennon and McCartney on a Helen Shapiro tour bus.

'The Wotsits Bop', a song that had been started by John and me the previous year, with Ian's help, was completed and given a tune identical to 'Jailhouse Rock'. You'll remember this was a song about Benjy Fenster's silly group Doctor's Wotsits, and it's fair to say that most of the songs penned during this period carried the themes of either taking the piss out of people at school or things that we didn't like very much.

Gary Steinberg was a slightly chubby kid that I had known many years before from my days at Gearies. In those days he sported National Health glasses that had lenses like the bottom of beer bottles. I'm not sure what happened to him during the years in between, but he turned up at Beal as a sixth-former, taller, sleeker and with those glasses replaced by contact lenses. Being, according to his own legend, a drummer of some repute, he naturally gravitated towards the musos at Beal. By all accounts, he was very full of himself and had a bad habit of describing almost anything as being 'really triff', and, more annoyingly, chose to end every sentence that he uttered with the expression 'say no more', which presumably had its origins in the Monty Python sketch.

We'd all become regulars at the Green Man, Leytonstone and would go there three or four nights a week and watch Deep Feeling, the resident band. Gary started tagging along with us and so I became acquainted with him once more. He thought it was rather sweet that I had just started learning the drums and offered to teach me. I declined. Not on the basis that he was being patronising, which of course he was, but more to do with a private performance that he gave me in his bedroom prior to one of these nights out at the pub. He told me that the drummer is the most important musician in a band and deserved far more respect than they got, and that it was his mission to ram this fact home to anyone who would listen. He then proceeded to get behind his drum kit, which was permanently set up in his bedroom, and informed me 'this is a little number that I've just written'. He laid down a bit of a rock groove and started singing.

I'm the drummer, I'm the singer
I'm the star of the show,
I'm a winner, you're the loser
It's now time for you to go.

I'm afraid I was unable to do anything but guffaw helplessly, and probably in his face, at which point he laid down his sticks and said, 'say no more'. I complied.

A week or so later John rang me up as excited as a small hamster presented with his first wheel. 'Have a listen to this Bear, a new song – 'Say No More''. He played the song to me over the phone. It was catchy – in the way that syphilis was catchy – and based on a two-chord verse.

At the Pub, the other day
Saw a big prat, walking my way
Didn't have time to get away
He said, say no more

Went to school, he was there
Seems he caught us unaware
Couldn't hide anywhere
He said, say no more

And then, and as if I didn't know it was coming, he interjected 'and this is the chorus'

Say no more to me today
Say no more, more no say
Say no more, it's really triff
Say no more, you're a biff

I did actually think that it was really triff – especially the 'more no say' bit. Although 'Say No More' obviously had to be the title, The Adverts had recently had a minor hit with 'Gary Gilmore's Eyes', and so there was a brief flirtation with the idea of calling the song 'Gary Steinberg's Contact Lenses'. We considered it, dismissed it, and said no more.

It was decided that seeing as Black Sabbath had a song called 'Black Sabbath' and Bad Company had a song called 'Bad Company', it was only fair that Gud Fungs should have a song called 'Gud Fungs' and so John and Ian went about their work. They had this idea that each member of the band would have their own verse and that should we ever get to the stage where we would perform this song in public, the stage would be set in absolute darkness and we would all have our backs to the audience. The plan was that each member of the band would turn around in a kind of jumping-turning-aroundy type way just before singing their own verse. We hadn't really worked out the logistics of how me as the drummer would have both my back to the audience or be able to do the turning around thing, but that didn't really matter at this stage.

At the next practice the finished song was presented to the rest of the band. The lyrics were made up of a combination of in-jokes, which no-one outside of the band would find in the slightest bit funny, and outright lies … but mostly the former. It went like this:

My name's Fraser, Fraser Cooper,
And no one thinks I'm very super
I'm the singer with this group
Do you like my crimplene suit?

Chorus

Gud Fungs, Gud Fungs
Ooo Gud Fungs, Ooo Gud Fungs
Gud Fungs.

My name's Budd, Budd John Graham
See these strings, I can really play 'em
Don't talk to me anymore
About fat little Gaynor, the piggy-eyed whore

Gud Fungs

Chorus

My name's Monty-Montague
And I like watching Raymond spew
I'm always having ego trips
And I'm proud of my three nips

Chorus

My name's Pearce, Pearce Ray Nowt
I can't talk, so I always shout
I call my friends 'stupid turd'
And throw-up peanuts in the kerb

Chorus

My name's Shelley, Shelley Bear
And I've got rather lovely hair
I used to beat on people's bums
Until I got a set of drums

Chorus

To a man we all loved it – well, apart from Fraser, who wasn't quite so enamoured with the fact that no one thought he was very super, but he took it in good spirit, which in itself was rather super. We never got to the stage (or on any stage for that matter) where we were all singing our own verses, so Fraser sang the lot and with gusto, like only a young boy in tight crimplene trousers can. The song was set to a tricky little drumbeat that Ian invented (oh yes, he could play the drums as well). If they knew where or what their laurels were, these boys were certainly not going to rest on them. Ian and John continued to fill their rough books with lyrics, and the songs were plentiful.

Every band chock-full of teenage boys needs the obligatory song about wanking and 'Bernard's Organ Recital' filled that particular hole, so to speak. Whereas previous songs of this ilk, like 'Teenage Kicks' by The Undertones, had disguised the theme, there was no room for such subtlety in the Fungs. The second verse was most lovely:

In raincoats of grey it must be too much
Dreaming all day of a girl's hairy crotch
You lop out your John Thomas and put it on the chair
And all that's left to see is the stain and curly hair

229

And just to ram the point home, a chorus of:

Up and down
Higher and higher
Take your aim
And let it fire (let it fire)

Another song, 'Grun', was about old women and just downright nasty ... but bloody funny. The music was set to a tango-style arrangement, probably because we imagined that all old women liked to tango in their spare time, when they weren't of course jumping the queue at bus stops or cultivating the whiskers on their chins.

Rheumatism in your legs with a bandage surround
I really like to hear it when you hit the ground
This is my favourite sound

All your life is one big moan
That's probably why you're gonna get shut up in an 'ome
You evil little gnome

And a delightful chorus of:

Snotty-nosed, shrivelled up, smelly old Gruns
You ain't nothing but a pain in our bums
You nag your little husbands till they drop dead
Then you ruin your children's lives instead

But it wasn't all about the nasty. When the challenge to write a love song presented itself, those boys rose to it like a fat bloke at an all-you-can-eat buffet. 'The Ballad of Milly Molly Nesbitt' takes a look at Laurence's holiday romance with a girl from Lancashire called Angie, whom he met during that week he and John had spent camping in the Lake District – and consequently rips it to shreds. It had these dramatic thrashy bits in the middle that went:

She said Laurence, I come from Preston
And I'd like to see you, with just your vest on
He said do you love me?
She said 'sure do boy'
Just look at your winkle
It's from an Action Man toy.

230

The chord progression was a little bit like 'Oh Diane', which was especially clever of us seeing as it would be another four years before the Fleetwood Mac hit would be written. We didn't sue – let them have their day, we thought.

All this was hilarious stuff for us, but in the meantime, whilst not taking ourselves seriously by any stretch of the imagination, we were all learning our instruments and becoming used to being in a band. It was still awful, but it was getting better. All these songs had a couple of things in common – they all sported a guitar solo played by Ian, where he would widdle and twiddle for about sixteen bars longer than was necessary – you can take the boy out of prog, but you can't take prog out of the boy. All our songs had to end with a thrashy power chord, brought to us directly from the Pete Townshend school of thrashy power chords. We were consistent if nothing else.

We recorded every practice and I listened to them all. This was the best learning process that I could find. When you hear your mistakes, you tend not to make them again – unless of course it's the bass solo in 'All Right Now'. The recordings revealed that I thought that if a song didn't have at least 15 drum fills in it then it wasn't worth playing. I tempered this and calmed down later ... much later.

Sometimes there were others present at our rehearsals. I'm not sure why anyone would have been interested in watching this wretched bunch of Billy No-Notes grinding their way through these songs, but for some reason they were. Indeed, on one occasion Gary Steinberg himself turned up and begged us to play the song that he had heard we had written about him (well he would, wouldn't he). Knowing the song was more disrepute than tribute, we were reluctant, but eventually his begging became so irritating and to make him say no more, we gave in.

Fraser wasn't there that day – he had started to miss practices due to him getting a Saturday job and so I was the one expected to deliver the vocal. I began the song and immediately after the 'saw a big prat walking my way' line Gary shouted out 'you cunt!' very loudly, but we didn't let that put us off and continued to the end of the song. I don't think he ever told us whether he liked our little song, but the chances are that he probably didn't. This magic moment was captured of course on tape, and I can clearly remember writing on the inlay card of the cassette box: *5. Say No More (You Cunt Version)*.

That very same day we had our first band photoshoot. Laurence dropped in with his camera and took some snaps. The resulting photos served as a bit of a timepiece, as we posed in my front room with our instruments amongst the swirly carpet and ashtrays that were moulded in coloured glass into the shape of clowns. It's probably fair to say that there's not much of a connection between punk rock and doilies, although we managed to find one. By doilies I don't mean those paper things posh people use on plates when serving cake and sandwiches for afternoon tea, I mean those lacy articles that working class people used to hang over the back of armchairs and sofas in the fifties and sixties to stop the teds in the family getting Brylcream all over the fabric. I've no idea why we still had them over our furniture in 1977, or at all, for that matter, as I don't remember there ever being any teds invited round to our house, but we did have a lot of doilies. Anyway, my favourite photo from this session was the one in which all five of us were crouched behind my mum's sofa with just our heads poking out over the top, each of us with a lacy doily on our hairy heads.

Still the new songs kept coming: 'Thin on Top' – a tale of a balding man who buys a mail-order toupée:

I've got a brand new toupée to wear on my head
I can remember the days when I could be a ted
It came through the post in a brown paper parcel
If my mates found out, I'd feel such an arsehole.

Another song, 'Balls in my Smalls' (occasionally referred to as 'Bollocks in my Smollocks), was written solely by Ian with nonsense verses, one of which went:

I've got my Balls in my Smalls
I've got my gland in my hand
I've got my thumb on my plums
But I'm a happy man

Similarly, childish couplets like snot on my bot, shit on my tit and chopper in my whopper ensued, but 'Smalls' had a chorus that was so catchy it would have no qualms about taking herring at the same table as something written by the beardy bloke out of Abba and a riff shamefully identical to that used many years later by David Brent in 'Free Love Freeway', But once these boys had left school and were unable to write together during dull A-level history lessons, the songs soon dried up. They would never have got together in their own time just to write songs – that would have been far too pretentious.

However, by this time we were able enough to tackle cover versions and did a couple of Pistols songs – 'Anarchy in the UK' and 'Pretty Vacant'. We also did 'Wild Thing', which was always a bit more 'Goodies' than 'Hendrix' in the way we interpreted it. We even tried different arrangements on some songs – improved starts, tighter endings and 'The Ballad of Milly Molly Nesbitt' was given a fast version in which we even managed to all come in at the same time – although it seemed to pass us by that 'The Ballad of Milly Molly Nesbitt' played four times as fast as it was intended didn't really make it a ballad anymore. In our final practice together Ray even managed to complete the bass solo in 'All Right Now' from start to finish.

A practice was arranged for the following Saturday but only John turned up. Fraser was working again, Ian was nowhere to be seen and Ray, after successfully completing that bass solo the previous week, probably thought there was nowhere else to go and subconsciously thought that the game was up.

Perplexed that we were on our own, John and I briefly speculated where the others could be but as the keepers of the flame, sat down at my mum's dining room table, opened a box of Peak Frean's Family Assortment and set to work on two new songs – 'Boogie Oogie (kick in goolie)' and 'She Was Only a Farmer's Girl (but look at her melons)'. Both complete dogshit that would never see the light of day, but we laughed and laughed all afternoon putting the words together.

The next day Ian called me and apologised for his no-show the previous day. He went on to explain that he had been working on some new songs with Steve Ricard (you may remember Steve from the school disco night with Sandy Richardson and the Wheelchairs). He then went on to explain that they had this idea of forming a new band in which they would share the lead guitar and bass guitar duties. They say that in the Kingdom of the Blind, the one-eyed man is king and whilst I'm sure Ian enjoyed munching his way through my mum's biscuit collection and playing the king amongst fools in Gud Fungs, it was now time for him to move on and do something more substantial. That was always going to be the deal.

Surprisingly, he asked if I wanted to be the drummer. I wondered if I was up to it but I'll admit I was flattered. This was to be a proper cover band, which wouldn't be playing songs about goolies, wigs or melons, but proper songs by proper bands. Steve was an excellent lead guitarist and so, excited about the prospect, I accepted the offer. Fraser was invited to join the new venture too. I was concerned about how John would feel about not being asked to join the new band. I knew Ray wouldn't be in the slightest bit bothered; I always felt that he was only in Gud Fungs to humour the rest of us and would rather be spending his Saturday afternoons over at Upton Park. John said he was ok with it but I'm not sure if I ever believed that he was.

The original line-up of Gud Fungs would never play together again. There was no big falling out or disgruntledness, no musical differences, no tears. Punk rock had opened its arms wide and five boys from Essex had gleefully dived in for an all-too-brief cuddle. Their talent was tiny, but their balls were huge, and most crucially, they kept them in their smalls – but now it was over. I enjoyed every single second of being in that band. They were some of the funniest moments of my life.

The new band, which was eventually christened Quasimodo, and only then because we actually had a gig and needed a name, would rehearse in a youth club in Newbury Park – a space that Fraser secured for us. It wasn't ideal; the room was echoey and live, and anyone from the youth club could just walk in whenever they liked and watch us rehearse, which was very off-putting and terribly annoying. One of the youth leaders would come into the room several times a night and tell us to turn it down. I can't remember his name – we just referred to him as 'the Bearded Cunt', for reasons that didn't soley relate to his facial hair.

We covered some great songs; 'I Can't Explain' and 'Substitute' by The Who, 'You Really Got Me' and 'All Day and All of the Night' by The Kinks, 'Rebel, Rebel' by David Bowie, 'Anything That's Rock n' Roll' by Tom Petty, Nick Lowe's 'So it Goes' and 'The Cowboy Song' and 'Little Darling' by Thin Lizzy.

Although this band was a lot more serious than Gud Fungs had been, it was not without its moments of silliness. Around this time, Cadburys were running a rock version of their TV ad for Flake. You know, the 'only the crumbliest, flakiest chocolate' thing. This version had searing great chunky rock chords and drums that went 'dugga-da-dugga-da-dugga-da-dug' like they were being thumped with a couple of goalposts. We decided it would be fun to try it and Fraser sang it with all the throatiness and gusto of a Ronnie James Dio, so much so that Louis Walsh would probably have commented that he had made it his own and then cried. When struggling for a name for this band, we were only a crumbly piece of chocolate away from going with 'Flake'.

The Bearded Cunt had heard enough to deem us worthy of a gig at the youth club and we rehearsed hard to fashion a set out of the songs that we had. He wasn't going to pay us, of course, but that wasn't really the point. We invited all our friends and they mingled with the usual youth clubbers, and on the night the room was packed. I was incredibly nervous about playing my first-ever gig. There wasn't a stage as such; we just set up on the floor and when the room was full there were people standing at the side of my kit, watching my every move, as if the pressure of my first gig wasn't enough. I seem to recall that it all started off quite promisingly. We opened with a minute or so burst of 'Flake', which may or may not have raised a smile on the faces of the audience – I'm not sure, I was too scared to look up. As that ended, we went straight into 'Rebel Rebel'. It amazed me that people were cheering and clapping at the end of each song. Even if it was out of politeness, it was still very warming to hear and helped to give us confidence, spurring us on. After about seven or eight songs, the Bearded Cunt, who was manning the disco that was planned for after our set, surprised us all by announcing over his microphone 'and that's all from Quasimodo for now folks, they'll be back in an hour. And now what you've all been waiting for … the disco – this is Earth, Wind & Fire'.

We stood there shell-shocked and open-jawed, as none of us were expecting there to be a break. He hadn't told us he was planning this and his timing was rubbish because we only had three songs left to do. The second half was going to be pretty much over before it had begun.

The band retreated to The Avenue pub across the road from the youth club to stroke our wounded egos and most of our friends that had turned up for the gig came with us to sympathise. We contemplated not bothering to go back to play our three-song second set. After an hour and a half, we all trooped back, very much worse for wear, and played the rest of our set. It was awful. Going back pissed had not really had the right rock'n'roll effect – we weren't very rock'n'roll. I can't remember what the other two songs were, but I remember we ended with the Sid Vicious version of 'My Way' and the whole thing just fell apart. I missed beats; Fraser forgot the words and the chords emanating from the guitar may have been the same ones that are used in the song, but I doubt it. Something that had started out quite promising had dissolved into musical slapstick.

It was deemed that we needed a second guitarist and we brought in a friend of Laurence's to fill the gap. The band struggled on for a while, but rehearsals became more and more infrequent.

Meanwhile, me, Fraser and Mark had booked a lad's holiday to Majorca for the summer of 1980 and I didn't have the money for the final payment. As the band had more or less ground to a halt after our solitary gig, I decided that I would sell my kit to fund the holiday. I had added various bits and pieces to it by then and sold it to a music shop called Cliff Owen in Seven Kings for £300. It was just about enough for my holiday. I was no longer a drummer and no longer in a band.

Nights out with John and Ian became infrequent over the next couple of years, but without entirely losing touch. I'm not sure whose idea it was to have a Gud Fungs/ Quasimodo reunion, but in 1982, that's what we did.

As I no longer owned a kit, we booked ourselves into a studio in Leyton one Saturday afternoon. The studio would supply all the amps and speakers etc. and of course a drum kit, and all we had to was turn up and play – if any of us could remember how to, or how any of the songs went.

Ray didn't take part in the reunion; he was now engaged to Denise and the chance to play that bass solo one more time was savagely trumped by the need to shop for soft furnishings in Ilford. The rest of Gud Fungs showed up, as did Steve from Quasimodo. We ran through most of the old songs and they came flooding back as if it had only been yesterday that we had last played them. We played 'Say No More' for the very last time until there was no more to say. The occasion was of course recorded, this time by Laurence's brother Gary, who not only had the patience to sit through four hours of this drivel, but also had a very nice tape recorder. He even got up and had a go on the drums, playing on an impromptu song called 'Egg', which lyrically consisted only of the word 'egg' – that's why it was called 'Egg'. I had a copy of Gary's tape but over the years forgot about its existence.

I pretty much lost touch with Ian and John after the reunion afternoon. Neither of them came to my wedding in 1983, which was a shame, whereas Fraser and Ray were my joint best men. There were sporadic meetings over the next couple of decades but these were brief and were of a one-off nature, and eventually we lost touch completely.

In early September 2001 and completely out of the blue, an email from Ian plopped into my inbox at work. I opened it and it read as follows:

Bear,

My name's Fraser, Fraser Cooper,
And no one thinks I'm very super
I'm the singer with this group
Do you like my crimplene suit?

Gud Fungs, Gud Fungs
Ooo Gud Fungs, Ooo Gud Fungs
Gud Fungs.

My name's Budd, Budd John Graham
See these strings, I can really play 'em
Don't talk to me anymore
About fat little Gaynor, the piggy-eyed whore

My name's Monty, Mont-e-gue
And I like watching Raymond spu
I'm always having ego trips
And I'm proud of my three nips

My name's Pearce, Pearce Ray Nowt
I can't talk so I always shout
I call my friends 'stupid turd'
And throw-up peanuts in the kerb

My name's Shelley, Shelley Bear
And I've got rather lovely hair
I used to beat on people's bums
Until I got a set of drums

Monty

Nothing more, just that. I was delighted and replied immediately. We started to rebuild our friendship by wasting hours endlessly emailing each other things that kept us amused and helped us get through the working day. Lists; lots of lists: Top 10 Bands You Really Should've Seen But Couldn't Be Bothered, 10 Song Titles That Become Funnier If You Replace the Word Love with Glove ('How Deep is Your Glove'– The Bee Gees, 'Where Did Our Glove Go?'– The Supremes, 'I'd do Anything for Glove (but I won't do that)' – Meat Loaf). We once spent two entire days remotely discussing whether or not Paul McCartney's hair in the eighties was an authentic mullet.

We started meeting regularly for a drink after work, and we spent a lot of time talking about music, just like we always had, particularly about our respective current bands. Ian was then in a country band called Middle Age Rampage and I was in my eighth year as drummer for the Fabulous Heseltines. We talked about Gud Fungs and how if only video had been around then, how great it would have been to have seen some footage of those days. There were never any awkward silences like you would expect from people that hadn't spent any time together for several decades. You see, the one thing that middle-aged men that have been in bands are really good at is talking about the bands they were in. If they didn't have their bands to talk about they would be forced to talk about their greenhouses.

It gave me an idea, and one evening I started rummaging through a big bin liner of cassettes that was tucked away in my loft. Since the invention of CD, I hadn't really needed to play any of the hundreds of old cassettes I had, and so they had been discarded, unloved and redundant in the black hole of the roof space.

To rummage is to half-heartedly look, and there were hundreds of tapes, so out on to the floor they went. I got waylaid by some of the old compilation tapes I had made over the years – 'Songs that are Quite Nice', 'Trapezium Discharge', 'Nice Breasts' etc. – but eventually I came across two cassettes that looked promising.

A TDK C60 marked up 'Gud Fungs Reunion 1982' was clearly exactly what I was looking for. The tape was hanging out of the bottom of the cassette and so I carefully reeled it back in with a pencil, just like I'd done countless times before in the seventies. Another cassette had 'Ratticus Norvegicus' (sic) written on it in Fraser's handwriting. His handwriting was instantly recognisable as it looked like the work of an epileptic spider. I wondered why I would have his cassette of 'Rattus Norvegicus' as I had the record – it didn't really make sense.

I took the cassette downstairs to my redundant cassette deck and gingerly placed the tape into the tray. With my headphones plugged in and almost too scared to hit play, I took a deep breath and went for it.

It was all there – in incredibly lo-fi, but all there nonetheless: 'The Wotsits Bop', 'Gud Fungs', 'The Ballad of Milly Molly Nesbitt' (fast and slow version), 'Bernard's Organ Recital' and even the 'Say No More (You

Cunt version)'. It felt emotional – really emotional. Not just because this terrible music had somehow been preserved all these years, but because what I was listening to was a little slice of our youth, saved, pressed forever onto this light brown magnetic tape. Little snippets of conversation between these five young boys who were trying to make some music and have a laugh at the same time. It took me right back there, to my mum's front room in 1977.

In my mind I was picturing those five boys, with heads still full of hair and flat stomachs and minds filled with not a lot more than simply pop music. It was a humbling experience and felt kind of historic, but with all sorts of funny stuff going on too, such as Fraser having extreme difficulty coming in at the right place in 'Balls in my Smalls'. Ian once skillfully observed that Fraser had trouble knowing where to come in on a song, and where to get out, but the bit in the middle was not too bad. This was never more evident than on 'Balls'. There is a count of five and then he should start singing, but in countless takes he either comes in after four or six. After about the eighth attempt you can hear me in the background, saying 'it's easy to remember it's after five because there are five of us'. Simple when you know how, eh.

I now had one of those CD recording machines where you can take another source such as LP or cassette, and record them onto blank CDs. It was time to prepare Gud Fungs for the new digital age. My original idea was that I would make this CD and present it to Ian the next time we met as a surprise, but my excitement got the better of me and I told him all about my discovery the very next morning in an email.

I listened to all the stuff and then recorded it onto CD so it was safe. The last thing we wanted was for the tape that had survived almost three decades to snap just as it suddenly had a purpose for existing. With the reunion tape there was enough there for a double CD. Ian and I decided that we should press five copies – one for each member of the band. I made a CD sleeve in bright yellow and pink (just like the *Never Mind the Bollocks* sleeve) and Ian wrote some amusing sleeve notes.

We spent some time coming up with a title for this Gud Fungs Anthology; *The Gud Fungs Anthology* being one of the names we came up with, but after narrowly rejecting *Where's the Biscuits?* we plumped for *The Bear Lies Down on Ilford Broadway*.

I dug out the photos that Laurence had taken at that photoshoot in 1977, and they went on the sleeve, along with some updated photos of each of us in 2001. The only problem was that no one knew where John was or how to contact him, so we didn't have an updated photo of him. All we knew was that he was now a policeman, and so I Googled a picture of PC Plod from the Noddy stories, and that went on the sleeve. We eventually caught up with John a few months later and were able to present him with his copy of the CD. He was unimpressed with the picture of PC Plod but enjoyed the sentiment.

The CD rather appropriately ends with Fraser shouting at the top of his voice 'SHUT UP – ALL BE QUIET!' at the end of a rather poor rendition of the 'Ballad of Milly Molly Nesbitt' (slow version). And shut up we did. Forever. A poignant ending for a not very poignant band.

Can You See the Real Me?

Sometimes with pop, it goes a little bit beyond the acknowledgement that this is a great song or that is a fantastic album. Not for everyone, I know, but for those of us that fully immerse ourselves into the pop experience, pop music returns the favour by throwing its arms around us and giving us a great big soppy hug.

These are the moments that separate pop from other media that are also able to create great feelings of euphoria or sadness. You might feel ecstatic when your team scores the winning goal in the cup final, or when you walk away from the cinema having just watched the most fantastic film, but however great these feelings are, there is still a distance between you and that movie or that winning goal that leaves you feeling detached.

It's hard to explain – impossible even, but when pop music speaks to you, it speaks to you on a personal level, like it is only speaking to you, even though you know deep down that it really isn't. We create situations in which the words of a song fit the exact way we are feeling at that particular moment, and lock us in that moment forever. It's magical. And it doesn't happen by accident – oh no, pop music knows exactly what it's doing when it delivers these emotions. R.E.M didn't create 'Everybody Hurts' for any one person in particular, they wrote it because they wanted everyone that was hurt, for one reason or another, to feel that song was written about them and their own personal situation, and to feel that emotion. Similarly, Paul McCartney didn't write 'My Love' just for Linda, he wrote it for everyone that was in love with their partner, to rejoice in that situation and to make everyone else that didn't feel that way about theirs wish they did.

And it's not just about these delicate emotions either. It sometimes speaks with a forked tongue. Pop can make you angry or rebellious; to all intents and purposes, that is what it was invented for. I've already talked about the angry men of punk and how that had been something for me to latch on to – the way I have always needed something to latch on to, but by the summer of 1979 it was all starting to wear thin. I was looking for something else.

I had been a fan of The Jam since the beginning. I had been attracted to them not simply by the records that they made, but because they had embraced the whole ethos of the sixties. It was like they brought a little bit of that decade along for the seventies generation that was too young at the time to enjoy it. Seeing The Jam live however, was never as joyous as it should have been. The band, as a three-piece, struggled to recreate the music that they had made on record live, without the use of the overdubs they had clearly used in the studio. Their gigs were all about the attitude though and they had that in abundance, or at least Paul Weller did. If I'm honest, Jam fans got on my nerves. They all seemed to be at least a couple of years younger than me, and to go to one of their gigs you had to be prepared to have sixteen-year-old-kids lolloping all over you in a sweaty suit and a Parka. It wasn't that I didn't like the mod style, I did; it was just mods that I didn't really like very much.

But then it all changed. I went to see the Who film *Quadrophenia* with Fraser. This was one of those rare moments when I was inspired by a film rather than the music that it contained. I'd been familiar with the *Quadrophenia* album for some years; it was one of those albums that when you first get it and look at what you've bought, you realise straight away that this is an important album. The imagery created by the mod in full regalia sitting astride his scooter on the front cover, and the photo of that same scooter floating alone in the sea on the back cover, demands that you find out what happened in between. The whole package felt bulky and heavy due to the book of black and white photographs and lyrics stapled to the gatefold sleeve. It was so fat it was a job to stuff it into a PVC cover. The book of photographs seemed to be random snippets of early sixties London (and Brighton). It all felt very stark, depressing even, but the music inside was bloody fantastic.

I hope I'm not putting myself out on a limb here, but did anyone really understand the story of *Quadrophenia* from the record? I know I didn't. But once the film came out it made complete sense. The film brought that music to life and gave a great insight into what it might have been like to be a teenager in the early sixties, which after all is what I had always wanted to be.

The film consolidated the rising of the mod movement for the seventies. The Jam weren't the only band that were going down that route – there were new bands like Secret Affair, The Purple Hearts, The Merton Parkas and The Chords doing it too.

Fraser and me threw ourselves wholeheartedly into the whole mod revival thing. We both had our hair cut short and bought two-tone mohair suits from a shop in Carnaby Street (where else?). Mine was green and grey, I seem to remember. More locally, there was a shop in Romford called Mintz & Davis that sold all the clothes – button-down shirts, skinny ties, Hush Puppy shoes and Fred Perry t-shirts. I was now spending more money on clothes than I was on records. I was going to say that this was when the rebellious side of pop spoke to me, but on reflection, how rebellious can you be in a pair of Hush Puppies?

The great thing about this fashion was that I could wear my tonic suit to work. I adorned the lapels with a single button each day. Some days The Jam, some days The Who and some days just a red, white and blue target. It felt great to look different to everyone else in the office, at a time where the pin-striped, double-breasted suit with turn-up trousers was king.

I had my ear pierced. Not like a normal person, of course. The proper

241

way to do this would be to have it done in a sanitary way at the hairdresser with a sterilised gun. My method of choice was to get one of Fraser's mates to ram the pointy bit of one of my sister's studs (by this I mean the pointy bit of one of her pieces of ear jewellery, not the pointy bit of one of her boyfriends) straight through my earlobe. It hurt like a bitch, but I liked how it looked. Boys wearing earrings was still frowned upon in the world of Banking, and therefore I had to go through the ritual of taking it out every morning and then trying to force it back through the congealed blood that had accumulated in the hole during the day when I got home from work. This was about as rebellious as I got, although rebelling against what, I wasn't sure. Thatcher? The National Front? West Ham getting relegated? Boney M? One of those … probably.

An ad in the *NME* one Thursday told me that all the Parkas that were used by the mods in the *Quadrophenia* film were going on sale at 'The Last Resort' – a shop in Petticoat Lane on the following Sunday morning. Fraser and I got ourselves down there early, and managed to get one. It cost me a tenner.

What a great piece of rock memorabilia! Mine had a Union Jack patch sewn on the back with The Who logo over it – the one with the arrow pointing up from the letter 'O'. It fitted me like a tent and smelt a bit like one too, but I was dead proud of it and wore it everywhere. I thought the bees had lent me their actual knees. I never went the whole hog though and bought a scooter. Why would I? If I wanted to break down on the side of the road I had a perfectly rubbish 1968 Mark II Cortina 1600GT that I could do that in.

On the August bank holiday 1979, a gang of us piled into the back of my dad's yellow Escort van (not me, obviously, I was driving and sat in the front to do so) and headed to Brighton – the location for that great scene in the *Quadrophenia* film, but more importantly the scene of so many battles between mods and rockers in the sixties. There were thousands of mods strolling about singing 'We are the mods', just like they did in the film. The place was lacking in rockers, but that didn't matter – we had a great day anyway and got a tiny taste of what it might have been like in those heady days.

I suppose I was a mod for about six months, but in the end The Jam were really the only mod band that had any sort of sustainability; all the others were a little bit rubbish and faded as quickly as they had arrived.

I still think *Quadrophenia* is a brilliant piece of work. By the time it came out in 1973, The Who were the self-claimed 'best rock band in the world' and so there is a touch of irony attached to them producing what is essentially a rock album about being a mod. The irony wasn't lost on me, but I think it is on a lot of Who fans. I saw what remains of The Who play live in 2015, and after a rousing rendition of 'My Generation', as the applause died down a large section of the audience started chanting 'We are the mods'. Pete Townshend, looking rather perplexed and, it has to be said, somewhat dismayed, retorted in his usual straight-talking manner, 'No, we're not the mods and neither are you – we're all just a bunch of old blokes that used to be the mods'.

Whether you were a mod, a ted, a skin or a punk, today's pop-tribe uniform eventually becomes tomorrow's fancy dress box filler and once I'd lost my mod mojo, my Quadrophenia parka lay dormant, hanging unloved in our coat cupboard. After I left home in 1982, I went back for it, just for old times' sake, and maybe as a future conversation piece, but I couldn't find it anywhere. I asked my mother if she knew where it was – she always knew where everything I couldn't find was – mainly pants, admittedly.

'What that ugly green coat?' she said. 'Oh, I threw that old thing out for the bin men years ago, it was stinking the place out.'

Feel It

When pop music and sex join forces they are a knicker-wetting combination that is hard to resist.

In 1978 I fell in love for the first time. Kate wasn't like anyone I had ever seen or heard before. Stunningly beautiful, and with a voice that fell somewhere between banshee and angel: deep from her boots one moment, then the highest note you could ever imagine the next. Her first hit, 'Wuthering Heights', seemed to be number one forever and her follow-up single 'The Man with the Child in His Eyes' was the most wondrously charming song ever written by a seventeen-year-old girl. Both songs came from an incredible record called *The Kick Inside* – a seventeenth birthday present from my sister. Kate followed that album up swiftly the following year with another record that was almost as good, called *Lionheart*. Shortly after its release, she (Kate Bush, not my sister), performed a run of stunning shows at the London Palladium. I went to two of them, and then a third at Hammersmith Odeon, at which both Steve Harley and Peter Gabriel also performed.

I was on good form with my ticket buying for that one, because not only did I manage to land myself a seat smack bang in the middle of row A, but it would also turn out to be the last live show she would do for thirty-five years. I'd like to think that the reason for such a long lay-off had nothing to do with the close proximity in which she spent that evening with me.

I had acquired a huge poster of Kate, which had been used to promote *The Kick Inside* from a record shop near to where I was working. It was the one with her in a pink vest, her nipples hard and poking so far through the tight fabric that you could probably hang a soggy duffel coat on them – sexy enough to give a stubborn pensioner a semi at least, but with an innocence in her wry smile – as if she'd just finished laughing at one of my hilarious quips. And eyes so wide, they followed you around the room – so much so, I was almost too embarrassed to undress in front of her. With the walls of my bedroom fully occupied with Beatles posters, I was forced to sellotape her to my bedroom ceiling directly over my bed. It was the perfect place for me to lie in bed and stare longingly at this beautiful creature and … well, I guess you get the picture, and occasionally so did I.

In 1978 most teenage boys were either in Camp Bush or Camp Harry, although, most would have liked to have been in both. Don't get me wrong; Debbie Harry was as hot as a sauna in hell. It's hard to shift the memory of her singing 'Denis' on *Top of the Pops* wearing just a shirt and knee-length boots, crouching purposefully down during the middle eight to give us just a momentary glimpse of her red knickers. But Debbie was just a singer, there was something more to Kate. Not only was she utterly gorgeous, she was also a brilliant writer who had this ability to get inside the characters that she invented and become them through her songs. And if the characters already existed, such as Heathcliff and Cathy, she breathed new life into them. She was totally original and never stood still, even if the next thing wasn't as good as the thing before, she still went with it and stood by it – very much like Bowie had done before her.

But Kate was just a poster on my ceiling, always available whenever I needed her; having sex with real girls was proving a little more troublesome. Finding them was a problem – I was quite picky for a ginger lad. I didn't mind if potential girlfriends weren't really interested in pop music, so long as they didn't mind listening to me talking endlessly about it, whilst they twiddled with their hair and stared blankly back at me. But preferably they would be into pop, and be suitably impressed by blokes who were in bands, because I was a bloke who was in a band. If that didn't so much as moisten their lips, they should at least pretend that they liked nothing as much as being talked at by a bloke who's in a band, about the being in a band, because blokes who are in bands like nothing more than to talk about the bands they are in. Those kinds of girls were hard to find. Most girls I knew just liked shoes.

I will admit that, back then, I could probably drive most people to the edge of distraction with insistent chatter about pop music or about being in bands. Even when I wasn't in a band anymore, I would somehow manage to turn the conversation back to the time when I was in a band. So, for example, a song would come on the jukebox whilst having a quiet drink in a country pub, and I would pipe up with 'we used to do this in the band'. I must admit that, when that band is Gud Fungs, this line of conversation was hugely flawed and had only a limited shelf life. Let's face it, it was highly unlikely that 'Say No More' or 'Bernard's Organ Recital' would ever pump their way out of any jukebox – anywhere – ever … unless the pub was owned by John Budd. I could extend it slightly by using the 'my mate's band used to do this one' routine, but that would make me sound more like a band-hanger-on rather than a proper musician.

Of course, the minute that you say 'we used to do this in the band', you are not only blatantly showing off, but you are also inviting questions about the band – about your rock'n'roll lifestyle, about the day you bought your first sizzle cymbal. Should things develop this far, the main thing to remember here is to never take her up to your bedroom and play her distorted cassette recordings of the band running through songs about people you didn't like at school in your mum's front room.

She may of course feign interest and ask to hear some stuff by this band that you have self-satisfyingly been banging on about for the last twenty minutes. You will then have to start making excuses before you even put it on, like: 'well, it's just some old thing we laid down on a Sony Cassette Deck' or 'the quality's really poor, but you can kind of get where we were coming from'. In my experience, though, the recordings should be avoided at all costs, because up until the point where she actually hears this band of yours, in her mind she'll be thinking Alice Cooper, and what she is about to get is ... Fraser Cooper. If things get out of hand and you do end up playing her something, remember never to start any sentence with 'I wrote this one because ...'.

There is some mileage to be gained by taking the 'going right over her head' road. This route to impressing girls is very popular amongst 'muso' types, and this is where you might talk about different makes of guitar, throw in a quick mention of humbuckers or headstocks for good measure, or even come out with something as clinically banal as saying 'yeah we used to do this one, but had to change the key cos Tonker couldn't get up there'. You have to be careful with this one, though, if you're looking for something that might raise your standing with a girl. Tread lightly, especially if you're not quite sure of your subject matter. If she knows the slightest thing about guitar pick-ups or musical keys, you're in trouble straight away and could come a cropper.

'So what key did you guys do it in, then?'
'Err, not sure – L sharp, I think?'

On a boredom scale of one to ten, I was cranking it up to eleven and beyond. If you're a girl and didn't put this book in the bin after the third chapter, then not only do I thank you for sticking with it, but I also recognise you as a fellow pop-bore and just the sort of girl that would have been right up my street, which begs the question, 'where the hell were you in 1979?'.

I've never really understood why, when you're young, the popular call is to have sex with music playing in the background. I'm of the opinion that having sex while listening to pop music is a combination made fashionable only by the sexually proficient, Prince fans or people who have no soul, and therefore no regard for pop music. It just seems odd that pop is used in this way as some sort of aphrodisiac. Does it work in the same way with other media? What do couples that hate pop use as a background aphrodisiac? Stick on a particularly gripping episode of *The Bill*?

When my time finally came, the scene was set: an empty house, a bottle of warm Black Tower pilfered from her parents' drinks cabinet and her bedroom decorated with posters of various bare-chested men in their pants, who appeared to be watching my every move.

We were ready to go. Well, she was, I was bloody petrified. She dimmed the lights and put on *Sgt. Pepper* because that's what she thought I wanted to hear. It really wasn't. It was my own fault; she only had it because I lent it to her as a 'must-hear' record during one of my pop music boreathons.

It's really the whole concept of background music that I struggle with. To me, pop music has to be played loud – there is no room for subtlety, because in the end, if music is playing, I generally want to listen to it – unless it's the Pet Shop Boys. And so trying to perform for the first time with one of the greatest albums of all time spinning away in the background is putting me at a disadvantage straight away. And the softer the music is, the more I am struggling to hear it, and the more I am struggling to hear it, the more I want to hear it, and the more I want to hear it, the less inclined I am to struggle with difficult-to-negotiate bra-clasps.

Singing along with the title track and emphasising the 'It's wonderful to be here, it really is a thrill' bit was just wrong, I know that now. I will also admit that asking her to stop what she was doing to just listen to McCartney's little bass runs on 'Lucy in the Sky with Diamonds' was just a delaying tactic, and putting off what would inevitably be the permanent association of the *Sgt. Pepper's Lonely Hearts Club Band* LP with my very first time.

Sgt. Pepper in this context, is a record that introduces all sorts of doubts and asks questions that need answering. What if I play that bit where the crowd cheers after Paul introduces the one and only Billy Shears, backwards, and listen through headphones with the sound turned right up, would I be able to faintly make out one of their number shouting 'get in there my son'?. What if I can only hold out till halfway through 'With A Little Help from My Friends'? What if I can't rise to the occasion at all, and then forever after, listening to 'Fixing A Hole' will be a sorry reminder of five tracks' worth of miserable, floppy failure? Did I really want to set that memory to music?

There's also the rhythmic issue to overcome. Different songs, different time signatures. How can one be expected to keep a steady pace when you have the ultra-slow 'She's Leaving Home' setting your tempo, and then have to writhe about to the odd rhythmic patterns of 'Mr Kite'? I'm sure the time signature thing must have been a particularly gritty issue for prog rock fans and probably explains why all fans of Jethro Tull are still virgins.

What if, miracle upon miracles, I actually made it to the end of side one? Then what? Stay exactly where I was, in a blissful silence, or waddle uncomfortably over to the turntable, trying desperately not to trip over the trousers and pants nestling clumsily around my ankles? Remembering, of course, to cover that huge spot on my arse with my hand as I waddled, just in case she thought I had a third buttock. Sex with pop is full of these tricky decisions, so you need to make your choice wisely. The silence wins hands down for me, because let's say I made it safely across the room to the turntable and flipped the thing over, the next two songs we are going to be trying to do it to are the appropriately named 'Within You, Without You' and 'When I'm 64' – and frankly, neither of these are sexy songs.

Rock, Paper, Slippers

A recent survey's results said that 65% of women asked had made love with Sade's *Diamond Life* album playing in the background. That fact alone is enough to convince me that doing it with the sound well and truly off is only right and proper.

(Just Like) Starting Over

I can't really think of another year that was anything like 1980. It was a year of extreme highs and rock-bottom lows.

Totally oblivious of the horrors that the eighties had in store, the seventies ended for me on a massive high note. Wings toured the UK for the first time since I'd been a fan. I am completely aware that when you put the words 'Wings' and 'fan' next to each other, the kind of image that pairing conveys is similar to when you do the same with 'speccy' and 'twat'. They're the band that you list last and slightly mumble the name of when reeling off the bands that you like – usually just before you concatenate the words 'Electric', 'Light' and 'Orchestra'. But they were the band that Paul McCartney was in so I loved them unconditionally.

I'd been marginally too late to catch them on the 1975 tour, but in December 1979 they played several dates in London in support of their latest album *Back to the Egg*. There was no way that I was going to miss them this time, so Fraser and I queued up half the night outside Wembley Arena when the tickets went on sale, securing reasonable seats for three nights there. I was ridiculously excited about seeing Paul McCartney in the flesh for the very first time. I'd been to over a hundred gigs by now, but this was the big one as far as I was concerned. Only a live performance by John Lennon would have been a bigger occasion, and seeing as John was enjoying his premature retirement from music, this was the one.

The countdown to Friday 7 December 1979 began the moment we had those tickets in our sticky little mitts, but now it was finally here. We headed to Wembley straight after work and waited impatiently for the lights to dim. After what seemed like an eternity, there was a flush of horns and there, standing in the same room, breathing the same air as me, was Paul McCartney out of The Beatles, singing 'Got to Get You into My Life' before my very eyes.

As great as it was to see my hero live, and, to be fair, he was on great form, I wasn't totally satisfied. Having spent entire days of my life listening to the *Wings Over America* live album as a kind of training session for the real thing, I have to say that the set he delivered on this tour wasn't what I was hoping for. Much of the set that he had performed in America three years earlier had been usurped by comparatively weaker material from the *Back to the Egg* LP. A personal highlight from the second show was when drummer Steve Holley threw his drumstick into the crowd and Fraser wrestled with another fan to secure it, handing it directly to me. A kinder gesture I have yet to witness. It was quite a humbling experience to hold a splintered drumstick that had been pounded to death to provide the beat that kept Paul McCartney out of The Beatles in time. It's a treasured possession that I still have. But, despite this, there was a little feeling of emptiness as we trudged away from the arena after the third show.

Out of the blue, as these things usually are, there was a humanitarian disaster in Kampuchea. Rock stars including Macca stepped up to the plate with a series of gigs at the Hammersmith Odeon in late December. Queen played a night, The Who played a night and the final show featured Rockpile, Elvis Costello & The Attractions, and Wings. We pulled out all the stops and managed to get tickets.

The pre-gig excitement for this one was built up by rumours that this show was The One – the one where all four Beatles would appear on stage together for the first time since 1966. The news buzzing around town was that George and Ringo were in London for Christmas and John was going to be flying in to take part. It seemed possible; it was for charity after all, and it was almost the last day of the seventies – could this actually happen? Well, I believed it could. I wanted to believe it could, and if it was going to happen, I had to be there. If you want something badly enough sometimes, just sometimes, it happens. Admittedly not very often for me, in fact hardly ever, but maybe this time it would be different.

It's not like there hadn't been rumours of a Beatles reunion before – the seventies had been awash them. They cropped up at least twice a year, every year, the most celebrated of these being an album by a Canadian band oddly named Klaatu. They had released an album of songs that sounded very much like the post-*Revolver* Beatles. Their album had no pictures of the band on it, no credits, just the name of the band – Klaatu. It was a mystery worth investigating and many did, searching feverishly for clues, much like they did with the 'Paul is Dead' conspiracy.

One little gem of a 'clue' that popped up was that the name 'Klaatu' was also the name of a character in the film *The Day the Earth Stood Still* – a character that Ringo had decided to dress himself up as on the cover of his *Goodnight Vienna* album sleeve. Well, if that wasn't proof enough, then I don't know what was.

The Klaatu album shifted plenty of copies because of the whole 'was it or wasn't it them' thing. Considering that nobody had heard of the band, these songs got an awful lot of airplay on the radio. Nicky Horne on Capital Radio played a couple of tracks from this album every night, fuelling the fire that this was just the sort of thing The Beatles would do. However, the harsh reality for those silly enough to bite was that anyone who knew anything about The Beatles would know that they would never, ever write a song called 'Anus of Uranus' or 'Calling Occupants from Interplanetary Craft'. Klaatu's second album sounded nothing like The Beatles and the rumour was binned. That one sold about seven copies.

Back at Hammersmith Odeon on the evening of 29 December 1979, the tension was building as Wings came towards the end of their set, with everyone speculating as to just when Paul would introduce the other three.

Paul and Wings left the stage after playing 'Band on the Run' just as they had on all the other nights of the tour that we had seen just a couple of weeks before. After a few minutes of chanting for more, Billy Connolly, strode out onto the stage and announced how lucky we all were to be witnessing what we were about to witness.

This was it. Fraser and I looked at each other knowingly. And then Connolly took out a piece of paper from his back pocket and starting reading out a list of musicians that were about to appear on the stage: Robert Plant, John Paul Jones, John Bonham from Led Zeppelin; Pete Townshend and Kenney Jones from The Who; a couple of Elvis Costello's Attractions; Dave Edmunds, Ronnie Lane and countless others – but no John, no George and no Ringo. The 'Rockestra', as they were called, all came on wearing silver jackets and matching top hats, except Townshend, who was far too cool to be wearing silly clothes.

They ran through the Little Richard song 'Lucille', 'Let it Be' and the 'Rockestra Theme' from the *Back to the Egg* album. There before us was probably the greatest collection of rock musicians ever gathered together on one stage, and they were of course brilliant ... but it wasn't The Beatles.

If ever there was an early indication of just how rubbish the eighties were going to turn out, the events of 16 January 1980 were it. As Wings embarked on their tour of Japan, Paul McCartney somehow thought it would be great idea to smuggle a pound of cannabis through customs in his suitcase – because that's what you would do when you already have a couple of drug convictions to your name, and you've previously been refused entry into a country that not only takes one of the hardest stands against drug use, but is generally not that keen on you anyway because you once foolishly in your youth had the chutzpah to play a song about holding ladies' hands in their sacred Budokan Hall. What was he thinking?

It was all over the news – Paul was sent to jail and the tour was cancelled. The red-tops probably ran with something punny like 'Macca in the joint', but I wasn't laughing – I was worried. In the pictures from Tokyo airport that appeared in the papers, Macca looked terrified, and all the talk was that he would be made an example of, and spend a number of years in a Japanese jail. There was one photo that I remember with a customs officer holding up the great big bag of dope with a huge grin on his face, absolutely chuffed to bits with himself. It all looked very bad for Paul. This was one of the first times I can remember making a point of watching the news every night. Well, the bit about this story anyway.

In the end, he spent sixteen days in jail and was eventually deported being told in no uncertain terms never to darken the doorstep of Japan ever again. (Their doorstep remained light for ten years, after which he was allowed to go back to play a couple of gigs in Tokyo.) It was a huge relief to have him back, and the pictures of him disembarking a plane at

Heathrow showed him looking a little dishevelled but with thumbs clearly aloft once more.

West Ham began the eighties in the old Second Division. The 1979–80 season was looking like it was going to be another failed attempt to get back in the First Division and indeed that was exactly how it panned out. However, our spirits were raised beyond all expectations by another great run in the FA Cup. I went to every cup game that season, taking in victories against First Divison teams West Bromwich Albion, Aston Villa and Everton, followed by West Ham surprising everyone by beating Arsenal in the final to win the cup. This time, both Ray and I managed to get tickets for Wembley. It was an amazing day. Trevor Brooking's swooping header went in after ten minutes and for the rest of the match we sang our hearts out with fingers tightly crossed as West Ham managed to thwart wave after wave of Arsenal pressure. We held out for eighty long minutes, which felt like about three days, but at the final whistle we were ecstatic. It was no mean achievement and West Ham still remain the last team from outside the top flight of football to win the FA Cup.

Later that summer, I met Melanie. She was very beautiful and I was very smitten. More importantly, she was a hardcore Beatles fan. She was perfect. We did Beatley things together like watching Beatle movies, listening to records and writing our names on the doors of the derelict Apple Offices in Savile Row. It's funny: years and years later, I paid a visit to the Beatles museum in Liverpool, and they had that very door as an exhibit. On close inspection, squeezed in amongst the hundreds of other fan inscriptions, I could still see 'Mel & Tony' written on it inside a heart shape. We went out for a few months.

Also that summer, Julie began working at Singer & Friedlander. I clearly remember seeing the memo that came around the office announcing the names of the new joiners. It amused me that her surname was Painting. I'd never heard of anyone having a name that was a verb before. She was from the Cotswolds (which I had heard of before) and spoke with an accent that I had only heard in episodes of Worzel Gummidge. We became friends and sometimes spent lunchtimes together in the pub. Julie was a year older than me and was engaged to a bloke called Tim, who didn't like people who wore suits. They had been together since they were sixteen, which surprised me because I thought he was a bit of an arse. She would sometimes bring him along to after-work drinks and on one such occasion a £20 note fell out of his pocket. I picked it up and took great pleasure in using it to buy a round for the suited types in our gang. We grew close under the safety net that we were both with other people.

By the beginning of Autumn, news had started to filter through that John

Lennon was back in the studio making a new album. This was pretty much the best news I had ever heard. He had retired just before I discovered he existed so this would be the first John Lennon record I would be buying as it came out. I was very excited about its arrival and of course bought it on the day of its release.

The album was preceded with a single, '(Just Like) Starting Over' – a medium-paced rocker and John's voice sounded as good as ever on it. The song was really about new beginnings in his relationship with Yoko, but could just as easily been about starting his music career again. I loved it and played it to death whilst I waited impatiently for the album to come out.

The album *Double Fantasy* finally arrived in November and, to be honest, when I got it home I was a little disappointed to find that the fourteen tracks on the album were shared equally (vocally) by both John and Yoko. I'd waited four years for this album and seven new John Lennon songs was not a great return for my patience. However, once I'd listened to the album a few times, it was clear that Yoko had learned far more from new wave than John had, and her songs sounded more modern and edgy; the main rule learned from punk rock being that you don't have to have a great voice to be a decent singer. After all, Yoko was making records like Siouxsie Sioux about ten years before Siouxsie thought she had invented that sound. It might even be fair to say that Yoko was the original punk rocker!

While John's songs were about embracing middle age and domestic bliss, Yoko's took a harder stance and sounded bitter, angry and exciting, and were laden with some of John's most vicious guitar playing. 'Kiss, Kiss, Kiss' was just pure sex and ended with Yoko (presumably) faking an orgasm, which was uncomfortable to listen to, but challenging at the same time.

Whilst the subject matter of John's songs was a little bit more mainstream, it was clear that in songs like 'I'm Losing You' and 'Watching the Wheels' he had written a couple of songs that were amongst the best of his career. On 'Woman' he sounded like Beatle John and what could be better than that?

It was great having John back in the news and on TV again. He did lots of promotional stuff for the new album – a photo-shoot for *Rolling Stone*, an interview with *Playboy* and a five-hour interview with Andy Peebles from Radio One, in which he was in the best of moods and seemed happier than he'd ever been. The best news that he gave us was that he was already halfway through making the follow-up album to *Double Fantasy*. It would be finished in 1981 and, when it was, he was planning to go on the road, and his first stop was going to be the UK. He hadn't been home since he left for New York in 1971. A second new Lennon album, the promise of seeing him live, West Ham were top of the league by miles and looking dead certs for promotion and I had a gorgeous girlfriend – who said the eighties were going to be rubbish?

On the morning of Tuesday 9 December 1980 my mum woke me with a jolt. This was no different to any other morning. I always relied on her to wake me up for school or work, posing difficult questions for the sleepy-headed such as 'what do you want for breakfast'. But this was earlier than usual and more forceful.

'Anthony – I don't know how to tell you this – John's been shot.'

'John? John who?'

'John Lennon.'

Her words resonated around my ears for a few seconds as I gradually came to. At first it never even crossed my mind that he might be dead. People got shot all the time in America, right? They didn't all die, did they? If he had been dead she would have said 'John's dead,' wouldn't she? This was John Lennon – he'd be fine.

I got dressed for work as normal and still in a bit of a daze crept down the stairs. As I got halfway down, I could hear the radio in the kitchen playing 'Imagine'. My mum always listened to LBC in the morning and LBC was a talk radio station – they didn't play pop music unless there was a bloody good reason. It was at that moment that I realised that John was dead. There could be no other reason. I slumped down on the stairs, with my face in my hands and wept like a baby. I don't remember another time in my life when I was so not in control of my emotions. I had lost two grandparents in the late seventies and not shed a tear, yet here I was in bits over a pop star whom I had never met, and who had no idea of my existence. I didn't want to go to work, but my mum insisted that it was unlikely I would be granted compassionate leave because one of The Beatles had died. They probably wouldn't view it with the same degree of importance as I did.

I got on the tube a puffy, red-eyed mess and looked around the carriage. Some passengers were laughing and joking or just chatting to each other without a care in the world, like it was just a normal day. How dare they? Did they not know what had happened? Did they not care? On reflection, it's possible that they didn't know. It happened too late at night to make the morning papers, and these were the days before Breakfast TV, so if they hadn't been listening to the radio that morning, then they probably didn't know, and even if they did, I doubt they would have cared as much as I did.

When I got to work, people were making a special journey down to my office to offer commiserations as if it was a member of my family that had died. On any other day, my office was usually full of banter and piss-taking between the five of us who worked there, but today was different –

it was dead quiet and seemly. They were all very nice.

Julie came to see me and threw her arms around me; it looked like she'd been crying too. I'm not sure if her tears were for John or me. On the way home from work I bought both the *Evening Standard* and the *Evening News*. The papers were now full of the story – pages and pages of it. Outpourings of lament and horrendous photos of John signing an autograph for Mark Chapman, the man who a few hours later would put four bullets through his back. The tube had a very different atmosphere that evening to the one earlier in the day. London's heart was broken after all.

When I got home, I drove over to see Melanie. We watched all the stuff that was on TV. The whole evening schedule was taken over with tributes and programmes about John and The Beatles. The most moving scenes were the news shots from New York, where thousands of fans were gathering outside John's home, the Dakota building. The gates were covered in flowers and the cameras panned across the fans, holding candles and singing Lennon songs with tears streaming down their faces. One thing that really struck me about looking at those fans was the different age groups that had gathered there. There were kids, mums and dads, ageing hippies, Hells Angels and pensioners. This was a man that had touched so many people's lives in so many different ways – ways that he didn't even know about. It was heartbreaking to watch and I wanted to be there. It felt kind of disloyal not to be, and in some stupid, misguided way, I wanted him to know that he had touched my life too.

After a while I left Mel's and went to see how Fraser was doing. We hadn't spoken yet that day. When I got to his house ITV were showing the Beatles film *Help!* We didn't laugh once. It was all very depressing.

The vigil outside the Dakota seemed to go on for days, with more and more people turning up every day from all over the world. I had just taken out a bank loan of £1,000 to buy a new car but considered using it to go to New York to join them. I was ready to do this until Yoko announced that she would like everyone to go home as the singing was upsetting her and Sean (their five-year-old son) and they needed some time. She promised that she would organise a worldwide vigil in a week or so. I bought a Triumph Dolomite.

'(Just Like) Starting Over' was slipping down the charts before John was murdered. The following week it was number one. And when it wasn't number one anymore, 'Imagine' was. And when Imagine wasn't number one anymore, 'Woman' from *Double Fantasy* was. John had never had a number one solo record before he was shot, now he had three – he would have been chuffed. The little flurry of Lennon chart activity in 1981 was brought to an abrupt halt by a comedy record called 'Shaddapa You Face' by Joe Dolce. Normal service in the charts had been resumed. I still haven't forgiven the British record-buying public for allowing that to happen.

Melanie was about to go on holiday to Australia with her family and I wouldn't see her for six weeks. Before she left, I tried to buy her a couple of John Lennon albums for Christmas but you couldn't get hold of a Lennon album for love nor money. However, our relationship had pretty much run its course anyway and we broke up shortly after, but I'm really glad we were together when John died.

I wasn't really in the mood for the Singer & Friedlander Christmas party but everyone talked me into going. Getting pissed out of my brain at the bank's expense wasn't really going to solve anything, but it might help. When the DJ played 'Imagine', Julie grabbed my hand and insisted that I danced with her. Unlike the Nolan Sisters, I wasn't really in the mood for dancing, but did anyway. We kissed for the first time – we'd been building towards this for some time and it wasn't completely unexpected.

Julie and I married in 1983. I was 22 – a child bride. We have two children; Daniel, who was born in November 1986, was always going to have the middle name of Lennon. It could have been worse – I could have been a fan of Steven 'Tin Tin' Duffy. It's with some relief that I can announce that he quite likes it. Sarah was born on the day West Ham got relegated in May 1989. There was no chance of her being named after the entire first team squad, nor was there any chance of her being named after Yoko. That honour was bestowed upon a Siamese cat that we once had.

I occasionally speak to Melanie. She has two children, 'Harrison' and 'Jude', which is lovely, but I fear all us Beatleheads may just be a little bit mental.

Julie and I divorced in 1991. With hindsight, the writing was on the wall the day we argued furiously on our honeymoon about how the money given to us for our wedding should be spent. She thought carpets and curtains for our flat would be a good idea. I, on the other hand fancied some new speakers for my hi-fi.

It seems strange to reflect upon the events of December 1980. If John Lennon had not been shot, would my life have taken the same twists and turns – Julie, the kids, the soft furnishings? I tend not to spend too much time dwelling on this, but I often think about John and wonder what he might be like today. I bet he would have loved the internet – I can imagine him ranting on Twitter. Would he have appeared at Live Aid? Would he have appeared at Live Aid with Paul? Would he still be preaching peace to anyone that would listen? Would he still be the cantankerous old rocker with a razor-sharp wit and the wordsmith skill almost unrivalled in pop? Which of course is what he really was, rather than the canonised saint and part-time philosopher/politician he became in death. Would he still be as nutty as a fruitcake, as an old man? I'd like to think so.

On December 8 2000, I found myself standing beside the Imagine mosaic in the area of Central Park, New York that is now called Strawberry Fields. Twenty years after the event, I had finally made that pilgrimage that I'd thought hard about making in 1980. The park looked beautiful and peaceful covered in snow and was populated by a smattering of guitarists who accompanied the choir of many in the singing of Beatles and Lennon songs. A crowd of people delivered flowers or candles to the mosaic. Others just stood and stared. It was the only place I wanted to be at that particular time. Having spent some time there chatting to some other fans, I was approached by a journalist and cameraman from Fox News who must have picked up on my accent and asked if I would do an interview. The reporter wanted to know what John Lennon meant to me, which I guess was his way of asking what is it that drives a man to fly 3,500 miles to stand in a park in the snow. It's a question that is impossible to answer in a news bulletin-sized sound bite.

I totally understand that to form some sort of meaningful bond with a celebrity that you never actually knew, and to grieve for their loss, can be construed by some to be the actions of a maniac. But the sadness is not because we knew them, but more because of the absolute joy that they brought us when we needed them most.

I would give almost anything to hear the music he would have made over the last thirty-six years. For people like me that never knew John personally, that is what we have been robbed of. I still miss him – I think the world misses him – and I have absolutely no doubt that it would be a much better place with John Lennon still in it.

... And the Lesson Today

I'll be honest. I didn't really get on with the eighties and they didn't really get on with me. These days, when I think about that decade it sends a shiver down my spine. I'm not just talking about the horrible stuff that we all know about – Thatcher, the Falklands War, the miners' strike, yuppies, Maradona's Hand of God, and all that 'Tell Sid' bollocks – there was just something about the eighties, and what it turned us into, that gives me the willies.

I don't suppose I was the only person who was glad to see the back of that hideous decade, and return to a time when we could go to shopping centres without the fear of being pounced on by breakdancers on street corners, or turn on the TV without having to see Timmy Mallet or Australian soap stars taking over *Top of the Pops*. We'd no longer have to wonder what that thing was on Mikhail Gorbachev's head, or worry about how to spell Czechoslovakia, or concern ourselves with fiddling endlessly with the tracking knob on our VCRs. And although the recession of the early nineties was vile, it was born out of the womb of the eighties and at least it stopped everyone talking about the value of their houses for a while.

To me the eighties represents a time when I was forced to grow up before I was really ready to. They remind me all too often about my lost youth. I moved out of Mum and Dad's house in 1982. When I lived there, my mum did everything for me. I'd never even made my own bed. And now I was spending my evenings learning how to iron, dust and peel spuds. Things were changing fast – too fast. I had a mortgage at 21, was married at 22, and by the time I was 25, I was a father. At the age of 27, I owned an electric screwdriver.

I'm a great believer in the fact that we can't be the same person in our early thirties as we were in our early twenties, and couples either grow up together or they grow apart as they head towards the big three-O. Having kids changes you, it reshapes everything forever. When I look at my own kids now, fully grown, beautiful and enjoying their own twenties, I'm glad that I had kids young, leaving me now still young(ish) enough to be roughly on their wavelength and still able to remember what it was like to be their age.

But for Julie and me, we drifted apart. I don't think it was either of our faults, it just happened that way. The reasons why don't matter anymore – it was too long ago, but for the record, I will say that it had nothing to do with her fondness for early eighties Rod Stewart albums. When it happened, it seemed to be a relief for both of us. One of the saddest aspects for me was that I no longer had regular contact with her family and friends, whom I adored. Damage limitation is important and the line was drawn quickly. We remain friends and have two fantastic kids together, who will always remain our bond no matter what. These are the important things.

We were really poor; mortgage payments took their toll, particularly on my record buying, which was just as well because pop went a bit rubbish in the eighties – to the point where guitars and drums became a luxury item that, for many bands of the time, were no longer needed.

Soulless bands like A Flock of Seagulls, OMD, The Human League and The Pet Shop Boys made empty-sounding records with just keyboards and voice, and they were mostly horrid. Other bands that did feel the need for minimum intervention from traditional instruments, such as Duran Duran, Culture Club and Spandau Ballet, made a few half-decent records but they weren't for me.

There were some bands, though, that made some great records in the eighties. I followed Paul Weller from The Jam into The Style Council, who sporadically did some great stuff. The Smiths from Manchester were as miserable as sin – mainly by reputation – but made one of the finest albums of the entire decade in the jollily titled *The Queen is Dead*. And good old Billy Bragg from just around the corner in Barking churned out quality tunes by the bucketful.

My record buying declined dramatically during the first part of the eighties. The records that I did buy had to be bought on the sly and sneaked into the row of LPs before anyone noticed that the line of albums was getting longer. We could barely afford to eat, let alone dance. And neither of us wanted to dance anyway.

The early eighties felt like a cold, selfish place in which the privileged seemed to be getting richer and getting away with wearing red braces in a built-up area. Tenants bought their council houses, and the government put out terrifying TV ads warning us that if AIDS didn't get us, then the nuclear bomb probably would. And then it all changed. Briefly.

I remember seeing Michael Burke's report on the famine in Ethiopia on the *9 O'clock News* one evening in November 1984 – the same report that Bob Geldof from The Boomtown Rats was watching in his own home just a few miles away. Within days he had assembled just about everybody who was anybody in pop and made a record – 'Do They Know it's Christmas', a song that he co-wrote with Midge Ure of Ultravox. It went straight to number one and stayed there for weeks, selling over two million copies and becoming the biggest-selling UK single of all time. It raised a few eyebrows, and a few million quid for the starving in Africa, but Bob wasn't stopping there.

We hadn't heard a peep out of Bob Geldof for a few years. The Rats had been the most popular band in Britain in 1979 when 'I Don't like Mondays' had been number one, but since then the hits had slowly dried up. But Bob still had enough about him, and still knew enough people in the music industry to put together what turned out to be the greatest concert in the history of pop.

When the Live Aid concert was first announced, I shrugged my shoulders and thought 'that sounds like a nice day in front of the telly'. But when the line-up for the concert was published, with particular reference to the fact that Paul McCartney was going to close the show, I knew I had to be there.

Julie and our friend Corrine went up to Wembley Stadium and queued for tickets. They managed to get four. The tickets cost £25, which was a huge amount for a concert at the time, and money that we couldn't really afford to spend. Corrine couldn't afford to go either, so the other two tickets went to Ray and his wife Denise.

Saturday 13 July 1985 was a blisteringly hot day. Ray drove us to Wembley and we got there in time for the doors opening. When they did, there was a huge stampede as everybody ran for all they were worth across the pitch, and headed for the stage. We ended up somewhere in the centre circle, pretty much in line with the royal box. As the clock ticked away towards midday, the tension built as the pitch gradually got covered with rock-hungry fans ready to feed the starving.

Status Quo opened the proceedings with the only song that they possibly could – 'Rockin' All Over the World' – and from the opening bars of the piano striking out, 72,000 heads bounced up and down in unison.

Each act was only on for twenty minutes maximum, some even less than that. Bands came and went: The Style Council, Ultravox, but when The Boomtown Rats took over the stage after an hour or so there was a moment. They kicked off their set with 'I Don't Like Mondays' and when it got to that bit in the middle, where Geldof sings 'and the lesson today is how to die', he paused, and stood there in his denim shirt, with his arm raised aloft holding the silence for what seemed like an eternity, just to remind everyone why we were all there. It was pop drama at its finest.

Phil Collins came out and did a couple of songs and then buggered off to catch a flight on Concorde to Philadelphia to perform the same two songs at the American Live Aid a few hours later. Adam Ant, who wasn't nearly as mental as he is today, was only allowed to do one song and chose to be the only artist to use Live Aid as a vehicle to promote his new product. He performed his new single 'Goody Two Shoes' and everyone sat down on the pitch and laughed. Proving, that ridicule is indeed, something to be scared of.

Around sixish it was getting towards the part of the show that I was most looking forward to: Queen, Bowie, Elton John, The Who and Macca.

Queen had lost a bit of their popularity during the early eighties. Of course, they still had their hardcore fans, but they had faded a little from view. No one was expecting what happened next. I can honestly say that I have never seen one person own a stage, a stadium, and actually a worldwide audience the way that Freddie Mercury did that day. He was everywhere, poncing about in his white vest and matching jeans. This was his finest half hour. They rattled out hit after hit. The sight of 72,000 pairs of hands raised aloft and clapping in unison to 'Radio Ga-Ga', which let's face it, is a bit of a rubbish song, was something to behold. If you weren't a fan of Queen before this performance, chances are that you probably would have been afterwards.

I felt a bit sorry for David Bowie, who had to follow them. He came on stage looking immaculate in his grey suit and bleached-blonde hair. It was the first time I'd seen this wonderful man in the flesh and he didn't disappoint. He sacrificed the song 'Five Years' (my very favourite Bowie song) from his original set to introduce a video, which was shown on the screens in the stadium and on TVs all over the world. The video was a compilation of clips of starving Ethiopians, screaming in pain from hunger and sadness, living – if you can call it that – in the most appalling conditions. The video was set to a soundtrack of The Cars' song 'Drive'. The words seemed to fit perfectly and really drove the message home. There was hardly a dry eye in the stadium. The image of a child on the ground, wrapped in a death shawl, with its parents saying their final farewells as the child is left to die in the baking sun, is an image that will stay with me forever. As the parents walk away, the child is still twitching with its last breaths of life. It was said that the biggest number of donations were pledged during the hour directly following the screening.

In another clip on the video there was a young girl, who was maybe around the age of two or three, being held by her father with barely enough energy to open her eyes, looking only minutes from death. In an incredible story, twenty years later this young girl was brought on to the stage at the Live 8 show and introduced to the audience by Geldof himself. Now an educated, healthy 24-year-old, her life was saved by the kindness of humanity on Live Aid day. This girl moved me to tears for the second time in her short life. This, folks, is the power of rock'n'roll.

It was also marvellous to see The Who for the first time. They had got back together specifically for this show, and they were in fine form. The TV broadcast broke down during their set and so only those of us lucky enough to be in the stadium saw them making the absolute most of their twenty minutes back together.

By the time Elton John came on, sporting a ridiculous Georgian-type wig, the heavens opened and some much-needed rain soaked us all. It was most welcome.

I began to get nervous as I waited anxiously for Paul McCartney to come on. It would be his first live appearance since John had died. He had become paranoid that he was next, and his public appearances had been minimal over the previous five years. The stage was set in darkness and we didn't see him come on to the stage, only realising he was there when he struck out the opening piano chords of 'Let it Be'. But as he began to sing, his mic failed, and so the entire audience sang the words for him and for the TV audience around the world. He was totally oblivious to the fact that his mic wasn't transmitting any sound and looked startled when the crowd let out a massive cheer halfway through the song, when the mic started working again and we could suddenly hear him. Towards the end of the song he was joined by Pete Townshend, Alison Moyet, David Bowie and of course Bob Geldof. When the song was over Geldof was raised on the shoulders of Townshend and McCartney like the hero that he was.

We got home around midnight, buzzing like a chainsaw in the Amazon. I stayed up till about 5am and watched the last few hours of the American Live Aid.

I consider this day to be one of the greatest days of my life and I feel extremely fortunate to have been there. Live Aid raised something like two hundred million pounds across the world and thousands of lives were saved.

Bob Geldof continued to be involved with the famine cause for years after the concert. There is some famous footage that shows him taking down Margaret Thatcher a peg or two when he felt that she wasn't doing enough to release surplus EU food mountains to Africa. She said to him 'It's not as simple as that, Mr Geldof,' to which he replies, 'Yes, it is, Mrs Thatcher'.

Live Aid was the day when the eighties got a social conscience. The work that Bob Geldof did to make this happen will never be forgotten, but it's a shame that when governments do so little, it's down to a bunch of silly old pop nincompoops to step in to save lives. And whatever the long-term failings of the African aid programme were, we can still look back at Live Aid day and remember that for a few hours in July 1985 pop music fulfilled what it had been threatening to do for three decades, and really did change the world.

A Design for Life

I think the first time that I heard about the compact disc was in a feature on *Tomorrow's World*. Not that I was an avid watcher – science really isn't my thing – but it used to be on directly before *Top of the Pops* on a Thursday evening. It seemed almost comical when Raymond Baxter, or that bloke off *Screen Test,* or whoever it was doing the feature, informed us that this little novelty 5-inch disc was about to revolutionise the way we bought music in the future.

Vinyl contained in 12-inch packages of cardboard was about to become obsolete. We'd heard it all before: first there was the pre-recorded cassette, then the eight-track, but here we all were, still buying our records on vinyl – great big cumbersome things that took up at least one entire wall of our homes, complete with beautiful artwork, and gorgeous labels adorning crisp black vinyl. Records were the king of the castle, and so Compact Disc feel free to come and display your wares if you like, but you'll be sent packing just like all the other formats that have been dreamt up, just to make us buy something that we already own all over again.

The presenter referred to them as CDs, like he was already familiar enough with the format to give them a nickname. He told us that we would hear our music with a quality of sound that vinyl could only aspire to if it had been granted one final wish from its fairy godmother. Not only that, but there would be no crackles, no pops and definitely no snaps as these things were indestructible. Apparently, we could chuck a couple of them on the barbie, douse them in ketchup and mustard and stick them in a bun, eat them, poo them out again and they would still play like they were brand new.

Seem far-fetched? Well, maybe, but it was claimed that because this was digital music, the sound would never deteriorate. Digital, schmigital – what did we know about digital? They could have told us anything and we'd be none the wiser. They seemed very confident, but how could they be so sure? Never was a long time, and science is a funny old beggar that, to be frank, couldn't be trusted. What if in five years' time they did lose all their digital wonderfulness and we were confronted, helpless, by the sight of our music physically dripping off the discs to form a pool of molten rock on our shag pile? Then what?

I wasn't really buying it – literally. I was happy with the vinyl format. I liked the crackles and pops; I felt they were part of my own personal pop history. A well-worn record is a well-loved record, and I loved big fat records in big fat record sleeves, with big fat pictures and big fat inner sleeves with lyrics printed on them that were readable without the aid of a telescope. Size is important, it really is.

And the history is important too – not just the crackles and scratches but the little reminders that sleeves give us of just how long we have had these records. It's an emotional attachment that no amount of modernisation or buffing up can ever dislodge. The little crease on the corner of my copy of *24 Carat Purple* is there purely to remind me of the time that I leaned so far back playing tennis racket guitar in front of the mirror to one of its solos, that I fell back on the bed and landed on top of it. Those inner sleeves where the record peeks through the bottom, or the sides have become unglued, commemorates the hundreds of times that the record has been plopped in and out of it. My copy of *This Year's Model* by Elvis Costello & The Attractions, where the word 'Model' disappears off the end of the sleeve halfway through the letter 'L', reminds me of buying it for 50p in 1978 from that shop in Barking that dealt only in records that were deemed to be 'seconds'.

I guess it was around 1983/1984 that CDs first started appearing in record shops. I was standing firm, but that didn't stop me having a look, just to experience what a CD case felt like in my hand. My first moment of weakness came when I spotted that Paul McCartney's *Give My Regards to Broad Street* album had an extra track on the CD that wasn't on my LP. It was only an instrumental, but I still had a little wobble as it meant that I now didn't own every single song that featured a Beatle. My resolve was being well and truly tested. Anyway, it wasn't an issue because I couldn't afford to buy a CD player even if I wanted to.

In March 1986 I changed my job, joining Hill Samuel Bank at an annual salary of £10,000. It was almost double what I had been earning, but money was still too tight to mention. We had moved from our flat in Ilford to a house in Newbury Park, and Julie was pregnant, so despite the salary increase we were still as poor as church mice (I have no idea why church mice are more poverty stricken than other mice – but until either Bono or Bob Geldof steps in to save them, they will have to continue to rely on the Sunday morning plate collection for their cheese). But, whatever the reason, we were as poor as them.

One Friday lunchtime, whilst mooching around the Barbican area, I bumped into Ian. We hadn't seen each other for about four years and headed off to the pub for a catch-up. It was during the Mexico '86 World Cup and we talked briefly about that, but mostly about bands. We made it a regular Friday lunchtime date so we could talk about the bands that we hadn't talked about the previous Friday. At that time Ian was running a secondhand record stall on a Saturday in Roman Road Market to earn some extra cash. He asked if I had any albums that I wanted to sell.

Now, let me make it quite clear that I do not now, nor have I ever, thought of records as a transaction. This is your pop past and your personal history – a record collection can say more about you, and who you were, than recounting old stories ever can. It's hard evidence, and so generally I would frown upon the flogging off of the past. Nicking away at it is reshaping it down to the highlights for others to admire. So what if you own 'Ain't Gonna Bump No More (With No Big Fat Woman)'? Yes, there is remorse now, of course there is, but you did it loud, and you did it proud and it's ok, we're all in this together. But like I said, times were hard, I had a baby on the way and I did happen to have some fucking awful records, so I agreed that I would have a root through and see which ones were now surplus to requirements.

In my mind, I'm thinking of this as 'the great record cull of 1986', but when it boiled down to it, out of the three hundred or so albums that I owned, I was only able to come up with twelve. You'll have to bear with me on this – to be honest there may have been more, it was a long time ago, but from memory, I now present the dirty dozen and the reasons for binning them.

Bad Company – *Desolation Angels*

This was one of three Bad Company albums that I owned. The eponymous first album was great, the second one, *Straight Shooter*, less great, but it still had some decent moments on it. *Desolation Angels* was their 1979 album, which I only bought because we had tickets to see them at Wembley Arena, a decision that I can only put down as one of loyalty to a band that we all once quite liked, who were now well past their sell-by date. We turned up late and left before the lighters came out. I hadn't played this album for seven years or, to put it another way, since the Tuesday after I bought it.

Ultravox – *Greatest Hits*

I was being ruthless with this one. This was only a year after Live Aid and, with this in mind, it may have been a little cruel to bin off Midge Ure and his band Ultravox. Midge, the finest exponent of the sideburn in pop, was after all Bob Geldof's co-writer of the Band Aid single and also his sidekick in the background work that made Live Aid happen. I based the decision on the fact that despite it being 90 degrees inside the stadium on Live Aid day, Midge chose to go on stage wearing a full-length leather coat – a decision he probably regretted from the opening bars of 'Reap The Wild Wind'. So long, Midge and your leather coat – you mean nothing to me.

Unknown Artist – *Unknown Album*

Sounds odd I know, but I really can't remember who this one was by or what it was called. All I know is it was an LP that was handed to me while I was walking down Oxford Street in 1980 by some very nice Hare

Krishna people in orange robes. They were giving them out to anyone that would take one. Most wouldn't – I did. The reason: George Harrison was name-checked on the back cover; I can't remember what for, but it was something very minor like making the tea or finger cymbals. However, this was enough for me to claim in my own mind that it was in some way Beatles-related. It was supposed to be an album of mantra chants. I say 'supposed to' because I don't know, as I never actually played it – not once. Ian said he would give me one new penny for it. We looked at each other and I made my way sheepishly to the kitchen and put it in the dustbin.

Supertramp – *Even in the Quietest Moments...*

If you've been paying attention, you probably knew that this one was going to make the list. It may as well have grown a pair of legs and walked all by itself from my record rack straight into Monty's waiting carrier bag, waving a white flag as it went, no questions asked. You might remember that this was the unwanted, second-hand present bestowed upon me for my birthday by some friends of my parents. Played it a couple of times, but with some relief I never liked it. My only regret concerning my involvement with Supertramp is that I didn't have any more of their albums to sell him. It was, at long last, out on its ear.

Sparks – *Indiscreet*

It was with a heavy heart that I handed this one over. The first proper album I ever bought all by myself was their earlier album *Kimono My House,* and so from that perspective I still had a morsel of affection for that album and the band that had made it. *Indiscreet,* which popped along two albums later was another story and unquestionably a bit of a loyalty purchase on my part, although I didn't think of it as such at the time. It was dreadful. It had the terrible 'Get it in the Swing' on it, and other songs about tits and pineapples and being with ladies under the table. Its only saving grace was the excellent 'Looks, Looks, Looks', which I had on a single anyway. But, despite all this, it was a record by the first band that I really liked and it felt wrong to be getting rid. Still, I bit my lip, mustered up the courage and it became not so much 'Get in the Swing' but more 'get in the swing-top bin'.

Mr Mister – *Welcome to the Real World*

The dreadfully monikered Mr Mister had a massive hit in 1985 with 'Broken Wings'. Now, I know what you're thinking: he made the most basic of schoolboy errors, i.e. liked the single and bought the album on the strength of it, but you'd be wrong. By 1985 I was an experienced record buyer and would never fall for something as stupid as that (who am I kidding?). *Welcome to the Real World* came into my possession via the wonderful Britannia Music Club. Remember them?

The Britannia Music Club used to advertise on the back of all those glossy magazines that were tucked inside our Sunday newspapers in the eighties. It was an offer that was very hard to resist – all the latest albums at 99p a pop. Of course there was a catch, and to be fair it was a rather clever one. The deal was that you picked five albums from the selection in the ad for £4.95 as your introductory offer and that made you a member of the club. Now, this is the good bit: a few weeks (yes, weeks) later, the postman knocks on your door and hands over a heavy parcel, and when you open it up, inside are your records. Sounds like nothing in these days of next-day deliveries of CDs from Amazon, which we all take for granted, but to receive records through the post was so exciting in the mid-eighties that we almost forgot that Norman Tebbitt even existed.

Also included in your parcel was the Britannia Music Club monthly magazine, chock-full of further albums to choose from. You had to buy at least one album from the magazine every month for a year at full price. Not too much of a hardship, even if they were a bit more expensive than you would pay in Our Price, and you were at least able to look forward to another exciting delivery every month. But here's the knock: every month they would recommend an 'album of the month' and if you didn't order your pick from the magazine by the deadline date that they set, you would automatically receive their album of the month whether you wanted it or not, and would have to pay for it.

Now, as a compulsive record buyer, you wouldn't think that it was beyond me to organise myself well enough to pick an album from the magazine thus avoiding unwanted albums by Mr Bloody Mister. But apparently not, and so it was revenge time for Mr Mister, who were told in no uncertain terms to take their broken wings and learn to fuck right off.

Various Artists – *Mods Mayday '79*

I bought this one because I was reading great things in the NME about a mod revivalist band called Secret Affair right around the time when I became a mod revivalist. I thought I was oh-so-cool buying an album by a bunch of unsigned bands. The album was recorded live in a pub and it sounded like it too. It had a great black-and-white photo of a mod on a scooter on the cover. As it turned out, Secret Affair were not bad at all. Their songs had great titles like 'Let Your Heart Dance' and 'Shake and Shout'. The album only had about three songs on it by Secret Affair though; the rest of it was filled by bands with predictable names like 'The Mods' and 'Beggar', which were populated with kids who wanted to be

Ray Davies or Steve Marriott. Although I thought this was a great album to have in 1979, the mod revival didn't last much longer than a keyboard solo on a Genesis track, and by 1986 it was looking very silly indeed. One of the Secret Affair tracks on the album was called 'I'm Not Free (But I'm Cheap)', which was all rather appropriate when Monty offered me 50p for it.

Thin Lizzy – *Fighting*

The night that I heard the news that Phil Lynott had died, I was sharing a huge spliff with my brother-in-law Kevin. Phil was only 36 and I was gutted. He was special to me; so imposing as the front man of Thin Lizzy and one of the greatest live performers I have ever seen. Whilst Lizzy had always been just about as 'rock' as I was willing to go, by the eighties they had taken the dark path into heavy metal and I lost interest. I hadn't bought anything by them since the *Black Rose* album (1979) and hadn't bothered to see them live since the tour that supported that album. I abandoned Phil long before he decided to abandon himself. But that didn't detract from the sadness I felt on hearing of his untimely death. The *Fighting* album came out just before they made it big and, to be truthful, whilst not being terribly good, it wasn't all that bad either. So why did I get rid? Mainly because of the cover, on which Phil and Brian Robertson were bare-chested and the band were standing there pouting and holding iron bars, looking as if they were about to kick someone's head in. It just wasn't necessary. On reflection, to bin off a Lizzy album five months after Lynott's death was probably a bit harsh.

Stevie Wonder – *Journey Through the Secret life of Plants*

Ahh, Stevie Wonder. Little Stevie Wonder. Little tiny, tiny, Stevie Wonder. To attempt a double album and succeed is a big ask. Many have tried, few have triumphed. There are some exceptions, such as Stevie's own magnificent *Songs in the Key of Life*. To follow this masterpiece with yet another double album was nothing short of foolhardy, and it stank. What does it even mean? What secret life do plants have? Do they sneak off when nobody is looking and go ten pin bowling with their mates? Utter tosh. Secret Life of Pants, more like.

The Stranglers – *Live (X-Cert)*

I'm not really a fan of the live album. There have been some real crackers I will admit: *Live and Dangerous*, *The Who Live at Leeds*, *Get Yer Ya-Yas Out,* etc., but generally the live album tends to be a contract-fulfilling obligation to the record label – full of songs just like they are on the studio record but not quite as good. *Live (X-Cert)* wasn't a bad live album; in fact, I should be pleased it was released because I am on it. The problem I had with this one was Mike Giles. Mike was a bloke in my office from my days at Singer & Friedlander, who bossed me about and quite often made my life a misery by giving me endless mind-numbing tasks to do. He was also smugger than Michael McIntyre on a chat show, and seemed to be ever so pleased with himself over the slightest thing. If that wasn't bad enough, he wore a multicoloured bow tie to work and told terrible jokes. What's this got to do with *Live (X-Cert),* I hear you ask? Well, he was a huge Stranglers fan and drove his Austin Allegro all over the country to see them play, which meant that he was probably on this album too. I found it hard to look at the black leather glove on the sleeve of this album, without picturing Giles' hands clutching the steering wheel of his Alegro in a similar pair of driving gloves. It had to go. So, basically, *Live (X-Cert)* was binned on the basis that Alegro-driving, glove-wearing Stranglers fans are wankers.

ELO – *Discovery*

It would be churlish of me to deny that there have been times when I embraced the guilty pleasures of the Electric Light Orchestra. *A New World Record* is a fine album. The follow-up, *Out of the Blue,* a bloated double album, less so. I went to see them at the Empire Pool, Wembley – the gig where they played their set from the inside of a spaceship. They were terrible, the sound was terrible and Jeff Lynne wore his sunglasses between the hours of 8 and 10pm in a venue that had a roof. So what it was that possessed me to continue the trend and buy the 1979 album *Discovery,* I do not know – a moment of weakness, maybe. All I know is that when Jeff Lynne out of ELO comes knocking on your door with a bunch of gorgeous Beatle-esque tunes tucked under his armpit, it's only the strongest amongst us that can resist opening the door and letting the bubble-headed, bearded, indoor-sunglasses-wearing buffoon in. However, when the door-knocking comes from the mumbling and a-fumbling Horace Wimp, it's best to hide behind the sofa until he gives up and goes away.

In 1979 ELO were pretty much at the peak of their power. This album boasted five (yes, five) hit singles and ELO wormed their way into the hearts of a nation and made their way up the charts. By 1986 the only place they were making their way to was Monty's stall in Roman Road market.

Rod Stewart – *Blondes Have More Fun*

It wasn't mine, it was Julie's. She never knew, but 50p is 50p. It was chucked out like Dino during the opening credits of *The Flintstones.*

So what's all this record selling got to do with the arrival of the CD? Well, in my mind, and indeed out of it, I had almost convinced myself that the selling of these albums was a deed of selflessness, an act of heroism no less, on behalf of my poverty-stricken family. In reality, what was really happening here was me raising money to put towards a shiny new CD player.

The final nail in my coffin of resolve was when Apple announced that the first four Beatles albums were going to be released on CD later in the year. I try and use this as the excuse but the reality of it was, not if I was going make the transition, but when. The resisting was over and the time for me to drop my trousers, bend over and yelp helplessly to Compact Disc 'take me, take me, I'm all yours!' was upon me.

By the end of the summer of 1987 I had saved the money and was ready to take the plunge. I had arranged with my friend Mark, who worked in the hi-fi shop at Gants Hill, to go in the following Saturday and he would sort me out with something that was in my price range, with a helping hand from his staff discount.

Before that could happen, I had to get through a camping trip to the New Forest. On the way down there we stopped for lunch at a Dorset town whose name escapes me now. I popped into Woolworths and bought my first CD in anticipation of Saturday's purchase – *Shaved Fish* – a John Lennon compilation. Now I was committed – there was no backing out; I had joined the CD generation.

Of course, being a camping trip, it obviously pissed down with rain from the moment we got there to the moment we decided to bugger off early and go home. The only difference between this camping trip and others that I had been on was this time I had a 10-month-old baby with me. Daniel hated camping as much as I did and screamed the tent down for three days, and who could blame him. I felt like doing the same.

When Saturday came I was excited about my new purchase. I went for a Denon CD player, which was black, and midi-sized. It didn't look great alongside my other silver full-size hi-fi components, but the midi version was cheaper than the full-size one so it was worth a little compromise.

I had owned the LP of *Shaved Fish* since 1976. My copy was secondhand and came complete with pops and crackles and a little jump on 'Instant Karma'. And here I was, eleven years later, listening to it as if it was a brand new album, hearing things that I hadn't heard before and feeling unfamiliar with 'Instant Karma' without the jump. CD was a revelation, there is no doubt about that; clinical and clean, and a little top heavy, with less depth and richness of vinyl, but a revelation all the same.

I made myself all kinds of rules and boundaries about how I was going handle the transition. One thing I was definitely not going to do was re-buy my entire record collection. I decided that I would buy compilation CDs of my favourite artists – compilations that I never owned on vinyl because I had all the albums and singles. I would be buying these purely for their sonic beauty.

I was aided with this rule by the record labels, who had yet to put out their artists' entire back catalogues on Compact Disc. But it wouldn't be long before each major artist was re-launching their entire works on CD. This basically meant that it wasn't long before my golden rule went straight out the window, and I was buying up pretty much my entire record collection all over again. They drew me in with the lure of bonus tracks of unreleased material and the anticipation of hearing the music that I had loved for years sounding all gorgeous and unhindered by the crimes of my old Bush music centre. I should have fought hard against it, but in the end I was – like T'Pau almost once said – putty in their hands. It didn't feel good and it certainly didn't feel very clever. As, piece by piece, my record collection was replaced by newer younger models, I could almost feel the sadness oozing out of my battered old records. I wanted to comfort them with words of hope and encouragement – tell them that they still had a purpose, an important job to do, and that there would be no wholesale redundancies, that I was just moving with the times … but it would have been a lie. What was actually happening was Thatcherism for records, right there in my front room. What I was doing was no better than what she did to the miners.

The idea of our old music sounding all new and shiny for the new digital era was a reasonable selling point, but the phenomena of the 'unreleased bonus track' was a gift that just kept on giving, and one that the music industry brought to us exclusively for CD; I lapped it up and used it as an excuse to buy my old records all over again. But with CDs costing around £10, not only could we buy something that we already owned, but we could also pay three times as much for the privilege of doing so. Genius really, when you think about it.

So what were these tempting bonus morsels of pop loveliness that were just impossible to resist? In the main, there were three different flavours:

• The Demo – These were the original tapes made by the songwriter playing around at home, on an acoustic guitar or piano, tinkering with chords and toying with first-draft lyrics – most of which wouldn't end up on the finished record anyway because they didn't scan or rhyme properly. But these were the very embryos of the songs that we ended up loving so much. It's a great leveller to contemplate that whilst these primitive recordings were being committed to tape for the very first time, the very wealthy and famous pop star was probably unshaven and wearing only his pants.

What price for that very first tape recording of 'Yesterday', in which, as legend has it, Paul McCartney woke suddenly from his slumber (almost certainly unshaven and wearing only his pants), with the song going around in his head? He searched frantically for his tape recorder so he could get it all down before he forgot it. Once he had located the recorder, he pressed the record button and sang in his best just-woken-up voice:

'Scrambled eggs, oh my darling how I love your legs'. The tune apparently remained unchanged.

• The Studio Outtake – These are much rarer to come by than the demo. This is because musicians have egos the size of small cities and they don't like us mere mortals hearing their mistakes. These are the versions of the soon-to-become-epic songs that went a little bit wrong. A wrong chord here, a missed beat there, a fumbled lyric. A kind of musical version of *It'll Be Alright on the Night*.

• The Live Recording – Speaks for itself really, or to put it another way, the track that was so badly recorded, or so badly played that it wasn't good enough to make it on to the live album that came out five years ago.

These extra bonus tracks were the stuff that had for years been the food and drink of the bootleg LP, and here they were being offered to all and sundry as part of a regular release without a by-your-leave.

I'm not sure if this had a detrimental effect on the sale of bootlegs, as I was never a big fan of them either. Bootlegs were overpriced and, as far as I was concerned, a big steaming pile of unlistenable do-do and I refused to get involved with them – especially the live bootlegs that sounded like they had been recorded through a doctor's stethoscope inserted into the bottom of the bass player. And as for outtake bootlegs – I once heard a bootleg that contained about fifteen versions of The Beatles having a go at 'Ob-la di, Ob-la-da'. Fifteen versions all going wrong – does anyone really need to hear that? After three or four takes, they all started to sound the same – probably because they were. Admittedly, there is some merit in hearing the evolution of a song from its embryonic demo to the final released version, but once I've heard it a couple of times, my curiosity is quelled and I'm ready to go back to the proper version.

But lots of other people did collect bootlegs, and took great joy in owning something rare. Getting on board the top deck of the school bus with the new Captain Beefheart 'boot' tucked under your arm was tantamount to saying to the other passengers 'Here's my penis, please admire it.'. The fact that it sounded more like Captain Birdseye didn't seem to matter.

I suppose bootlegs had a certain amount of coolness attached to them because they were illegal and not easy to come by. Record shops would have a sign up behind the counter announcing: 'We do not sell bootlegs – so don't ask' – but they did, and you had to if you wanted one. And when you did, record shop staff were ready and waiting with their instant platitudes of ridicule as the great unwashed sidled up to the counter on a Saturday afternoon and whispered, without a shred of dignity, into the waiting lug-hole: 'You got the Lindisfarne *Live at the Dog and Duck* boot?'.

So here was CD, putting paid to all this under-the-counter record shop shenanigans with its fancy new additional tracks. After a while it occurred to me that actually, if I was going to have to buy my old records again, I wanted them to be exactly like the old ones and not have all this inferior material tacked on the end, cluttering up the original album and making it sound all unfamiliar. Track running orders are there for a reason, and an album ends where it ends because that was the best way of ordering the music at the time – agreed and sealed in blood by the artists themselves and not the silly old duffers at the record labels. An album should not end with a track that at the time was deemed not good enough to be on the album in the first place.

With all things new to market, CD brought dilemmas a-plenty. There was the issue of brand new albums; LPs were still costing £4.99, which now seemed like a bit of a bargain compared with the price of their Compact Disc cousins, which were a tenner a go. This made buying new albums a little bit risky. If you spent a fiver on a record and it turned out to be a stinker, well that was annoying, but not the end of the world. But to spend double that on a CD of a terrible album was veering on the side of heartbreaking. So I had to become a lot more selective about which new albums I was going to give a go.

Once you got your CD home you then had to go through the trauma of getting it out of its box. These brittle plastic boxes that housed CDs were called jewel cases. I have often wondered why, but then again I have also spent time wondering why a shoe is called a shoe. I have a theory that calling what amounts to an awkward plastic container, a jewel case, is yet another attempt by the music industry to big-up the value of the Compact Disc. It's as if they wanted us to believe that the contents of these boxes was so precious that opening one up and revealing the treasure inside is similar to extracting the pearl from an oyster. Perhaps that's why they made them so bloody difficult to open.

Getting into these things was an ordeal. They were tricky blighters to negotiate and they took no prisoners – plenty of fingernails, but no prisoners. I don't mind admitting it took me quite a few goes to get the hang of it. Jewel cases, once opened, would reveal the CD sitting on a several-spoked hub which also needed the technique known as 'pressing down on it a little bit' to release the disc from its captor. Doing it wrong (as I often did) would leave you with snapped spokes and a CD that would forevermore slide and rattle around inside the case – which didn't really matter because CDs were indestructible, right?

On the inside left of the case was where the CD booklet was housed. We really needed a different word for what was the CD equivalent of the album cover. I can't really think of a word that is less 'rock' than booklet. Getting the booklet out of the case was no mean feat either. It was held in place by a couple of plastic tabs and you had to somehow slide it carefully underneath these tabs to avoid ripping it. This seems like an awful lot of effort, which ultimately led to disappointment because the booklet was most unsatisfactory.

With old records that were being released on CD, they tried to replicate the artwork and contents of the original LP in the miniature booklet. This didn't work at all, especially with regards to albums that had originally come complete with huge posters such as *The Beatles White Album* or *Dark Side of The Moon*. These great posters were now replicated over a few pages of the booklet in bite-size five inch pieces, with two filthy great staples through the middle, and completely missed the point. What were we expected to do with these broken-down posters? Extract the staples and tear the poster sections out of the booklet, reconstruct them and go and put them up on the walls round at Ken and Barbie's place?

With records, we listened to all the tracks – the good, the bad and the utterly bizarre. Short of getting up and down to move the needle on every time a track came on that you didn't like, you suffered or enjoyed it all accordingly. CD players changed all that with their fancy track-programming facilities – they conveniently allowed us to skip the bad tracks so that we never had to suffer them ever again. Fast forward (or use the skip button if you like) thirty years and we now observe that CDs changed the way we listened to music, just like they promised on *Tomorrow's World*. They formed the prototype for how we listen to music today.

In 2016, the CD is hanging on to its status as music's premier format by the very spokes of its spindly middle bit. Vinyl, unbelievably, is making a comeback but nobody except me owns a record player anymore so that won't last long. Digital music is the way to go for many music buyers these days and with this format, not only do we not have to listen to the rubbish tracks – we don't even have to buy them in the first place if we don't want to. Whilst I like the idea of being able to buy a single song without having to buy the whole album, this is the only scenario in which I have embraced the digital download era. I still buy physical CDs because I can't bring myself to accept that simply having a download of an album counts as actually owning it. Luckily jewel cases have all but disappeared and CDs generally come in cardboard packets just like records used to. They still have booklets, but I never read them anymore. I figure that if life is too short to spend time pairing up my socks, I certainly don't have the time to find out who plays triangle on track seven.

Pumping on Your Stereo

I don't suppose there is ever a really a good year to get divorced, but if we're going to pick one, 1991 would have been a good one to avoid. Britain was as bleak a place as I can remember it ever being, and house prices were dropping faster than Edwina Currie's knickers in the back of John Major's car.

When it came to sharing out the spoils, we were very short of spoils to share – hardly anything of any value worth arguing about – a Vauxhall Cavalier and a three-piece suite. It was simple: Julie had the car, I had the sofa. Job done. Our house was sold with a huge negative equity, which the mortgage lender said I could pay back at £15 a month, which was very nice of them. I would be 723 by the time it was paid off.

Of course, when there is a property market crash, it's a great time to buy ... as long as you don't tell your new lender about the ten life sentences you still have with the old one. I found a flat in Wanstead and moved back in with my parents whilst I waited for the paperwork to go through. It was only for a few months, but it was a very strange thing to find myself living back in the house that I grew up in, with the parents that I grew up with. As an adult, I noticed things that I hadn't spotted the first time around – such as my mum watching TV whilst eating bowls of ready-salted crisps and pouring vinegar over them rather than just buying salt and vinegar crisps, or discovering that she ironed bras and socks. On one occasion we were sitting on the sofa together watching a film, when my mother piped up 'Anthony, don't you think it's time you went to bed, you have work in the morning?' Once I'd reminded her that I was 31 years old and was the father of two children, she took the point, and let me stay up until the end.

I took very little with me to my parents' house. All my bibs and bobs (have you noticed how it's impossible to have bibs without having a selection of bobs to accompany them?), including my hi-fi, records and CDs went into storage, leaving me reliant on a few homemade compilation tapes that I could play on my Walkman, whilst I prayed for their safe deliverance.

By the early months of 1992, it was time to move into my new bachelor flat. Single once again, I was my own boss – the captain of my own destiny, the master of my own carpet slippers, and when single men have no one to tell them not to, they buy stuff.

I'd spent more of my time at my parents' house than could be considered rational plotting an upgrade of my hi-fi system for my new home. I think when I viewed the flat for the first time, I had already planned where the hi-fi rack and the speakers were going to be located – it's even possible that I plumped for this flat purely on the basis that the lounge was the perfect shape for the consumption of lots of lovely pop.

The arrival of CD had taken care of the front-end of pop music, consequently making me pay more attention to the sound quality of the music that I listened to – almost to the point where I could enjoy late-seventies disco music just because the percussion and chinking guitars sounded great. Now it was time to consider the back-end.

Buying hi-fi equipment is a huge investment, but it still troubles me that the research of hi-fi components totally consumes me. There are whole hosts of magazines on the shelves stacked full of sexy photos of beautiful black and silver boxes, just seducing me from the glossy pulp. Those magazines should be top-shelfers, as this stuff is unadulterated hi-fi porn. Speakers are so brazen these days; they don't even have the modesty of the black gauze covering their ample woofers. I was finding myself buying these electrical 'jazz mags' even when I wasn't looking for new bits of hi-fi to buy. In fact, it's only recently that I have managed to wean myself off them, and that's only because they now send me emails twice a week, teasing me, in lieu of the monthly mag. However, during this time of residential flux, I would curl up in my old bed, in my old house, just like I used to, the only difference being my bedtime reading of *Sounds* had been usurped by *What Banana Plug?*

Looks are unimportant and never more so than with hi-fi equipment. You can almost tell how a component is going to perform from the number of lights it has. Those that light up like a Christmas tree are saying: 'I am a clown with a squirty flower!' and their only statement of intent is a big fat exclamation mark. Whereas those that only have an on/off light are deadly serious items of kit, which wouldn't crack a smile even if you told them the joke about the bloke with an orange for a head.

I knew what I wanted and went to see Mark in the hi-fi shop once again. I was lucky that I had a friend that worked in the hi-fi business, because salesmen in hi-fi shops were usually even more standoffish than those that work in record shops. I've seen them at work. They ask difficult questions.

'What sort of wattage are you looking for in your speakers, sir?'

Always a strange question I think, as watts are very rarely visible to the human eye.

To the hi-fi novice the wattage guess could be anywhere within the range of 3 or 5,000; hi-fi salesmen can spot the sonically unwashed a mile off and will hone in and prey on these poor unsuspecting beings, just so they can have a snigger and spill their hilarious war stories with their hi-fi salesmen colleagues.

'… and then, he asked if the CD player had Dolby – bwhhhhaaaaa!'.

They will also try to convince you that it's not just the hi-fi components that are going to help you create the cacophony of musical delight that you crave – it's the little things like your speaker cable, speaker stands and even the rack that you sit the whole lot on that are going to make all the difference. They may even refer to the place where you listen to your music as your 'listening space' but ignore this – they mean the sofa.

I came away from Mark's shop with a Rotel amp and CD player, a Denon cassette deck and a pair of Linn speakers, which came with some stands made out of concrete and granite that were heavier than a couple of Sumo wrestlers carrying a Rammstein box-set. Even though I was now committed to CD, I wasn't prepared to box up my albums and stick them in the loft just yet, that would be too heartbreaking – so I also went for a Thoren's record deck, which did the whole record-playing thing just great.

When I got it home, the whole set-up process was a bit of an ordeal – cables all over the shop with the back of the rack looking like a big plate of spaghetti. This is the bit where I spend an age fiddling about with speaker positioning. A little bit to the right, a little bit to the left, raise the feet on the stand, lower the feet on the stand, go back to where I first started, until finally I find that sweet spot where both channels of sound meet my anxious ears smack bang in the middle of where I'm sitting, and finally I'm satisfied. But it never ends there. Well, not for me anyway. Just when I think I have achieved the optimum sound out of my system, I will read something in *What Pissing About With Your Hi-Fi?* offering practical tips on how I can improve my sound with a few minor, yet cheap tweaks.

Simple home improvements such as stapling a small beaver (check *What Beaver?* before deciding) to the wall directly opposite your listening position can make a big difference, and if that isn't quite doing it for you, you can always try chopping up all your kitchen appliances into tiny pieces, dipping them in Dijon mustard and hurling them at the wall until they stick, as apparently that works a treat too.

That does all sound a little far-fetched and, of course, it is, but talking of kitchen appliances, let me invite you to take a retrospective look into my freezer on one particular day not long after I moved into my new flat. Now, you'll have to excuse the sparseness of its contents, but I am a newly single man, remember, so don't judge. When I open it up, you'll see one pack of Findus Crispy Pancakes (minced beef), one bag of Birds-Eye garden peas, a bag of frozen chips, an ice tray with only three ice cubes left in it and *Goodbye Cruel World* by Elvis Costello & The Attractions.

What? Why? I can hear you exclaiming in horror. Well, because blokes never re-fill the ice tray, everybody knows that, don't they? Oh, you mean the Elvis Costello CD?

Well I did say it had to be on one particular day, and on this particular day, I had read in *Q* magazine a letter from a reader who claimed that if you stick your CDs in the freezer for a couple of hours prior to playing them, this would improve the sound no end.

It did make me wonder what on earth would instigate such a bizarre idea in the first place? And, furthermore, what sort of person has these dark thoughts? Retrospectively, I've come to the conclusion that it's probably someone who is never satisfied and is constantly striving for perfection out of their system – someone, I suppose, just like me. So what did I have to lose? I tried it. *Goodbye Cruel World* – an album so poor that when the album was re-released and expanded in 1995, Elvis himself wrote in the sleeve notes: 'Congratulations you've just bought the worst album of my career!'. So thinking that this album could do with any help it could possibly get, I popped it into the freezer for a couple of hours, and then gingerly placed it straight into the waiting tray of my new CD player. Did it sound any better? Of course not – it was a Bejam freezer, not Paul bleedin' Daniels.

The Things We Do for Love

My opening gambit with Kim was to walk into her office after a lunchtime drinking session and perform the playground routine of 'Turn round, touch the ground, bagsie not included', and then scamper back to my own office across the corridor without saying another word. I wasn't proud of this. I was an adult and shouldn't have still been using words like 'bagsie'.

Her colleagues briefly looked up from their accounting ledgers, shook their heads and promptly looked down again and continued with their work as if what they had just witnessed didn't really happen. She roared with laughter – I had found a kindred spirit.

The main purpose for my visit to Kim's office was not to carry out some sort of infantile pulling routine, but to borrow her copy of the first Paul Weller solo album, and in truth, my interest in Paul Weller was probably going to earn me more points with her than the turn-round thing.

When I did eventually get to hear the Weller album, it turned out to be great. A real return to form. I, like many other fans of The Jam had given up on Weller after hearing The Style Council's difficult third album, *The Cost of Loving*. But he was back and making great music again and all this needed discussing … and for several nights a week over a cheeky drink after work.

I had form with office romances. Not particularly good form either. The office romance is a tricky bedfellow that encompasses lots of sneaking about and clever ruses, whilst attempting to keep it under wraps before it gets a mention in the quarterly staff magazine. You can't really take anything for granted as far as any type of dalliance in this area goes, but when Kim revealed that she had recently seen Weller live and her ex-husband fell asleep and snored during the gig, I thought I might be home and dry.

For our first date we went to a record fair in London. The perfect date for a couple of pop-heads. Kim had mingled in record fair circles before – not to the point where she would receive a nod of acknowledgement from the stall holders, but she had certainly dabbled. For me, it was my first time. The record fair is a funny old creature that scratches the itch record shops just can't reach. They sound cool, but in reality are inhabited by pop's trainspotters – the anoraks replaced by a faded jean-jacket with a sew-on Quo patch, but otherwise, the same beast.

I'd been to quite a few London Beatles Days and flicked through the unkempt cardboard boxes full of imports, bootlegs and rarities, disappointingly filed in a system that could be best described as higgledy-piggledy. They also had all the regular Beatles albums, and all the solo albums, all of which I already owned, now on both vinyl and CD, but here they were again, and here was I, browsing through them for no apparent reason. The prices were greatly inflated from the prices that I had paid, but it didn't stop me from thinking how brilliant it would be if I didn't already own all these records – then I could buy them and discover them all over again.

The two of us perused every stall, slowly flicking through albums that we really had no intention of buying, and buying up stuff that we both knew we would never play, but it was great to own them anyway. It's not every day that you come across an Indonesian import of Dire Straits' *Love Over Gold,* is it?

We made each other compilation tapes full of our favourite songs – songs that meant something to each of us. I would listen to hers on the way home from our sneaky nights out after work. It somehow seemed more authentic to be able to listen to her choices whilst I could still smell her on my coat. The songs that we chose were songs we wanted each other to listen to the lyrics of because they were relevant to what was happening. It was much easier to get Paul McCartney to sing the words of 'Maybe I'm Amazed' (*Wings Over America* version) to her than for me to say them out loud. Macca was good at that sort of thing, and I wasn't.

Before we knew it, we were making a weekend of it at out-of-town gigs and even more record fairs, and plotting our future together. Moving in with someone is an activity that causes many dilemmas for record collectors. There was never any question that our record collections would be amalgamated and forced to swell to ridiculous proportions. This meant that she would have free reign over my records and me over hers.

You can get to learn a lot about a person by spending some time alone with their record collection. Their pop credentials are right there to be admired or to pour scorn upon. But this was a girl whose record collection was as important to her as mine was to me. There were no records in the wrong sleeves (I checked). Not even any records in the wrong inner sleeves and certainly no records, heaven forbid, that had been plonked straight into their sleeves without an inner sleeve. The signs were good. She even had some records in protective PVC covers. Yes, the signs were very good.

But when the joining of collections happens, questions have to be asked. What do we do with our duplicate albums? Do I really want my record collection infested with the complete works of Simply Red? Does she want *Beaucoups of Blues* by Ringo Starr infiltrating hers?

The duplicate records are key of course, because what you do with them says everything about how you see your future together. If you box up your duplicates and take them down to the charity shop, then what you are actually saying is 'I don't need these anymore – the pair of us will be together forever'. Or you can hedge your bets and stick them in the loft, until a time when you might need to reinstate them if it all goes pear-shaped.

Whatever the dilemmas were, they were unimportant. Imagine that –

something more important than pop music? I had found someone that understood my obsession because it was hers too. I loved everything about her – even her bent towards ginger-dreadlocked pop stars.

One lunchtime she met her friend Jo to tell her about her new domestic situation. Jo and her boyfriend Christian had a band that had recently split up due to the departure of their drummer. On learning the news that I used to be a drummer in a former life, Jo was very keen for us to meet.

Just What I Needed

Meeting Jo and Christian would turn out to be one of the most important introductions of my life. The fact that I had once known which end of a drumstick to hit a drum with seemed to be the only requirement for them to invite me to join them in a makeshift band called Mission Groove.

There was a gig. Nothing big, just six songs. On the night, we would be just one of a number of bands performing and far enough from being the main attraction to be fairly comfortable. But I hadn't held that drumstick for ten years, and even then it was only for a few hours at the Gud Fungs reunion in 1982. It had been twelve years since I had played regularly, and I had no drum kit and no idea whether or not I was still able to play one even if I did. Let's be honest, I wasn't that great when I was playing regularly and the passing years would certainly not have improved my skill.

Jo and Christian were heavily involved with an environmental centre in Walthamstow called Hornbeam and the gig was to be a fundraiser to help get it off the ground. Green issues were not really something that concerned me. To say that I was not very 'green' is a bit like saying Bernard Manning is not very politically correct. But having not been invited to take part in Live Aid or Nelson Mandela's birthday bash, the thought of playing music to raise money for a cause appealed to me.

I was really nervous about taking this on but Kim really wanted me to, and secretly so did I – more than anything, if I'm honest.

There was time for three rehearsals before the gig. In normal circumstances this would have been plenty of time to prep six songs, but with my lack of practice it was always going to be touch and go whether or not I'd be up to the job. I would use the kit provided by the rehearsal studio and the songs that I had to learn would be delivered to me on a cassette. Just six songs – how hard could it be?

Mission Groove, for this one-night-only performance, would consist of a guitarist called Dave and his sister Elaine, Jo, Christian plus Rob and Pete from Jo and Christian's regular band The Fabulous Heseltines, who were currently in a state of flux having recently lost their drummer. To completely lose a drummer is a careless act at the best of times – drummers are rubbish at hiding due to the fact that they find it impossible to keep quiet for more than five seconds and gongs are very difficult to conceal.

The songs we performed that night were: 'Hands Off, She's Mine' (The Beat), 'Sorrow' (David Bowie), 'The Dark End of the Street' (The Commitments) and a very horrible k.d. Lang song called 'Big Boned Gal'. The other two songs that were in the set have been lost to memory.

As it transpired, I could just about handle the songs on the night and somehow managed to hold the band together with some sort of slovenly beat. At the end of the night Rob approached me and said 'Well, you weren't all that, but probably good enough for this band. We're trying to get The Heseltines together again – wanna join us?'.

If I'd taken a moment or two to think about it, I probably could've come up with a hundred reasons not to – I was 33 years old and all grown up now; I had kids; I owned a lawnmower and a barbeque – but before I could think of a single one of them, I found myself saying 'Yes please, when do we start rehearsing?'. When Mistress Rock comes calling, only a damn fool would deny that girl her wicked way.

The first thing I needed to do was get myself a drum kit and I went for an unbranded cheapo 5-drum kit, finished in jet black, from a music shop in Romford. There seemed no point in spending lots of money on a kit, as this project (like all the other projects I start but never finish) would probably only last five minutes.

The Fabulous Heseltines had history. In 1990, the arse-end of Thatcher's Britain, the country was drowning in Gazza's tears and interest rates were higher than Bez on a pair of stilts, and so a bunch of old school friends from Walthamstow, East London, decided to form a rock band – it was the least that they could do, they had no choice.

They had hair, big hair. Nice hair but big. Nice big hair. They toiled relentlessly fashioning not only their big hair, but also a set of pub-rock beauties into a collection of songs perfected for public consumption. The Hezzas (as they became known amongst the 'Stow Massive') were up and running and they were good – very good actually. Gigs were hard to come by, but when they did eventually earn an appearance at the Walthamstow YMCA, the town turned out in force to support them. It was chronicled that the night The Heseltines played their first ever gig, the local constabulary recorded the lowest crime rate ever. Some naysayers might point out that the suicide rate was up slightly, but that wasn't the point. The next morning it was not unusual to spot some of the locals parading merrily down Hoe Street, sporting copy-cat big hair whilst whistling one of the previous night's triumphs – the theme tune to *Joe 90*.

The gigs came flooding in. There was a wedding in 1991 at which it was claimed that more than three people got up to dance at one point, and who can forget the gig in Hatfield in 1992 where nothing particularly interesting happened, apart from the drummer crashing the van, turning up very late, leaving the others wondering whether he was going to show up at all and then running off with all the money to pay for his van repairs.

But despite this little set back, they moved on, becoming tighter and tighter, plying their trade with aplomb in front on anyone who would listen – which was mostly friends, and friends of friends, workmates and their mums and dads (the band's mums and dads, not their workmates' mums and dads – that would be ridiculous). This bunch of young bucks had balls, but unlike Gud Fungs, they didn't hide them away in their smalls – they wore them on their sleeves, right next to their massive hearts, and occasionally as earrings. But all was not rosy in Camp Hezza.

The drummer was called Fal and as far as I know was of no fixed surname. He wore fingerless gloves to play the drums and owned a huge kit that hung together across a structure that looked a little like a five-a-side goal, and took roughly an hour to assemble. It has never really been explained to me why he decided to quit the band, but apparently one day, he just threw down his fingerless gloves, packed up his gong and buggered off and was never seen again, leaving The Heseltines drummerless, penniless and pretty much talentless.

Suddenly, The Fabulous Heseltines were not feeling quite so fabulous. What now?

They were hurt and all retired to their various corners of E17 to lick their collective rock wounds. They indulged themselves in solo projects while they waited for something to happen. Guitarist Rob developed an unhealthy interest in Peruvian mime, but alas it was to be short-lived. His debut performance – *La Alegria de los Pollos* (*The Joy of Chickens)* failed miserably. Nobody came. Disheartened and broken, he grew a goatee beard as a protest statement. Jo and Christian started work on their never-to-be-heard concept album *Desmond Tutu's Sandals,* which allegedly included the songs 'Don't Bash the Bishop', 'Vegetarianism (It's Not Rocket Salad)' and the touching 'Can You Hear Me Griff Rhys Jones?'. Meanwhile guitarist John, who didn't really like anything in particular, couldn't find a project to immerse himself in and so indulged himself in buying lots of effects pedals, and spent the hiatus trying to work out how to cable them all together. Singer Phil briefly became the front man for Scottish prog-folk outfit Stumpy McTrumpy.

It may have once been said that The Fabulous Heseltines had worked their way up to being East London's 16th or possibly 17th best covers band, and had been on the verge of approaching something that may have been described as quite good – but it was probably them that said it. But when such a beast is hurt and injured, it is at its most dangerous, and that is where I came in, I guess. By all accounts Fal was a great drummer and it was now down to me to fill those fingerless gloves.

They gave me a cassette recording of their last gig so that I could go away and learn the songs before we could reconvene and start working on them. All I had to do was do what the old drummer did.

The first time we had the band over to our place for a band meeting, I was expecting the place to be turned into a rock den of iniquity. I warned Kim that there would probably be drugs and we'd better get a mountain of beer in. When they showed up, the only refreshment they required was a nice cup of tea and a chocolate Hobnob. This was going to be my kind of band.

So who exactly were The Fabulous Heseltines? Well, let me introduce you to the band:

Phil Brierley – *Lead Vocals, Backing Vocals* – A Scot by nurture but as cockney as a jellied eel stall in Petticoat Lane by nature; a Jockney, if you will. Phil was a fine vocalist with a rasping rock voice, who knew exactly when to hold back and when to let go. This applied both to his voice and his bottom. Phil was always the last to arrive at rehearsals and when he did eventually turn up he would get to work building a spliff whilst he explained to us in great detail the reason for his lateness. He was something important at Thames Water, like some sort of drain surgeon. Phil once described the last bit of a long road trip – you know, the bit when you've already played all the good music you have on board the car apart from *One More from the Road,* as the 'Lynyrd Skynyrd miles'. It's a phrase that has stuck with me. Rumour has it that Phil once bumped into Woody out of the Bay City Rollers in Londis in Dundee and told him that he had nice trousers. This is unsubstantiated though– his trousers were generally horrible.

Jo 'Hairy-Arse' Slade. – *Lead Vocals, Backing Vocals, Percussion.* When I first joined the band Jo really only did backing vocals, but later she developed into an excellent lead singer whose voice can sometimes give me goose bumps. Her work with a rattley egg remains unrivalled in rock and vocally she made 'Hanging on the Telephone' her own. Her musical influences include Posh Spice, Kirsty MacColl and some French shit that no one has ever heard of. Little-known facts about Jo include: she once made a pubic wig for Noel Edmonds and that she has been monitoring the price of an egg and cress sandwich from Pret A Manger since 1997 in the back of a notebook that she keeps tucked in her bra. As far as I'm aware she doesn't actually have a hairy arse but I am aware that she is most probably the kindest individual that I have ever met.

Rob Mellor – *Lead Guitar.* A guitar virtuoso who could make his instrument sing like an angel one minute, and wail like a piglet that had just had his trotter stamped on the next. It was a regular occurrence at Heseltine gigs for fans to bow at Rob's feet doing the 'we're not worthy' thing as he widdled and twiddled his way through his solos. Some wore badges that claimed 'Mellor is God', others – 'Mellor is Odd'. Rob played a bright red guitar, which he called Simon and he dusted him every week before putting plectrum to string. On the rare occasions when he played a bum note during a solo he would stop in his tracks, stick out his bottom lip and stare in bemusement at Simon as if it was the guitar's fault. He would then proceed to smack it around the neck and send it to its room without any supper. Rob was the funniest Heseltine, with a sense of humour drier than a fortnight in the Sahara. A little-known fact about Rob is that he once successfully guessed the identity of fourteen Revels chocolates on the bounce.

Christian Mountney – *Bass Guitar*. Christian spent his formative years dressed as a pirate. Back in the day, when he had hair that would flop of its own accord, he was a New Romantic. However, despite this obvious fashion faux pas, he was the most melodic bass player I ever played with. Christian was most definitely the leader – the glue that held the band together with the stickiness of semen on a teenager's duvet. He was great at coming up with ideas of how we could make our covers sound different from the original without actually playing them wrongly. He was in charge of nodding. Nodding is one the most important roles in a band. It's an action that needs to be taken to remind the rest of the band that something in the song is about to change – like a little stop or where the solo kicks in. He was great at nodding, it was one of the things he did best, and he got very cross if anyone else did the nodding. On one occasion, someone else in the band tried to do the nod to indicate we were about to go into the outro of 'The Boys are Back In Town'. He stopped the song dead and said 'Who put you in charge of nodding? I've done the nod for twenty years and I'm not stopping now – I'll do the nod, ok?' Not only did he nail the nod, he also once nailed several planks of wood together and built us a portable stage.

John Rutter – *Rhythm Guitar*. The first time I met John, I was frightened. He looked very scary with his long hair that stretched over halfway down his back, combat trousers and steel toe-capped Dr. Martens, but as it turned out he was as gentle as a lamb. John said 'fuck' with a greater regularity than Roy 'Chubby' Brown, but was a lot funnier. John was simply a fantastic guitarist – an absolute natural with an amazing ear for music. Back in the day when there was no Internet packed with guitar tabs and chords, cover bands had to work songs out by ear. John was brilliant at this. He had the ability to listen to a song, and by verse two he was playing along with it. I enjoyed playing with John as part of the rhythm section in this band. We had a lot of eye contact (we didn't dare to nod), and he would always acknowledge a nice fill with a little pout of approval, but at the same time any fuck-up would be greeted with a glower so fiery, it could fry an egg. He could be a miserable old bastard though, and he never seemed to like any of the songs that we played … apart from 'A Forest' by The Cure – he really liked that one, mainly because it was miserable. Known within the band simply as 'Butler', for reasons too tedious to explain.

Pete Harvie – *Saxophone*. Pete was older than the other Heseltines and played out-of-tune sax like no other. As the complete opposite to John, Pete couldn't play anything by ear, and had to write all his parts down on manuscript paper like a proper musician. He once turned up at a rehearsal but forgot to bring his sax with him and had to go home to get it. On his return to the studio he found the rest of the band hiding behind my drum kit. Pete left the band around a year after I joined. These days he fronts a Kings of Leon tribute band called Sax on Fire.

We used to rehearse regularly at 'The Premises' studio in Bethnal Green. At first I found rehearsals a struggle. I had a lot of catching up to do, but the rest of the band made me feel welcome and made allowances for the fact that I hadn't played drums for twelve years.

At home I set my drums up in the front room of my flat and dampened them down with tea towels so as not to drive the neighbours mental. I practiced the songs over and over again until I eventually got them; I was probably practising three or four times a week just to keep up.

I really enjoyed rehearsals with this band. The sessions were always relaxed and full of laughter. If I'm totally honest, I preferred rehearsing to the gigs – especially in the early days. I would get ridiculously nervous at gigs, and although the nerves kept the adrenalin pumping, it took away some of the enjoyment.

One of my favourite rehearsal moments was when we were learning the Cars song 'Just What I Needed'. There is an eight-bar passage in the song that on the record was played on keys. With the band lacking a keyboard player, it was decided that Pete should take this part on sax. He carefully wrote down each note on manuscript paper and placed it on his music stand. But despite having the notes written down, he just couldn't get it right. Every time we got to his part, he would play a wrong note and the whole thing would collapse into a heap of uncomfortableness. Christian suggested that it would be better for Pete to play his part on his own without the distraction of the rest of us playing along until he got it nailed. But even without us, he was still struggling. Over and over again he would play it, but at some point during the eight bars there would be a wrong note or two and each time he played it, it would be a different note that was wrong. If it wasn't a note that was wrong, it would be the timing. The more he messed it up, the more we laughed. Not that we were ridiculing him, but it was just so funny that he couldn't get this simple passage right. He knew he could play these notes blindfolded, back to front and inside out, and that's exactly what it sounded like he was doing. There didn't appear to be any logical reason why. After well over twenty attempts he finally got it right and the rest of the band cheered and danced excitedly around the rehearsal room. So Christian made him play it again just to make sure that it wasn't a fluke. Again spot on. One more time just to make sure. Spot on again. Now it was time to do it with the rest of the band.

So, once more we begin the track. We get through the first verse ok, and then it was the sax part – to a man, we held our breath in anticipation. Three notes in and the puff coming out of the end of his saxophone, to our delight, caused all the sheets of manuscript paper to float up in the air and off his music stand and we all just fell about laughing uncontrollably for about five minutes. When it came to gigging the song for the first time, we all felt very tense as we approached the sax part. A collection of 'will-he-wont-he' looks, spread across the stage. Of course, he nailed it – no problem.

Pete left the band shortly afterwards. Having mastered the sax break in 'Just What I Needed', he'd made a statement that ended with a full stop. There was nowhere left for him to go. Like a sax-playing Kevin Keegan, he quit while he was on top of his game.

Pete was the last Heseltine to leave the band for several years, and so after a period of comings and goings, the band at last had a steady ship. It's not unusual; building a band is a bit like building a football team – you can't get all the right players in at once, but for now the tinkering was over. Lots of big bands suffer multiple line-up changes – look at The Stones for example, or Deep Purple. No one talks about the Coverdale or Bolin years with any affection, do they, and The Heseltines were no different, so between 1995 and 2000 the band enjoyed their most successful period with the classic yet somewhat tragic Brierley/Slade/Mountney/Mellor/Rutter/ Shelley line-up.

I suppose The Heseltines' main mission statement was not to have a mission statement. Nothing reasonable was off limits, but we mainly covered songs that were well known, whilst making sure we stayed well clear of the usual cover band fodder trotted out by every other band on the circuit. There was no 'All Right Now's or 'Jumping Jack Flash's, although we had no issues whatsoever with knocking out the odd TV theme or two. John knew the *BBC Snooker Theme* from start to finish and wasn't coy about giving it a workout during slow rehearsal moments. We always tried to add something of our own to the songs that we covered. Nothing subtle or clever – subtlety wasn't our middle name – 'Fabulous' was, obviously. We used to call this tampering 'Heseltine-ing them up', which generally meant that we would rock them up a bit to make them more muscular – particularly those songs whose original versions were a little bit lame, stuff like 'Greased Lightning' and the Abba song 'Mamma Mia'.

I think it's fair to say that The Heseltines were probably East London's least prolific rock band. We would only gig once or twice a year. If we ever did three, that more or less qualified as a tour warranting t-shirts with the dates printed on the back. The way things usually worked out was that we would rehearse for three months, replenish our pantry of rock with lots of new songs, play a gig, have three months off to recover from the trauma, and then start all over again.

We played to packed houses – public houses mostly, where the audience often tipped the one hundred mark, some of them even paying to get in. Our performances were loud, raunchy and convicted, if not always convincing. We did most of our gigs at The Heathcote Arms in Leytonstone. It became our spiritual home.

We didn't have our own PA, so we used to hire a bloke called Steve who did – we called him Steve the PA Man. He was ably assisted by his girlfriend Sue, whom we referred to as 'The Goddess'. They would turn up (usually late), with an extraordinary collection of speakers, mixing desks, fold backs and miles and miles of cables. That amount of gear was probably more suited to U2 live at Wembley Stadium rather than The Heseltines live in Leytonstone, and it all took hours and hours to set up. It was very boring waiting for all this gear to get assembled so that we could sound check, but we didn't waste this time idly. We discovered that if we took the plastic covers that protected those enormous speakers and placed them over our heads and then attempted to stumble blindly around the room, crashing into tables and chairs that had been arranged into a sort of slalom, we had invented a new game for *Jeux Sans Frontières*. Simple things, for simple musicians. Here come the Belgians? Here come the bellends, more like.

By the summer of 1996 we were at our peak. Admittedly there was the 'Down Down' debacle where we just couldn't get the thing to sound anything like Status Quo. We didn't dwell on it, it wasn't our fault – we just put it down to The Quo being a bit crap and happily moved on. It was a nice time to be in a band though and generally a good time to be British. The country seemed to be buzzing on a wave of new identity known collectively as 'Cool Britannia' and everyone from Land's End to John O'Groats could name all of The Spice Girls. Blur and Oasis were at war in the charts and being very rude to each other in the papers.

We dabbled with Britpop for a while, including songs by Oasis, Blur, Supergrass, Ocean Colour Scene and Paul Weller in our set, and suddenly we were 'current' and ready to air our new songs at a gig at The Heathcote at the end of June.

Somewhat overshadowing our gig in terms of public interest was the fast-approaching Euro '96 tournament. '3 Lions' was the anthem that heralded it, but we didn't bother learning that one.

Two days before the tournament started I played in my work's Inter-Department 5-A-Side football tournament. I was far too old to still be play-ing football, but 'Football's Coming Home' fever had got the better of me. I was playing in goal, so nothing too strenuous ... or so I thought.

Oddly enough, Alvin Martin, the former West Ham and England centre back, came along to watch the tournament because his best mate Geoff worked at our place.

Anyway, the first shot that I attempted to save was a piledriver from some distance. I got a hand to it and palmed it clear. I was dead chuffed that I'd pulled off a decent save in front of Alvin Martin, no less – I think he clapped and shouted something out in affluent Scouse. The stinging that you usually feel after making a save usually only lasts for a few seconds, but something wasn't quite right – my hand continued to throb until half time.

I pulled off my glove very gingerly and to my horror the thumb on my right hand seemed be hanging on in there only by the tenderest of threads and I couldn't move it. After the obligatory photo opportunity with Alvin (his thumb aloft, mine just hanging), it was off to hospital for me.

The young doctor that I saw said that I had dislocated my thumb and wasted no time at all in yanking it back into its socket. I can't say that I have ever felt a greater pain than in those few seconds. He told me that I was going to have my arm in plaster up to my elbow for two weeks. After learning that I was right-handed, he announced that I would be signed off work for the duration.

'Look on the bright side,' he said, 'at least you'll be able to watch all the afternoon matches'.

This cheered me up temporarily and then I remembered that Heseltines gig.

'I play the drums in a band,' I declared, with an element of minor shame. 'How long before I can play again?'

'Well you won't be playing anything until the plaster comes off – then we'll assess it when we see how much movement you have back.'

Detecting the dejection on my face, he attempted to cheer me up with: 'There's no reason why you shouldn't make a full recovery. You'll be able to play the drum solo from 'Moby Dick' in no time at all once it's fully healed and strong again'.

That's amazing, I thought, as I hadn't a clue how to play it before the injury. The miracles of modern medicine, eh?

We managed to rearrange the gig for a few weeks later, but I hated being out of action. Taking heed of the commitment advised by Roy Castle on *Record Breakers*, I continued to go to rehearsals with my arm in a sling and cast. I could still muster some sort of beat with just kick-drum and snare and that kept things ticking over for me, but I knew exactly how the bloke out of Def Leppard felt.

We didn't just play at the Heathcote, certainly not. We played them all – the biggies – The Chestnut Tree, Walthamstow, The Bardstock Festival and of course the daddy of them all, a garage in Wivenhoe, Essex where the walls were decorated with several pairs of coloured Y-fronts.

We sometimes did functions such as birthday parties. Functions are the trickiest of gigs for cover bands – mainly because aunties and uncles and sometimes even grandparents are in the audience, and they really don't want to hear 'Teenage Kicks' any time, ever. Family functions are full of people that haven't seen each other for ages, catching up and pretending that they like each other. When you're the entertainment at one of these dos, it always feels like you're a bit of an inconvenience. We once played a surprise 40th birthday party for a Billy Bragg fan, and at the request of the birthday boy's wife, learnt Billy's reading of 'The Red Flag' specifically for the lad to get up on stage and sing it with us. He was horrified and clearly scared shitless, to the point where we might have just ruined his evening, his reputation and possibly his entire life.

At one such function, Rob pointed out that the paper plates on the buffet table were decorated with paper doilies. Always a nice touch, but then he pulled out our set list for the evening from his pocket and pointed to the doilies and then to our set list and muttered 'doilies – "Smells Like Teen Spirit"' and then gave a facial expression that had 'I don't think this is gonna work' written all over it.

In March 2000, we decided that it was time that the Heseltines made an album. It's not every band that has the cheek to release a live album as their debut, but that's what we did. The Fabulous Heseltines were not about convention (unless it was a VW camper van convention, and then we were most compliant). We were just six young upstarts who wanted to rock, and if we really had to wear pants, then we were gonna rip them off a garage wall in Wivenhoe and wear them on our heads – so a live debut album it was. We just didn't care.

We hired some recording equipment and attempted to record a gig. There was an extra measure of nervousness for this gig as we had to get it right, and to be fair we did. We delivered that night like a postman with a huge parcel from Amazon – a huge parcel of rock. It turned out just great.

We decided to call the album *Piss on Yer Chips* (known within the inner sanctum of hardcore fans simply as 'Piss'). 'Piss on Yer Chips' was a phrase coined by John which, in our world, referred to that moment when someone makes a mistake, and the rest of the band look round at the culprit. He insisted that no one outside the band would even notice that a mistake had been made and so used to say: 'If you make a mistake, don't piss on yer chips'.

For the cover of the CD we took things to a Pan's People-esque literal interpretation level. We took a photo of a portion of chips sitting in their wrapping paper, which was so greasy that it actually looked as if someone had pissed on them. *Piss on Yer Chips* sold 77 copies. Fourteen of the people that bought it actually played it. It didn't trouble the charts.

I have just listened to *Piss on Yer Chips* for the purpose of writing this chapter. It is currently fifteen years old and without the need to big up my own band, I have to say that it still sounds as fresh as it did back in 2000.

Well as fresh as some stale old pub rock tunes can ever sound. But I am proud of this record, and of this band, and our reading of 'Song 2' by Blur still makes me want to jump up and down and shout 'woo-hoo'.

Kicking against the pricks of convention once more, we were forced to do another gig shortly after the recording to try and sell the thing. This was pretty much Rob's final involvement with the band. When we reconvened for rehearsals after this gig, he suggested that we might want to have a look at the Duran Duran song 'Hungry Like the Wolf' as an addition to our set. He was laughed out of the room and quit the band in a huff on his way out. Well that's how we like to remember his departure, but the real reason was that he was moving to Berkshire and that was quite a long way to travel to rehearse every week.

Rob's departure left us with a dilemma. Should we risk bringing in an outsider to fill the lead guitar-shaped hole that he had left? We were a pretty tight bunch and decided that we didn't want to risk upsetting the band equilibrium with a random stranger who might turn out to be a complete nob. That would make us very cross indeed. Luckily, singer Phil, a complete nob whom we already knew, had been quietly turning himself into a pretty nifty guitarist and volunteered to step into the breach.

It's funny, but in my opinion we did some of our most interesting songs in the time after Rob left the band – stuff like Bowie's 'The Man Who Sold the World', 'Babylon's Burning' by The Ruts, a Heseltined-up version of Kylie's 'Can't Get You Out of My Head', 'I Can't Stand Losing You' by The Police and The Stones' disco song 'Miss You'. The dynamics of the band definitely changed. We had to become tighter with there only being five of us, and Jo had to really step up to the plate as a lead singer, as Phil was becoming more and more preoccupied with guitar parts. We recorded our second album 'Suburban Papoose' in Christian and Jo's home studio, but never got as far as putting it out.

We limped on with a few more gigs as a five-piece, but it wasn't the same without Rob. Around this time Ian and I had got back in touch and I invited his current band – the country flavoured Middle Age Rampage – to support us at a couple of gigs. Funny how things turn out – it felt odd that a band that he was in were supporting a band that I was in, but that's how it was.

There was a band meeting sometime in 2002 at my house, in which John and Phil both decided that they didn't want to carry on with the band and The Heseltines were no more. I think I can say quite confidently that this was the first time in the history of rock that a band has split up whilst the drummer was wearing brown suede moccasin carpet slippers.

I was gutted. I'd been in this band for nine years and our weekly rehearsals were the highlight of my week. There was going to be a massive hole to fill. It's been really hard for me to describe in words the rapport that existed within this band and do it justice. All the others were connected through Christian: Jo was his partner, he was at school with John and Rob and he met Phil at College. They had shared history and I was the outsider, the Johnny-come-lately, yet not once in those nine years did these fine people ever make me feel like I was. This wasn't just a band to me; it was a bunch of people that I loved spending time with as well as making music with – friends for life. Everyone in the band brought something to it in equal parts; there were no stars, no egos, no fights or arguments. Just six people making some great music and having loads of laughs doing it.

I had become a much better drummer thanks to my time in this band. The Heseltines might have been over but I wasn't ready to hang up my drumsticks just yet. Whatever was to happen in the future band-wise, The Fabulous Heseltines will always be my band, the band I want to reminisce about, but mostly the band I want to play in.

(I'm Not Your) Stepping Stone

The morning after The Heseltines decided to call it a day, I emailed Ian to tell him the news. He said that he was looking for another band to supplement Middle Age Rampage so he could play some stuff that wasn't country, and would I fancy doing something together.

I liked this idea and asked Jo and Christian whether they wanted to be involved – they did. For the final piece of the jigsaw, I contacted my friend Carl. I'd not known Carl that long. In the early stages of our friendship he had mentioned that he played a bit of guitar. The way he spoke about it so modestly, I had assumed he played guitar in the way that I played guitar – just a bit of casual strumming of a few simple chords on an old acoustic to pass the time. As it turned out, Carl was a magnificent lead guitarist who owned a whole host of guitars and so many effects boxes that they had to be kept in a large trunk at the bottom of his garden. He could also play the mandolin and banjo, and was a virtuoso wobble-boarder who had made quite a reputation for himself in the St. Albans branch of the Rolf & Anita Harris Occasional Players. I thought he would be perfect for the new band and so I asked him to complete the line-up. Emails were traded back and forth and within an hour a new band, So Last Century, was formed.

Apart from the fact that we had both male and female vocalists, So Last Century was a very different band to The Heseltines. The material that we did was a lot gentler and sometimes subtler than the kind of stuff that we had covered in The Heseltines. Ian played acoustic guitar on a lot of the songs and that encouraged the gentler material. There was still some muscular stuff though – '(I'm Not Your) Stepping Stone' by The Monkees, 'Rocks' by Primal Scream, Rod Stewart's 'Hot Legs', Terrorvision's 'Oblivion', with all these tunes sitting alongside some quieter songs like 'Outdoor Type' by The Lemonheads, 'Creep' by Radiohead and 'Distant Sun' by Crowded House.

In the summer of 2002 we made our live debut out in the wilds of Essex. The organiser of the Bardstock Festival, Dave Moist (we called him that because his name was Dave and he was in a band called The Moist), invited us to appear. The Heseltines had played the event for the previous couple of years so it was going to feel strange going back there with the new band. Possibly even stranger for Carl, who the previous year had come along just to watch the Heseltines – this year he would be playing. Thus far, we had only managed to cobble together a set of around ten songs, so we played somewhere in the middle of the bill. We'd only been a band for a few weeks but it was an encouraging debut. Things were looking promising.

By the winter of that year it was time to peddle our wares in front of a local audience, and we were blessed with a massive turn-out for our first proper gig at The Chestnut Tree in Walthamstow. I didn't get nervous playing live anymore and I particularly enjoyed this gig because it was the first time that my kids came to see me play. The audience was mainly friendly and a large proportion of its number was made up of former followers of The Heseltines, inquisitive to see what the three of us would do next, and I imagine there would have been expectations from the erstwhile Fab fans – many of whom had grown up following The Heseltines – some of them still hadn't. There were members of that audience that may have shared their first kiss whilst watching The Fabulous Heseltines many years before. It may have even been possible that some of them may have named their pets or even children after members of that band. Our followers were loyal. It was a great gig and feedback from most people was really good. Even John from The Heseltines came to see us and gave us his nod of approval, which was surprising seeing as he doesn't like anything much (apart from 'A Forest' by The Cure).

There is a video that still exists of this gig, which, although I haven't watched it for a long time, I remember has some great moments. The bit where Carl and Chris playfully lean back-to-back, Quo style, as Carl widdles his way through his fantastic solo in 'Moonage Daydream', and where they bounce up and down like a couple of teenagers in 'Hot Legs'. The link where Ian introduced Jo as 'a lady that sings like a thrush ... or stings like thrush'. But my very favourite moment is where during the bit in 'Rocks', where it breaks down to just drums and vocals, Ian raises his hands above his head and gives a solitary clap – the moment where, for a split second, he forgot to be cool and then quickly withdraws them as he remembers again.

We played gigs with a little more regularity than we had in the Heseltines – sometimes we even got paid handsomely. We played at UFJ Bank's Christmas Party for a whopping great £500. UFJ was a Japanese Bank and, at the time, my employers. Playing drums in a band in front of my colleagues made it an odd gig for me. It was quite strange for the rest of the band, too. I had been to these Christmas parties before, but didn't really warn the others that Japanese ex-pats, let off the leash and full of alcohol, tend to go a bit crazy at these sorts of things. None of the band really expected to be greeted by a circle of tiny Japanese men acing with their ties tied around their heads like a kind of Samurai Legs & Co. tribute troupe – not during 'Subterranean Homesick Blues', anyway.

It has to be said that this band wasn't without its tensions. It wasn't a massive thing, there were never any out-and-out arguments, but sometimes you could feel that there was a bit of uneasiness at rehearsals as we assembled our gear in stony silence – a sort of grumbling by proxy.

Christian and Carl would often intersperse rehearsals with a funky jam of their own and this used to frustrate the hell out of Ian. They couldn't help themselves – they were, after all, just a couple of little black boys from the 'hood' funking out – but Ian never liked the in-between song noodling and his body language told the tale that he thought time was being wasted. If he was particularly irked, he would let out an audible 'shall we?'. In The Heseltines, we had all been used to working in a much more relaxed way, where comedy interludes were as much a part of rehearsals as the making of music. Ian is a very good musician, with the ability to listen to what everyone else is doing during a song even when concentrating on his own playing, and if he heard something that he didn't like, he would let it be known that he didn't like it with varying degrees of harshness.

However, sometimes these little moments of tension worked in a positive way and despite (or maybe because of) them, the music we made was good. We had a good sound and Jo and Ian sang really well together. There were some notable triumphs, especially when we were all contributing ideas. We came up with a version of the Soft Cell song 'Tainted Love' which we played around the riff from 'Green Onions', turning a fairly mundane-sounding eighties electronic workout into something far more pleasing.

Ian came up with the masterstroke of doing the old David Essex song 'Gonna Make You A Star' – a song that he would have absolutely loathed back in the seventies, but given a rocked-up treatment it sounded great and became a crowd favourite at our gigs.

We were the first name on the team sheet as far as parties were concerned, with a lot of our friends turning forty around this time. We played my friends Hilary & Martin's joint 40th party, at which for the most part, our audience was mainly several children sitting cross-legged in front of the stage. Of course, children never sit cross-legged for very long unless *The Simpsons* is on the telly. Have you any idea just how disconcerting it is to watch from the stage as several pre-ten-year-olds skip around the room whilst you're playing 'Psycho Killer'?

For Kim's 40th birthday party we all dressed up in ridiculous eighties clothes. Not to herald a new direction for the band – it was an eighties party, silly. When I say we all dressed up, I mean we all dressed up apart from Ian. He didn't really do dressing up anymore, although that hadn't always been the case. I remember a party in the eighties when his 'Arthur Fowler – The Breakdown Years' turned heads as only an unshaven man in a dressing gown and slippers can. By 2007 he felt wigs were for solely for balding men with hair envy. He was right to shun the wig – I sweated like a hog under mine.

We didn't really do that much eighties material in our normal set so we had to learn a load of extra songs just for the party. One of these was the XTC song 'Senses Working Overtime'. Not an essential party song by any stretch of the imagination, but a good song nonetheless. We struggled in rehearsals to make it work but eventually cobbled something together that we were happyish with. On the night, it didn't quite go to plan. I can't remember what exactly went wrong, but wrong it went. Ian was great at engaging the audience with in-between-song banter – sometimes totally random stuff like playing the theme tune to *Brookside* on his acoustic as a tenuous Liverpool link to introduce The La's' 'There She Goes' – but he always seemed to have the right quip, for the right moment. At the end of 'Senses Working Overtime' he announced: 'that was the sound of a cover band overstretching itself'. The division in the band was widening. Ian left the party as soon as our set was over – possibly to weep, possibly to catch the end of *Match of the Day* – I'm not sure. It turned out to be our last gig.

We reconvened after Kim's party but finding new material that we could all agree on was becoming more and more difficult. Even changing our name to The Undercoats hadn't helped. We were five individuals with differing eclectic musical tastes, who all thought we knew which songs would suit the band best, and which songs would go down a storm. Every song that got suggested would be rejected by someone for one reason or another. The final nail in the band's coffin came when Christian and Carl's funky leanings got the better of them and they made some very loud noises about having a crack at the Grace Jones song 'Pull Up to the Bumper'. For Ian, who would freely admit to not having a funky bone in his entire body, this was the final straw. In the end, he emailed me and said he was leaving the band to concentrate on some self-penned material he had been working on. What actually happened was that he turned Middle Age Rampage into a great seventies cover band called Cheesecloth.

I think we may have all given a sigh of relief when Ian called time on the band – there wasn't so much as wimper from the rest of us. It just felt like the right time. I was particularly pleased. What musician doesn't want to be in a band that splits up due to musical differences?

The rest of us went on to form a drum-free acoustic band called The Ya-Ta-Ta-Ta's, a band in which for reasons best known to the others, I was allowed to play acoustic guitar and sing a bit. Still, it kept me busy for a while. A strange sort of busy though.

I'd never really considered myself to be much of a singer, but I'd enjoyed learning how to harmonise with Jo in that band. However, a guitarist I most certainly was not, and I needed to start drumming again. It was time to look for a new band.

Pop music is so forgiving – it just lets you keep coming back to it whenever you are ready. Football is much harsher. With football you know that once your legs have gone, it's over. You can faff around, hoofing the ball about if you want, but once you're relegated to The Red Lion's third choice centre half – only getting a game when the pub cat has a groin strain – the game is well and truly up.

Not so with pop – look at the likes of Jagger, McCartney, Townshend and countless others – rock'n'roll pensioners, still out there doing it and not ready for a deckchair on an allotment just yet. It's no different for the ordinary folk of cover bands; we can keep going until the public never want to hear 'Mustang Sally' ever again.

I put an advert on the Essex section of a website called 'Join My Band'. This site was a coming together of musicians looking for bands, and bands looking for musicians – a sort of Tinder but with guitars.

A singer called Tony contacted me almost immediately and I was invited to Basildon to audition. The songs he'd asked me to learn were all standard pub rock fodder: 'Mustang Sally', 'I'm A Believer', 'Play That Funky Music' – you get the picture. These were all songs I'd played before in other bands so my preparation was minimal. I'd never done an audition for a band in which I didn't know any of the members; being judged by total strangers was new but got the adrenalin pumping. It all seemed to go quite well and after a brief discussion I was invited to become the new drummer for Fat Bloke Band. They weren't actually called Fat Bloke Band and not everyone in the band was fat – to be fair, not everyone in the band was a bloke either – but most of us were both, and we never came up with a proper name so it'll have to do.

The band were actually pretty good, but Tony was a typical cover band stalwart who, despite there being a squillion songs out there for bands to cover, didn't want to look any further than the songs he knew as tried and tested material. For example, he'd say 'we really need a Stones song', so I suggested 'Tumbling Dice' – he gave it five seconds thought and come back with 'how about 'Jumping Jack Flash?''. That's how he was. He's not unique; the circuit is fraught with dozens of cover bands all trotting out the same twenty songs – it's something that bewilders me beyond comprehension. The band lasted about eight months.

So it was back to 'Join My Band' for me and I was soon talking to a bass player called Mike Simmons about joining an Upminster-based band called Strongbox. I liked the idea of this band – a female-fronted five-piece who had regular gigs waiting and a forty-song set list, hardly any of which I'd played before. We exchanged recordings, but on seeing their show reel, I almost backed out. The band were good but they had a singer who screeched like a set of worn out radials hurtling round the North Circular. I went to the audition anyway believing that she couldn't be as bad in the flesh as she sounded in the video. I was right, but it still wasn't pleasant – her voice made me wince.

Strongbox were a fairly new band on the circuit who hadn't done too many gigs, but had gone through drummers faster than Freddie Starr goes through hamsters. I had prepped around fifteen songs from their set for the audition, which seemed to impress them and I was offered the gig – I was to be the tenth person to fill the Strongbox drum stool. I immediately took to Mike (bass), Mark Hewitt (rhythm guitar/vocals) and Mark Foster (lead guitar), and soon felt part of the gang. After a while the singer was dispatched and replaced by Warren 'Wozza' Bean and things improved no end, until his inner diva got the better of him and he left in a huff after refusing to sing 'Blitzkrieg Bop'. When our current singer Natalie Jupp joined the band, it felt like the jigsaw was finally complete. She can't assemble a music stand to save her life, but luckily she is brilliant at singing and engaging an audience.

I love being in this band; we do around twenty paying gigs a year, playing mostly pop, with a bit of rock and some new wave thrown in – which, after all, is all I've ever wanted to play. I'd go as far as to say that our ever-evolving set list is probably the most interesting I've ever played with any band. They indulge me by allowing me to choose songs by 10cc and even occasionally let me sing lead vocals on a few songs – in public, in front of actual real people! Now that's something that I would never have thought I was capable of or would have had the nerve to do a few years ago. We even have a bit of a following, but the point is, that being in this band allows me to continue to do the thing that I love doing most.

I can't really explain what it is about playing in a band that keeps drawing me back and makes it impossible to let it go. When I think about the endless humping about of gear, the setting up, the packing up, the thousands of pounds spent on equipment and the hours put in at the rehearsal studio; fretting about getting that fill just right when absolutely no one cares about it or will even notice it except me; the endless twiddling and tuning of my floor-tom that drives me nuts until I get it just how I like it – for what? – who cares? When you break it down, it's just pretending to be pop stars by playing other people's songs to a handful of pissed-up people in a pub on a Saturday night for fifty quid – it's hardly living the dream.

But then again, when you're up there with your mates alongside you, all in it together, each of us contributing equally to the cause of making this noise – this beautiful noise – and those same pissed-up people in the pub are digging it, singing at the top of their voices, dancing, laughing and bouncing around the room like a gang of well-worn spacehoppers, it makes my pulse race that little bit faster and makes my heart happier than almost anything else I know.

So no, not living the dream ... but it's as close as I'm ever going to get, and if I could choose the way that I eventually pop my clogs, the emphasis will be on the pop bit, and it will be in a pub on a Saturday night, slumped motionless across my drum kit – preferably whilst playing 'Ace of Spades'.

Live and Dangerous

I have a problem with gigs. Not the ones that I'm expected to play in, but the ones that I have to pay money to go and see. This isn't a new thing, but it seems to have escalated now that I'm a grumpy old bastard.

Let's start with the tickets. In the old days it was so simple. You read the news section of the *NME*, it tells you that your favourite band is about to embark on a UK tour and you send off a little letter stating the number of tickets you want and for which venue with a cheque for the value of the tickets. Oh, and also a stamped self-addressed envelope so they can either send you back the tickets or the un-cashed cheque depending on which way it's gone. Hmmm, ok actually, it wasn't that simple at all, was it? So these days logging onto a website is probably a little bit simpler, but much more time-consuming.

First of all, I have to register with the ticket agency before I can even get a sniff of the button that needs to be clicked to buy the tickets. Once registered, I then have to carefully negotiate the pop-up box offering me a special VIP package for that Tears for Fears reunion gig in Gothenburg, or for some other godforsaken eighties band who weren't any good the first time around. One wayward click, and I'm on the plane and picking up my Swedish krona. If I manage to get past that little hurdle, I'm finally in the waiting area, where I wait nail-bitingly, with all the other hopefuls for the clock to strike 9am, when the virtual cyber-bundle for tickets can begin.

What is totally beyond me is how it can be possible for all the tickets to be sold out by three minutes past nine? It says on my text message that I have priority booking rights. Priority over whom? It seems that every man and his dog's uncle's goldfish have higher priority booking rights than me. They must have, or how can 15,000 tickets selling out in three minutes be explained?

On the occasions where I have been able to get to the stage where I can actually plop a ticket into my basket, I get to the checkout and find that I have been charged an extra fiver per ticket as a booking fee! The tickets are already the price of a small Greek Island, and now I'm being charged a booking fee on top – why? I'm the one who's been up half the night waiting for the things to go on sale, and when they eventually did, I booked my own ticket! So what exactly am I paying you robbing bastards for?

But my main issue at gigs is with rock audiences. This isn't something that has developed as I've got older, although I must admit I probably feel it more acutely these days than I did in the past. It was back then that it occurred to me that, actually, 90% of people that go to gigs are wankers. I think this opinion was born out of going to a lot of gigs at standing-only venues back in the seventies. Although fans of bands who played at seated

venues back then are not immune or exempt from criticism in this
department – especially those that spent the entire gig swirling those
luminous green swirly things all over the shop.

But let's start with the standing audience. There doesn't seem to be any
kind of etiquette with these people. When I go to an all-standing venue, I
know that if I want to be near the front for the main act, then I have to get
there early, get myself down the front and suffer the worst support band of
all time. If I'm honest, this has led on occasion to the discovery of a few
good support bands/artists, but mostly they are terrible.

I once saw some support band whose name I wouldn't have remembered
the next day, let alone forty years later, introduce an instrumental by telling
me that the song was about the time when the band left all their gear on the
baggage carousel at Gatwick Airport. Who wouldn't agree that it's a fascinating story that simply had to be told, but how an instrumental can be
about something I have no idea – that's musos for you – mad as hatters,
the lot of them. I understand that instrumentals at their best can be
evocative or atmospheric and used maybe as an extended intro into
something more purposeful – take The Who's fabulous 'Overture' from
the *Tommy* album, for example, which does that job brilliantly – but more
often than not, instrumentals are just unfinished songs that the writer didn't
love enough to write lyrics for – and if they have to explain to me what the
instrumental is about, then they have failed somewhat in their mission,
haven't they? Oh, but hang on, was that little bass run, just there, the
guitarist chasing after the airport baggage manager to ask him if he's seen
a headstrong wah-wah pedal hanging about? No, I'm not buying it, so let's
just come clean and concede that it's just a little throwaway and get on
with the next song – preferably one with words, that's not about lost
property.

Anyhow, I digress, so yes, I get there early, get up the front and allow
my ears to be assaulted by Clitheroe's finest. Then, the second they finish
their set, the bar at the back suddenly empties, and all the pissed-up
fuckers who have been feverishly downing as much lager as they can
possibly fit into a 45-minute window, are burrowing their way through the
masses.

'Scuze me mate, I'm just trying to get over there, where my mate/
girlfriend/grandma/pint is'. 'Scuze mate', 'scuze mate', 'scuze mate',
'scuze mate' – aaagggghhhhh! Because I am physically incapable of
standing my ground, or brave enough to say 'actually, no, fuck off, I've
been here for two hours', before I know it, I'm now standing somewhere
near the back, and can't see a thing because I'm stuck behind the mixing
desk and the huge haystack of a bloke who's working it.

The thing that bugs me most about these 'space invaders' is, once they
have blagged their way to the front, they never stay there. They spend the
rest of the gig going back and forth in a constant cycle of: go to the bar/

come back from the bar with pint/drink pint/go to the loo/come back from the loo/go to the bar – and so it goes on, and I'm starting to wish that I hadn't paid forty quid just to watch people go to the toilet. I think it's high time that venues started installing urinals just in front of the stage; maybe I should patent the idea – I could call it 'The Slosh Pit'.

I remember an incident in the mid-nineties when Kim, our friend Darryl and I went to see Ocean Colour Scene at the Hammersmith Palais. Ironically, I had discovered Ocean Colour Scene as a support act for Paul Weller a few years previously. They were supported by a band from Liverpool called The Real People, who double-ironically, were actually very good, but let's ignore that for a second and pretend my point about rubbish support bands is still a relevant one. We watched The Real People, and even managed to hold our ground during the bar-emptying interval ritual. So, still standing in the second row, we were quite proud of ourselves and prepared for a great view of Ocean Colour Scene. But as they struck up the opening notes of their first number, 'The Riverboat Song', the whole place went absolutely nuts, there was a huge surge, and I think I actually saw Darryl's feet leave the floor as she was flown from one end of the hall to the other, very, very quickly indeed. It was very annoying for her, but a hilarious spectacle to watch. Arms and legs everywhere, they were.

It's no better at seated venues. There was one time at a Paul McCartney gig at the 02 Arena in London, where this huge fella had squeezed along the row seven times, forcing everybody to curl themselves up into the size of a ping pong ball so he could pass, each time returning with a pint of lager. On his final return I had to say something. 'You do know that's Paul McCartney down there, don't you? Paul McCartney out of The Beatles?' 'Yes,' he replied – 'I come from Brazil'. I had no response to that. He must have missed about thirty minutes of the show going backwards and forwards to the bar. All the way from Rio to drink warm beer at the 02 out of a plastic cup. Makes you wonder.

And here's another thing: the ceaselessly unanswered question – why do I always seem to get The Singer directly behind me at gigs? Have you ever met The Singer? No, of course you haven't, because it's always me that he's standing behind and not you. So let me introduce you to The Singer.

The Singer is the bloke who knows the words to every single song that the artist on the stage has ever written, and spends the entire gig yelling them at the top of his voice. It's not the fact that he chooses to do this in a completely different key and with a totally new melody to the original that drives me nuts, it's the fact that I've paid a fortune to hear the bloke on the stage sing the songs and I can't do that when this idiot is bellowing in my ear 'ole.

Don't get me wrong, grumpy old goat I may be, but I'm not totally against people having a good time at gigs, however the singing, nay yelling, is not about having a good time, it is purely about showing off. And this has brought me to the conclusion that all bad behaviour at gigs is about showing off. And this isn't showing off to other fans, this my friends, is about showing off to the artist themselves – it's a demonstration that says 'Look at me, I'm your greatest fan!'.

Don't ask me why, because I'm buggered if I can explain it, but in some remote corner of their brains – a corner that nobody or nothing has visited in some years, there is a nagging voice that is telling them that if they can attract the attention of the artist in some small way, and demonstrate what a huge fan they are, then said pop star will love them forever, ask them over for a cuppa, which will ultimately lead to an invitation to be a bridesmaid at their pop star wedding.

It's not just The Singer either. There's The Whooper as well. The Whooper is the one (predominately female, but not exclusively), who will greet the intro of each and every song with a very shrill whoop. They usually barge The Singer out of the way to do this so I can really enjoy it to its full whoopiness. In her mind, this scores double points on those songs that the band just go into without announcing what the song is called, because this demonstrates to the artist that she recognises it purely on a musical basis and that she has already bought and thoroughly devoured the album even though it only came out two hours ago. She'll whoop at the end of the guitar solo, and bookend the whole thing with an extra loud whoop at the end. A triplet of whoops, all of which take place directly in my eardrum.

Festivals introduce a whole new set of annoyances. When you see the length of the queues for the toilets at a festival, I can almost excuse the 'pissing in a bottle of Evian' brigade, but is there any reason on god's sweet earth why we have to have girlfriends sitting on the shoulders of giants? Yet again, more showing off. In fact, this is a two-fold showing-off scenario. On the one hand the giant is inciting the crowd to admire his girlfriend and her jiggly breasts, and on the other, the bouncing girlfriend is saying 'hey band, look at my jiggly breasts – aren't they great, oh and by the way, I've got your new album – can I be your bridesmaid?'. Don't get me wrong, breasts jiggling about like Jimmy Sommerville and Michael Stipe head-butting each other in a small hammock are all very well in their rightful place – a beach volleyball match perhaps, preferably between Sweden and the Netherlands.

Finally, The Facebooker. The Facebooker will firstly post a photo of the empty stage before things get underway, with the location tagged just to let their friends in Facebookland know that they're at a gig. The message will generally read something like 'waiting for Satan's Scrotum to hit the stage'. Once the action has started, and despite there being a floor-to-ceiling screen on either side of the stage, and some actual pop stars playing some nice music on it who can be watched through their very own eyes, they prefer to watch huge chunks of the gig through the tiny screen on their mobile phones or digital cameras. The consequence of this is that they spend half the concert with one arm in the air as if they've got a really important question to ask or worse still, resting it on my shoulder, using me as some sort of human tripod, and I have to spend the gig bobbing my head in between the sea of smartphones to catch a glimpse of the band.

It's funny – back in the seventies we would be thoroughly frisked by the security staff for cassette recorders, dictaphones and cameras before entering a venue. Recording the band in any shape or form was punishable primarily by the death penalty, but now if you don't record at least a couple of videos and post them on Facebook, then you weren't even there. It's almost compulsory.

Of all the irritants at gigs, The Facebooker is the one that I can least readily accept. Mainly because I've just realised The Facebooker is me.

Hello, Goodbye

I will freely admit that I am still totally in awe of the Internet. The novelty of its wonderfulness hasn't worn off yet. I don't know how we ever coped without it. I have lost months of my life to this gorgeous creature. Especially YouTube – so much music, TV and footy content on there that I will never have enough time to watch everything I want to. It's that little 'related videos' bar down the side that does me every time. The videos in it that I spot out of the corner of my eye and think 'Ooh that looks good, I'll watch that one next'. And when I get to that one, my related video bar is then replenished with even more things that I just have to watch. And on and on it goes, and before you know it, it's almost time for breakfast. But you can find anything on YouTube – ridiculous types of anything.

There was one occasion when I accidentally dropped an SD card into the CD drive slot on the side of my iMac. Both slots are close together on the side of the screen, granted, but only a complete idiot would drop their tiny little SD card into the great gaping hole reserved for CDs. I had no idea how I was going to get it out. I tried everything, even turning the computer on its side and shaking it, which always worked for me when I dropped a pick into the hole in my acoustic guitar, but doesn't work quite so well with an iMac. You can shake it all you like, but it isn't ever coming out. Eventually, I turned to the Internet for help, not thinking for a single second that there would be anyone else on the entire planet who would do anything this stupid. But blow me down with a feather duster, there it was in the list of search results – a YouTube video showing me exactly how to retrieve the lost SD card from a CD drive. It worked, too. If you're now wondering how you do get your SD card out of the CD slot, I'm not going to bother to explain it because you're not stupid enough to ever need to know.

But on this particular day in December 2006, it wasn't YouTube that I had to be thankful to the Internet for, it was just a Beatles fan forum. I arrived at work that morning and as soon as I found myself with not too much to occupy my brain, I logged onto the forum, just like I did every morning, to check up on what the American members had posted overnight and what today's chatting topics were going to be.

But today I had a private message from a woman who lived in Michigan USA, and with whom the usual discussions involved me trying to convince her that Yoko Ono was actually a very nice lady, or that *Wings Wild Life* was a decent album. We would argue about the most trivial of things, but this particular Monday morning was different.

'Tony, did you know that Paul is doing a book signing at Waterstones in London on Friday? Anne'.

No, I didn't know this, but this is the wonder of the Internet; I can get a message from a complete stranger, who I have never met, and who lives on the other side of the world, telling me about something that is happening in my own backyard. I checked the Waterstones website to find that she was absolutely right. McCartney had written a children's book called *High In The Clouds* and would be signing copies of it at the Waterstones store on Piccadilly this coming Friday.

'This is a wristband event' the website boasted, as if to say: 'There will be no bundles to get in involving smelly rock fans, thank you very much'. This meant that if I wanted to go, I had to get myself along to the store on Wednesday morning at 9am, when they would hand out wristbands to the first hundred people in the queue. Those with wristbands would get to meet Macca on the Friday, and get their book signed.

One hundred people – that's not very many out of the millions of Beatles/McCartney fans that could potentially be lining up for wristbands. A very slim chance, I thought, but this was a once-in-a-lifetime opportunity to meet the man who had meant so much to me for over thirty years. I had to pull out all the stops to try and get one.

I planned to get to Waterstones by 4am on the Wednesday morning. I went to bed early on Tuesday night, but I couldn't sleep. I lay awake tossing and turning, playing over in my mind the scenarios of both getting a wristband, and not getting one. By 2.30am, I'd had enough. I took a shower and waited quietly by the front door for my cab to arrive.

I arrived at Waterstones just before 4am, and there was already a queue that stretched a fair distance from the shop's doors. Some people near the front were asleep in sleeping bags on the pavement, others just stomping their feet either out of impatience or just to keep warm. I pondered whether it would be possible for the rest of the queue to tiptoe quietly past the campers, leaving them asleep while the rest of us got our wristbands. I tried to count the heads that were in front of me to see if I was in the first hundred, but it was impossible to tell as people were leaving and re-joining the queue constantly to take toilet breaks. My counting got up to the high eighties just from my vantage point, but I couldn't see the people that were sitting or lying on the pavement. It was going to be touch and go.

It was 4am on a dark December morning, I had five hours to wait and it was freezing. I got chatting to the people who were immediately in front and behind me in the queue. Some were teenage girls, sporting Beatles sweatshirts, who weren't even born the last time McCartney had a hit record. It never fails to amaze me the universally timeless power and appeal of The Beatles. You see kids at McCartney's gigs with their parents, and they know the words to every song he plays.

Behind me were a couple from Connecticut, who had arrived at Heathrow not two hours previously, just for a stab at getting to meet their hero. That was impressive. I talked to them a lot during the wait, sharing Macca memories and discussing favourite albums and songs. I hoped that they wouldn't be going back to the States until after Friday, but they were behind me in the queue and if I happened to get wristband #100, I wouldn't be complaining.

I heard a bloke a few people in front of me boasting about how he is a professional signing-event attender. These are the people that would go to the signing of a cheque if it meant they could sell it for a fortune on eBay immediately afterwards. He was talking about how he was here last month when Britney Spears did her book signing. It made my stomach churn listening to him bragging about his wins, especially in light of what the couple behind me had done to be here. These events should only be for real fans, not leeches like him – here just to make a fast buck. The thought of him getting a wristband and me missing out was unthinkable. Macca fans are a considerate bunch; it wasn't until the reasonable hour of 7am that the ghetto blasters came on, playing Beatles and Wings tunes, and the queue bounced along moderately to keep warm.

By 8am I may have had icicles dripping from my nose, but there was only one hour to go. When I looked behind me the queue stretched further than I could see. Those people were certainly not going to be getting a wristband. Maybe they didn't know that it was only a hundred that would get one, or maybe they did, and were just waiting, hoping, that the people in front of them would give up and go home or possibly die of exposure.

Around 8:30am, staff from Waterstones came out and started counting people in the queue. The fact that they counted me and beyond must mean I was getting in, I thought. I didn't know for sure, but in my head that's what it meant. Then they spread themselves down the queue and started to explain what was going to happen when the doors opened. We were told that the first hundred people would receive blue wristbands, and that would mean that they would definitely be attending the signing. The next fifty would get a red wristband that would be numbered, and if any of the blue-wristband holders didn't show up they would be reserves, in numerical order. They then went on to explain that Paul would only be signing for ninety minutes but if, when all the blue-wristband holders had had their books signed, there was time left before he had to leave, he would see as many of the red-wristband holders as possible. I supposed this was good news – a kind of sloppy seconds, but better than nothing, as sloppy seconds always seem to be.

With the efficiency of a German banker, bang on 9 o'clock the store doors opened, and I started to shuffle my way slowly towards them. It was all very orderly, which surprised me considering what was at stake, very civilised. There was plenty of 'will-we-wont-we' talk, as the minutes ticked by and we edged ever closer to the Holy Grail.

By twenty past I was through the doors and it was just a short distance to the table that had been set up to dish out the wristbands, and I could see the members of Waterstones staff who were doing the dishing. I could even see the Tupperware pot that contained the wristbands; I couldn't make out how many were left, but they were still blue.

Eventually it was my turn and a very kind lady fastened a nice shiny blue wristband on my wrist. I was in, and I was going to be meeting Paul McCartney out of The Beatles! The lady told me that I was not to take the wristband off before Friday, because if the seal was broken in any way I wouldn't get in. This was a precaution to stop people making money from selling their wristbands for what was essentially a free event. 'See you at noon on Friday – don't be late,' she said. Are you fucking kidding, I thought? I glanced down at the Tupperware pot, there were two blue wristbands left. And guess who got them? Yeah, Gordon. No, not Gordon at all, it was the couple from Connecticut. I was chuffed for them.

I sped away down Piccadilly, heading to work, literally skipping and punching the air and just hardly believing that this was going to happen. This was big – absolutely huge. I rang Kim to tell her the news. I looked at my reflection in a shop window as I did so. There were two of me looking back – I was beside myself.

As soon as I got to the office, I logged onto the Beatles Forum and posted a thread titled 'I'm meeting Macca on Friday'. There were many posts of congratulations and virtual back-slaps from all corners of the globe (why do we say that – since when does a globe have corners?).

After the longest Thursday in the history of Thursdays, Friday finally arrived. I got into work early to compensate for the long lunch I would be taking. I don't why I bothered really, as I couldn't keep my mind away from what I was going to be doing at lunchtime. I normally spent my lunchtime on the forum talking about The Beatles, but today I was going to be meeting one of them.

I'm not that great at meeting celebrities. Who is? What do you say to them? It's really hard to have a normal conversation with someone famous without sounding like a sycophant. But you only know them because of their career, so if you don't talk to them about that, what do you say to them? I needed to think long and hard about what I was going to say to him. I would imagine that some celebs are very obtuse and deliberately difficult to have a conversation with. I would have loved to have met John Lennon, but I'm pretty sure that if I had caught him on an off day he would have been a nightmare, and I would have gone away with the impression of my ultimate hero in tatters. Conversely, Bob Geldof, another I would love a one-to-one with, I imagine would be easy to talk to and would put you at ease.

The most chilled-out celeb that I have met is Glen Tilbrook from Squeeze. We once went to the premiere of a film that he made called *One for the Road*. Before the film was about to start, the fire alarm went off and we all had to file off down the fire exit to the street. On our way down we found Glen and his wife directly behind us. He engaged us in some small talk, but mid-sentence (and mid-staircase), there was an announcement over the Tannoy that said it was a false alarm and we could all go back to our seats. Glen said, 'Let me squeeze [ah ha ha ha] past and go and tell everyone they can come back in'. To which his wife said, 'I don't think you actually have to be the one to do that, love'.

Apart from that, my celebrity interface CV amounts to Blakey from *On the Buses*, Tom Baker, Black Beauty, Alvin Martin and Yoko Ono. I'd met Yoko when I attended one of her concerts in London in 1986. Her show was surprisingly very good, and she came out afterwards to greet the fifty or so fans who were waiting outside the stage door. She signed my programme and shook my hand. I said 'Great show, Yoko,' and she said 'Thank you'. That was it. Others spoke to her for longer and she seemed really lovely and happy to chat. There were so many things I would have liked to have said to her, but I lost my nerve.

When I told my sister about the meeting with Yoko, all she could say in response to my rather lame conversation piece was 'Well, at least you shook her hand. Actually, let me touch the hand that's touched the hand, that's touched John Lennon's nob'.

So I had to make my conversation with Paul count, and I was determined to not to say anything stupid or sycophantic. I had it all planned in my head. I was going to be fine.

When I got to Waterstones, after waiting a short while outside, we were led into a sealed-off area where we had to buy the book that he was going to sign. Even though it's true that I would buy pretty much anything unusual that was Beatles-related, I must admit that if Paul wasn't going to be signing it, a kiddies' story book was not something I would have normally bothered with even if it was written by Paul McCartney. I've never been a collector of autographs either, but it seems rude not to ask – they kind of expect it, don't they. But if he was going to sign something, my CD booklet from his latest album *Chaos and Creation in the Backyard* would be a good thing for him to sign. I had that it my pocket just in case, along with a digital camera.

Once the book was purchased, we were then taken to another holding area on a different floor of the store. We were told that Paul wouldn't be long, but he was doing a reading of his book to some school children in another area. We were also briefed on the rules. We had to leave our coats and collect them afterwards. We were also told that we must not give anything else to Paul to sign, and must not under any circumstances reach into our pockets for anything while standing in front of Paul, and there was to be absolutely no photography. If we broke any of these rules we would be pounced on by the security guards and removed from the store. So that was my plan of a nice photo of me and Paul together, with arms around each other's shoulders holding up my signed *Chaos and Creation* booklet, out the window then. We were told that we would have approximately one and a half minutes with Paul. Ninety seconds – I really had to make this count and try my best not to soil my pants.

I had decided that I was going to ask him about his American tour, from which he had recently returned home, and whether he had any plans to play any shows here. And if I didn't lose my nerve I was going to say to him that I thought 'Nineteen Hundred and Eighty-Five' would be a great song for him to do live (he'd never played it live before).

Despite the disappointments of the camera and CD booklet thing, I was still excited beyond the realms of stupidity. In no time at all, Paul arrived to huge cheers from us all. He gave a wave, said hello and sat down at a desk, and the first person stepped up for a chat. I'd seen him many times at concerts and had even seen him at the premiere of the Wings film *Rock Show*, but I'd never seen him so close – just a few yards away, and I was going to get a whole lot closer very quickly indeed.

I watched as a woman who was maybe in her mid-sixties arrived at his desk and just burst into tears before either of them had a chance to say a word. I wondered whether she was maybe a first-generation Beatles fan – they were prone to that sort of thing. There was a time when I would have thought something like that was just bloody stupid, but not today. You could feel the cocktail of tension mixed with overwhelming joy in the air – it was thick with it. Paul cuddled her and gave her his handkerchief out of his actual Paul McCartney trouser pocket. He was clearly used to this sort of thing happening.

As I moved closer to his desk, I was starting to feel very nervous. Fuck, fuck, fuckety fuck! In about two minutes I am going to be standing in front of, and speaking to, Paul McCartney out of The Beatles in a one-to-one situation. A bloody Beatle. A real live bloody Beatle. Just me, Tony Shelley, drummer out of So Last Century and you, Paul McCartney, bass guitarist out of The Beatles.

The gentleman in front of me stepped up to Paul's desk holding the hand of his three-year-old son. Waterstones had given Paul some toast and jam to eat while he was doing the signing. Well, it was lunchtime after all, and even rock royalty have to eat something. I was close enough to overhear their conversation. 'Want some jammy toast?' Paul said to the kid. That was the last thing I heard before I started to stride purposefully towards the desk.

Paul looked amazing, much younger than his years, his hair dyed a chestnut brown to hide the grey, but smart as you like in his white shirt and grey suit. He stood up and offered an outstretched hand. My heart wanted to shout, 'I bloody love you, man!' because I really did, but thankfully my head stopped that from happening. As we shook hands, it was all I could do to not think about Mads and the John Lennon nob thing, although I was pretty sure that Paul's hand had never touched John Lennon's nob.

'Hi, what's your name?'
'Tony.'
'Really nice to meet you, Tony'.

Oh my god, Paul McCartney just called me Tony.

'Really nice to meet you too, Paul'.

Oh my god, I just called Sir Paul McCartney, plain old Paul like he was a mere mortal or the bloke that trims my hedges. That's only a tiny slap on the back away from calling him Macca. Go on, say it, say it, please say 'you can call me Macca'.

As he signed my book I asked him my planned question:

'How was the American tour?'
'It was great – we had a great time, we only got back last week.'
'Any plans to bring the tour to the UK next year?'
'Yeah, we're looking at a few venues here and in Europe and hoping to do a few old songs that we've not done before.'

Ha, you played right into my hands, sucker!

'You should do "Nineteen Hundred and Eighty-Five" and "Back Seat of My Car"'.
'Yeah? You like those ones?'
'Yeah, they are both fantastic.'

With that, he handed me my book.

'Thanks for coming.'

This was too much. Macca had just thanked me for coming to one of the greatest moments of my life. It was at this point that I lost it, and I did what I had promised myself not to do.
'No, thank you. We know you don't have to do this, but it means so much to us that you do'.
'I know, I do understand, I do it cos it's fun and great to say hi to everyone. Have a great Christmas, Tony'.
'You too Paul, and thanks again'.

And with that, I was gone. Maybe a little more than my ninety seconds, maybe a little less – I don't know, but while I was there it seemed like ages. I was shaking as I left the shop, totally overwhelmed and very emotional indeed. I could have consumed a mountain of very high-quality hard drugs, and not felt as high as I did at that particular moment.

What I took away from this very brief encounter was the bit where he said he understood. I wondered if he really did. How could he? How could he possibly understand what it meant to someone like me? Someone who has bought every record, read every book, been to gigs on every tour, videoed every fleeting TV appearance and a whole lot more over the preceding thirty years. Yet from his humility, and the way he went out of his way to appear ordinary and make everyone feel comfortable, I believed him – I think he really did get it. I remembered him once talking about the time when The Beatles met Elvis, and how totally in awe of him they all were, so yes, he knows what it's like to stand before greatness.

The UK tour of 2007 that Paul had mentioned never happened, but when I next saw him live in 2010, he performed 'Nineteen Hundred and Eighty-Five'. Coincidence? Of course it is. I know that Paul would have forgotten about me the moment I turned my back and walked away from his desk, but I will never forget a single second of the day that I met Paul McCartney. I take this one to the grave. I really do love you, man.

Fat, Fifty and Finished

I don't remember the exact moment when my mid-life crisis, Colin (the bastard), first reared his ugly head. Like when you get a boil on the bum, there were no early warning signs that he was coming, he was just suddenly there. Now, don't get me wrong, Colin wasn't anything as serious as, say, depression – he was just this thing that seemed to take great pleasure in reminding me that I was old now. He mostly did this when he knew I was feeling it most and didn't want to.

A Colin, or a similarly named bastard, doesn't drop in on everyone – he mainly visits those of us that heap overblown expectations on ourselves, when we sit back and reflect on why we haven't achieved them. Was I ever going to be a pop star or a footballer? Of course I wasn't, these were just dreams, fantasies – absolutely tremendous dreams, but dreams all the same, and in the end just something to keep me going through the mundane business of everyday life. But Colin made me feel like I should have achieved more, or at least should have tried to. He made me reflect on past times and made me yearn again for my youth. He didn't think I could be a pop star or a footballer either, but he reminded me that my twenties had passed me by, whilst I was too busy pretending to be a grown-up, trying to meet crippling mortgage repayments, raising children and doing the vacuuming, when I should have been out taking drugs and having vigorous sex with women whose surnames I would never know, and were so numerous that even if I did know them, I couldn't possibly be expected to remember them.

He reminded me that I loathed my job more than I loathed rap music, and whispered in my brain that it was a totally pointless job anyway, and asked me why I was wasting so much time at the office doing this pointless, loathsome job, when I actually had so little time left. He was there watching as I panted my way up the stairs, and when I couldn't fit into any of the clothes that I'd bought because, in some remote corner of my brain, I had told myself that they might at least make me look younger. Not just watching, but pissing himself laughing too. I have no doubt that it was he who pointed me towards the Blue Harbour range at Marks & Spencer.

He even got involved in the music stuff. It was him that was making me feel the lyrics of songs more intensely than ever before, and deduce that every song was talking about me – just the sad ones, the happy songs were obviously written about someone else. I don't think it's normal for 'Spice Up Your Life' by The Spice Girls to reduce anyone to tears. That was Colin.

The most common thing that men who suffer a mid-life crisis do to make themselves feel better and combat these feelings of inadequacy is to buy themselves a drum kit or a sports car. And this is where I had him. I already had a drum kit, and I've always thought that people who drive sports cars were borderline nobbish – unless they have a comedy personalised number plate like NOB 1, and then it's ok.

The other thing they do is join a band again. The world is full of middle-aged blokes who used to be in bands when they were young. They get married and have kids, whilst their guitars lay dormant for twenty years gathering dust at the back of their wardrobes, along with all those clothes that they insist they will one day be slim enough to squeeze into again. And then suddenly they are divorced, or their kids have all grown up and left home for university, and they have all this free time and disposable income again. Shorter of breath and much shorter of hair, that dusty old guitar is the first thing they reach for. The strap fits a little snugger than it did all those years ago and the guitar sits a little further away from the body than it used to, but it feels great to hold it once again. Time for a quick glance and a guitar pose in the bedroom mirror? Of course. They look lovingly at the fretboard, which was once adorned with their slender digits and remember how those fingers danced up and down it with the agility of a young Hendrix. They gingerly place those same fingers, which these days resemble a packet of pork sausages, back on that same fretboard and lo and behold, they can still remember how to play the riff from 'Sweet Home Alabama'. Now all they have to do is call up a few old mates and get the band back together again. This is because we never give up, and more to the point, never grow up.

I'd recently met up again with my old school chum and Gud Fungs rhythm ace, John Budd. He and an old mate of his, Tish, who was in Cheesecloth with Ian, thought it might be a rather nice idea to form a Clash tribute band, and they asked me to fill the Topper Headon drum berth. Another old mate, Steve, who was in a band with Ian and Tish in the early eighties, was to play bass. It sounded fun, and I liked the idea of playing with John again after all these years. I didn't really know Tish from the old days, but he was a lovely bloke and I enjoyed playing with him. It was never on the cards that we would try and be one of those lookalike-type tribute bands, that would be ridiculous; how would a bunch of near-fifty-year-olds look like a band in their late teens even if we had wanted to? But we did decide that we would wear the gear. I bought myself a new black Harrington jacket (with authentic tartan lining) and a pair of white 501s to celebrate. If I left the top two buttons undone I could just about squeeze into them.

John's Vox Stroller was long gone; he now played a Les Paul and a Les Paul Junior and his playing style suited the Clash stuff that we were trying out. The original idea was that Tish was going do the singing, but he found this hard whilst playing the guitar and so history repeated itself once more as we asked Ian to help out and do the vocals, just as we had thirty years previously with Gud Fungs. Being in a band with John and Ian again had a certain feeling of full-circleness about it. Life is a funny old thing and bands can be very incestuous beasts at times.

We called ourselves Black Market Clash. It was a good tribute band name. We mainly covered songs from the first Clash album and a few of the other singles. We put together a decent-sized set of twenty or so songs, and thrashed them out with as much aggression as a bunch of old duffers could muster. Although John and Tish were hardened Clash fans, and loved playing these songs, I wasn't crazy about doing only Clash songs (which is a bit of a problem in a Clash tribute band), but if nothing else it still felt great to be playing again and it was a great excuse to see my old pals every couple of weeks.

A pub in Bishop's Stortford foolishly booked us for our first gig. With a week to go, we had the most appalling rehearsal. I'm not sure what went wrong but we were on terrible form. This, I've found over the years, is not an unusual thing for the last rehearsal before a gig, and because of this I have always lived by the maxim: 'shit rehearsal – great gig'. It's stood me in good stead as the last thing you want going into a gig are the thoughts of a disastrous rehearsal playing in the back of your mind. Ian, with his usual bluntness and hoping to chivvy us up a bit, commented 'If we play like this next week, we're gonna look like a right bunch of cunts'.

We left the rehearsal room that night a little bruised, but confident it would be all right on the night. The next morning John rang me around midday to say that Tish had suffered a stroke on the train on the way to work that morning. Another followed when he got there, and a third in the ambulance on the way from work to hospital.

It transpired that during the rehearsal the night before, Tish had been giving everything in his backing vocals in preparation for the gig, and had ruptured a vocal cord. The consequence of this had caused the stroke. He lost the use of an arm, a leg and temporarily lost his speech. He was only 53. It shook us all to the very core, this was serious shit.

Tish's speech came back pretty quickly and after many weeks in hospital and much physiotherapy, he eventually got full use of his arm and leg back again. However, his recovery was not sufficient to enable him to do the thing that he loved doing most – playing the guitar. For poor old Tish, the game was up and it spelt the end for Black Market Clash too.

In the week preceding my fiftieth birthday, I received a Skype call from my dear friend of over thirty years, Darryl. She was living in New Zealand with her husband Alistair – who was my best man when Kim and I married in 1997. We had these pre-arranged Skype calls regularly and she was due to fly over here for my birthday party, so I presumed that the call would simply be about firming up on the arrangements for her arrival at the end of the week. What she was actually calling for was to tell me that she wouldn't be able to make it, and went on to deliver the bombshell that she had been diagnosed with ovarian cancer – it knocked me for six. I, along with all our mutual friends, was absolutely devastated. She may not have made my party, but in the following months she attacked this horrible bastard head-on with such positivity that it was truly inspirational to watch.

I was so proud of her, and the way that she dealt with this vile disease. She wasn't going to let it get the better of her until there was absolutely nothing she could do about it. She was determined to live what time she had left in the way that she had lived the forty-nine previous years – to the absolute limit.

Suddenly all those little things that Colin (the bastard) was making me feel and think about seemed insignificant. I started to re-evaluate and began to embrace my middle-agedness and how good it was to be alive. I might have tits like an aged aunt and be almost fifty, but I wasn't quite finished yet. What Tish and Darryl went through – these are the real mid-life crises, not the self-pitying stuff that I was going through. I felt pathetic.

There's that really annoying saying: 'don't sweat the small stuff'. It's good advice and we should take it. Growing old is not that bad when you have similar aging creatures to grow old with. It's a beautiful thing.

Admittedly, there are things that I'm still not entirely comfortable with. Leo Sayer for one thing. I find it hard to reconcile his song 'Moonlighting', which I still adore, with the man that went into a fit of rage on national TV because no one would wash his pants for him. But there are things that I am comfortable with, things that I never thought I would feel ok about. Does it really matter that I own a barbeque and some Black & Decker tools (that I don't know how to use), or the fact that I need to read online reviews before making a decision to buy such items? Barbeques are very middle-aged affairs I must admit, but as long as I don't wear an apron or a chef's hat whilst I'm cooking, then what's not to like? And it's ok that I enjoy gardening so long as I never refer to it as 'pottering about in the garden'. I can't really get on with cardigans, but they do keep the chills out. I no longer mind staying in because, after all, there is rather a lot of really great telly to be watched and I have a nice sofa – the cushions of which, have rather thoughtfully, moulded themselves into the shape of my arse. I still haven't got to grips with the metric system, nor with the fact that half of the presenters of *Top of the Pops* turned out to be paedophiles apart from, most ironically, the one that called himself Kid, but I have come to terms with my bald patch – you could say I've taken a shine to it.

I'm stuck in my ways; I know I am. But I like my ways. I like them a lot, that's why they are my ways. I've even started getting myself into a tiz over modern expressions that seem to be finding their way into everyday speak. 'Reaching out' – that's one that drives me potty. I hear this a lot at work. 'Can you reach out to Bob and find out what his calendar is looking like tomorrow?' What does that even mean? I'm sure his calendar looks pretty much like any other calendar – a collection of square boxes with numbers in them representing the days, and sure, I can ask him if he's free – asking is good, reaching out however, is just cock-fodder. Just say what you mean, don't wrap it up in ridiculous buzz words, because I'm not playing. And whilst I am prepared to take on some modern expressions, there are others that I refuse to bend on. As far as I'm concerned a 'season' is something that should only be used to differentiate between weather patterns and football fixtures, and not a TV series. In restaurants, I still say to the waiters 'can I have' and not 'can I get' just in case they invite me to 'get' it myself. And as for people who greet me with a throaty 'Whaaatsup!' Sweet baby Jesus on a tricycle, when did we allow this meaningless salutation in? Nothing's fucking up, and if it was, the last person I would want to discuss it with would be someone who says 'Whaaatsup'. A cheery 'hi' is still working for me.

I haven't yet shown any leanings towards liking opera, and I still have never heard *Bat Out of Hell* all the way through. I still can't abide hip-hop or trip-hop or flip-flop or plip-plop or whatever the hell it's called these days. Nothing much has changed – essentially, I'm still Jenny from the Block. I have slightly changed my stance on tattoos though. Not enough to actually go out and get one, but I now accept if they are small, pretty, represent something personal and not on your forehead, then they are ok. I don't understand 'sleeves' though. I can't even contemplate the amount of excruciating pain one would have to go through only to end up with an arm that looks like an unfinished colouring-in book. I've also stopped using rude words as passwords on my work computer. The problem with work computers is that at some point they will go wrong and when they do, you're going to have to call the bods on the IT Help Desk and tell them your password – a harsh lesson learned during 'The Shameful Beefcurtains Incident of 2004'.

I don't sit down all night at weddings and then suddenly get up and start frantically kicking my legs up like John Cleese, the minute the DJ puts on 'New York, New York' – I don't want to play any part in that sort of behaviour. I still get annoyed when vocal groups like One Direction or Take That get referred to as 'boy bands' – they don't play any musical instruments, so therefore they are not a bloody band. I have no idea how to use Twitter or what a Jaegerbomb is, and what's more I really don't care.

There was a time, lasting approximately fifteen years, when I could name every song in the top twenty in order, but right now I couldn't even tell you what the number one record is. I've been known on occasions to dabble with country music. Christ, I've even seen Sting in concert ... and he was bloody good!

I have an amazing family and circle of friends that understand my foibles and tolerate them, and for this I thank them. Middle-age and me –

we are ok, and I look forward to being much, much older when I can own a cat and grow my ear hair to a sizeable length in order to annoy young people by pretending to be deaf. Recognise your age, turn another page, it's a middle-age rampage, yeah!

I am at peace with it now. In the words of Supertramp: 'Crisis? What Crisis?' Who the fuck was this Colin, anyway?

Fields of Gold

'In My Life' by The Beatles is, for me, one of the greatest songs ever written. It's Lennon's genius at its most evident and a song that when I'm in a reflective mood can make me a little dewy-eyed, but I guess that's why he wrote it that way. It's a song about nostalgia and reflection, which is essentially what this book is about too – the difference being that Lennon manages to say it all in less than a hundred words, where as it has taken me thousands.

The song makes me think of certain places that have been part of my life for so many years and the people that I specifically associate with them. 'I know I'll often stop and think about them,' Lennon says, and whenever I hear this song, that is exactly what I do. Pop music is so wonderful when it manages to connect you to things that are real and important.

Today I am in Stratford, East London – at its shiny new Westfield shopping centre, actually. You see, Stratford is one of those places that has changed forever, but taking the opposite stance to how Lennon tells it in the song, this place really has changed for the better. The Stratford of my youth was terribly run-down, filthy and dangerous to walk around at night – to be blunt it was a bit of a shithole.

I didn't go there that often if I could help it, but my outstanding memory of Stratford was spending a very drunken night with Ray in one of its pubs celebrating the 1980 FA Cup Final win over Arsenal. We stopped off there on the way home from Wembley. Our intention was to spend the night in Bobby Moore's pub, Mooro's, but by the time we got there it was rammed to the rafters and we didn't have a hope in hell of getting in. And so we ended up in some pub on Stratford Broadway whose name escapes me now, singing our hearts out and getting very drunk with all the other fans who also couldn't get into Mooro's.

When London was awarded the Olympics in 2005, part of the bid was to build the main stadium at Stratford – just a fifteen-minute tube ride from my house. It was all very exciting passing the site every morning on the tube journey to work, watching the piles of rubble miraculously metamorphose into an arena of absolute beauty. What was even more exciting was the announcement that when they had finished with the games, work would begin again on changing the Queen Elizabeth Stadium into the new home for West Ham United Football Club.

Roll forward to 2012, when the games got going, the whole country got ensnared with Olympic fever as the gold medals for Team GB came rolling in. I wasn't really that bothered beforehand about going to any of the events, but I got sucked into the whole occasion just like everyone else; by then however, it was too late to get tickets for anything. I only really wanted to go to an event that was held in the stadium, purely out of interest of seeing what it was like and to imagine how it might be watching the Hammers play there every other week. So I was delighted to be offered a ticket for the Paralympics a month or so later.

On the day I had a great seat and, by an unusual stroke of good fortune, in the first event of the day, the gold medal went to a Brit. It was in the wheelchair discus event and, to be absolutely honest, I think my mum could have probably thrown it further than the winner, but that wasn't the point. The medal ceremony was very moving, with everyone in the stadium standing as the British flag was raised and the National Anthem was played.

A few events later, the wheelchair shot put was won by a German girl who had no legs. This left me with a bit of a dilemma. By now I knew the medal ceremony drill, and as the German flag was raised and 'Deutschland, Deutschland Über Alles' rang out over the Tannoy, I stood. But then I thought 'Hang on, I'm not standing for the German National Anthem,' and sat down again. But then I looked at the screen and saw the athlete sitting there in her wheelchair with a grin spread across her entire face and I stood up again. The next minute or so was spent alternating between standing up and sitting down, whilst I wrestled with my conscience and my brain chanted the mantra German, Legs, German, Legs over and over again, until the ceremony was over.

Back at Westfield's state-of-the-art shopping mall, I'm now just outside having a ciggie and reflecting on just how much this place has changed and I can see the empty Olympic Stadium from where I'm standing. And inside the mall there is a brand new cinema complex, boutiques selling designer clothes that the residents of the old Stratford could only dream of affording. And restaurants. Loads of them. One of them is a salad bar called 'Tossed'. A salad bar in Stratford – a concept that even John Lennon, no matter how hard he tried, would never have been be able to Imagine.

It's a sad reflection on the youth of today that in the three years that 'Tossed' has inhabited the food court at the Westfield centre, not one teen-ager has got up to the sign and spray-painted the word 'off' on it. That's what the Stratford youths of the seventies would have done – probably within hours of the sign going up.

It poured with rained earlier, and as I stub out my ciggie, a man in an orange boiler suit is operating what looks to me like an industrial-sized vacuum cleaner and Hoovering up the puddles. When, as a nation, did we start Hoovering up puddles? Yes, it's a very different world that we live in these days.

Still Crazy After All These Years

From the moment I discovered that my fiftieth birthday fell on a Saturday, there was never any question that there was going to be a party, and it was going to be a big one. The thing that I wanted most for my birthday was to get The Heseltines back together on stage for one final hurrah, so what could be a more appropriate occasion to reassemble the band than my fiftieth birthday?

My band at the time, Black Market Clash, were not right for a party, but The Heseltines were perfect for this sort of thing. It had to be The Heseltines, the question was, how was I going to make this happen? It had often been said that the band were all over the shop musically, but now we were geographically too. Like an elephant attempting to ride in a hot-air balloon, this wasn't going to be an easy thing to get off the ground, what with Phil being holed up in Scotland, Rob in Berkshire, John in Kent and Jo and Christian in Norfolk. It had been nine years since we had last all played together. All I had to do was get these five people in the same room, at the same time, which had sometimes proved a bit tricky even when we were all local. Well, six actually, as I decided that I wanted Carl (from So Last Century) involved as well. Although Carl wasn't an authentic Heseltine, I figured that any band with Carl in it is going to be better than one without him. I wasn't sure how we would accommodate two lead guitarists, but that was a minor detail.

And so on 3 January 2011, I drafted an email …

Subject: Rock, Jelly and Ice Cream

Dear Former members of The Fabulous Heseltines pop group,

Hezza New Year to you all. I hope this mail finds you all as well as can be expected under the circumstances. The circumstances being, devoid of rock. Good news on that score, I'm here to relieve you of this unfortunate affliction. To that end, I was wondering if any of you still have any musical instruments. I'm thinking mainly guitars and voices, but if these have been replaced by Stylophones and combs and crispy bog paper, this may be ok too.

'Why?' I hear you cry, or am I just hearing you cry?

Well, I'll tell you. 19 March 2011 is the day that I will be 50 years old, and I'm having a party. I'm hoping to get a new gong for my birthday, and was thinking that there's no one I'd like to try it out with more than you lot.

I haven't really thought about the logistics of getting us all together yet, nor what we might be able to play, but I'm thinking about an hour's worth

321

of material – something old, something new, everything borrowed and absolutely nothing by Blue. Well maybe not the something new bit, but if we were to try something new, it would almost definitely be 'Hungry Like The Wolf', Rob.

But we need to organise some rehearsals because I want us to be good and deliver like the milkmen of rock we are. So we'll worry about how this is going to happen later but if you can answer these four simple questions then we can take it from there.

1) Are you free on 19 March 2011?
2) If not, what is the fee?
3) If so, are you up for it?
4). What's the capital of Peru?

Come on, it's my birthday, it's a Saturday night in Essex, it's The Heseltines and it'll be quite good.

Love Tone x

So the wheels were set in motion, and these were some of the replies I got.

From: Philip Brierley
Re: Rock, Jelly & Ice Cream

Hippo New Queer to you too! I'm up for it if everybody else is. When do we rehearse?

Phil.

From: John Rutter
Re: Rock, Jelly & Ice Cream

Yes, but I'm not doing 'I Fought the Law'. Can we do 'A Forest'?
Butler.

From: Robert Mellor
Re: Rock, Jelly & Ice Cream

1) Yes.
2) N/A.
3) Yes.
4) Lima.
Please note my normal gig rider applies:
• Own dressing room (heated to 73° precisely)

- A bowl of M&Ms (blue ones removed)
- Coffee (Ethically-sourced – Guatemalan or Nicaraguan medium roast only)
- 1 pint of fresh breast milk, and a tin of banana Nesquik
- Two unopened bottles of still mineral water (potassium content not less than 5mg/l)
- A straight glass with 2 flexible straws (no pink or green ones)
- Clowns to the left of me, jokers to the right
- One orthopaedic shoe.

Let me know if you need the exact specifications for the bendy straws. Ideally I'm looking for about 60cm in length with a flexible section about 12–15cm from the top, but I'm not that fussed.
Boutros, boutros ghali
Robinson P.

From: Carl McAndrew
Re: Rock, Jelly & Ice Cream

It was touch and go mate but I've managed to persuade Sue that it's not necessary for us to attend the opening of the new stationery cupboard at Maia's school, so I'm in. She put up a fight though! Delighted to be a fully-fledged Heseltine for this one-off performance despite the amount of work I have to do to learn whatever songs we will be playing. I have scientifically calculated this out to be roughly 'a fucking lot'.
Looking forward to it.
Carlos.

I'd like to be able to tell you that the reassembling of The Fabulous Heseltines was a little bit more 'rock' than this; that Jo had to be kidnapped from rehab following an intense crystal meth addiction, or that Christian was living as a recluse in a tent at the foot of the Andes refusing to speak or eat anything other than sautéed straw. Or that John had been slung in Turkish prison for playing 'I Fought the Law' without due care and attention in a built-up area. But it was just an email.
And so The Heseltines were back and it was all systems go. We eventually managed to find dates for three rehearsals between January and March that we could all make. I was really impressed with Phil for making the effort to fly in from Scotland to prepare for this gig. I cobbled together a set list of songs that we might be able to remember without too much difficulty:

Teenage Kicks
I'm A Believer
Heatwave
Heroes
Thinking of You
Play That Funky Music
Can't Get You out of my Head
(Come Up and See Me) Make Me Smile
Drop Dead Gorgeous
Boys Are Back in Town
Basket Case
Venus/Song 2
Hanging on the Telephone
I Fought the Law
Weak
Tainted Love
Greased Lightning
Waterloo
Gonna Make You A Star

I Saw Her Standing There
Sgt. Pepper's Lonely Hearts Club Band / Sgt. Pepper (reprise)

It looked like a strong set to me; now all we had to do was try and remember how to play them. Nine years is a long time in rock. I sent out some recordings that I had from the old days, which weren't great quality – mostly taken from old video tape recordings of our gigs. I wondered if Rob still had his little blue book in which he used to write down all the chords and where his solos came in – it could be a lifesaver.

The first get-together was held at Jo and Christian's barn on the last weekend in January. They had, rather considerately, built this barn complete with a recording studio, which doubled up as a great rehearsal space. We all arrived on the Friday night, and sat around their kitchen table drinking, catching up and talking about the old days, just like any other group of friends who had just met up again after getting back in touch through 'Friends Reunited'. The conversation flowed non-stop as if it was only yesterday that we had all been together. From what I remember, it was mostly talk about the band and not too much of the 'so what are you driving these days' type of chat. We were always a band of self-deprecators, so most of the memories that we shared that night were about the disasters rather than the triumphs, because, of course, these are much funnier to discuss. The out-of-tune backing vocals in 'She's Electric', the time that we totally lost our way in 'Suffragette City', or the fact that John had 15 effects pedals, none of which ever had working batteries in them.

All these little in-jokes that are exclusively funny to people who have spent the best part of a decade in the same band, but no use to anyone else – so I won't burden you with the details.

As the night drew on, we all got drunker and drunker, and I can quite honestly say that I can't remember a single time where I have laughed as much as I did that night. I actually ached. Not that I can remember very much about what we were saying, I just remember it hurt. It's a shame that we had to interrupt the frivolities by playing some music.

The next morning, a little worse for wear, we gathered in the studio. The morning is never the best time to try and make music, but there was a lot of work to do. The aim for the day was to try and cover all the songs on the set list and at least work out who was playing what parts, and to sort out endings and intros, stops and starts etc.

With everyone in position, it suddenly occurred to me that this band had been apart for as long as we'd been together. With Kim poised with her omnipresent camera, we launched into 'Heatwave' and after a couple of false starts, miraculously it all came flooding back – it was as if we had never been away, and it felt good – really good. In shock, we had to retire to the kitchen for a nice cup of tea and chew the fat over this minor triumph. There were hiccups, of course there were – it had been a long time – but by the end of the day we had fashioned ourselves some sort of presentable set that only required a bit of tightening up. The Hezzas were back in business – the business of rock. We would be able to do this, and I was delighted.

That evening we sat around the table having dinner, and chatted about how our lives had changed over the last ten years. I was the only one of the band still living in Essex; we had all changed jobs; some of us had changed wives. If there had been a great aunt there, she could have told us how much we had all grown since she last saw us – outwards obviously. We talked about getting old and decrepit, our aches, our pains, our lawnmowers. There was a gap, a tiny moment of silence from the incessant chatter and clinking of glasses, then Phil looked up from his plate and said, 'I've started baking cakes. I do a fantastic lemon drizzle.'. His words hung awkwardly in the air for a few seconds. The silence this time was slightly longer and more poignant. He looked down again, slightly ashamed, and mumbled 'So, what songs are we gonna do tomorrow then?'.

Ahh hello, you've found the secret chapter then. A sort of literary version of those hidden tracks that appeared on just about every CD that came out in the nineties, and scared the shit out of you when, without warning, they'd come crashing out of your speakers half an hour after you thought the album had ended, and were just about to settle down to watch *Casualty* with a takeaway curry.

They were always a little bit whacky, weren't they? I blame The Beatles. They started it, just like they started everything else. I believe that little snippet of laughing and gibberish that announces itself at great volume just as the needle hits the run-off groove at the end of Side 2 of *Sgt. Pepper*, was the first. It lulls you into a false sense of security. Just as you think you've finally heard the last of that everlasting C Chord that closes 'A Day in the Life', it comes crashing in unannounced and uninvited like the musical equivalent of the ending to the movie *Carrie*, and soiling just as many pairs of pants as it does so. They said that if you played the 'Sgt. Pepper Run-off Groove' (as it became known) backwards, by moving the record anti-clockwise with your finger, you could hear a secret message from The Beatles themselves that said 'we'll fuck you like supermen, we'll fuck you like supermen', which was nice. When I tried this, it just sounded to me like 'waddyhmphperdaddy, waddyhmphperdaddy' repeated over and over again – which was a bit of a relief really.

On vinyl, it was much harder to disguise a hidden track, because we could see the track bands, but on a CD who knows what witchcraft is going on inside that little tray when nobody's looking? It was like a free-for-all as far as the hidden track was concerned. Sometimes there was even more than one hidden track, and albums became longer and longer and longer. This coincided with the time when I was becoming less inclined to listen to entire albums in one go – I just didn't have the time to sit down for eighty minutes to listen to one album. What I really needed was a kind of 'highlights' version of an album for those of us that just can't sit still for that long without needing a wee.

With that in mind, I am fully aware that the same could be said about this book, and I know it's gone on a bit, and so for those of you that are in bit a bit of a hurry, and don't have the patience to read this tome of mediocrity all the way through, I present in a single paragraph *Rock, Paper, Slippers – The Highlights*:

Redundant ginger bank clerk has mid-life crisis and decides to write a book. Drones on for a while about the sixties. Starts school and learns how to swear and how not to jump off the roof of Gants Hill Odeon. Doesn't learn much else. Some stuff about seventies telly, adverts and football. Meets Blakey from *On the Buses* and Black Beauty, who is a horse. Discovers pop music and allows Gilbert O'Sullivan and Sparks into his life – they take advantage, and 10cc take the absolute piss. More stuff about the seventies, finds The Beatles, punk rock and mods. Forms a band. Gets married, has kids, gets divorced, gets a lawnmower, gets married again. Moans about the eighties, and who can blame him. More stuff about being in bands and just about liking bands and stuff. Meets Paul McCartney out of The Beatles – has to change pants. Gets bewildered by the modern world and then gets unbewildered again and then it's all ok and everyone shouts hoorah. The End.

Printed in March 2021
by Rotomail Italia S.p.A., Vignate (MI) - Italy